Youth Information-Seeking Behavior II

Context, Theories, Models, and Issues

Edited by
Mary K. Chelton
Colleen Cool

The Scarecrow Press, Inc.
Lanham, Maryland • Toronto • Plymouth, UK
2007

SCARECROW PRESS, INC.

Published in the United States of America
by Scarecrow Press, Inc.
A wholly owned subsidiary of
The Rowman & Littlefield Publishing Group, Inc.
4501 Forbes Boulevard, Suite 200, Lanham, Maryland 20706
www.scarecrowpress.com

Estover Road
Plymouth PL6 7PY
United Kingdom

British Library Cataloguing in Publication Information Available

Library of Congress Cataloging-in-Publication Data

Youth information-seeking behavior II : context, theories, models, and issues /
edited by Mary K. Chelton, Colleen Cool.
p. cm.
Includes bibliographical references and index.
ISBN-13: 978-0-8108-5654-7 (pbk. : alk. paper)
ISBN-10: 0-8108-5654-9 (pbk. : alk. paper)
1. Information behavior. 2. Information retrieval. 3. Internet and teenagers.
4. Internet and children. 5. Youth—Information services. 6. Children—
Information services. I. Chelton, Mary K. II. Cool, Colleen, 1952–
ZA3075.Y69 2007
025.5'24—dc22   2006032922

Contents

Preface

Lynne (E. F.) McKechnie

Youth Information-Seeking Behavior II, edited by Mary K. Chelton and Colleen Cool, continues the work of the earlier volume of the same title published by Scarecrow Press in 2004. This collection of an introductory article and ten further contributed chapters is not a purposeful or thematic sample of youth information-seeking research. Nonetheless, as with the earlier book, it provides a snapshot of this work at this particular time, which will be useful to many people in a variety of ways. Individuals not familiar with young people's information seeking— including students, practitioners, and established scholars in Library and Information Science (LIS) and related fields such as education— will appreciate this book as a first place to start exploring this topic. It is an excellent resource to support information behavior and youth services courses. It identifies, in one convenient place, many important researchers and research projects. And it will stimulate discussion and thinking among information behavior scholars and youth services librarians.

As with the previous volume, the articles collected here address varied topics. Five fall within the rubric of Savolainen's (1995) everyday life information seeking (ELIS). Fisher and her colleagues at the University of Washington report on the preliminary findings of a National

Science Foundation funded study of the everyday information behaviors of children nine to thirteen years of age, so-called tweens. This is the first study to specifically target this age group, and some of the findings are particularly interesting. For example, the authors discovered that tweens differentiate between the sorts of questions and information asked of peers and those asked of adults, that the curiosity-fuelled drive toward information seeking that is characteristic of this age group was often tempered by peer pressure, and that adults frequently give children information they either do not want or regard as incorrect. What emerges in this chapter is a fascinating picture, captured from the perspective of the children themselves, of an information world that differs substantially from that of adults.

Hughes-Hassell and Agosto also firmly situate their work within the perspective of their participants, in this case urban teenagers fourteen to seventeen years old. The twenty-seven young adults who took part in this study were very active research partners, completing surveys, and for one week keeping written activity logs, maintaining a tape-recorded audio journal, and using disposable cameras to photograph places in their communities where they go for information. Hughes-Hassell and Agosto derive two models from their data, one that postulates how urban adolescents use ELIS behavior to support their development and another that provides a typology of their ELIS information needs. They note "[u]rban teens want and need information to support their emerging sexuality, their pressing financial needs, their attempts to understand the social worlds in which they live, their self-doubts about who they are and what role they can play in society."

Jennifer Burek Pierce explores one of these adolescent information needs, the need for sexual health information, more closely. What differentiates this chapter from others in the book is that it is a meta-analysis of a sort, a literature search that focuses primarily on "contemporary peer-reviewed medical and public health research on adolescents' sexual and reproductive health information" and associated public policy. Pierce identifies many findings common to both LIS and the health sciences literatures—significant information gaps; the importance of media of all types, especially the Internet; the problem of limited confidentiality protection for minors; teens' poor information search skills; and differences between urban and rural contexts. While Pierce argues for more cooperation between LIS and health sciences researchers, she also identifies significant differences in research culture and intellectual traditions that will prove challenging.

Mehra and Braquet's work, based on narrative interviews with adults recalling adolescent experiences, "proposes a model to better understand the process of information seeking during "queer" youth coming-out experiences." Resources appropriate for different stages in the coming-out process are identified, and the author provides recommendations for realistic and achievable changes to library collections and services to better support these information needs.

Studies of reading practices such as those conducted by Catherine Ross and her colleagues at the University of Western Ontario, are now regarded as part of the literature of ELIS behavior. Howard and Jin's chapter makes a substantial contribution to this area. They report the results of a survey of teen reading, book purchasing, and library use patterns in Nova Scotia, Canada. The pilot study for a future national survey, this work has the potential to provide badly needed benchmark data to track trends.

The formidable task of understanding and deconstructing the complex everyday information lives of children and young adults resonates in the chapters discussed above. This collection also includes four chapters that address the information seeking of youth in their role as students. Interestingly, all reflect a continuing interest in students' use of electronic, online, and digital resources.

Dhillon focuses on an older cohort, third-year undergraduates in the United Kingdom studying leisure, tourism, and adventure. Unlike much of the work related to online resources and online searching, in addition to identifying use patterns, Dhillon's survey explored how students behaved and felt while searching databases. This single case study of a particular group at a particular institution serves as a fine model for other practicing academic librarians wishing to understand and support student information-seeking behavior in their own programs.

While study after study indicates that students seldom use libraries when seeking information, Valenza's chapter indicates that the students in a least one high school do use their high school's virtual library. Through focus group interviews the students indicated they frequently used the school library website for academic research, appreciated having online access to resources and tools, had greater success with the school's virtual library than with available commercial tools, and recognized the website as acting like a quality filter to help them find appropriate information they could trust. Further, excerpts from the focus group interview transcripts construct a picture of the students that is radically different from that of the more prevalent image of an inept, detached, and information-illiterate searcher. The participants were aware of many information sources, spoke about the varying authority and usefulness of the tools, and were self-reflective about their own abilities in information searching and seeking. This is a feel good study—we see the school library as being successful and students as active, self-reflective information seekers—which reintroduces a positive perspective to the research agenda needed to improve school library services and students' experiences of them as information seekers.

Silverstein uses a systematic and innovative approach to study the use of what she refers to as traditional children's digital reference services (TCDR) services. She starts with the premise that while children use such services, the services themselves typically are characterized by child-oriented content delivered through platforms developed for adults. Through a literature review Silverstein develops a list of "assumptions" about children's use of TCDR services, which she then tests through an analysis of 297 questions submitted to a TCDR called "Ask a Scientist or Engineer." Some of the assumptions (e.g., very young children use TCDR services less) were supported by Silverstein's data, while others were not (e.g., children tend to ask broad rather than specific questions). More important, the author identified trends that were not anticipated through her examination of earlier literature (e.g., duplicate questions, which suggest that children experienced difficulty or confusion in using the TCDR service) and that merit further exploration. Silverstein's chapter concludes with a call for a theoretically informed research agenda centered upon the information behavior of children themselves to inform the design and evaluation of CDR services.

Andrew Large and his team of researchers from McGill University in Montreal appear to have done just what Silverstein has suggested. They have been working on a multiyear, multistage project funded by the Social Sciences and Humanities Research Council of Canada on the design and evaluation of web portals for use by elementary school students seeking information to support class projects. This chapter provides a synthesis of this work and is likely to become one of the landmark publications associated with this project.

A final chapter by Andrew Shenton falls neither within the framework of youth everyday life or school information seeking, but rather is holistic in its approach. Addressing information-seeking failures experienced by young people four through eighteen years of age, it might be appropriately subtitled "Close encounters with information sources." Focus groups and individual interviews identified five categories of underlying factors associated with failures: "need/source mismatch, knowledge deficiency, skill shortcomings, psychological barriers, and social unease and inhibitions." Shenton carefully points out that information-seeking failure is not always associated with deficiencies in children and young adults and provides implications and suggestions for practice in terms of collections and information literacy education.

Overall analysis of all the contributed chapters yields some interesting trends. Youth information behavior researchers, with only three of the ten chapters referencing child or adolescent developmental theory, appear to still not be seriously attending to the intrinsic developmentally different characteristics of young people in either the design or discussion and interpretation of studies. This is unfortunate, as the examples provided by Hughes-Hassell, Large et al., and Silverstein demonstrate that developmental theory can provide powerful tools for research design, data analysis, theory building, and simply understanding what one is observing. Only half of the studies used other theory (from either within or outside of library and information science) to frame and inform their work. This rate is lower than that for information behavior research in general (58.9 percent) as reported by McKechnie, Pettigrew, and Joyce (2001). However, in three of the chapters, new empirically based theories are proposed. Mehra and Braquet use grounded theory to develop a model of information seeking during queer youth coming-out experiences. Hughes-Hassell and Agosto derive a typology of teens' preferred everyday life information sources. Large et al. describe the development of a new "Bonded Design Model" of technology design, arising from over three years of multimethod fieldwork with elementary school children. It may be argued that the "Bonded Design Model" is the first to adequately describe the process in terms of children and has the potential for application to some contexts involving adults as well.

Chelton and Cool's second book on youth information-seeking behavior is as pleasing and useful as the prior volume in terms of its diversity. The contributed chapters are almost equally divided between the everyday life and school information-seeking contexts, reflecting an increasing interest in the full dimensions of children's and young peoples' lives. While the information worlds of teenagers were addressed in the most chapters (eight of ten, six exclusively), preschoolers (two of ten chapters), children (four of six chapters, two exclusively) and older youth (one chapter) have also been represented. Methods used across the reports of empirical research (nine of the ten chapters) include surveys, focus groups, interviews, and activity and question log analysis, with one-third of the studies using a multimethod approach and an overwhelming majority (seven of nine) choosing qualitative approaches. Clearly the exploration of youth information-seeking behavior is continuing to become methodologically richer. Contributing authors come from diverse backgrounds and include academics, students, and practitioners from the United States, Canada, and the United Kingdom.

I will not comment on Anthony Bernier's chapter. His compelling call to develop a new research agenda for youth information-seeking research that puts the "joy" back into this work and encourages us all to think of children and young adults in different ways stands on its own and informs our responses to and understanding of the work that follows.

REFERENCES

Chelton, Mary K., and Colleen Cool, eds. 2004. *Youth information-seeking behavior: Theories, models, and issues.* Lanham, MD: Scarecrow Press.

McKechnie, Lynne (E. F.), Karen F. Pettigrew, and Steven L. Joyce. 2001. The origins and contextual use of theory in human information behavior research. *The New Review of Information Behavior Research* 2: 47–63.

Savolainen, Reijo. 1995. Everyday life information seeking: Approaching information seeking in the context of "way of life." *Library and Information Science Research* 17(3): 259–94.

Acknowledgments

The editors wish to thank various referees who assisted in reviewing manuscripts for this book: Linda Cooper, Eliza Dresang, Patrick Jones, Peter Scales, Hester Coan, and Ross Todd.

We extend special thanks to Professor Tatjana Aparac-Jelusic, Department of Information Sciences, Faculty of Philosophy, University J. J. Strossmayer in Osijek, and Ivanka Stricevic, director of Children and Youth Services at Zagreb Library, for their commitment to providing worldwide dissemination of scholarly writings in youth information-seeking behavior through their translation of an article about our work into Croatian, the annual LIDA conferences, and their encouragement to us to produce this second volume.

Introduction: "Not Broken by Someone Else's Schedule: On Joy and Young Adult Information Seeking"

Anthony Bernier

Scholarly research on youth information-seeking behavior through the 1980s emerged largely from teacher and librarian concerns with discrete student research and retrieval skills. Since the 1990s, researchers have sought to correct what has been viewed as that literature's under-theorized approach to issues of cognitive development and its various relationships to information behaviors and learning. In other words, the research agenda shifted from examining *what* young people knew and learned, to *how* they learned.[1]

This shift into issues of cognitive development and its relationship to information behaviors has yielded many and important insights into the ways young people gain bibliographic skills. Among these findings emerged an enhanced understanding that young people learn and acquire bibliographic skills differently from adults and that their instructors must take these differences more seriously.[2] We also learned that pedagogy itself must become more pliable, flexible, and take social factors into account, such as the ways in which student self-confidence contributes to higher functioning on discrete tasks like composing search statements.[3] Among the more rich and promising innovations in this work is the pressing of ethnographic research methods into the service of pursuing what young people themselves actually do and say about how they learn.[4]

As this concentration on cognitive development matured, however, it naturally also began to reveal many important gaps in our understanding of how young people seek and behave with information. First, young people are reduced to rather one-dimensional student beings, for instance. Second, especially at odds with adolescents' developmental needs, they are nearly always constructed as individual information seekers. Third, they are nearly always portrayed as lacking and deficient. Finally, given this scholarly backdrop of constructing or imagining young people as individual students with deficient skills is the construction of young people merely as information consumers.

At base, however, the current research agenda would be well served by dramatically expanding the scope of what counts as information gathering, of literacy tasks, and what mental labor in general qualifies as "information behavior." We need to begin asking the "why questions" about youth information-seeking behavior and taking young people more on their own terms than exclusively on terms dictated to them.

CURRENT RESEARCH

What becomes immediately apparent in reviewing recent research on youth information-seeking behavior is the nearly ubiquitous conflation of all "youth" into "student" identities, and nearly all actions reduced to "skills." Long a research imbalance in many disciplines, this self-imposed limit on the narrowly defined instrumental behaviors, skills, and cognitive development of young-people-as-students in librarianship has impaired the ways in which we conceive of and serve them across the wide spectrum of the library's service profile.[5] Among the topics more recently illustrating this pattern are concentrations on school discipline—specific information-seeking behavior, issues of school assignment plagiarism and report research skills, student perceptions of information technologies, as well as studies on student Web searching and Boolean search statements.

What research considers as worthy information behavior is really the information seeking of students toiling away at curricular goals. While it seems logical, of course, that teachers and school librarians would represent young people as students, this ought not necessarily hold true of examining young people from the public library standpoint.[6] When they do, however, public libraries risk excluding nearly all the complexity young people actually embody as well as contradicting the myriad ways in which young people themselves may want to be identified in the public sphere.

Closely related to a current research agenda reducing complex young people into one-dimensional students is the idea that information seeking is individuated. In an effort to test research model validity, to render findings more "relevant," to measure skill acquisition against prescribed standards, scholars feel compelled to pluck young people from their often higher-functioning developmental postures as members of small groups and shoehorn them into lonely learning silos. Learning may be an intimate thing, but it does not always take place alone. This, too, is a function of constructing young-people-as-students. On the other hand, were we to investigate the information-seeking behavior of a youth group planning to raise money by hosting a neighborhood car-wash, one wonders how our perceptions of their behaviors would change. What might researchers find by examining the hierarchical and relationship recognition capacities, the strategizing and analytical skills, the multivariable problem solving exhibited by three fourteen-year-old boys in the participatory cognitive workout called computer gaming?

In addition to constructing nearly all young people as lone academic agents, much of the research on information-seeking behavior engages a rhetoric that, perhaps inadvertently, portrays young people in a decidedly negative light. In a 2002 study, students are characterized as "novice searchers" lacking in the ability "to form effective search plans and queries," or to "cope with searching obstacles," or "assess, refine and select results and synthesize data."[7] Young people are commonly referred to as "copying" from one another, as "cheating" or "plagiarizing," when evidence goes wanting that they actually understand these often difficult-to-define behaviors, whether or not they know that these practices are inappropriate, or even how to tell the difference between collaborative learning and "cheating." Further, while "copying" certainly can be an academic miscue, adolescents are widely known to work more effectively in successfully guided collaborative efforts. Public librarians will immediately recognize that young adults much prefer using the library in small groups. Librarians even increase bibliographic instruction efficiency when they use collaborative pedagogical models. That common bibliographic pedagogy itself, however, may lag behind our understanding and incorporation of youth's developmental needs is seldom factored into the research design.

Likewise problematic is how young people are widely viewed in the research literature as "having difficulty" learning information-seeking techniques or are "challenged" by certain technical interfaces. It is usually their low skill levels, their short attention spans, lack of systematic planning, superficial browsing, inabilities to manage and reduce large volumes of information, difficulties in making relevance and authority judgments, and other inabilities and skill deficits that researchers identify as preventing or retarding an otherwise attained maximum efficiency in navigating search syntax execution.

Rarely does the research examine the field for the ground. Rarely cited, for instance, is software deploying highly technical language or unforgiving interfaces that render it not-yet-ready for serving its nominal customers. Hardly mentioned, identified, or evaluated are skill standards tailored to economic, demographic, linguistic, cultural, or ability-specific youth audiences.[8] One interface apparently must fit all. And, considering that the content being taught may not capture the intrinsic interest of the young people involved, seldom do we read a study measuring information topics selected or nominated by young people themselves. And where is the research stream evaluating and recalibrating the skills, lessons, and pedagogies of school librarians and instructors, to say nothing of public librarians?[9]

Some researchers actively caution against making searching simpler and more transparent, risking that young people might be "handed information on a plate." No advanced features for you! "No pain, no gain," one supposes. A contrary argument would justifiably posit that that is precisely what we should be doing.

In both the scholarly literature, as well as in practitioners' journals, one generally does not need to look too far to find varying degrees of subtle denigration of the research subjects themselves. Young people are characterized as "impatient" and "unprepared," and nearly always just an act or two away from violating behavioral expectations.

Current research on information-seeking behaviors of young people is really less about "information seeking" than it is about constructing youth as library or database or Web users and about improving *student* achievement.

In all of this resides a curious tension. We lean toward treating young people as both entitled to our serious concerns for their information-seeking needs while at the same time constructing them as teetering on the precipice of their own failings: facing a desperate future without bibliographic skills.

Finally, in constructing young research subjects as individual information consumers, current scholarship eclipses any view that young people are increasingly *producers* of information as well. The nation is currently at perhaps only the beginning of a revolution in youth-produced media. In nearly every possible form, young people are individually and collectively growing their own sets of "information vocal chords" in various forms of print media, online, and in broadcast media as well. Each of these expressions requires high levels of information and literacy skills.

Aside from our need to eliminate denigrating, if perhaps only rhetorical slippages, from our scholarship, perhaps a more beneficial way to consider our young subjects would be to engage a more youth-centric approach. Rather than constructing them as impatient, we might alternatively view them as demanding. Rather than view them as unprepared or as needing instruction in this software application or that, we might view them as customers requiring better design from engineers and information managers. Rather than viewing young people as merely gatherers of information we can also begin to view them as entitled agents of literary production. And we might begin to do all this by opening up the domains of youth experience from which we draw our research questions.

NEW POSSIBILITIES FOR RESEARCH

Among the most obvious possibilities for a new research direction lies in balancing the vast majority of scholarship currently devoted to chil-

dren with more concentrated emphasis on adolescents. While researchers have valiantly attempted to stretch their theoretical formulations
across wide boundaries, the results frequently stretch beyond where we
know it should go, beyond developmentally significant frontiers. It may
be true, for instance, that database software needs to provide better
skill-appropriate search options to allow for children's budding linguistic skills. But the array of options required to better facilitate the searching of a sixteen-year-old girl just learning English will differ
substantially. In scenarios like this, however, the literature is silent.
Given the current demographic explosion of adolescent-age youth, both
native born and those new to the United States, this long-established
and inequitable focus on children seems a bit puzzling.

The barriers young people find to information seeking likewise differs by age. Where children are still learning to manipulate basic cognitive categories, young adults confront far more complex barriers to
information. As Ross J. Todd and Susan Edwards point out in a recently
published article on adolescent information seeking about drug use,
libraries were not viewed as effective resources for common, "real-life"
information. And school libraries, they explain, were "perceived as a
mechanism for control, a source of only socially sanctioned material."[10]
We need to test, validate, and feather out the complexities of these adolescent perceptions before we can address them.

But Todd and Edwards introduce an important and exciting new vista
for young adult literacy-behaviors research: "daily life" and other "life
concerns." Their study of teenage girls and drug usage information
reveals large gaps in our prevailing research agenda. They recognize
that adolescents were "not passive, robot-like processors of information" but "active creators of new knowledge, manipulating information
selectively, intentionally, and creatively to build opinions, viewpoints,
arguments, explanations, and to change and/or verify facts."[11] This is
literacy capacity at some of its highest levels. On the other hand, their
work begins to shed light on how social contexts drive a good deal of
adolescent information behavior. Their study shows, for instance: "that
no matter how compelling or authoritative information might be in the
minds of others, no matter how useful someone else might think the
information is, these qualities do not guarantee its receptivity and utilization."[12] So, like it or not, all adolescent literacy acts come embedded

in social contexts. All literacy is local. And research ignores this critical developmental fact at the risk of our own efficacy.

Todd and Edwards begin to pry open a way for future research. Daily life for a large percentage of American youth, however, extends far beyond information about illicit activities. It also includes work and the information behaviors connected to it. As sociologist Stuart Tannock points out, "texts are ubiquitous in the youth workplace."[13] Tannock's study highlights the growing information demands on teenage grocery store bagging clerks. Like so many entry-level occupations to which teenager labor is confined, the workplace requires the management of a "remarkable proliferation of texts." Baggers contend with work schedules and time sheets; accessing, completing, and maintaining forms and documents; print and online store inventory records; work-order databases; tracking advertising promotions (such as discount coupons); training and performance review documents; and ever-increasing "customer service scripts." All of these tasks constitute literacy behaviors.

Clara M. Chu's work on the often weighty family responsibilities of immigrant children also sheds light on everyday information-seeking behaviors, revealing another arena thick with research potential on what counts as "literacy." Chu documents a long list of important information-based responsibilities assumed by immigrant children "mediators," young people who must translate, research, negotiate, and facilitate the demands of a new culture for their elders. Among these responsibilities are finding and completing forms for immigration and tax requirements; locating bureaus, offices, and services; researching and translating information about schools and communicating with landlords, doctors, home repair specialists, and mechanics; writing letters and paying bills; and many other tasks. All of these literacy behaviors cross the boundaries of curricular support, but few of them register on the current research agenda.[14]

JOY AND DAILY LITERACY

Expanding beyond the boundaries of bibliographic skills for curricular support, beyond the examination of common information behaviors of young adults, however, there remains much more to be studied. Young people read, seek, use, transfer, and interpret information well beyond the boundaries of life's "concerns" as well. Not all of their literacies help solve "problems" or make a serious decision. In other words, they also seek joy.

Somewhat outside the perimeter of the community of academic research, comes the Pew Internet and American Life Project study that pushes further into the "daily life" of young people. Along the way, however, it also helps reorder how young adults are constructed as research subjects as well. The Pew's study views young people as leaders in new and proliferating online information behaviors, not mere students lacking skills.[15] Responding to its more youth-friendly accessibility, 87 percent of U.S. teenagers report using the Internet, up 14 percent from Pew's previous study in 2000. Online computer gaming has grown 52 percent since 2000. Online teen news gathering has climbed to 76 percent of U.S. teens surveyed, up 38 percent since 2000. Without reference to school or "problems," teens reportedly increased their access to health information (47 percent during the same period). And teens also now nearly rival adults in seeking digital religious and spiritual material (26 percent of teens versus 30 percent of adults).[16] The Pew study moreover contextualizes a broad array of teen/tech overlap: 84 percent report owning at least one "media device," such as a laptop, cell phone, or a PDA (personal digital assistant)—nearly half own two or more such devices.

In the complex daily world of young adults, capacities for adaptability are outstripping the jokes told at their expense about e-mail addictions, too. Teens now consider e-mail "something you use to talk to 'old people.'"[17] Instead, so-called instant messaging (IM) has rocketed to the top of their technical world. Young adults report using IM for social purposes, for communicating with parents, as well as for talking to friends, even "about homework assignments."[18] In IM, this "multi-channel space of personal expression" contains a rich information gathering and sharing mélange of website links, photos, music, video, text, games, news, and more. One Pew subject, a high school girl, narrates the point nicely: "I know I rely a lot more on the internet for everyday stuff—looking up things that you know, I would have had to call a couple of people to find out. . . . I know I rely on the internet a lot more as I've gotten older."[19]

Little of the joy young people exhibit in this environment connects to curricular standards and search-strategy metrics. Yet, like the school hallway between third and fourth periods, the excitement manifested in young peoples' literacy responses is palpable.

Are they by mere chance better at searching for what they want using these devices, as opposed to our databases, indexes, and shelved collections, or are these devices (driven as they are largely by market forces) simply better and more interestingly designed for their intended customers? In other words, *why* do they so quickly adapt and thrive with some tools and not others? *Why* do they so successfully engage some literacy acts over others?

Also, where the research literature finds young people as impatient and lacking in analytical skills, the Pew study finds young people's literacy and communications skill sets sophisticated and strategically efficient. In the technical and information atmospheres of young people, in the domains over which they exhibit the greatest control, teenagers analytically select, modify, collect, and discard online identities. They cunningly open and close personal access, as illustrated by this young woman:

> I can have my away message up, but I can still talk to people and my away message won't go down. So if I don't want to talk to somebody, I just put up [that] away message and talk to the people that I want to and the other people I can avoid.[20]

Teenagers also carefully monitor social behavior as well as critically evaluate the tools and skills that best fit their discrete and fluid literacy demands. They quickly determine, for instance, when it is more advantageous to send a text message rather than placing a cell phone call or engaging IM. Their quick mental labor considers timing, purpose, cost, amount of information required, and degrees of privacy desired, among other factors. In many ways they have become more facile at deploying these skills than adults. And unlike constructions of young people found in the research literature, this Pew study portrays young adults as sophisticated consumers as well:

> I think text messaging is still too new. It's too expensive and it doesn't come with enough programs. And it's not compatible enough between different kinds of cell phones and stuff for it to work as well as instant messaging yet. Maybe it will be someday, but right now it's not worth it.[21]

THE JOYFUL LITERACIES OF
MARGINALIZED YOUTH

Many other daily forms of adolescent literacy abound, and nearly all of them fall outside of the current research agenda on young adults. Many are not even connected to technology. "I probably read magazines most often," wrote one young adult public library survey taker, "because you don't have to start on a certain page for reading. You can choose what you do and don't want to read."[22]

One of the valid criticisms of the Pew study is that it selected young people from more affluent and mainstream circumstances. But young people considered more on the "margins" of society also exhibit literacy skills in their own daily experiences, and few of those connect to achieving curricular goals. Elizabeth Birr Moje's standout scholarship with young people reflects, for instance, how they synthesize meaning from a variety of creative forms in their literacy enactments. In one interview with a young women named "Chile," Moje noted that Chile

recounted stories from novels and movies that she had seen describing them all in exacting detail . . . providing me with seven pages of interview transcript that described the movie, *Bound by Honor* . . . [and] scenes from *Always Running: La Vida Loca: Gang Days in L. A.*, a novel. Chile was obviously a reader of both traditional print forms and many other forms of representations in the world.[23]

Moreover, Moje is quick to point out that "*virtually all of these literacy practices occurred outside of school.*"[24]

Indeed, the joy young people seek through their literacy enactments comes much less through keyboards, search boxes, and hardcover fiction, than it does through satisfying their real-world needs to develop and maintain relationships and to make their own meanings out of a complicated world.

In his outstanding ethnography of a community of young people in a small northern California town, architect Herb Childress documented one such magical moment in which youth deploy their own definitions of the literacy they had acquired, an instance in which they came together to enlist literacy in the very shape and substance of their relationships. The passage bares quoting at length:

Irene and Mara and I left school on a Wednesday and stopped at Julian's house at about 3:30. We'd intended to drop off his script for our upcoming performance and just take off; but we went in and sat down for a minute, and that became ten minutes, and that became five hours. And during that five hours, we discussed which soliloquy from Hamlet was our favorite. All three of them were actually passionate about their choices, interrupting one another to finish a passage in unison, as thought discussing a favorite song from the radio. We talked about thirty or forty movies, both current and historical; and about another dozen or so books; and about going out dancing at the Run Club in Port City; and about possible careers; and why Julian was confused about whether or not to keep on going toward being an elementary school teacher. We talked about friends and lovers; talked about why it's so hard to have a really affectionate relationship between men; talked about the differences between friends and best friends. We talked about ideal educations and how we aren't really close to them yet. In short . . . we had a five-hour-long, erudite, skilled conversation; the sort of wide-ranging and fearless talk that can only occur among people who trust one another, in settings not broken by someone else's schedule, surrounded by visible proof of aspirations and desires.[25]

This utopian scene brings information and literacy together in a youth community context, a local context. Young people defining for themselves (that is to say constructing themselves) in terms of how they will seek, define, and deploy their synthesized literacies. Those terms include integrating personal experiences, deepening relationships with conventional and unconventional texts, blending them toward visions of their own futures, all mixed together in an atmosphere of trust, community, and joy. For young people at least, there are local literacies of joy.

YOUNG PEOPLE AS LITERACY PRODUCERS

Finally, in addition to the research and scholarship constructing young people as solitary skill-lacking students, recent work also imagines their information-seeking skills and literacies exclusively within the context of information consumption. In other words, young people's contribution to their own literacy experiences consists largely of consuming the instructional endeavors of teachers illuminating dazzling new databases or buying new digital communications products. Youth literacy has worn the face of a consumer. Increasingly however, they produce their own.

Young people *themselves* have begun to bend and twist new and ever cheaper communications and information technologies toward developing literary vocal chords of their own. I call the manifestations of these new literary vocal chords "fugitive materials" that engage "subversive" literacies. Perhaps needless to say, these otherwise pejorative terms refer to how our institutions and research agendas have treated them early on, rather than how young people themselves characterize them.

Fugitive literature is produced by and delivered to the youth market not in huge, industrywide jobber tonnage, but in relatively small lots, one-time printings, *non*-sequential, *non*-serial productions. Frequently this is the kind of stuff designed to fly below the radar of the official mediators of "true," "legitimate," and "profitable" literature.

The otherwise professional term for much of this body of work is "ephemera," a polite synonym for "not valuable." And not without some practical reasoning. These fugitive materials present researchers and librarian allies of young people alike unique challenges with respect to institutional embrace. Cataloging such ad hoc publications, for instance, or shelving and providing access to these "fugitive" materials threaten to drive librarians to distraction. Even subscribing to or collecting these acts of fugitive or subversive literacy challenge us in unusual ways. As important and culturally relevant as these materials have become to young readers and writers, however, few of our institutions or our research models, appear ready to respond to them.

Nevertheless, fugitive productions embody a vast and rapidly growing landscape of young adult–produced literacy. In the San Francisco Bay Area, to highlight just one growing media empire of young adults, resides the Pacific News Service's "Youth Communications Team" (YCT), promoting no less than seven market-viable formats. These formats range from hefty weekly literary newspapers containing the original and creative content of incarcerated youth (*The Beat Within*), to online collaborations of young poets and spoken-word artists (Poetry Television). Other YCT formats include quarterly zines produced by Bay Area young workers, artists, and activists; one-off resource publications; and websites featuring practical information, personal stories, and art "by America's nomadic homeless youth population (*Road-*

dawgz)"; as well as a full-grown glossy-covered regional magazine circulating over twenty-five thousand copies monthly (*YO! Youth Outlook*).

And there are of course other non-YCT-affiliated youth-produced publications from the Bay Area. Oakland's *NexGeneration* publishes quarterly on local and national news, profiles, and editorials. It's motto: "Da magazine of truth from da youth." The Bay Area is also home to, among other growing institutions, the Youth Media Council (YMC). YMC is a media watchdog outlet dedicated to "amplifying the public voice of marginalized youth and their communities." In 2002 YMC published an essential and blistering media critique in "Speaking for Ourselves: A Youth Assessment of Local News Coverage."[26]

Of course, the Bay Area does not hold a monopoly on burgeoning youth-produced media. Locally produced school newspapers, for instance, are published from one end of the nation to the other. *New Expression* has published monthly from Chicago since 1977. *LAYouth* in Los Angeles, rising from the ashes of the 1992 civil disturbances, publishes young journalists and writers monthly during the school year. The magazine *represent* publishes the writing exclusively of New York's foster care youth.

And youth-produced radio is itself flowering. Witness the Peabody Award–winning Youth Radio, from Berkeley. Youth Radio's journalism and editorials are syndicated across the country on National Public Radio. The Blunt Youth Radio Project comes from youth in Portland. Radio Diaries comes from New York. Voices of Youth broadcasts from Austin. RadioArte broadcasts live performance, news, local features, and music bilingually from Chicago. And this is not to mention numerous television programs produced throughout the nation in large and small cities alike informed by and/or entirely brought to air by young people.

These youth-produced formats are attracting the attention not only of their young audiences and the institutional supporters who help launch them, but increasingly of mass market advertisers, educators, and service organizations as well. As YCT says themselves, "communication enables America's diverse youth cultures to come of age and find their place in society at large. They are the voices and stories that will shape the future, and they will not be ignored."[27] Well, perhaps they reveal a bit of unwarranted youthful optimism on that last point. Generally speaking, our research agendas and collections holdings have indeed ignored them.

All of these formats, from newspapers through broadcast media, require not only high-level organizational skills and sophisticated resources management, but a wide and deep array of literacy capacities, including research and information seeking. Few of them, however, are executed by youth-as-students. None of them view youth literacy merely as a consumptive endeavor. And none of them are brought to audiences by lone rangers.

SUMMARY

As with the ever-increasing use of new communications devices, fugitive literacy exhibits new manifestations of youth vocal chords. Youth communication is coming alive during our current technical age, defined by its prevailing features: instantaneity, temporariness, portability, flexibility, and high customization . Neither do new communications devices nor fugitive literacies rely completely on national demographic or marketing trends. They rely instead on the up-close neighborhood, the local concerns of students at XYZ High School, on particular music affinity groups, around specific and youth-defined lifestyle identities and youth culture rituals. For so many young people, literacy is a highly local affair. On the other hand, the rather sinister coinage of "fugitive" accurately implies the negative attitude with which our research and institutions currently approach these emerging trends in young adult information seeking, literacy, and culture.

Youth literacies, in all their manifestations, are quickly becoming an ever more complex and fantastically exciting landscape. And if we are responsive to these changes, at least *more* responsive than we've been in the past, we can look forward to enjoying better and richer relationships with young people than we have ever had before.

Focusing on these emergent, fugitive, and subversive literacies is where at least some of our future research should go. But in so doing, we should focus on the "why" questions about young adult literacies. *Why* do so many boys, for instance, read so deeply about Darth Vader? *Why* is youth journalism (in all its forms) exploding? *Why* are Chicano youth drawn to Old English texts? From *there* we can pick up the challenge as information professionals to link those interests, or, as Frances Jacobson Harris recently put it, "merge bridging functions" at the crossroads of information and literacy in its many forms and flows. In this context, literacy is not an end in itself, and it does not reduce young people to one-dimensional utilitarian functionaries.

At least part of the answer to why boys seek Darth Vader, why young journalists flourish, and why Old English is popular is because that is how many young people find joy and meaning in their own definitions of literacy. Building on those reasons and practices should be as important to us as improving narrowly defined database retrieval results in the service of curricular goals.

NOTES

1. M. K. Chelton and C. Cool, eds., *Youth Information-Seeking Behavior: Theories, Models, and Issues* (Lanham, MD: Scarecrow Press, 2004), vii–xiii.

2. J. S. Watson, "'If You Don't Have It, You Can't Find It': A Close Look at Students' Perceptions of Using Technology," in *Youth Information-Seeking Behavior: Theories, Models, and Issues*, ed. M. K. Chelton and C. Cool, 145–80 (Lanham, MD: Scarecrow Press, 2004).

3. D. Nahl and V. H. Harada, "Composing Boolean Search Statements: Self-confidence, Concept Analysis, Search Logic, and Errors," in *Youth Information-Seeking Behavior: Theories, Models, and Issues*, ed. M. K. Chelton and C. Cool, 119–44 (Lanham, MD: Scarecrow Press, 2004).

4. R. J. Todd, and S. Edwards, "Adolescents' Information Seeking and Utilization in Relation to Drugs," in *Youth Information-Seeking Behavior: Theories, Models, and Issues*, ed. M. K. Chelton and C. Cool, 353–86 (Lanham, MD: Scarecrow Press, 2004); and D. Bilial, "Research on Children's Information Seeking on the Web," in *Youth Information-Seeking Behavior: Theories, Models, and Issues*, ed. M. K. Chelton and C. Cool, 271–91 (Lanham, MD: Scarecrow Press, 2004).

5. As long ago as 1978, Mary K. Chelton was calling for research on "non-school-related motivation factors" in public library use. It seems as though the introduction of information technology delayed the school bell from ringing for more than a quarter century. Cited in M. L. Shontz, "Selected Research Related to Children's and Young Adult Services in Public Libraries," *Top of the News* 38, no. 2 (1982): 125–42.

6. In her broad and synthetic treatment of Information and Communication Technology (ICT), school librarian Frances Jacobson Harris advocates for combining, rather than resisting, the ways in which young people are rapidly adapting information technologies for social purposes. Yet her purpose is nevertheless to

improve student learning. See F. J. Harris, *I Found It on the Internet: Coming of Age Online* (Chicago: American Library Association, 2005).

7. J. Branch, "Helping Students Become Better Electronic Searchers," *Teacher Librarian* 30, no. 1 (2002): 14.

8. For a rare glimpse into the complexities of teaching students with disabilities, see J. Murray, "Teaching Information Skills to Students with Disabilities: What Works," in *The Whole School Library Handbook*, ed. B. Woolls and D. V. Loertscher, 253–56 (Chicago: American Library Association, 2005).

9. Only one recent study advocates a partnership between teachers and students in both the learning and teaching of new information resources. Watson, "If You Don't Have It," 176–77.

10. Todd and Edwards, "Adolescents' Information Seeking," 358.

11. Todd and Edwards, "Adolescents' Information Seeking," 358.

12. Todd and Edwards, "Adolescents' Information Seeking," 381.

13. S. Tannock, "The Literacies of Youth Workers and Youth Workplaces," *Journal of Adolescent and Adult Literacy* 45, no. 2 (2001): 140–43.

14. C. M. Chu, "Immigrant Children Mediators (ICM): Bridging the Literacy Gap in Immigrant communities," *New Review of Children's Literature and Librarianship* 5 (1999): 85–94.

15. Pew Internet and American Life Project, "Teens and Technology: Youth Are Leading the Way to a Fully Wired and Mobile Nation," http://www.Pewinternet .org/pdfs/PIP_Teens_Tech_July2005web.pdf (accessed August 3, 2005).

16. Pew, "Teens and Technology," 42.

17. Pew, "Teens and Technology," ii.

18. Pew, "Teens and Technology," iii.

19. Pew, "Teens and Technology," 13.

20. Pew, "Teens and Technology," 25.

21. Pew, "Teens and Technology," 29.

22. P. J. Jones, "The Hip and Well-read: The Reading Interests of Older Teens," in *Serving Older Teens*, ed. S. B. Anderson, 112 (Westport, CT: Libraries Unlimited, 2004).

23. E. B. Moje, *"All the Stories That We Have": Adolescents' Insights about Literacy and Learning in Secondary Schools* (Newark, DE: International Reading Association, 2000), 39.

24. Moje, *"All the Stories That We Have,"* 39 (emphasis in text).

25. H. Childress, *Landscapes of Betrayal, Landscapes of Joy: Curtisville in the Lives of Its Teenagers* (Albany: State University of New York Press, 2000). 209–10.

26. Youth Media Council, "Speaking for Ourselves: A Youth Assessment of Local News Coverage," http://www.youthmediacouncil.org/pdfs/speaking.pdf (accessed May 22, 2005).

27. Pacific News Service, "PNS Youth Communications Team," http://news.pa cificnews.org/news/view_custom.html?custom_page_id=51 (accessed June 8, 2005).

1

Tweens and Everyday Life Information Behavior: Preliminary Findings from Seattle[1]

Karen E. Fisher, Elizabeth Marcoux,
Eric Meyers, and Carol F. Landry

As *Time* magazine featured in its August 8, 2005, issue, children age thirteen face pressures today that are far different from those experienced by recent generations (Gibbs 2005). Beyond the earlier onset of puberty for both sexes (Herman-Gidden et al. 2001; Kaplowitz 2004; Kaplowitz et al. 2001; Zuckerman 2001), today's children live in a world of unprecedented social change due to technological advancements, commercialism, and terrorism—among others, often publicized by different media. While the *Time* articles shared insights into the everyday lives of thirteen-year-olds across the country, it focused little on the role of information in kids' lives—a phenomenon also unaddressed by researchers of library and information science (LIS) and the academy in general. This chapter thus holds two objectives: (1) to review LIS studies of kids' everyday information-seeking behavior (more broadly referred to as "information behavior"), and (2) to share the methodology and preliminary findings from a 2005 qualitative study funded by the National Science Foundation about kids aged nine to thirteen and everyday information.

THE TWEENS YEARS: FINDINGS FROM
SCHOOL AND BEYOND

During the preteen or "tween" years, roughly from age nine to thirteen, kids undergo significant physical, emotional, and cognitive development. As kids transition from childhood dependence to adult independence, their social interactions demonstrate a switch in emphasis: parents become less important than peers in decision-making processes, identity formation, and in validation of behaviors (Harter 1983, 1998; Kellet & Ding 2004; Kroger 2004). These years also mark two important transitions that affect tweens' motivation, behavior, and self-perception: the move from the elementary grades to middle school, and then to high school (Wigfield et al. 1996). While sociologists (e.g., Lesko 2001; Miles 2000), educators (e.g., Bransford et al. 2000; Wigfield et al. 1996), and marketers (e.g., Delvecchio 1997; Quart 2004) have focused extensively on understanding tweens, little is known about how life changes influence their information behaviors, particularly those that occur outside the school context. In general, non-LIS studies report that adolescents struggle to carve out a sense of "place"—physical, social, or virtual—in order to cope with the stresses of their changing lives (Elkind 1984; Perret-Clermont 2004), and that they seek new information types and information sources as they try to make sense of their evolving identities in an increasingly postmodern and uncertain society (Lesko 2001; Miles 2000; Wyn 2005).

The vast majority of LIS research on minors focuses upon the school context—usually specific information-based tasks or assignments—and thus the development of information literacy and problem-solving models that are both descriptive and instructionally prescriptive. The most refined and widely cited models include Kuhlthau's Information Search Process (ISP) (1990, 2004), Eisenberg and Berkowitz's Big Six Process (1990), Eisenberg (2004), and Gross's imposed query (2004). Lesser known but highly similar approaches to the challenge of disseminating and building information literacy skills include The PLUS model (Herring 1996), the Peer-Tutoring Model (Deese-Roberts & Keating 2000) and The Pitts-Stripling Model (Stripling & Pitts 1988). While validated repeatedly in academic and library contexts, these models offer little insights into kids' everyday information behavior and, specifically, interpersonal information seeking. Related "school" studies report that children's information search-and-retrieval skills differ from those of adults, and that electronic resources pose problems for children with limited conceptions of resource relevance and authority (Agosto 2002; Bilal 2000, 2001; Fidel et al. 1999; Gross 2004; Hirsch 1999; Large et al. 1998). Along this line, researchers identified how specific media include affordances that influence information searching and retrieval, as well as how students use these media to resolve information needs (Kozma 1991; Marchionini 1989). These studies, however, are limited in that they focus on a particular information tool (e.g., CD-ROM or the Internet) or exclude the complex nature of children's personal inquiries, which may incorporate interpersonal and tool-mediated strategies to solve an information problem.

To date, studies of everyday information behavior have largely focused on adults (cf., Case 2002) or teenagers (e.g., Agosto & Hughes-Hassell 2005; Latrobe & Havener 1997), two populations with significantly greater autonomy and mobility than preteens, and thus greater capacity for creating and using social networks that might facilitate interpersonal information behaviors. Given teenagers' proximity in age to tweens, the two primary studies of teenagers are particularly significant. Agosto and Hughes-Hassell (2005) performed semistructured group interviews with twenty-seven urban teens (aged fourteen to seventeen) in two Philadelphia venues to identify their information needs, sources, and preferred media. Using Savolainen's (1995) ELIS framework, they reported that teens identified friends and family as their preferred information sources, and cell phones as their most preferred method of tool-mediated communication. Top non-interpersonal sources were the telephone, television, school, and the Internet. A typology of their needs listed schoolwork, time/date, social life, and weather as their primary information needs. Furthermore, these teens were highly skeptical of libraries and books as sources of everyday information, casting library staff as negative social types. Latrobe and Havener (1997) studied eighteen teens (sixteen to seventeen years old) in an eleventh grade honors math course. Through surveys and individual interviews, they reported that teens were most in need of course-related information, but also sought information on relationships, work, future plans, recreation, health, and lifestyles. All students reported using teachers, peers, and course-related materials to fulfill their information needs.

A third related study by Shenton and Dixon (2003) found that "youngsters" of all ages turn to adults and peers for information. Conducting focus groups and interviews with 188 students aged seven to seventeen in a rural town in Great Britain, they revealed a typology of thirteen different information needs: advice, spontaneous "life situation" information, personal information, affective support, empathetic understanding, support for skills development, school-related subject information, interest-driven information, self-development information, consumer information, preparatory information, reinterpretations and supplementations, and verification information. The study further identified that some young people take three general social types into consideration when selecting persons to consult about an information need: (1) people of convenience; (2) friends or peers of comparable experience; and (3) experts, such as teachers. Teachers and librarians were cast as negative social types by some students, who were loath to approach them for particular information needs. Unfortunately, Shenton and Dixon's typology fails to distinguish information needs developmentally, or enumerate qualitative differences in strategies among the developmental periods of childhood, preteen, and teen.

Collectively, these three studies are the first to address the everyday information behavior of minors; however, research is needed that focuses upon minors at specific developmental stages and, hence, age groups.

NSF-FUNDED STUDY OF TWEENS

Our investigation of the everyday information behavior of tweens (children ages nine to thirteen) is part of a larger study entitled "Talking with You: Exploring Interpersonal Information-seeking" funded by the National Science Foundation (NSF).[2] This larger study is the first to focus specifically on why people turn to other people for everyday information,[3] ranging from finding new jobs and lower mortgages to healthcare, housing, childcare, social activities, and other aspects of daily life. The collective results will be used to derive a theoretical model of interpersonal information seeking that can be used to design and deliver information systems and services. From over thirty populations tweens were specifically chosen for their conceptual interest: it was hypothesized that rich insights would be obtained from a population nurtured from birth to seek information interpersonally and at a life juncture of becoming independent from the adult-oriented family/school structure, while also marked as society's most technically savvy generation. It was further hypothesized that tweens would engage in media-rich interpersonal information-seeking behavior, using all available synchronous and asynchronous media (e.g., face-to-face, telephone, e-mail, chat rooms, newsgroups, etc.).

Against a backdrop of several information and everyday life theories, including Dervin's sense-making (cf., 1992), Chatman's normative behavior (cf., 2000), and Fisher's information grounds (cf., Fisher & Naumer 2005) along with principles of everyday information behavior discussed by Harris and Dewdney (1994) and Case (2002),[4] the tweens study was guided by the following research questions:

- What types of everyday information do tweens perceive themselves as needing?
- How do tweens seek everyday information?
- What barriers do tweens encounter in seeking and using information?
- What criteria do tweens use in assessing and sharing information and information sources?
- What are the roles of information grounds in tweens' lives?
- What roles are played by different social types regarding information flow?
- How do tweens manage their accumulated everyday information?

These questions were explored using the "Tween Day" approach, which we designed to optimize the quality and amount of data possibly collected from a minor population during a single five-hour (10 a.m.–3 p.m.) timeframe. Initially we planned a series of focus groups and follow-up interviews with individual tweens in youth agency settings over a three-week period. This design, however, was abandoned because the benefits of prolonged engagement were far outweighed by difficulties of gaining agency access, parental consent, and minor assent, and preventing a high dropout rate.

Tween Day was held twice:[5] first in May 2005 at The Information School of the University of Washington (UW), and second in July 2005 at an Outreach Christian Ministry in a low-income neighborhood on the west side of Seattle, as a means of confirming early findings with a less advantaged population. Both Tween Days employed the same approach.[6] At UW, a recruiting flyer was posted on a community lists-erv, emphasizing that anyone between ages nine and thirteen could participate in the study regardless of an official affiliation with UW. At the Ministry, a key contact distributed the flyer to members of the congregation indicating that anyone could participate.

At each Tween Day, after the tweens arrived, parental consent and minor assent forms were collected, name badges were distributed, and mini-snacks provided, the tweens and researchers were introduced and the study procedures explained. One-hour focus groups comprising five to six tweens each were then conducted, followed by a snack and a second, one-hour focus group comprising the same members and researchers. After lunch, the tweens participated in a Webquest computer lab activity at UW, and a collage-making activity at the Ministry because we could not bring along computers and Internet access. During the activity, tweens were asked to participate in individual, thirty-minute interviews. In return, the tweens received UW T-shirts, a fancy certificate of participation, and a lootbag containing a UW mug and tchotchkes, an Internet guide, and candy. To improve accuracy and facilitate question asking, all focus groups and interviews were audio recorded. During the focus groups, two researchers were present of opposite sex; the interviews were held in rooms that afforded both privacy and public viewing. While parents were invited to attend Tween Day, at each locale only one female parent was present.

During focus group #1 the tweens were given the scenario of a new kid (their age) moving to their neighborhood. The tweens were asked to describe what everyday life would be like for the new tween and what types of things s/he would need to know. Then the tweens were asked to discuss how the following information sources would be used:

- peers with whom the tween is close
- peers with whom the tween is not close
- adults with whom the tween is close (mainly family, teachers)
- adults with whom the tween is not close
- websites
- television
- books and magazines

Focus group #1 ended with the tweens identifying the information grounds that their new neighbor might utilize. As explained by Fisher and Naumer (2005), information grounds are social settings where people go for a particular purpose (e.g., get a bike fixed, get a haircut, to eat, etc.) but wind up sharing information in the course of interacting with other people.

During focus group #2, the tweens were asked to expand the information grounds previously identified in terms of how frequently one would go there, who else would be present, what one would talk about, what one liked about it, and so on. Tweens were also asked to explain under what circumstances the sources discussed in the focus group #1 would not be used to seek information.

In the individual interviews, tweens were asked to recount a recent incident in which they sought non-school-related information as well as a time when they shared non-school-related information with someone. The recounts were based on Dervin's (1992) sense-making, micro-moment time line approach. After the tweens explained how they manage or keep track of all the everyday information that they pick up, they were asked to explain why they agreed or disagreed with ten generalizations of tweens and information that were designed to be thought provoking.

In total, twenty-one tweens participated: sixteen at UW (ten female; six male) and five at the Ministry (two female; three male). The UW tweens were Caucasian; the Ministry tweens were African American. Average age was 11.5 (11.3 at UW; 12.2 at Ministry). At UW and the ministry, respectively, five and three tweens did not show despite earlier confirmation.

Overall, the tweens were very engaged with the focus groups and interviews, providing rich insights into their information worlds. Before discussing our findings, we wish to remark upon two methodological concerns. First, Tween Day, itself, was neither designed to be nor studied as an information ground in its own right. While it is possible that some elements of an information ground might have occurred, the basic premise and core elements were not in play. Second, a portion of the study focused upon the tweens' interaction with adults, including those whom they do not know well, while seeking information. We, the researchers, of course, fit into this source category. Based on our analysis of the incidence of observer effect,[7] however, we did not identify any strong events in which the children's behavior or responses seemed altered due to our presence, the study methodology or instruments used. Along this line, to ensure trustworthiness (the study's reliability and validity—in quantitative terms), we implemented several measures as recommended by Chatman (1992) and Lincoln and Guba (1985). Dependability (or reliability) was ensured through: (1) consistent note taking, (2) exposure to multiple and different situations using triangulated methods, (3) comparing emerging themes with findings from related studies, (4) audio taping interviews, (5) employing intracoder and intercoder checks, and (6) analyzing the data for incidents of observer effect. We addressed different forms of validity as follows:

- Face validity: asked whether observations fit an expected or plausible frame of reference;
- Criterion/internal validity (or credibility): (1) pretested instruments, (2) rigorous note taking, (3) triangulated methods, (4) peer debriefing, (5) negative case analysis, and (6) member checks or participant verification;
- External validity: provided "thick description" and comprehensive description of our methods and theory so others can determine if our findings can be compared with theirs; and
- Construct validity: examined data with respect to information behavior principles and theories of normative behavior, sensemaking, and information grounds.

Moreover, learning and adopting the tweens' "language" greatly improved the efficiency of the study and increased the trustworthiness of the data. By employing interview and observational methods we listened for and adopted the tweens' language, thus allowing for subsequent interpretation from the participants' perspectives.

In the remainder of this chapter, we share preliminary findings regarding the tweens' interview responses to the ten generalizations. Collective findings about the tweens' perceptions of specific sources, their information-seeking and -sharing incidents, as well as their information grounds and information management practices are the focus of a forthcoming report.

GENERALIZING ABOUT TWEENS: PERCEPTIONS OF SOCIAL TYPES AND INFORMATION SOURCES

To gain insight into how tweens understand the role of social types in the exchange of information, including parents, teachers, and adults in general, the fifteen interviewed tweens were asked to respond to a list of ten provocative "generalizations" about information behavior. These generalizations were largely tied to Chatman's (cf., 2000) theory of normative behavior—which posits, in essence, that information seeking is a healthy and sanctioned activity within a social group—as well as Fisher's (Fisher and Naumer 2005) information grounds. Responses were initially analyzed using three codes: *agree* (full or nearly full agreement); *disagree* (full or nearly full disagreement); *both* (equal or nearly equal parts agreement and disagreement) (see table 1.1). We then qualitatively analyzed the tweens' open responses regarding why they assumed their positions. While the responses from the tweens interviewed at both UW and the ministry were largely in agreement, except for the last generalization, their rationales or stories differed markedly at times. In general, the tweens at UW were from advantaged backgrounds, all had computer and Internet at home if not in their bedrooms, and were connected in someway to the UW. The tweens from the ministry, on the other hand, did not have a UW link, had televisions instead of computers in their bedrooms, and could only access the latter at school (and they were on summer break during the study) or library, which they seldom visited.

Generalization 1: Teachers Can Answer Any Question of a Preteen

Our tweens (14/15) largely disagreed with this statement, asserting general human fallibility where "nobody knows everything" (Mr. Blackwood at UW)[8] or more specifically that "teachers don't know everything" (Sydney at UW). Other students documented specific instances of teacher fallibility. Aeisha (Ministry), for example, said "No, it's not true, because when I asked my teacher how many people died on the Lewis and Clark expedition, she couldn't answer it." Other

Table 1.1. Tween Interview Responses

Alias	Age	Gender	Ethnicity[a]	1	2	3	4	5	6	7	8[b]	9[b]	10
												Responses	
Aeisha	12	F	XXX	D	D	D	A	D	A	D	A	D	B
Austin	13	M	XXX	D	D	D	D	D	D	D	A	D	B
Brooke	13	F	XXX	D	D	D	B	B	D	B	D	A	D
Ellen	13	F	XXX	D	B	D	D	B	D	D	D	D	D
Kylie	10	F	XXX	B	D	D	D	D	B	D	A	D	D
Ladarius	13	M	XXX	D	D	D	B	B	A	D	A	D	B
Lauren	11	F	XXX	A	D	D	B	B	B	D	A	D	B
Madison	11	F	XXX	D	D	D	A	B	B	B	B	N/A	B
Mr. Blackwood	11	M	XXX	D	D	D	D	B	D	B	A	D	B
Mr. Henderson	11	M	XXX	D	D	D	D	A	A	B	A	A	B
Omar	13	M	XXX	D	D	D	D	D	B	A	B	D	A
Peyton	13	M	XXX	D	D	D	D	D	B	D	A	A	D
Rose	10	F	XXX	D	D	D	D	B	B	B	D	D	B
Shaniqua	10	F	XXX	B	A	D	B	A	A	D	N/A	A	D
Sydney	11	F	XXX	D	D	D	D	D	D	D	D	D	D
Totals: Disagree (D)				12	13	15	9	6	5	9	4	10	6
Both (B)				2	1	0	4	7	6	5	2	0	8
Agree (A)				1	1	0	2	2	4	1	8	4	1

1. "Teachers can answer any question that a preteen might have."
2. "Parents can answer any question that a preteen might have."
3. "Preteens always tell an adult when they have a question."
4. "Preteens don't like to seek information unless they absolutely have to."
5. "Preteens don't like it when people give them information."
6. "Preteens don't like it when other preteens seek information and then know more than they do."
7. "It's not cool to tell a preteen something unless he/she asks/or brings it up first."
8. "Preteens have lots of places where they can go and share information with other preteens."
9. "Society encourages preteens to gather wherever they want and socialize."
10. "Adults make it hard for preteens to talk about everyday life with other preteens and share information."

[a] IRB restrictions prevent the researchers from sharing this information due to sample size.
[b] Totals = 14 for responses #8 & #9. For all others Totals = 15

tweens noted that teachers' subject specialties prevent them from answering wide-ranging questions or in content areas outside their certification. Lauren (UW), the only tween who agreed with the statement, limited her answer to her own experience, saying it is "mostly true to me" but admitted that another student had once stumped the class's student teacher. Overall, teachers were perceived by these preteens as providing content for specific academic subjects, but limited in the range of information they could provide to curious adolescents.

Generalization 2: Parents Can Answer Any Question of a Preteen

The tweens (14/15) also largely disagreed that parents can answer any question. While most felt that parents were more capable of answering personal or social questions than teachers, there was a palpable distance between teachers and pupils that limited their discourse with teachers to academic matters. As Mr. Blackwood (UW) explained, "The teacher is more focused on making sure you learn things in class; the parent is the person who is looking out for you." Ellen (UW) clarified the difference between *teacher knowledge* and *parent knowledge* in saying: "Parents can answer social questions but a teacher can't. There are a lot of academic questions that a teacher can. Once you've got teachers and parents, you've got a lot of resources you can talk to." On an opposite note, Aeisha and Peyton, who were interviewed at the Ministry, felt that social information was parents' greatest weakness as an information source. They explained that a generation gap prevents parents from understanding the problems faced by modern tweens. More generally, Aeisha remarked that the "world changes every generation" and that even though parents were "once our age, things are different now." As illustrated in the following excerpt, Peyton said that social contexts, including more violent schools, are different than in the past, requiring different social information than parents can provide:

Interviewer: What types of questions might appear that parents wouldn't be able to answer?
Peyton: [They can answer] about schoolwork, like chores or something, but not like anything about your personal life.
Interviewer: Why's that?

Peyton: Because they might not be able to understand what you're going through. That situation.
Interviewer: What about parents who say I was that age once?
Peyton: Their time may have been different than our time. People might have been nicer or more talkative back then. Like now, there's a lot of violence that happens or something like that. But back then there wasn't any violence that happened between schools. So their time frame is probably different than ours.

Generalization 3: Preteens Always Tell an Adult When They Have a Question

Everyone (15/15) disagreed with this generalization, saying that they have questions that are reserved from their parents, that they either "keep to themselves" or ask only of peers. According to Sydney (UW), posing questions to friends is a way of demonstrating some level of autonomy from adults: "Sometimes I can ask my friends, and they'll tell me. And so I don't always need an adult's help." Aeisha (Ministry) added a different spin saying, sometimes "it's a question that's meant for a kid to answer, that an adult might not understand." The idea that there are *kid questions* asked of peers and *adult questions* reserved for adults was a prevalent theme. Brooke (UW) identified three reasons why preteens might not go to an adult with a question: "They might be too embarrassed to ask, too proud to ask, or they just don't think it's important enough to ask." Mr. Henderson (UW) said it would be "uncomfortable" to ask certain questions of adults. Rose (UW) explained that parents will inadvertently embarrass tweens in public if they are aware of information that is "really personal," such as "the boy you like." The perceived disconnect between adults and preteens makes conversation with peers "easier," even if they perceive the information source to be less accurate or helpful, as Peyton (Ministry) explained:

> Like a relationship between a girlfriend and a boyfriend, you might not go to your parents for advice or something because they might blow something out of proportion. Something like that. But if you talk to your friends, they probably won't know what to say, but it will be easier to talk to them.

Within a peer group, our participants said that there are "close friends" or "good friends" whom one can trust with more sensitive information. Other members of the peer group may be called friends, but are less trustworthy—people whom Peyton described "friends that I just say hi and bye to." Within the broader "friends" social type, our participants identified friends who were *strong ties* and others who were *weak ties*, and shared different information with them based on tie strength.

Generalization 4: Preteens Don't Like to Seek Information or Ask Questions Unless Absolutely Necessary

Most (13/15) tweens disagreed with this statement, feeling that tweens are naturally curious, and at a point in their lives when they are asking questions regularly, if not constantly. Mr. Henderson (UW) explained that the preteen years are "a time when we're trying to find out about as much as we can." Austin (UW) also disagreed, remarking: "I think exactly the opposite of that. [G]eneration Y is named that for a reason, spelled w-h-y, and that's because this generation tends to ask a lot of questions. And usually, our teachers have to slog through a barrage of questions flying at them all day." Participants who agreed with the generalization, or provided a mixed response, focused on the perceived social cost of asking questions, particularly at school or in group settings. Thus some tweens reserve their questions, hoping they will be answered at "a later time." Admitting ignorance is scary for adolescents, acknowledged Omar (Ministry), who emphasized that "some preteens are scared because other preteens might laugh at them and say, 'You don't know that?'" Madison (UW) provided an example from her experience:

> Sometimes people just think . . . that the question will be answered later on. And sometimes preteens get embarrassed because maybe somebody else knows the answer and they'll laugh at them for something like that. I've seen it happen in my classroom before. Somebody asks the question and the other person knows the answer, and starts laughing, and it gets kind of embarrassing.

For tweens in our study, curiosity was balanced by a keen awareness of peer pressure, and the implications of how information seeking might be perceived in a social context.

Generalization 5: Preteens Don't Like It When They Are Given Information

Most tweens (13/15) either disagreed or agree/disagreed with this state-ment, suggesting that information giving is closely related to the proc-ess of information seeking, and a natural part of communication. Kylie (UW) explained that getting and giving information is a reciprocal process, "I like it when I'm given information and I'm a preteen. Because when I ask for information, I like giving it back. And so, I like giving information." Sydney (UW) emphasized the comforting aspects of information exchange with close ties, such as a parent: "It is fine with me when people give me information. Sometimes my mom tells me something at night before I go to bed, and then I sleep on it, and then I remember it in the morning. It makes me happy to know that people want to tell me information."

Two participants were in strong agreement with this statement, since they perceived the information given would be critical, rather than con-structive. Shaniqua (Ministry) explained that preteens "don't like to be corrected." Other responses reflected the importance of situationality and the nature of the information being given. Mr. Blackwood's (UW) answer was typical of these: "it depends on what [preteens] think of the information." Adult criticism, reprimand, or notice of failure was the type of information that preteens were not interested in receiving. Aus-tin (UW) provided a nuanced reply, which recognized the constructive value of critical information over time: "I usually like it when I'm given information, unless it's criticism. And then I'll like it in the long run, but not in the short run." All of the negative information types involved academic or behavioral issues addressed to the tweens by adults, which is closely tied to the developmental insecurities of this age group. Tweens perceive that adults are often the providers of negative informa-tion or information that they do not wish to receive, reinforcing the tension between preteens and adult social types illustrated in General-izations #2–3.

Generalization 6: Preteens Don't Like It When Other Preteens Seek Information and Then Know More Than They Do

Responses were greatly mixed with roughly equal numbers agreeing (4), disagreeing (5) or both agreeing and disagreeing (6) with this statement. Differences stemmed primarily from perceived motivations for information seeking, and how knowledge was used in social contexts and within peer groups. Lauren (UW) summarized the general sentiments on this issue: "Some kids get kind of jealous about what these other kids know about all this other stuff, but some kids just really don't care." Four tweens agreed with the statement, indicating that school in particular can be a competitive information environment. Ladarius (Ministry) said that students make fun of each other for being less knowledgeable: "I know at my school they'll be like, 'I'm smarter than you,' and they'll laugh at you if you get the question wrong." Omar (Ministry) identified the "know-it-all" type that can make other preteens feel inferior. Mr. Henderson (UW) explained that he is competitive within his own circle of friends, and that information is a source of bragging rights in his social group, albeit with benign intent:

> I think that is true because me and my friends, we're competitive about how much we know. And a lot of times when I find my friends know more, they gloat, they try to rub it into the other one's face. It's not like we're making fun of each other. We have good intentions, we're not trying to make the other one feel bad.

The five participants who disagreed with the generalization saw information seeking by others as a positive activity from which they could benefit. They chose to see information-rich peers as a resource, rather than a detriment: "If someone knows more than I do, I can ask if I need anything. And it makes me feel good that there is someone I can ask" (Sydney, UW).

Generalization 7: It's Not Cool to Tell a Preteen Something Unless She or He Asks for It, or Brings It Up First

Most tweens (9/15) disagreed with this statement. They said it was socially acceptable to offer unsolicited information to preteens, which mirrors responses under Generalization #4 where tweens portrayed themselves as naturally curious and taking a positive stance toward information seeking. In explanation, tweens said they occasionally withhold questions themselves, or that they perceive others need information but choose not to ask questions out of insecurity or self-consciousness. According to Shaniqua (Ministry), "it's okay to [tell a preteen something] because they might be too shy to ask." Ellen (UW) revealed that there is potential discomfort on both sides of an information transaction, and that there is a social context that preteens should recognize when they share information:

> Normally no, but you don't want to barge into the subject right away. If you're uncomfortable about it, or if there's other people in the room, that she doesn't want to talk about it. She should try to bring it around at a time when they feel comfortable about it, but it's not necessarily—you wouldn't do it if you don't feel comfortable but it's not necessary.

The mixed responses revealed the tensions that sometimes surround giving unsolicited information to tweens. Rose's (UW) response illuminated that giving tweens information is generally good, but can become unpleasant if too persistent: "No, if they did that all the time, it'd probably get annoying, but if they do that occasionally, it would probably be just fine." Mr. Henderson's (UW) response points to a poignant perception on the part of tweens: that information giving by adults can make the younger recipient feel subordinate or resentful. He explained: "I think it's a yes and a no. We want to know stuff as much as we can, but at the same time, when adults are constantly telling us stuff that we didn't ask for, a lot of times it seems like they're trying to tell us they're superior." These responses emphasize how some tweens are conscious of the inherent power relationships that pervade some information-giving incidents, particularly those that occur between adults and young people. They are also conscious of information giving within their peer group as a kind of social power play, sometimes equating it with "bragging" (Rose, UW) or talking "smack" (Ladarius, Ministry).

Generalization 8: Preteens Have Lots of Places Where They Can Go and Share Information with Other Preteens

Only four tweens strongly agreed (with two others agreeing to some extent) that there are many places (i.e., information grounds) where they can go to share information with their peers. These places included physical and virtual environments, as well as communication technologies that facilitate information sharing. Participants identified school, home, friends' homes, church, shopping malls, and public parks as places they routinely gather with friends to socialize. Within schools, recess and lunch were noted as times of the school day when preteens were most likely to share information. Lauren (UW) explained:

> You can always do it at school. You can always do it at recess, you can always do it at lunch. You can do it after school, you can do it before school, if you got there early enough. And if they come over to your house, they can always do it there. So I think there are plenty of places where kids can talk to each other.

Tweens also noted that they use asynchronous virtual spaces, including chat rooms, weblogs, and multiuser websites to "display their feelings" (Mr. Blackwood, UW), "write whatever you want," or "have an interesting conversation" (Austin, UW). Communication technologies that preteens reported using with their peers were e-mail, instant messaging (IM), and telephone. Six tweens, however, identified significant barriers to information sharing, either for themselves or for other kids they know. These barriers fell into three categories: the safety of public spaces, concerns for tween privacy, and the authority or parents and adults. Omar (Ministry) suggested that some neighborhoods are dangerous for preteens, preventing them from gathering conveniently: "Some kids live in neighborhoods where you can't just walk down the street and go talk to other kids your age." Rose (UW) responded that tweens often do not want to share information in the presence of adults, particularly personal issues, and this limits the number of places they can socialize or the type of information that will be shared: "some places have grown-ups, and some preteens don't really like to talk about private stuff once grown-ups are around." Tweens were aware of the limitations adults imposed on their information sharing, both on their mobility and on the types of communication media they could use with peers. Madison (UW) explained how some preteens have more freedom and mobility than others, and this is a product of parental or family dynamics:

> Sometimes preteens, their parents want them to stay in the house and help do chores and that kind of stuff, so they don't get to hang out with their friends very much. And other preteens, they're parents don't care where they go. So they can go anywhere, and just get information from there. But other preteens

that have to stay home, I think they get information from their family and
sometimes they can call their friends if they really need it.

Sydney (UW) did not feel that she had many places where she could
talk to friends outside of school: "I don't have a lot of places except for
my room, or if I have my friend over or something." Kylie (UW)
expressed the limitations of parental permission to engage in some
forms of information sharing: "I'm not allowed to go on IM or chat
rooms, so I basically have the phone, and e-mail, and face-to-face."

Generalization 9: Society Encourages Preteens to Gather and Socialize Wherever They Want

Also linked to the information grounds framework, this generalization
was not supported by ten of fourteen tweens, who said that the precise
opposite is the truth—that society discourages preteens from socializ-
ing. Many acknowledged that this was a social restriction based on
adult concerns for a child's safety and welfare, while others remarked
that it was largely an issue of authority and control. Austin (UW)
asserted that "kids are kept out of a lot of places . . . for a lot of reasons
that I can see." Omar (Ministry) also saw restrictions based on safety:
"Some moms don't let us go to [certain places] and they don't trust the
world enough to let preteens to go down there." Ellen (UW) pragmati-
cally saw school, which many tweens in our study acknowledged as a
place where socialization can occur, as a highly structured environment
where adults discourage social opportunities:

> We have almost no time for socializing except for lunch. We get five-minute
> breaks between hours. You get five minutes to walk from one end of the
> school, take a detour to the locker, pick up our five pounds of stuff, walk
> around to the other side of the school, sit down, unpack all by the end of the
> bell. And go back to the bathroom and get Kleenex. It feels like a lot of work,
> and I don't see how they expect us to socialize in that time as well.

Two barriers to information sharing analyzed under Generalization
#8—safety and adult authority—were evident in these responses.
While the tweens generally agreed that they have places and tools that
mediate their information behavior, there are restrictions imposed by
the adult world. Tweens perceptions of these restrictions are important

to understanding the relationships that evolve between adults and tweens, and tweens and their peers, particularly as they influence information choices. Peyton (UW), who agreed with this generalization, approached the statement from a different perspective. He suggested that adults encourage good behavior, and use socialization opportunities as a reward: "they're always saying 'don't start anything, or don't do anything to jeopardize your freedom to go anywhere.'" Shaniqua (Ministry) supported this view, recognizing that "sometimes [adults] want us to have fun." Mr. Henderson (UW) saw socialization as a learning opportunity that society endorses: "when you're out there, it kind of encourages you to be able to learn as much as you can."

Generalization 10: Adults Make It Hard for Preteens to Talk about Everyday Life with Preteens and Share Information

Most tweens (14/15) disagreed (or partially disagreed) with this statement, perceiving that adults fulfill an assistive role in their information seeking. Kylie (UW) explained: "I don't think adults really get in the way very much because they're usually just there to help you and to help you understand stuff." Ladarius (Ministry) noted that in school there is a time when talking is not allowed, namely when the teacher is talking, "But you can talk, when it's time to talk." This view seems to accept adult restrictions on tween communication as reasonable, and nondetrimental. While tweens did not attribute negative intentions to adults, they attributed miscommunication, misunderstanding, or "not getting it" to the difficulties that adults pose in tween information sharing. Madison (UW) revealed a disconnect between what parents and preteens see as appropriate information sharing, particularly about matters adolescents see as private:

> Sometimes parents don't get it. I know my mom, whenever I tell her something, and she just doesn't get it, she'll ask questions and sometimes I just don't want to answer them. And it does get hard because when you're talking on the phone about guys or something, and your parents are all saying that you're too young for guys. You know, and you're like fourteen. It's like, hello, I'm a teenager. And it just gets more difficult as you go.

Peyton (UW), who earlier perceived that adults are not capable of understanding some preteen issues, suggested in the following exchange that adults make communication difficult between adults and preteens:

> **Peyton:** Like they might not understand what you're going through, so they'll just automatically give an adult answer instead of a kid answer so we could understand. Instead of us getting in trouble or something.
> **Interviewer:** So adults make it hard for kids to talk to other kids?
> **Peyton:** No, not other kids. They make it hard for us [preteens] to talk to them [adults].

According to Peyton, tweens seek information from their peers on social issues because they have difficulty communicating with adults, who might otherwise be a preferred source. He distinguishes between two types of answers: *kid answers*, which can be understood by young people, and *adult answers*, which are perceived by tweens as inappropriate and punitive.

DISCUSSION

Collectively, the tweens reactions to the ten generalizations suggest that they are highly aware of their own information needs and the roles played by and barriers inherent in different sources. Moreover, their reflections indicated that they view information seeking as a healthy activity but that their needs, particularly for social and personal situations, are not easily met: sources are not easy to access and communicate with, and those that can be accessed may not have the best information. The following themes arose from our analysis of the generalization data:

- Trust, as part of social cost, is highly significant: in choosing a source, tweens indicated that the ability to trust someone with their situation (or secret) far outweighed the source's likelihood of providing accurate information.
- There are levels of disconnect between tweens and adults that affect tweens' access to information sources, including media, places, and people. Kids are trying to break away, parents are try-

ing to reign them in. The youngest participants found comfort in sharing information with parents, while the oldest ones were skeptical that parents knew what is best for them.

- As tweens mature, adults are seen less often as persons they can consult for information, due in part to gaps in communication practices, perceived understanding of tween social situations, and the well-documented issues regarding tween self-esteem.
- Tweens think their peers are easier to talk to, and thus they are more likely to seek information from them, even if the information is not as good as the advice they would get from adults.
- Tweens withhold information from parents due to such adolescent tendencies as high self-consciousness or low esteem, but they also think parents are: (1) clumsy with sensitive data and might embarrass them, and (2) prone to blowing things out of proportion and punishing them.
- Tweens see differences within the adult group: teachers can only answer academic questions, not social/personal questions; parents are better at social questions than teachers, but still don't understand many tween issues in a changing social scene. Tweens seem to have primitive conceptions of what adults know; for example, tweens don't tend to see that teachers can also be parents, or that parents could have experienced tween social issues that are relevant to today's generation. Moreover, parents are viewed as strong ties; teachers are weak ties.
- Tweens see differences within their own group where some friends are strong ties and others are weak ties. Weak ties cannot be trusted with sensitive information, like dating and relationships, because it might get "blabbed." Also, some peers use information as a status symbol or form of social capital, almost a kind of "info bullying." This intimidates tweens who might ask questions and seek information in social contexts. Fear of peer ridicule influences what questions will be asked when, where, and of whom. This conflicts with their natural inclination to be information seekers, and sate their curiosity.

While these themes are also supported by our analysis of the focus group and other interview data, two primary areas for future examination include: (1) testing the generalizations with tweens in other parts of the country and from varying socio-demographic backgrounds to see how their responses compare with those of the tweens in our study; and (2) conducting further focus groups with tweens of the same gender (to increase participants' comfort levels, although the mixed-sex groups proved provocative as boys responded to generalizations by the girls and vice-versa) and more similar age, as we found that the youngest members of our groups were at different developmental stages than the twelve- and thirteen-year-olds.

NOTES

1. This material is based upon work supported by the National Science Foundation under Grant No. 0414447. Any opinions, findings, and conclusions or recommendations expressed in this material are those of the author(s) and do not necessarily reflect the views of the National Science Foundation.

2. The second population of study is stay-at-home mothers. For information about this NSF research, visit our IBEC (Information Behavior in Everyday Contexts) website at http://ibec.ischool.washington.edu.

3. While "other people" has been documented in literally hundreds of studies across varied disciplines as the primary source through which individuals seek information (and in context of both everyday and workplace settings), virtually no investigation has explored this phenomenon in-depth and posited a conceptual explanation that reflects its affective, cognitive, and physical elements. Hence the purpose of the "Talking with You" project.

4. These frameworks are explained in-depth in a forthcoming report.

5. A third Tween Day was held in November 2005 at an elementary school, which was specifically chosen to identify the effects of a school setting on the reporting of non-school-related information behavior. Data from this event will be included in future reports.

6. For an in-depth discussion of the Tween Day methodology, including data analysis, observer effect, and trustworthiness, see Meyers, Fisher, and Marcoux (n.d.).

7. Observer effect is a study limitation that occurs when the participants' behavior is affected in ways that affect the quality of the data collected. Since all qualitative studies contain some degree of observer effect (except perhaps when unobtrusive observation is used), researchers employ different strategies to reduce its occurrence as well as to identify and analyze its impact on the data, especially through the consideration of observer effect counterexamples.

8. Aliases are used to refer to all our participants. Mr. Blackwood chose his own alias. In brackets after each alias we list the site at which the tween was interviewed, i.e., UW (University of Washington) or the Ministry.

REFERENCES

Agosto, Denise E. 2002. A model of young people's decision making in using the Web. *Library & Information Science Research* 24(4): 311–41.

Agosto, Denise E., and Sandra Hughes-Hassell. 2005. People, places, and questions: An investigation of the everyday life information seeking behaviors of urban young adults. *Library & Information Science Research* 27(2): 141–63.

Bilal, Dania. 2000. Children's use of the Yahooligans! Web search engine. I. Cognitive, physical and affective behaviors on fact-based search tasks. *Journal of the American Society for Information Science* 51(7): 646–65.

———. 2001. Children's use of the Yahooligans! Web search engine. II. Cognitive and physical behaviors on research tasks. *Journal of the American Society for Information Science and Technology* 52(2): 118–36.

Bransford, John D., Ann L. Brown, and Rodney R. Cocking, eds. 2000. *How people learn: Brain, mind, experience, and school.* Washington, DC: National Academy Press.

Case, Donald O. 2002. *Looking for information: A survey of research on information seeking, needs, and behavior.* Amsterdam: Academic Press.

Chatman, Elfreda A. 1992. *The information world of retired women.* Westport, CT: Greenwood.

———. 2000. Framing social life in theory and research. *Information Behaviour Research* 1 (December): 3–17.

Deese-Roberts, Susan, and Kathleen Keating. 2000. *Library instruction: A peer tutoring model.* Englewood, CO: Libraries Unlimited.

Delvecchio, Gene. 1997. *Creating ever-cool: A marketer's guide to a kid's heart.* Gretna, LA: Pelican.

Dervin, Brenda. 1992. From the mind's eye of the user: The sense-making qualitative-quantitative methodology. In *Qualitative research in information management,* ed. Jack D. Glazer and Ronald R. Powell, 61–84. Englewood, CO: Libraries Unlimited.

Eisenberg, Michael B. 2004. It's all about the learning: Ensuring that students are effective users of information on standardized tests. *Library Media Connection* 22(6): 22–30.

Eisenberg, Michael B., and Robert E. Berkowitz. 1990. *Information problem solving: The big six skills approach to library and information skills instruction.* Norwood, NJ: Ablex Publishing.

Elkind, David. 1984. *All grown up and no place to go: Teenagers in crisis.* Reading, MA: Addison-Wesley.

Fidel, Raya, Rachel K. Davies, Mary H. Douglass, Jenny K. Holder, Carla J. Hopkins, Elisabeth J. Kushner, Bryan K. Miyagishima, and Christina D. Toney. 1999. A visit to the information mall: Web searching behavior of high school students. *Journal of the American Society for Information Science* 50(1): 24–37.

Fisher, Karen E., and Charles M. Naumer. 2005. Information grounds: Theoretical basis and empirical findings on information flow in social settings. In *New Directions in Human Information Behavior*, ed. Amanda Spink and Charles Cole, 93–112. Amsterdam: Kluwer.

Gibbs, Nancy. 2005. Being 13: What's on their minds? *Time*, August 8. http://www.time.com/time/archive/preview/0,10987,1088663,00.html (accessed August 12, 2005).

Gross, Melissa. 2004. Children's information seeking at school: Findings from a qualitative study. In *Youth information seeking behavior: Theories, models and issues*, ed. Mary K. Chelton and Colleen Cool, 211–40. Lanham, MD: Scarecrow Press.

Harris, Roma M., and Patricia Dewdney. 1994. *Barriers to information: How formal help systems fail battered women*. Westport, CT: Greenwood.

Harter, Susan. 1983. Developmental perspectives on the self-system. In *Handbook of child psychology, socialization, personality and social development*, vol. 4, ed. Eileen Mavis Hetherington and Paul H. Mussen, 275–385. New York: Wiley.

———. 1998. The development of self-representations. In *Handbook of child psychology: Social, emotional, and personality development*, vol. 4, ed. William Damon and Nancy Eisenberg, 553–617. New York: Wiley.

Herman-Gidden, Marcia E., Lily Wang, and Gary Koch. 2001. Secondary sexual characteristics in boys: Estimates from the National Health and Nutrition Examination Survey III, 1988–1994. *Archive of Pediatrics & Adolescent Medicine* 155(9): 1022–28.

Herring, James E. 1996. *Teaching information skills in schools*. London: Library Association Publishing.

Hirsch, Sandra G. 1999. Children's relevance criteria and information seeking on electronic resources. *Journal of the American Society for Information Science* 50(14): 1265–83.

Kaplowitz, Paul. 2004. *Early puberty in girls: The essential guide to coping with this problem*. New York: Ballantine Books.

Kaplowitz, Paul B., Eric J. Slora, Richard C. Wasserman, Steven E. Pedlow, and Marcia E. Herman-Giddens. 2001. Earlier onset of puberty in girls: Relation to increased body mass index and race. *Pediatrics* 108(2): 347–53.

Kellet, Mary, and Sharon Ding. 2004. Middle childhood. In *Doing research with children and young people*, ed. Sandy Fraser, Vicky Lewis, Sharon Ding, Mary Kellet and Chris Robinson, 161–74. Thousand Oaks, CA: Sage.

Kozma, Robert. 1991. Learning with media. *Review of Educational Research* 61(2): 179–212.

Kroger, Jane. 2004. *Identity in adolescence: The balance between self and other*. 3rd ed. New York: Routledge.

Kuhlthau, Carol C. 1990. Information search process: A summary of research and implications for school library media programs. In *The research of school library media centers: Papers of the treasure mountain research retreat*, ed. Blanche Woolls, 111–20. Castle Rock, CO: Hi Willow Research.

———. 2004. Zones of intervention in the process of information seeking. In *Seeking meaning: A process approach to library and information services*, 127–44. Westport, CT: Libraries Unlimited.

Large, Andrew, Jamshid Bheshti, and Alain Breuleux. 1998. Information seeking in a multimedia environment by primary school students. *Library and Information Science Research* 20(4): 343–76.

Latrobe, Kathy, and W. Michael Havener. 1997. The information-seeking behavior of high school honors students: An exploratory study. *Journal of Youth Services in Libraries* 10 (Winter): 188–200.

Lesko, Nancy. 2001. *Act your age! A cultural reconstruction of adolescence.* New York: Routledge Falmer.

Lincoln, Yvonne S., and Egon G. Guba. 1985. *Naturalistic inquiry.* Newbury Park, CA: Sage.

Marchionini, Gary. 1989. Information-seeking strategies of novices using a full-text electronic encyclopedia. *Journal of the American Society for Information Science* 40(1): 54–66.

Meyers, Eric, Karen E. Fisher, and Elizabeth Marcoux. n.d. Studying tweens: Notes from the field. (Under review.)

Miles, Steven. 2000. *Youth lifestyles in a changing world.* Philadelphia, PA: Open University Press.

Perret-Clermont, Anne-Nelly. 2004. Thinking spaces of the young. In *Joining society: Social interaction and learning in adolescence and youth*, ed. Anne-Nelley Perret-Clermont, Clotilde Pontecorvo, Lauren B. Resnick, Tania Zittoun, and Barbara Burge, 3–16. New York: Cambridge University Press.

Quart, Alissa. 2004. The great tween marketing machine. In *Branded: The buying and selling of teenagers*, ed. Alissa Quart, 63–76. New York: Basic Books.

Savolainen, Reijo. 1995. Everyday life information-seeking: Approaching information-seeking in the context of "Way of Life." *Library and Information Science Research* 17(3): 259–94.

Shenton, Andrew K., and Pat Dixon. 2003. Youngsters' use of other people as an information-seeking method. *Journal of Librarianship and Information Science* 35(4): 219–33.

Stripling, Barbara K., and Judy M. Pitts. 1988. *Brainstorms and blueprints: Teaching library research as a thinking process.* Westport, CT: Libraries Unlimited.

Wigfield, Allan, Jacquelynne Eccles, and Paul R. Pintrich. 1996. Development between the ages of 11–25. In *The handbook of educational psychology*, ed. David C. Berliner and Robert C. Calfee, 148–85. New York: Simon & Schuster MacMillan.

Wyn, Johanna. 2005. What is happening to "adolescence"? Growing up in changing times. In *Re/constructing "the adolescent": Sign, symbol and body*, ed. Jennifer A. Vadeboncoeur and Lisa Patel Stevens, 25–48. New York: Peter Lang.

Zuckerman, Diana. 2001. Boys to men. *Youth Today* 10(9): 26.

2

Modeling the Everyday Life Information Needs of Urban Teenagers

Sandra Hughes-Hassell and Denise E. Agosto

There are over 34 million teens living in America's cities of one million or more,[1] yet there is little research focusing specifically on urban young adults and their information needs or use. The Urban Libraries Council's initiative has been the most significant user-centered examination of urban young adults' library use patterns, and it concluded that urban youth view the public library as an "uncool" and uninviting place.[2]

This chapter presents selected results of a 2002–2005 Institute of Museum and Library Services (IMLS) research grant designed to investigate this gap in the research literature. At the core of the project is the conviction that young adults themselves are the best sources of data about their information needs. The study asked urban teens to describe their everyday life information-seeking patterns. Specifically, it sought to determine the people sources/channels urban teens consult when engaging in everyday life information seeking (ELIS), the types of media most commonly used, and urban teens' most frequent everyday life information needs topics. This chapter focuses on the theoretical and empirical models of urban teens' common everyday life information needs that resulted from the research.

Both models have direct relevance to the practice of librarianship. It is widely recognized that an understanding of human information behavior is fundamental to the provision of high-quality library service. Armed with knowledge of the common reasons why urban youth seek information and the types of information they seek in their everyday lives, librarians may engage in collection development, provide reference services, and develop programs that not only more effectively address the ELIS needs of urban youth, but also positively impact their perceptions of libraries.

LITERATURE REVIEW

This work builds on two main areas of theory: ELIS and adolescent information behavior.

Everyday Life Information Seeking (ELIS)

Everyday life information seeking refers to the type of information seeking that "people employ to orient themselves in daily life or to solve problems not directly connected with the performance of occupational tasks."[3] In other words, information seeking for non-work-related, non-research-related, or non-school-related purposes. For example, the average person might turn on the television in the morning while dressing to hear the day's weather forecast, search the Internet during lunch for information related to applying for a home equity loan, skim newspaper advertisements on the train home from work, and so on throughout the day.

There has been renewed interest in the topic of everyday life information-seeking behavior within the ELIS research community in the last decade.[4] The ELIS behavior of diverse groups, such as homeless parents, lesbians, and adolescents making career decisions, has been studied. Savolainen, who developed one of the most frequently cited models of ELIS behavior, suggests that ELIS habits and attitudes allow people to use their personal values and beliefs to make meaningful life choices.[5] He introduced the concepts of "way of life" and "mastery of life" for understanding the role of information seeking in an individual's daily problem-solving activities. "Way of life" is defined as "the order of things," or preferences given to life activities such as household tasks and hobbies.[6] "Mastery of life," which can be cognitive or affective, and optimistic or pessimistic, serves to keep things in order; that is, it is "a general preparedness to approach everyday problems in certain ways in accordance with one's values."[7]

Williamson developed an ecological model of ELIS that emphasizes the context of social and cultural factors that affect information-seeking behavior.[8] The model suggests that although people purposefully seek information in response to perceived needs, they also receive information incidentally through their daily monitoring of the world. How they monitor the world is determined by their social-cultural backgrounds and values, physical environments, personal characteristics, and socioeconomic situations and lifestyles. Intimate personal networks (i.e., family and friends) are perceived by users as the most easily accessible sources of information for both incidental information acquisition and purposeful information seeking. Wider personal networks (i.e., clubs, churches, voluntary organizations, etc.) and the mass media are perceived as less accessible, but are still commonly used for both types of information gathering. Institutional sources (i.e., government agencies, information professionals, etc.), on the other hand, are perceived as least accessible and are less likely to be sources of incidental information.

McKenzie proposed an ELIS model based on social interaction that further emphasizes the role of social relationships and social contexts in ELIS source selection and information-seeking patterns.[9] The model describes two stages of the information process (making connections and interacting with sources) and four modes of information seeking (active seeking, active scanning, nondirected monitoring, and obtaining information by proxy). The mode(s) users employ depends on the information needed and situational factors.

Much of the ELIS research has employed qualitative methodologies.[10] Interviews, diaries, participant observation, and other ethnographic methods have proven to be effective for not only procuring rich, authentic ELIS data, but also for gaining participant trust, a critical element in understanding information behavior.[11]

Adolescent Information Behavior

Two streams of research on adolescent information behavior are particularly relevant to this project: (1) general adolescent information needs, and (2) everyday life information seeking of adolescents.

General Adolescent Information Needs

The general information needs of adolescents have been the focus of a number of studies since the 1970s. Minudri identified five areas of teen information needs: school and curriculum needs, recreational needs, personal development needs, vocational and career information needs, and accomplishment skills and information needs.[12]

Fourie and Kruger characterized adolescents' basic information needs as physiological (security and safety), affective (achievement and self-esteem), and cognitive (self-actualization), and concluded that their urges to seek information may be intrinsically or extrinsically motivated.[13] For example, a teen may seek information to reduce uncertainty or to reach a higher level of achievement (intrinsic motivation). On the other hand, a teen may seek information because of the expectation of a reward, such as a grade, to be gained from others for the effort (extrinsic motivation).

Latrobe and Havener studied the personal and school-related information needs and behaviors of eighteen honors students.[14] They identified six categories of information needs: course-related activities, current lifestyles, future plans, relationships with others, health, and general information. Course-related informational needs dealt primarily with test preparation and school assignments. Current lifestyle issues included extracurricular activities, part-time jobs, money, sports, movies, cars, and other recreational activities. Future plans included college and career choices. Relationships included family, friends, peers, and other acquaintances. Health information dealt primarily with fitness, beauty, alcohol/drugs, sex, and birth control. The last category, general information, encompassed areas such as current events, politics, religion, and social issues.

Shenton and Dixon created a typology of children's and teens' informational needs categories.[15] The typology included eleven major types of information that teenagers need: advice, personal information, affective support, empathetic understanding, support for skill development, school-related subject information, interest-driven information, consumer information, self-development information, reinterpretations and supplementations of information, and verificational information.

Adolescents and Everyday Life Information Seeking

Several research studies have focused on the ELIS behavior of teenagers. Poston-Anderson and Edwards used qualitative methods to study the role of information in helping twenty-eight adolescent girls address their life concerns.[16] When asked to identify problems or worries they had in the last month, the girls' concerns fell into two groups: "relationships" and "education and work."[17] While most of the girls thought information was available to assist them with their problems, few of them believed that libraries would contain the information they needed. Instead, the girls turned to family, friends, and teachers.

In a later study specifically focused on how adolescent girls seek information about jobs and education, Edwards and Poston-Anderson found that the teens engaged in little or no formal information seeking. When they did seek information, they tended to approach their mothers the most often, and to a lesser extent their fathers.[18] Formal human information sources, such as teachers, career advisers, and librarians, were seldom approached for this type of information. The teens believed that adults, other than their parents, did not believe seeking information on future plans was an appropriate topic for twelve- to fourteen-year-olds. Surprisingly, the girls also seemed to avoid friends completely with any questions concerning their life concerns.

Julien's study of barriers to adolescents' information seeking for career decision making showed that many adolescents do not understand what decisions they need to make about their futures and that this lack of clarity leads them to feel anxious and overwhelmed.[19] Forty percent of the teens she surveyed said they did not know where to go to get help to make their decisions, and a similar proportion felt that there were too many places to go for their help in information seeking. In addition, the teens reported that when they were offered assistance, they often did not know what questions to ask, and they frequently encountered problems accessing information systems.

The findings of Todd's study of how adolescents utilize information about heroin seemed to contradict the findings of the above studies.[20] Rather than finding adolescents to be passive processors of information, Todd found that when teenagers are engaged in the information-seeking process they are active creators of new knowledge who intentionally and deliberately seek and manipulate information to adapt and create pictures of their world.

METHODOLOGY

We used qualitative methods for this project. As is common in qualitative research, multiple forms of data were collected to serve as data triangulation and construct validation.[21] The variant contexts that framed these multiple data collection methods also resulted in a fuller picture of the participants' ELIS behaviors.

Study Participants

Twenty-seven Philadelphia young adults aged fourteen through seventeen participated in the study on a volunteer basis and were paid modest compensation as encouragement to complete the study. All were Philadelphia public high school students in grades nine through twelve who lived in inner-city communities and were predominantly from the lower socioeconomic stratum. Twenty-five were African American, one was Asian American, and one was Caucasian. The participants represented two different populations: sixteen were members of the Free Library of Philadelphia's Teen Leadership Program, and eleven were participants in the Boys & Girls Clubs of Philadelphia after-school programs.

Each of the Free Library participants was employed at one of the Free Library branches as a Teen Leadership Assistant (TLA), assisting school children with homework and taking part in program preparation and delivery. Data from participant surveys indicated that the majority (11, or 68.8 percent) had home access to computers. They used public and school libraries infrequently for their own purposes, even though they were employed at the Free Library of Philadelphia at least two days a week.

Survey data from the eleven Boys & Girls Club participants indicated that about half had access to computers at home (6, or 54.5 percent). They too were infrequent public and school library users.

Data Collection and Analysis

Data were collected in two stages. For stage one, the participants provided data over the period of one week in the following ways:[22]

1. Written surveys: The surveys included questions relating to age, grade in school, access to computers, school and public library use, and perceived computer skills.
2. Audio journals: Participants were given tape recorders and asked to keep an audio journal for seven days. The teens were instructed to discuss the kinds of issues that came up each day that required them to get information and to describe any efforts they took in addressing their information needs.
3. Written activity logs: The participants were asked to record questions that arose each day during the week and to indicate where, or to whom, they looked for related information.
4. Camera tours: The participants used disposable cameras to take pictures of the places in their neighborhoods where they typically go for information.

After these initial data were collected, we analyzed the written activity logs using iterative pattern coding with QSR NVivo 2 software. Iterative pattern coding involves repeated readings of the transcribed data leading to the development of a coding scheme for continued analysis.[23] This process is comparable to the constant comparative method, the most common method for analyzing qualitative data.[24]

For the second stage of data collection, we presented the coding scheme developed from analysis of the activity logs to the participants in a series of semistructured group interviews. Four interviews were conducted, two at the Boys & Girls Club and two at the Free Library of Philadelphia. The interviews served as participant verification of the preliminary data analysis results and as a means of gathering additional data. The participants in each group discussed the coding scheme, rearranging existing codes and suggesting additional codes. Each participant was also asked to describe a recent significant incident involving an everyday life information need.

We then reanalyzed the data from the written logs, as well as analyzing the remainder of the data from the initial data collection phase and the group interview transcripts from the second data collection phase, to develop a final revised coding scheme.[25] The final coding scheme, or typology, included four major categories of codes: people sources/ channels, mediated communication media, media sources, and information needs topics:

1   **People Sources/Channels**
1.1   friends/family
1.2   school employees
1.3   mentors
1.4   customer service staff
1.5   other teen (not friend)
1.6   librarians
1.7   passers-by
2   **Preferred Communication Media**
2.1   face-to-face
2.2   telephone
2.3   computer
3   **Media Sources**
3.1   computer
3.2   TV
3.3   book
3.4   print ephemera
3.5   newspaper
3.6   magazine
3.7   radio/CD player
3.8   telephone (automated)
3.9   school notebook
4   **Information Needs Topics**
4.1   daily life routine
4.2   social activities
4.3   creative performance
4.4   academics
4.5   personal finances

4.6   current events
4.7   goods and services
4.8   emotional health
4.9   friend/peer/romantic relationships
4.10   popular culture
4.11   familial relationships
4.12   fashion
4.13   college
4.14   health
4.15   physical safety
4.16   self-image
4.17   job responsibilities
4.18   social/legal norms
4.19   philosophical concerns
4.20   creative consumption
4.21   career
4.22   school culture
4.23   sexual safety
4.24   sexual identity
4.25   religious practice
4.26   civic duty
4.27   heritage/cultural identity
4.28   self-actualization

MODELS OF URBAN TEENS' COMMON EVERYDAY LIFE INFORMATION NEEDS

Two models of urban teens' common everyday life information needs were derived from the information needs and topics represented within the typology shown previously—a theoretical model and an empirical model.

The Theoretical Model

In building the theoretical model, we decided that an integrated theoretical model of urban teen ELIS topics, media, and human information sources/channels was premature. Instead, we focused on the information topics represented in the fourth section of the coding scheme. These twenty-eight categories represent topics for which the study participants actively sought information, or for which they needed information but did not seek it. For example, some of the teens wanted information relating to "heritage/cultural identity" (topic 4.27). An excerpt from an audio journal helps to illustrate this type of information need:

> I really am interested in Savannah, Georgia, because that's where my grandma was born, and I'd like to go back to my roots. If I could go to school down there and could find more about my heritage, that would be great. (021[26]; 136–39[27])

After developing the typology, we looked for a preexisting model or theory that could bring added meaning to the information topics represented in the coding scheme. While a comprehensive theoretical model of teen information behavior did not exist, Havighurst's developmental tasks of adolescence did prove useful in understanding some of the various areas of teen development.[28] Havighurst created a typology of tasks to describe developmental changes that occur during adolescence. His typology is often used as a basis for examining adolescent behaviors across the spectrum of the social sciences.[29]

Havighurst's 11 developmental tasks are:

1. adjusting to a new physical sense of self
2. adjusting to new intellectual abilities
3. adjusting to increased cognitive demands at school
4. expanding verbal skills
5. developing a personal sense of identity
6. establishing adult vocational goals
7. establishing emotional and psychological independence from his or her parents
8. developing stable and productive peer relationships
9. learning to manage his or her sexuality
10. adopting a personal value system
11. developing increased impulse control and behavioral maturity

Havighurst's typology of tasks could be correlated to a number of the behaviors captured within the study data and reflected in the final coding scheme, such as tying information relating to "sexual safety" to Havighurst's ninth task, "learning to manage his or her sexuality." However, Havighurst's typology proved inadequate to support all of the information needs topics included in the final typology. It was therefore necessary to create additional tasks to supplement Havighurst's original list.

For instance, under the information needs task "social/legal norms" (4.18), one participant wrote the following question on his activity log: "What kind of attire is bad to wear at a funeral?" (003; 79). Questions of this type did not correlate to any of Havighurst's eleven developmental tasks. The new task "understanding and negotiating the social world" was added to encompass these types of questions.

Combining the ideas presented in Havighurst's typology and the additional tasks we developed with the twenty-eight information topics in the coding scheme led us to identify seven major areas of teen development: development of the social self, the emotional self, the reflective self, the physical self, the creative self, the cognitive self, and the sexual self. These seven areas of teen development were arranged into the visual model shown in figure 2.1.

As explained above, each of the seven areas of development is comprised of one or more tasks. The following list shows the tasks associated with each developmental area. The tasks followed by numbers came from Havighurst's typology; tasks without numbers are our additions to Havighurst's list.

- **Social self:** developing stable and productive peer relationships (8); understanding and negotiating the social world
- **Emotional self:** establishing emotional and psychological independence from his or her parents (7); developing increased impulse control and behavioral maturity (11); seeking emotional health and security; establishing relationships with adults other than parents/guardians
- **Reflective self:** developing a personal sense of identity (5); establishing adult vocational goals (6); adopting a personal value system (10); developing a sense of civic duty; establishing a cultural identity; questioning how the world works
- **Physical self:** adjusting to a new physical sense of self (1); devel-

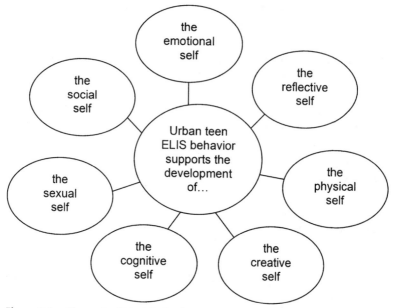

Figure 2.1. Theoretical Model of Urban Teen Development

oping physical self-sufficiency; seeking physical safety and security
- **Creative self:** expressing artistic preferences; expressing aesthetic preferences
- **Cognitive self:** adjusting to new intellectual abilities (2); adjusting to increased cognitive demands at school (3); expanding verbal skills (4); understanding the physical world
- **Sexual self:** learning to manage his or her sexuality (9); learning to recognize and accept his or her sexuality

These seven areas of teen development are not mutually exclusive. They often overlap, as some information needs support the development of multiple "selves." Considering the data excerpt shown above, the teen's interest in learning about Savannah, Georgia, serves to support the development of the reflective self (of which a sense of cultural identity is a part), as well as the development of the cognitive self (of which gaining new knowledge is a part), in that the teen's desire for information about Savannah is motivated both by a desire to understand her cultural heritage and by intellectual curiosity about an unfamiliar location.

The Empirical Model

The next step in modeling the ELIS behavior of urban teens was to create an empirical model encompassing the information needs topics from the final typology. These codes were arranged into the visual model shown in figure 2.2 to indicate their relationship to each of the seven areas of urban teen development represented by the theoretical model.

Reading the model from left to right, the first column lists the dependent variable: "urban teen ELIS needs." The middle column lists the seven components of the theoretical model, that is, the seven areas of urban adolescent development. The right-most column lists the twenty-eight empirical variables, derived via the data analysis process. These are the specific areas of development that fall under each of the seven theoretical variables.

For example, there are three empirical variables tied to the theoretical variable "cognitive self"—"academics," "school culture," and "current events." Each of these three empirical variables describes a thematic topic for which the study participants sought, gathered, mentally considered, or needed but did not seek information.

RELATING THE THEORETICAL MODEL TO THE EMPIRICAL MODEL

In this section we discuss the relationship between the theoretical and empirical models. Specifically, we use representative excerpts from the raw data, both to define the theoretical and empirical variables and to show how the models are supported by data from the participants.

The Social Self

> I wanted to know what parties are going on this week. I'm a very sociable girl and I like to go out and have fun, so I wanted to know

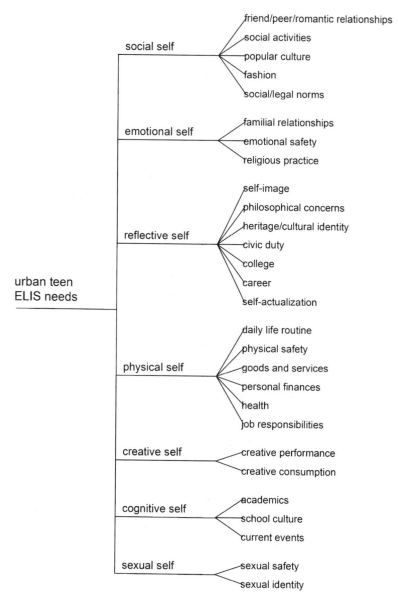

Figure 2.2   An Empirical Model of Urban Teens' Everyday Life Information Needs

what parties or any type of entertaining thing for me [there was] to do this week or weekend. So I called my friends on the phone and I asked them. (010; 283–86)

"Social self" refers to a teen's understanding of the human social world and to learning how he or she fits into that world. The social self includes Havighurst's task of "developing stable and productive peer relationships" (Havighurst's task 8) and the additional task of "understanding and negotiating the social world." Participants needed information pertaining to "friend/peer/romantic relationships," "social activities," "popular culture," "fashion," and "social/legal norms" to support their developing social selves.

Friend/Peer/Romantic Relationships. A number of the participants reported romantic relationship issues during the data collection period. As a female participant wrote in her activity log: "I asked Jasmine, 'Should I tell the boy I like that I like him?'" (001; 41). Many of the teens also dealt with friends who were fighting, and the study participants themselves engaged in a number of conflicts with friends and other members of their peer group. For example, one of the female participants described an altercation with another teen that would have resulted in a fight except for her friend's intervention:

My only issue that came up today was me attempting to fight. . . . My friend asked me why I was going to fight this girl, and I was like, 'I don't know.' So my friend went over to the girl and asked her why she wanted to fight me. After my friend returned back to me with her response, she said that we weren't going to fight over anything so petty, so therefore that day, I did not fight. I think if my friend wouldn't have solved the problem, then I would have gotten arrested, if the girl and I had fought. (004; 45–54)

Social Activities. The participants sought information relating to a number of social activities, such as going to parties, seeing movies, and attending sports events. Much information gathering related to social activities involved consulting with friends to generate leisure plans:

On my way to school, I happened to see my old friend, Terry. We then began conversating [*sic*], and I decided that we should go out this weekend. So we then brainstormed places that we would like, or we would enjoy to go this weekend, and came upon: parties, movies, and malls. (004; 19–23)

Since data collection occurred during the spring, prom was a prominent social activity in the data, e.g., "Where can I go after the prom? A teacher suggested [we could] go to AC [Atlantic City] or stay in the city. I decided to go to AC and try to have fun" (011; 30–32).

Popular Culture. Celebrities, sports figures, musicians, and hip-hop culture were some of the most common subtopics relating to popular culture. As one participant explained in her audio journal:

> Today, especially, I wanted to get the latest gossip or scandal, so I continued to listen to Power 99 because Wendy Williams came on in a couple of seconds. She's, like, the gossip queen, and so I listened to her and she gave all the latest gossip in Hollywood and on celebrities and all that other good stuff. (010; 47–50)

Fashion. Clothing and hairstyles were also frequent topics of information-seeking. A number of the participants looked for photographs and magazine articles about prom hair and clothing styles. One of the female participants ran an informal hair-braiding business, and she consulted her private collection of styling books a number of times during the data collection period.

Other fashion-related queries were more general. For example, one participant explained in her audio journal that:

> This evening I was curious, after watching TV, what the latest fashions were. So I picked up my April issue of the *Cosmo Girl* magazine where I found a bunch of things and a bunch of trends for this spring. (010; 66–70)

Social/Legal Norms. The participants reported a number of questions relating to expected patterns of behavior. Some of the teens wanted to know what types of clothing were appropriate to wear to formal functions, such as school ceremonies, funerals, and awards banquets. Others were interested in knowing the age at which minors could engage in legally restricted activity. For example, in her audio log one female participant explained, "I wanted to know how old do you have to be to date an older guy. So I went on the Internet to www.ask.com and they said it was okay. Sixteen was a legal age" (011; 10–12).

The Emotional Self

> I really hate having arguments with my mom, but I'm a teenager. You're going to have arguments with your parents . . . so I just been

> thinking about some hotlines I can call, maybe like a Boys and Girls
> Club kind of hotline. I think that's what it's called, to call to ask them,
> you know, give me some advice or something, on how to deal with
> arguments with your mom or dad. . . . From what the commercials say,
> I guess they can help out in those kinds of situations. (014; 12–18)

Whereas the social self refers to the external world, the "emotional self" refers to a teen's inner world of feelings and emotions. The development of the emotional self includes: "establishing emotional and psychological independence from his or her parents" (Havighurst's task 7); "developing increased impulse control and behavioral maturity" (Havighurst's task 11); "seeking emotional health and security;" and "establishing relationships with adults other than parents/guardians." Information topics related to the emotional self include: "familial relationships," "emotional health," and "religious practice."

Familial Relationships. Establishing and maintaining familial relationships is a crucial aspect of the study participants' lives. For example, in his audio journal one participant talked about visiting a sick uncle: "I wonder what time I should go to check on my uncle? My guardian wanted me to check on my uncle because he's a little sick." Another one reported:

> I'm just worried about my cousin sometimes, 'cause I think about him, how
> he's in trouble a lot, and how he's always in the middle of something, or how
> he's seen something that involves the cops or something. (002; 306–9)

Development of the emotional self also includes the process of becoming independent from parents, which often involves conflict between social norms or mores. As one female participant explained:

> My sock hop is a tenth grade dance for the tenth graders in my school, and
> it's like a little prom. You bring a date and you dance and stuff. I want to wear
> something casual, like not all dressy-dressy, but casual. But the only thing is,
> I want to have a little bit of my cleavage out, but I'm scared to ask my mom.
> If I do ask her she might say no. So before I get my outfit made, I gotta go
> over it with my mom. (001; 19–24)

Emotional Health. A number of the participants sought methods of protecting themselves from emotional harm, or struggling to heal after an emotional setback. For example, students wrote in their activity logs,

"Who should I talk to when I'm mad?" (027; 31), and "Where can I find teenage help hotlines?" (006; 7). In the group interviews many of the teens explained that they actively seek adult mentors who can guide them in their lives, especially for employment, career, and health information. One young woman periodically visited her physician to discuss issues relating to sexuality; one young man sought out his minister for advice on a number of life issues.

In one particularly compelling example of an emotional struggle, one of the participants was struggling to come to terms with her sexual identity. Although much of her information-seeking relating to this issue pertains to the empirical variable "sexual identity," much of it also pertains to "emotional health." She was searching for a person with whom she could discuss the emotional side of her growing realization that she was gay. She initially identified her school counselor as a person who could offer her emotional support, but fear that that her discussions with him might not remain confidential made her hesitant to seek his help:

> On the way to school, I was wondering if I was going to get to talk to Mr. L. about the papers he had gave [sic] me. [I needed] to talk to somebody about what was going on, some personal issues. And he told me that the information was confidential and stuff, but I still wasn't sure if I wanted to go along with it. (003; 201–4)

Religious Practice. Religion figured less prominently in the participants' lives than did emotional concerns, yet religion was a method by which at least two of the participants found some emotional fulfillment. One participant commented in his audio journal that "I came back from church. It was a good service today. I like what the preacher had said." (020; 65–66) Another mentioned in her audio journal that "Today I went to church with my cousin. The pastor preached a real good sermon today" (023; 33–34).

The Reflective Self

> I was thinking about many things that concerned me. For example, why can't I say who invented diseases? Why do people get sick? Why are so many people dying? Sometimes I ask myself these types of questions. These are the questions that you won't discuss with anyone except your inner self. (001; 52–61)

The reflective self also refers to a teen's inner world, but differs from the emotional self in that the focus is more introspective. It involves "developing a personal sense of identity" (Havighurst's task 5), establishing adult vocational goals (Havighurst's task 6), adopting a personal value system (Havighurst's task 10), developing a sense of civic duty, establishing a cultural identity, and questioning how the world works. In relation to the development of the reflective self, the participants needed information relating to "self image," philosophical concerns," "heritage/cultural identity," "civic duty," "college," "career," and "self-actualization."

Self-Image. The emotional fragility of adolescence was readily apparent in the self-musing of the study participants. A number of them questioned their self-worth in the eyes of others, as can be seen in one participant's written log question: "Why do people hate me for dumb reasons?" (001; 3). Others worried about their physical appearance and wondered how they looked to their peers.

Philosophical Concerns. The participants engaged in a number of instances of searching for a general understanding of society's fundamental beliefs and values, as in asking, "What's the difference between love/hate?" (001; 95), or, "Why does death come so suddenly?" (003; 55).

The Iraq war generated especially rich data relating to philosophical concerns, as is evident in this male participant's audio journal:

> And as I was watching the news, it started to make me think of those people in Iraq, and how they are being treated—how they weren't being treated, and how they're being treated now. It shows that these people, they needed the— our troops to help them, our coalition forces to help free Iraq under a dictator- ship government, and to make it a free one. So it made me start to think about how much they have suffered, and how much it was not—it was not fair to them. (002; 273–80)

Heritage/Cultural Identity. Twenty-five of the twenty-seven partici- pants were African American, and a small portion of their information behavior involved topics related to African American culture. One young woman noted that she wanted to find a "Black poetry sight [*sic*] . . . I love poetry, and Black poetry is one of my favorites because I can definitely relate" (010; 43). This same participant was interested in learning about voodoo practices because she was of Haitian descent.

Another participant wanted "to find a book on Malcolm X because I'm very interested in this and Black history" (004; 265-266).

Civic Duty. In addition to questioning values and practices of the society in which they live, many of the participants questioned their own value to society as they struggled to define future roles for themselves. For example:

> When I go to the Club, I do my hour of community service because I am in the Keystone Club. Keystone is a club for community service and free enterprise, education, and career development, leadership, unity, and self-recreation. (021; 17–27)

Again the war in Iraq figured prominently: "I really don't want to go to war; I'm against it" (019; 34-35); "Today at school there was a walk-out on the war on Iraq. Some of the kids walked out to address the issues" (025; 8-9).

College. Many of the older participants were interested in gathering information about higher education. They asked activity log questions such as "Where can I get information [about the] Penn State main campus?" (013; 33); "Where can I find books that will prepare me for the SATs?" (010; 115); and "Who do I go to if you need to know where to get a college loan?" (015; 9).

Career. Questions pertaining to career-related information ranged from the childlike "What do I want to be when I grow up?" (025; 35) to the more mature "What career offers the best satisfaction and income for me?" (010; 19).

Most of the participants' audio journal discussions about their future careers indicated that their plans were still uncertain. As one teen said, "I can't wait 'til I go to college. I want to be a teenage psychologist, actress, and fashion designer. And I also want to travel the world" (001; 146–47).

In some cases, queries relating to college and career overlapped. For example,

> In English my teacher taught us about SATs and that we should try to go to college.com to see what grade areas you need to get on the SATs. So when I go home, I'm gonna do that. . . . I need my SATs 'cause I want to go to college. . . . I want to go for teaching. (020; 35–43)

Self-Actualization. Maslow proposed that after fulfilling basic human needs, such as the need for shelter, safety, and nourishment, humans seek to fulfill the need for self-actualization, or their need to realize fully one's potential.[30] Whereas civic duty describes a desire to improve society, self-actualization describes a desire to improve oneself. For example, one of the participants expressed pride in the achievements of other teens in her inner-city neighborhood, pride that led her to aspire to attend college:

> It make my heart feel good to see that the kids in my neighborhood, the older kids like my sister's age, everybody [is] in college. Ain't nobody just home not doing nothing. That's where I hope to be in a couple of years. I only got two years left of high school. Right now, I be on the Internet looking up colleges to see which one is the best for me. (021; 82–93)

The Physical Self

> At my school there are some safe havens, like some quiet places [where] nothing goes on: the office, the counselor's office, and the library. Other than that everywhere else is a wild zone. That's why I spend most of my [free] time at the library, looking up books or on the Internet, even if I'm just surfing the web. (021; 71–75)

With the physical self, the focus returns to the external world. Development of the physical self includes: "adjusting to a new physical sense of self" (Havighurst's task 1); "developing physical self-sufficiency;" and "seeking physical safety and security." The participants needed and/or sought information relating to six areas of the physical self: "daily life routine," "physical safety," "goods and services," "personal finances," "health," and "job responsibilities."

Daily Life Routine. Much of the participants' information behavior related to daily life routine, or minor recurring events that served to bring order to their daily lives. Common activities falling under daily life routine included checking the time of day, selecting clothing, monitoring weather reports, and choosing meals. For instance, "Once again, I have to get my weather, so basically I listen to Power 99 in the morning" (010; 44–45), and "This morning I was off to a late start as usual. When I got dressed I checked out this website, www.septa.org, to see what subway I would be able to take" (006; 33–34).

Physical Safety. The study participants painted a dangerous picture of life in the inner city. Physical safety was often a threat, particularly in school. Much attention was given to describing fights between students at their various schools and to the security measures that the schools employ. As one participant explained, "When I got to school, I scanned in. . . . I went through the metal detectors" (006; 6–7).

Goods and Services. The participants had many information needs related to commercial products, such as pricing and availability questions. In their activity logs, participants wrote questions such as "What kind of car can I by with only $1,000?" (015; 39), and "Where can I find good deals on a Fax/Scan/Printer/Copier?" (010; 117).

In some cases, comparison shopping efforts were quite sophisticated. For instance,

> We decided we were going to throw our friend a surprise April Fool's birthday party, so everybody got their assignment. My assignment was to go to Party City and get the balloons and everything. So when I got home I went to www .mapquest.com to find out where the nearest Party City was, went to their website, priced balloons and other decorations, and then stopped by Shop Rite and priced the cake. (006; 41–46)

Personal Finances. The participants often needed information relating to money management. In many cases, they wanted to increase their work hours or take on additional part-time jobs:

> This morning after getting to school I went to my computer lab and I searched for where can I find another part-time job. I'm looking for another part time job to keep the money coming. (010; 255–56)

Much of the information behavior in this area, as well as much information behavior relating to goods and services, pertained to the management of cellular phone accounts. Cell phones were largely viewed as status items, and all of the participants had them.

Health. Information pertaining to health-related issues was also a frequent need. Some participants asked questions about the health conditions of friends and family members, such as, "If my friend thinks she's pregnant, where can she find a clinic?" (016; 11). Others asked questions related to their own health issues, such as, "What is more comfortable, a tampon or a pad?" (011; 41), and "How does one go about getting free insurance?" (016; 47).

Job Responsibilities. Job-related queries were also frequent. Most of the participants had part-time jobs, and, as explained above, all of the Free Library participants were employed at various library branches as TLAs. The TLAs displayed considerable interest in finding information that would help them improve their job performance. For example, one participant wondered, "Where can I find ideas on kids programs to do at the library?" (010; 7).

The Creative Self

> It's Tuesday afternoon. Me and my friend are wondering where we can get some recording studio time, 'cause we're trying to write— trying to make a demo or CD to get it out there so people will start—so we can look at some contracts or something. So we could get signed to a record label or something. So I think we should listen to the radio and get a phone number and ask them, call them, do they know anything about it. (009; 60–65)

The creative self refers to the fulfillment of aesthetic needs. It includes two tasks: "expressing artistic preferences," which involves the creation of a creative product, such as writing a story, performing a dance, or playing a musical instrument, and "expressing aesthetic preferences," which involves the judgment of or appreciation of a creative work, such as evaluating the quality of a movie or a musical selection. The related empirical variables include information pertaining to "creative performance" and information pertaining to "creative consumption."

Creative Performance. Only two of the participants sought information relating to the creation of creative products—the male participant quoted above and a female participant who wanted to locate dance studios where she could study dance:

> I also wanted to know some dance studios in my area. I am really interested in dance. Dance is one of my favorite hobbies, and I just love to dance. So I wanted to find a studio in my area that'll have the dancing things I like to do—you know, like, R&B, hip-hop, tap, jazz. So I looked in the yellow pages on yahoo.com, and I searched for that. I found a couple. (010; 268–72)

Creative Consumption. The majority of activities relating to the development of the creative self involved the consumption of creative works, such as listening to music or watching a dance performance. Activity log entries included a number of questions relating to movie and television viewing (e.g., "When does *Soul Food* air?" [012; 27]), and many questions relating to popular music (e.g., "Where can I find the lyrics to Sean Paul's new song?" [005; 11]). Questions about video games and sporting events were also prevalent, especially in the logs of the male participants. For example, "What cheat codes can I get for a game called *Dead or Alive 2*?" (009; 17), and "What is the [Philadelphia Seventy-]Sixers' record?" (002; 1).

Similar examples occurred in the audio journals, as well as incidents reflecting a wider range of aesthetic appreciation. For example, one participant discussed her appreciation of the sound of a British accent:

> I had bought the new Floetry CD yesterday, and it's a great CD. So I wanted to find interviews about them, like hear them talking and stuff. I love their accents, because they're from England, and I love their accents. So I just wanted to hear them talk. I didn't care what they talked about; I just wanted to hear them speak. (003; 152–56)

The Cognitive Self

> I have a five-page term paper due on Down's Syndrome and sickle cell anemia for 3rd marking period. I researched for my paper on three different days. . . . I know someone with sickle cell anemia so I interviewed her and asked her questions about her life and how she grew up. And then I combined what she said with the information I got off the Internet with what she said and for Down Syndrome. I looked on the Internet and encyclopedia. (021; 41–47)

The cognitive self refers to intellectual processing and navigation of the physical world. The development of the cognitive self includes: "adjusting to new intellectual abilities" (Havighurst's task 2), "adjusting to increased cognitive demands at school" (Havighurst's task 3), "expanding verbal skills" (Havighurst's task 4), and "understanding the physical world." The participants dealt with information relating to three areas of the development of the cognitive self: "academics," "school culture," and "current events."

Academics. As it is used here, the term "academics" refers to the various scholastic disciplines, such as biology or history. In some cases, the participants needed this type of information for homework purposes, for example:

> Since we had math homework, I needed to find out what my math teacher's phone number is because I think she would be a better resource for getting what we need to do. She'll make it more clear, instead of calling my friends. (014; 265–67)

In other cases, it was evident that personal curiosity was the motivation, as in this audio journal excerpt:

> This morning after I got to school I wanted to know the meaning of the word innuendo. I was curious because I just like basically to have a good vocabulary, so I looked it up in the dictionary and I also looked in the vocabulary workbook which has similar meanings and ways to put innuendo into sentences and stuff like that. (010; 79–83)

Often, however, it was impossible to discern from the data whether the participants sought academic information to satisfy personal curiosity or to fulfill school requirements since they did not provide the context of the information need.

School Culture. School culture involves information pertaining to the rules, norms, customs, and methods of school operations. For example, one participant wondered, "What is the purpose of taking tests?" (001; 113). Another mused, "We [are] like guinea pigs. They give us tests all the time" (003; 303–4). Still another commented in her audio journal, "I wanted to see if we were still having a sock hop because I know that we're supposed to. But my school's kinda unorganized. . . . Our committees and student government that's [*sic*] supposed to hold these things aren't really that organized" (014; 92–95).

Current Events. The participants showed varying levels of curiosity about world news and events. Many questions dealt with the newly declared war in Iraq, such as a male participant who reported keeping a "war journal about the war, Iraqi Freedom," (007; 12–13), or the female who wondered, "If we lose [the war], will we have a back up planned?" (025; 195).

Other teens wanted information about more general current events.

One participant wrote in his activity log simply: "What's happening in the world?" (004; 53). Another "wanted to find out what does S.A.R.S. mean" (007; 5). Still another asked, "How much snow did some people get?" (009; 67).

The Sexual Self

> My friend, she keeps telling me that she's pregnant. . . . Before she told me this, her boyfriend, her old boyfriend, gave her a disease. And she broke up with him. She thought she was pregnant. She went to the doctor's, got herself checked out and everything. And they gave her the antibiotics and everything, pregnancy test, everything, and she wasn't pregnant. So next thing you know, she comes and tells me a couple months afterward that she thinks she's pregnant; she didn't get her period; her period [was] late. So I said to myself, "Don't let me find out that you still doing it to the boy after he gave you something."
> (001; 30–38)

The sexual self refers to understanding issues related to human sexuality. The tasks related to the development of the sexual self are: "learning to manage his or her sexuality" (Havighurst's task 9) and "learning to recognize and accept his or her sexuality." Under the development of the sexual self, the participants sought, gathered, or needed information relating to "sexual safety" and "sexual identity."

Sexual Safety. Many of the participants expressed worries about contracting sexual diseases, the females more than the males, even though both sexes were exposed to warnings about possible health risks of sexual behavior. As one female explained in her audio journal:

> An issue that came up today that scared my class and myself was the STD talk. The purpose of the talk was to allow teenagers to be aware of STDs. Especially gonorrhea and Chlamydia. I was quite sure everyone knew about STDs, but what made this scary was the way he [the guest speaker] displayed and verbally said his information. For instance, he would talk low one moment, and then get hyped the next. (004; 56–61)

Sexual Identity. As discussed above under "emotional health," one of the participants was struggling to understand whether or not she was homosexual. She engaged in a number of related information behaviors, primarily searching for an agency where she could talk to a counselor or other objective adult. For example, she explained that:

> I was trying to figure out how I was going to get to this center. . . . The kids can come on certain days, and I was trying to figure out where it was at, for transgender, bi/gay youth. . . . So I looked in the PGM [*Philadelphia Gay Magazine*] . . . . That gave me the information . . . the phone number and stuff like that if you want to call. (003; 216–25)

Another participant was trying to understand the concept of homosexuality more out of general curiosity than personal experience. She wrote that she was trying to understand "Why do girls like girls?" (001; 109).

SIGNIFICANCE OF THE MODELS

The two models that resulted from this study provide valuable information to both practitioners and to researchers. Specifically, the models: (1) make the role of serving the urban teen clearer, and (2) expand previous research on young adult information needs.

Significance to Practitioners

The models clearly demonstrate that the essence of urban teens' ELIS is the gathering and processing of information to facilitate the *multifaceted teen-to-adult maturation process*. ELIS for these teenagers is self-exploration and world exploration that helps them understand the world and their positions in it, as well as helping them to understand themselves now and to understand who they aspire to be in the future. Urban teens want and need information to support their emerging sexuality, their pressing financial needs, their attempts to understand the social worlds in which they live, their self-doubts about who they are and what role they can play in society, and so on.

Experts in the field of young adult services have been saying for decades that library services for teens need to support the entire person—the physical, cognitive, affective, and social person—yet many libraries still support primarily homework and pleasure reading needs.[31] Librarians can use these models to examine their services and modify or expand them to include the many equally important types of everyday life information needs of urban teens. Several possibilities exist:

1. At the most basic level, librarians might hold their libraries' collections, websites, programs, and reference services against the twenty-eight information needs topics identified in the empirical model to see how well their libraries support the wide range of teens' information needs.
2. A more user-centered approach might involve a discussion of the models, including the developmental areas and the corresponding information needs categories, with the members of the Teen Advisory Council to receive suggestions about how the library might meet these needs more effectively.
3. A more research-based, but still user-centered, approach might involve using the models as the basis for a survey that would be administered to the community's teens. The survey approach would allow librarians to determine the importance of each developmental area and corresponding categories in the lives of the teens living in their service area and to mold their services to their specific needs.

Another important aspect of the study that has direct relevance to practitioners involves the people sources/channels that urban teens most commonly use. Whenever possible these inner-city teens consulted humans as favored sources of information, turning first to friends and family to fulfill their information needs.[32] They decided which people to consult based on established human relationships, question topics, and the location of the information seeking. As the teens themselves explained, their choices were guided by the "it depends" principle.[33] Again, this finding has several implications:

1. Librarians must develop personal relationships with urban teenagers in order to meet their needs the most effectively. Librarians must be viewed by teenagers as credible, approachable, and concerned allies in the maturation process.
2. Librarians must work to establish relationships with the families of urban teens, not just the teenagers themselves. It may well be a family member who turns to the library for information that is then shared with the teen.

Finally, while these teens actively sought and manipulated information, they were hesitant to visit libraries. As two of the participants explained in the group interviews:

> My personal opinion of the library, I do real well in school, but I never really had to go to the library. They should make it so it should welcome not only children but also teens.

> It's a waiting list at the [public] library. You gotta wait at least 25 minutes; then you get 10 minutes on the computer. Who can wait all day when they give you almost no minutes?

Librarians need to focus on outreach efforts that can help teens understand how libraries and librarians can support their everyday life information needs, not just their homework and leisure reading needs. Librarians should also launch teen-friendly public relations campaigns to show that they value teens and want to serve their wide-ranging information needs.[34]

Significance to Researchers

As table 2.1 shows, the information needs previous researchers found with more advantaged, nonminority groups of teens are consistent with the seven areas of urban teen development represented by our theoretical model. This finding is significant because it suggests that: (1) teenagers have similar information needs across socioeconomic, ethnic, cultural, and geographic boundaries; and (2) other researchers studying the information behavior of adolescents might find our theoretical framework useful in interpreting their findings. Due to the exploratory nature of this study, however, additional research is necessary to confirm these possibilities.

CONCLUSION

While this chapter has described the ELIS behavior of urban teenagers and proposed two models to represent their everyday life information-seeking needs, it must be remembered that the findings are tentative and

Table 2.1.   Relating Our Theoretical Model of Urban Teen Development to Other Adolescent Information-Seeking Research Categories

Areas of Urban Teen Development	Categories from Other Research
Social self	Advice; affective support[35] Relationships[36] Current lifestyle issues; relationships[37] Recreational needs[38]
Emotional self	Advice; affective support[39] Relationships; current lifestyle issues; general information[40] Relationships[41] Personal development needs[42]
Reflective self	Affective support; self-development information; interest-driven information[43] Future plans; current lifestyle issues[44] Achievement; self-esteem[45] Education and work[46] Personal development needs; vocational and career information[47]
Physical self	Personal information; advice; affective support; consumer information[48] Current lifestyle issues; health information[49] Security and safety[50]
Creative self	Self-actualization[51] Accomplishment and skills; recreational needs[52]
Cognitive self	School-related; subject information; interest-driven information[53] Course-related information needs; general information[54] Self-actualization[55] Education and work[56] School and curriculum needs[57]
Sexual self	Health information[58] Personal development[59]

context bound, as is appropriate for qualitative inquiry.[60] Further study in other urban contexts, with a different, more racially and more ethnically diverse group of teenagers, is necessary to determine whether the results are transferable to the ELIS behaviors of other teenaged populations.

Lastly, the findings of this study illuminate the ability of urban teenagers to provide rich data. Not only did the participants exhibit enthusiasm for the project, they were able to describe and analyze their own behavior in sufficient detail and with sufficient clarity to support in-depth behavioral analysis. We encourage other researchers interested in the information behaviors of youth to consider this often-ignored segment of the population as future study participants.

ACKNOWLEDGMENTS

This research was supported by a grant from the Institute for Museum and Library Services (IMLS) under the National Leadership Grants for Libraries, Research and Demonstration. The contents of this chapter do not carry the endorsement of IMLS. The opinions expressed in this work are those of the researchers.

NOTES

1. Annie E. Casey Foundation, "KidsCount," www.aecf.org/Kidscount (accessed July 7, 2005).

2. Karen Pittman and Nicole Yohalem, "Public Libraries as Partners in Youth Development: Lessons from the Field," *Urban Libraries Council*, 2003, http://www.urbanlibraries.org/plpydpdf.html (accessed July 7, 2005).

3. Reijo Savolainen, "Everyday Life Information-Seeking: Approaching Information Seeking in the Context of Way of Life," *Library & Information Science Research* 17, no. 3 (Summer 1995): 267.

4. See, for example, Laura Reiner and Allen Smith, "Placing the Internet in Information Source Horizons: A Study of Information-Seeking by Internet Users in the Context of Self-Development," *Journal of Academic Librarianship* 31, no. 3 (May 2005): 301; Pamela J. McKenzie, "A Model of Information Practices in Accounts of Everyday-Life Information-Seeking," *Journal of Documentation* 59, no. 1 (2003): 19–41; Amanda Spink and Charles Cole, "Information and Poverty:

Information-Seeking Channels Used by African-American Low-Income House-holds," *Library & Information Science Research* 23, no. 1 (Spring 2001): 45–65.

5. Savolainen, "Everyday Life Information-Seeking," 259–94.

6. Savolainen, "Everyday Life Information-Seeking," 262.

7. Savolainen, "Everyday Life Information-Seeking," 264.

8. Kristy Williamson, "Discovered by Chance: The Role of Incidental Information Acquisition in an Ecological Model of Information Use," *Library & Information Science Research* 20, no. 1 (1998): 23–40.

9. McKenzie, "A Model of Information Practices," 19–40.

10. See, for example, Savolainen, "Everyday Life Information Seeking," 259–94; McKenzie, "A Model of Information Practices," 19–40; Williamson, "Discovered by Chance," 19–40.

11. Robert F. Carey, Lynne E. F. McKechnie, and Pamela J. McKenzie, "Gaining Access to Everyday Life Information-Seeking," *Library & Information Science Research* 23, no. 4 (Winter 2001): 319–34.

12. Regina Minudri, "Library and Information Services for Young Adults and Students," in *Library and Information Service Needs of the Nation: Proceedings of a Conference on the Needs of Occupational, Ethnic, and Other Groups in the United States*, ed. Carlos A. Cuadra and Marcia J. Bates, 155–61 (Washington, DC: Government Printing Office, 1974).

13. Jacqueline A. Fourie and Jan A. Kruger, "Basic and Developmental Information Needs of Secondary School Pupils," *Mousaion* 13, nos. 1–3 (1995): 225–49.

14. Kathy Latrobe and W. Michael Havener, "Information-Seeking Behavior of High School Honor Students: An Exploratory Study," *Journal of Youth Services in Libraries* 10 (Winter 1997): 188–200.

15. Andrew K. Shenton and Patricia Dixon, "The Nature of Information Needs and Strategies for Their Investigation in Youngsters," *Library & Information Science Research* 26, no. 3 (Summer 2004): 296–310.

16. Barbara Poston-Anderson and Susan Edwards, "The Role of Information in Helping Adolescent Girls with Their Life Concerns," *School Library Media Quarterly* 22, no. 1 (1993): 25–30.

17. Poston-Anderson and Edwards, "The Role of Information in Helping Adolescent Girls," 26.

18. Susan Edwards and Barbara Poston-Anderson, "Information, Future Time Perspectives, and Young Adolescent Girls: Concerns About Education and Jobs," *Library & Information Science Research* 18, no. 3 (Summer 1996): 207–33.

19. Heidi E. Julien, "Barriers to Adolescents' Information Seeking for Career Decision Making," *Journal of the American Society for Information Science* 50, no. 1 (January 1999): 38–48.

20. Ross Todd, "Utilization of Heroin Information by Adolescent Girls in Australia: A Cognitive Analysis," *Journal of the American Society for Information Science* 50, no. 1 (January 1999): 10–23.

21. G. E. Gorman and Peter Clayton, *Qualitative Research for the Information Professional: A Practical Handbook*, 2nd ed. (London: Facet Publishing, 2005).

22. Past research has proven a one-week period to be optimal for journal-based data collection. Few research participants are willing to cooperate for longer periods; shorter periods generally yield too little data to form complete pictures of participants' behaviors.

23. Matthew B. Miles and A. Michael Huberman, *Qualitative Data Analysis: An Expanded Sourcebook*, 2nd ed. (Thousand Oaks, CA: Sage, 1994).

24. Barney G. Glaser and Anslem L. Strauss, *The Discovery of Grounded Theory: Strategies for Qualitative Research* (Hawthorne, NY: Aldine de Gruyter, 1967); Yvonna S. Lincoln and Egon G. Guba, *Naturalistic Inquiry* (Newbury Park, CA: Sage, 1985).

25. For a more detailed explanation of the data analysis process see Denise E. Agosto and Sandra Hughes-Hassell, "People, Places, and Questions: An Investigation of the Everyday Life Information-Seeking Behaviors of Urban Young Adults," *Library & Information Science Research* 27, no. 2 (Spring 2005): 141–63.

26. Denotes participant numbers, which were randomly assigned from 1 to 27.

27. Indicates the line numbers from the transcripts.

28. Robert J. Havighurst, *Developmental Tasks and Education*, 3rd ed. (New York: Longman, 1972).

29. See, for example, René A. C. Hoksbergen, "Turmoil for Adoptees During Their Adolescence," *International Journal of Behavioral Development* 20 (1997): 33–46; Sandra Hughes-Hassell and Erika T. Miller, "Current Trends in Public Library Websites for Young Adults: Meeting the Needs of Today's Teens Online," *Library & Information Science Research* 25, no. 2 (Summer 2003): 143–56.

30. Abraham Maslow, *Motivation and Personality,* 2nd ed. (New York: Harper & Row, 1970).

31. See, for example, Eric Leyland, *The Public Library and the Adolescent* (London: Grafton & Co., 1937); Margaret A. Edwards, *The Fair Garden and the Swarm of Beasts: The Library and the Young Adult* (New York: Hawthorn, 1969); Patrick Jones, *Connecting Young Adults and Libraries*, 2nd ed. (New York: Neal-Schuman, 1998); and Virginia A. Walter and Elaine Meyers, *Teens & Libraries: Getting It Right* (Chicago: American Library Association, 2003).

32. This preference for humans as information sources is a common finding across socioeconomic and age divisions. See, for example, Andrew K. Shenton and Pat Dixon, "Youngsters' Use of Other People as an Information-Seeking Method," *Journal of Librarianship and Information Science* 35, no. 4 (December 2003): 219–33; Heidi Julien and D. Michels, "Source Selection Among Information Seekers: Ideals and Realities," *Canadian Journal of Information and Library Science* 25, no. 1 (April 2000): 1–18.

33. This finding supports the emphases on the social context of ELIS behavior discussed by Williamson, "Discovered by Chance," 23–40 and McKenzie, "A Model of Information Practices," 19–41.

34. Many good guides exist that offer librarians directions for launching simple, low-cost PR campaigns. See, for example, Jeanette Woodward, *Creating the Customer-Driven Library: Building on the Bookstore Model* (Chicago: American Library Association, 2005), and Rashelle S. Karp, ed., *Powerful Public Relations: A How-To Guide for Libraries* (Chicago: American Library Association, 2002).

35. Shenton and Dixon, "The Nature of Information Needs," 296–310.

36. Poston-Anderson and Edwards, "The Role of Information in Helping Adolescent Girls," 25–30.

37. Latrobe and Havener, "Information-Seeking Behavior of High School Honor Students,"188–200.

38. Minudri, "Library and Information Services for Young Adults and Students," 155–61.

39. Shenton and Dixon, "The Nature of Information Needs," 296–310.

40. Latrobe et al., "Information-Seeking Behavior of High School Honor Students: An Exploratory Study,"188–200.

41. Poston-Anderson et al., "The Role of Information in Helping Adolescent Girls with Their Life Concerns," 25–30.

42. Minudri, "Library and Information Services for Young Adults and Students," 155–161.

43. Shenton and Dixon, "The Nature of Information Needs," 296–310.

44. Latrobe and Havener, "Information-Seeking Behavior of High School Honor Students,"188–200.

45. Fourie and Kruger, "Basic and Developmental Information Needs," 225–49.

46. Poston-Anderson and Edwards, "The Role of Information in Helping Adolescent Girls," 25–30.

47. Minudri, "Library and Information Services for Young Adults and Students," 155–61.

48. Shenton and Dixon, "The Nature of Information Needs," 296–310.

49. Latrobe and Havener, "Information-Seeking Behavior of High School Honor Students," 188–200.

50. Fourie and Kruger, "Basic and Developmental Information Needs," 225–49.

51. Fourie and Kruger, "Basic and Developmental Information Needs," 225–49.

52. Minudri, "Library and Information Services for Young Adults and Students," 155–61.

53. Minudri, "Library and Information Services for Young Adults and Students," 155–61.

54. Latrobe and Havener, "Information-Seeking Behavior of High School Honor Students," 188–200.

55. Fourie and Kruger, "Basic and Developmental Information Needs," 225–49.

56. Poston-Anderson and Edwards, "The Role of Information in Helping Adolescent Girls," 25–30.

57. Minudri, "Library and Information Services for Young Adults and Students," 155–61.

58. Latrobe and Havener, "Information-Seeking Behavior of High School Honor Students," 188–200.

59. Minudri, "Library and Information Services for Young Adults and Students," 155–61.

60. Lincoln and Guba, *Naturalistic Inquiry.*

3

Research Directions for Understanding and Responding to Young Adult Sexual and Reproductive Health Information Needs

Jennifer Burek Pierce

What is known about young adults' information-seeking activities has increased markedly in recent years, yet youth efforts to obtain health information, particularly in the specialized and often controversial area of sexual and reproductive health, remain little explored by library and information science researchers. Research on youth information-seeking on sexual and reproductive health topics, though, is taking place in other fields. That research, generated primarily in areas such as medicine, nursing, and public health, nonetheless correlates to areas of interest in library and information science; further, the health sciences research calls for attention to matters like selection and use of information resources, information literacy, and privacy and confidentiality. Thus, health sciences findings on adolescent information seeking have significant interest and implications for library and information science researchers who study youth information behaviors. The former body of research presents ideas that sometimes are at odds with those articulated in library and information science publications, while exploring otherwise familiar terrain. The common element in this work involves researchers' efforts to understand relationships between information seeking and sexual and reproductive health.

Few researchers would contend that simply providing reproductive health information ensures healthy behaviors. Adolescent health is a multifaceted matter. The Chicago-based work of Felton Earls and a team of researchers indicates that adolescent sexual health is affected by factors including neighborhood levels of social cohesion and poverty. Further, Earls observes that findings on adolescent sexual health reflect a much larger picture. Researchers from the Project on Human Development in Chicago's Neighborhoods write, "The findings on adolescent sex are representative of a much larger body of data on health issues that deeply affect young people, from mental health to substance abuse."[1] Similarly, national perspectives on the ways neighborhoods influence adolescent sexual behavior have been obtained by Cubbin, et al.[2] Even as researchers acknowledge that multiple and dynamic contexts influence health behaviors, much research on reproductive health outcomes suggests that better health is more readily achieved when information is made available than when it is not.

This essay briefly reviews library and information science research that explores youth information seeking related to health, then focuses on contemporary peer-reviewed medical and public health research on adolescents' sexual and reproductive health information seeking. Attention is also given to the work of major public policy associations in this area. Health sciences and public policy research provides valuable perspectives on young adults' needs for and efforts to find information about their developing bodies and physical relationships; the research also raises questions about adolescents' abilities to obtain and evaluate appropriate information sources, often arguing that more must be done to ensure that adolescents have access to reliable information supporting their developmental needs. Despite this seeming congruence, disciplinary differences that result from dissimilar foundational assumptions must be understood before deriving directions for further research or forming interdisciplinary research partnerships. Discussion of these disparities concludes this exploration of health sciences research that pertains to as yet nascent work on sexuality in library and information science studies of adolescent information seeking.

UNDERSTANDING SEXUAL HEALTH IN THE
CONTEXT OF ADOLESCENCE

Defining sexual health is a necessary preliminary to interpreting this body of research. Simply put, the policy groups and academic researchers whose work seeks to define the norms of adolescent sexual and reproductive health do not always use the same terminology and sometimes disagree upon key concepts or even optimal outcomes. A number of professional and academic fields contribute to our understanding of youth sexual health information seeking, and those research projects evince multiple research cultures, and foci. Consequently, even though the meaning of sexual health may seem to a certain extent self-evident, in the research literature it entails a range of related concepts that must be explicated in order to delineate the terms and the boundaries of this discussion.

Different uses of the word *sex* and related terms appear in the published literature. Aspects of such differences, sources of definitions, and their relationships to characterizations of sexual health will be considered here. A pivotal distinction concerns biology, including physiology and behavior, as distinct from matters of identity and desire; these meanings are sometimes differentiated by using *sex* to refer to intrinsically physiological matters and *sexuality* to describe issues involved with values, perceptions, and feelings. While the Sexuality Information and Education Council of the United States defines the physical and psychosocial aspects of sex as intrinsically inter-related,[3] this understanding has not always prevailed. The medical and public health literature on adolescent information seeking historically has tended to emphasize sex rather than sexuality. This means adolescent actions and beliefs that either promote or jeopardize their health are more often the basis for study than elements that contribute to the individual's sense of him- or herself as a sexual being. Physiological and psychological components of sexuality are, however, sometimes studied in tandem.[4] More recent articles tend to incorporate sexuality as an essential consideration.[5]

The role of wellness and preventative care in ensuring sexual and reproductive health is gaining increasing attention, particularly where adolescents are concerned. Sexual and reproductive well-being involves more than the treatment of disease. As writers for the Alan Guttmacher Institute observe, some sexual and reproductive health conditions, such as pregnancy, are not ailments but nonetheless benefit from the provision of evidence-based medical information.[6] Although they have been underserved in this regard, youth benefit from preventative care as well as health maintenance.[7] Elsewhere it has been argued, "The health system must adapt to the needs of adolescents, and their needs reside as much in preventative medicine as they do in curative medicine."[8] Sexual health information pertains to positive as well as compromised states of health and, particularly in the case of adolescents, researchers must consider a range of issues such as confidentiality in order to support reproductive health and wellness.

Risk is a particularly important consideration in sexual health research. Risk has been defined as the "possibility of loss, injury, disease, or death" and recognizes that individuals, behaviors, or environments may be "characterized by high risk or susceptibility" to disease or poor health outcomes.[9] Risk is a broad term; it encompasses not only the actuality of individual health but also more abstract concepts such as future achievement, like education and employment potential. Risk sometimes is used to describe, largely through statistical assessments of negative outcomes associated with risky behaviors, adolescent sexual and reproductive health. As Brindis has argued, "sexuality—and particularly adolescent sexuality—has been conceptualized within a context of the negative and the problematic, a context of behavioral risk."[10] An example of this occurs on a Centers for Disease Control Web page intended to promote sexual health among adolescents, which opens by presenting teen sexual health in terms of less than optimal health outcomes:

> Unprotected sexual intercourse and multiple sex partners place young people at risk for HIV infection, other sexually transmitted diseases (STD), and pregnancy. Each year, there are approximately 19 million new STD infections in the United States, and almost half of them are among youth ages 15 to 24. Thirty-four percent of young women become pregnant at least once before they reach the age of 20—approximately 820,000 each year. In 2003, 47% of high school students had ever had sexual intercourse, 14% of high school students had four or more sex partners during their lifetime, and 37% of sexually active high school students did not use a condom at last sexual intercourse.[11]

This sort of statistical portrait of a teen population prone to risky behaviors has become a trope in policy debates over youth services, yet increasingly, health sciences research and public policy work argues that health and healthy behaviors are more than the absence of ill health or risk.

This concern, though, does not downplay the empirically demonstrable harms that result from adolescents' risky behavior. The health literatures conclude that adopting risky behaviors of one sort means that teens are more likely to experience other threats to health and well-being.[12] Sexual activity carries greater risks for younger adolescents, with those who are age fifteen and younger evincing heightened risk of infection.[13] Thus, adolescent risks are not simply matters of personal or cultural values about premarital sex and may be regarded as the result of information deficits representing barriers to long-term well-being. Risks, then, constitute behaviors or conditions to be addressed through information and counseling in order to make progress toward health outcomes carrying personal and public benefits.[14]

These definitional claims rest on a research-based understanding of the role of sexuality in youth development. Two recent articles conclude that sexuality is a normal part of human development, even prior to adolescence. According to Duncan, Dixon, and Carlson, "Curiosity about changes in sexual maturation is a normal part of childhood and adolescence. The development of a healthy sexuality should be a part of a child's physical and emotional development."[15] Other researchers acknowledge the extent to which this proposition may inspire controversy or even fears about sexual abuse and describe normal and appropriate sexuality in youth, as well as identifying sexual behavior that reflects knowledge or experience inappropriate to a young person's age.[16] These findings imply that seeking information about sex is a normal, even inherent, part of maturation.

A final definitional matter concerns the naming of young adults. The library literature, chiefly through professional associations concerned with services to teens, such as the Young Adult Library Services Association (YALSA), understands teens, adolescents, and young adults as synonymous entities. YALSA defines a young adult as someone between the ages of twelve and eighteen, and other prominent guides to youth librarianship[17] do not define young adults as a population. Library and information science researchers may see somewhat different conventions of nomenclature in the health sciences literature, where the term *young adult* most often refers to individuals who are eighteen or older, into their early twenties. Adolescence is more commonly used as an indexing term in the health sciences for the population referred to as young adults in library and information science.

These definitions ground the need for sexual health information for adolescents. Throughout the literature, calls for providing teens with information abound. Health professionals have identified information as of value in addressing risky adolescent behavior, observing that lack of understanding of basic reproductive facts has been demonstrated to be one factor influencing teens' decisions to take risks.[18] In addition to forming a normal part of growth and development, such information contributes to improved health outcomes. Typically, this research strives to identify ways reduce risk and improve health outcomes, and more holistic approaches recognize that peers, family, environment, and ethnic heritage or culture influence adolescents' motivations to seek or to disregard information concerning sexual and reproductive health. In turn, these more comprehensive efforts can result in a complex, multifaceted context for research on adolescent information seeking.

LIBRARY AND INFORMATION SCIENCE LITERATURE ON ADOLESCENTS AS HEALTH INFORMATION SEEKERS

A scattering of library and information science research offers some perspective on young adults as health information consumers. This research can be divided into three categories: studies that investigate youth health information needs broadly, writings that analyze available sources of health information in library collections, and studies that offer insights into actions and attitudes involved in youths' every day information seeking. Despite Lukenbill's assertion in 1979 that "we are beginning to collect data on the information needs and the information-seeking habits of young adults in relation to topics such as sex, drugs, and career information,"[19] library and information science researchers have given little attention to the former, even in some contemporary studies that attend to youth information seeking. The work to date provides, at best, limited conclusions about young adults' efforts to obtain health information related to the processes of physical maturation that play a part in marking the transition from childhood to adult life.

Some publications in the field directly acknowledge that young adults seek sexual and reproductive health material and respond with guidance for collecting and evaluating this content area. Foremost among these works is Campbell's *Sex Guides*, which sketches the development of sexual health materials for younger audiences and articulates guidelines for collection development, including fiction, in this area. Campbell indicates that much written with the ostensible goal of helping young adults develop a mature and informed perspective about sexuality is value laden, offering dated or even erroneous information.[20] Gross identifies more recent titles in this area and argues that libraries, through outreach, can do a better job of meeting pressing if unarticulated needs for reproductive health information.[21] These publications urge attention to the quality of sexual health information made available and promotion of these resources to increase awareness of their availability. Additionally, two other recent practitioner-oriented articles have considered the issues involved in teens' access to online sexual health sources.[22] These authors posit that young adults' sexual health information needs are inadequately met.

Studies making broader assessments of youth information-seeking activities provide limited conclusions about teens' and children's efforts to acquire health information. It has been shown, for example, that queries about sensitive subjects like sexuality sometimes provoke negative judgments about young adults who seek such information, leading them to defer information seeking or to conceal their activities.[23] Walter's identification of youth information needs as perceived by supportive adults includes health information topics from AIDS to "Western medicine."[24] Assessment of adolescent use of public library nonfiction holdings indicates use of titles on puberty.[25] These articles offer preliminary indications that adolescents have reproductive health information needs and make efforts to satisfy them in libraries, but it is difficult to assess the outcomes of these information-seeking behaviors.

Strikingly, some recent prominent publications in the field elect not to address this dimension of youth information seeking. For example, Case notes the growth of studies on children and young adults but does not give much attention to them beyond observing the multiple indicators that show young information seekers rely on the World Wide Web as the medium of first resort,[26] which, coincidentally, is a preferred teen medium for access to sexual and reproductive health information.[27] Large, who also observes this omission in Case's work, construes sexual material on the Web only in terms of prurient, threatening content.[28] While protecting youth from online predators and illegal or even simply inappropriate Web content is no mean matter, to represent the sexual content of the Web solely in these terms is misleading. The presence of sexual health information on reputable sites, such as those supported by federal government agencies that have historically carried high presumptions of reliability,[29] and authoritative nongovernmental organizations, must be considered. This is particularly crucial as federal information policies now restrict print publishing to a short list of titles, making the Web the primary outlet for federally produced information in most content areas, including reproductive health. Scholarly efforts to account for youths' everyday information-seeking behavior must depend on fuller understandings of their use of the Web to acquire health information.

From these studies it may be inferred that young adults' health-related inquiries may not be resolved in satisfying or meaningful ways, and some LIS researchers have sought attention to the shortcomings of research within the discipline. Dresang calls attention to the fact that "the environment for youth has changed dramatically in the digital age, but our paradigm for studying their behavior has not."[30] A key direction into which research should be extended, according to Dresang, is young people's autonomous, rather than imposed, information seeking. Reproductive health needs are one category of information seeking more often driven by youth interests than by the curriculum.[31] More directly, Chelton has observed, "The sexual health field has studied youth information seeking for years with little collaboration with LIS researchers."[32] It is this literature external to library and information science that constitutes major focus of this review.

FINDINGS FROM THE HEALTH SCIENCES LITERATURE

The health sciences literature on adolescent sexual and reproductive health is vast, comprising numerous subfields, and proliferating. Brindis has described the field's range this way: "Adolescent reproductive health is a broad area that encompasses sexuality education, pregnancy prevention, prepregnancy-related health services, pregnancy, abortion, and childbearing."[33] There are other ways of delimiting the scope of this field as well. Accordingly, this survey of the literature is selective rather than comprehensive, mapped to particular issues in library and information science research on everyday information seeking by adolescents. The library and information science literature suggests potential issues regarding adolescents' efforts to meet their sexual health information needs; in broad terms, these include access to information, confidentiality, and the ability to conduct queries in nonjudgmental environments. Use of the World Wide Web is another significant avenue of information seeking for adolescents. This overview of peer-reviewed medical, nursing, and public health literature identifies studies addressing potential barriers to teens' ability to obtain information, matters involved in confidentiality, and use of the Web to obtain material about reproduction and its associated health issues. These topics sometimes invoke other contexts, but an effort to collect the work most closely aligned with the issues represented by LIS investigations of adolescents' information seeking drives this review. The focus on access, confidentiality/privacy, and electronic sources of information excludes the significant number of articles that examine practitioner-patient interactions, even though these face-to-face communications serve a potentially important role in adolescents' willingness to ask for sexual health information.[34]

Further limitations characterize the research represented here. Chief among them is recentness. Literature published before 1990 is excluded from this study, and the most recently available information is prioritized. While there are parallels between sex education and sexual and reproductive health information, there are also differences between these areas. This review emphasizes teens' unstructured and undirected information seeking about reproduction, rather than the historically more structured and programmatic approach to information provision implied by the former. The material incorporated, for the most part, is written in English and refers to U.S. populations, as cross-cultural differences can strain efforts to draw conclusions about youth information behaviors. One internationally comparative study has observed that while "all cultures recognize and mark the transition from child to adult" the measures of this change are far from universal.[35] The chief exception to U.S.-based research is in the case of websites providing health information, although some world-based comparison studies are included as well. The literature on AIDS education, which almost constitutes a field in its own right, is not considered here. The primary focus of this assessment of the literature is peer-reviewed material, particularly the genre of medical publication known as the review article; however, policy research providing descriptive statistics, guidelines, and research findings have been used to develop the context for this assessment of the scholarly literature.

STATES OF SEXUALITY KNOWLEDGE AND IMPLICATIONS FOR ADOLESCENT INFORMATION SEEKING

The research on what adolescents know and when and how they came to know it is diverse, accounting for cultural influences such as friends and mass media outlets, as well as doctor-patient interactions. Recent findings pertaining to adolescent understanding of sex are presented here. These studies reveal environmental factors, including peer attitudes, that factor into information-seeking processes and decisions about whether to seek information. This section seeks to describe, through the presentation of targeted research findings, generalizations about teen sexual activity that lead to questions about teens' information-seeking behaviors.

In recent years, mass media attention to teen sexuality has suggested the prevalence of oral sex as a component of adolescent sexuality, describing it as a norm in a culture of casual sex[36] and as a perceived means of preserving one's virginity.[37] Because the data behind these stories is local and anecdotal rather than generalizable, some recent literature has attempted to examine the basis for these reports by assessing adolescents' knowledge and attitudes about specific sexual practices. A 2005 data analysis by the National Campaign to Prevent Teen Pregnancy derived these factual conclusions from a national sample of teens:

> More than half of teens have had oral sex and it is now more likely that a teen has had oral sex than it is that he/she has had sexual intercourse. Almost all

of those who have had sexual intercourse have had oral sex (although we do not know the actual sequence of behavior). Moreover, about one in four teens who have *not* had sexual intercourse have had oral sex.[38]

Also significant among this research is a study that indicates most young women who participated in a focus group perceive engaging in many sexual acts other than intercourse as practicing abstinence.[39] Halpern-Felsher et al. conducted a related survey and reached similar conclusions, which are borne out by the National Campaign to Prevent Teen Pregnancy analyses as well.[40]

Although these studies, which explore recently developed research questions, cannot be said to document teen sexual behavior in absolute terms, they do provide empirical data about sexuality issues reported by popular media and explore important attitudinal issues in relation to statistics compiled by units such as the Centers for Disease Control. Researchers observe that beyond verifying or contradicting media reports about adolescent sexual activity, these findings point to information deficits with regard to sexual health that effectively discourage adolescents from seeking information about safe sex practices; that is, teens who engage in sexual behaviors but believe themselves to be abstinent are unlikely to seek information or other resources to reduce risks to sexual health. As National Campaign to Prevent Teen Pregnancy researchers concluded, "Too many teens view oral sex as safe. . . . These data suggest that teens need to be better informed about the potential physical risks of engaging in oral sex."[41]

Researchers routinely advocate providing valid sexual and reproductive health information to adolescents. Still, international, comparative studies of adolescent attitudes suggest that knowledge of healthy or safe sexual behavior is not always sufficient to motivate teens to act in ways that health professionals endorse as safe or preventative. Metcalfe is one of many who note the prevalence of sexual risk-taking behaviors in adolescence.[42] These tendencies are further characterized by figures showing that in recent decades U.S. teens have experienced higher rates of sexual activity, sexually transmitted disease, and pregnancy than teens in other developed nations, conclusions confirmed by multiple studies.[43] Zwane et al. cite World Health Organization data demonstrating that "As a group, young people tend to be uniformed or misinformed about sexuality and reproductive health, and they are reluctant to take action to protect themselves." Zwane's findings indicate that peers and social perceptions influence adolescent decisions about safe sex practices, rather than clinicians or authoritative information resources.[44] Significant, then, are adolescents' tendencies to take health risks even when they possess knowledge about causes and prevention strategies. This remains a matter for continued study and action.[45]

Additional research characterizes the nature of adolescent knowledge deficits regarding their sexual and reproductive health. An article titled "Will the Pill Make Me Sterile?" signals the prevalence of misunderstandings about contraception.[46] Other studies have documented, in additional ways, indicators of teens' lack of knowledge about reproductive health; a burgeoning question concerns adolescents' awareness of the availability of emergency contraception. Brindis has observed that mass media sometimes contribute to adolescent misinformation:

> A major source of information on sex and sexuality that remains relatively unmonitored is the popular media. It is unfortunate and ironic that the "lessons" provided through this source have much less to do with the facts of anatomy and birth control than with the acceptance of passion leading directly to unprotected intercourse and, thus, the implied acceptability of forgoing the use of contraceptives.[47]

Brown and Keller assess the roles that all kinds of media, from television to the Internet, may play in shaping adolescent knowledge of sexual and reproductive health; citing international research findings, they argue the value of encouraging teens to make sound reproductive health decisions through media campaigns.[48]

Special information needs within the adolescent community have also received some scholarly attention. National longitudinal studies, like the Youth Risk Behavior Surveillance survey, document differences in sexual activity for male and female students and for white and minority group members. The 1997 survey indicates, for example, that black adolescents report having had four or more sexual partners at higher proportions than adolescents in any other ethnic group and that white teens were likely to use condoms.[49] Some shifts are evident in the 2003 analysis.[50] These statistics invite the inference that adolescents from different racial and ethnic backgrounds experience different health information needs,[51] and that these needs will change continually.

Other research confronts special populations' needs more directly. The problems presented by violence in intimate relationships have been proposed for further study.[52] Researchers also observe that while female reproductive health is an acknowledged area of concern, male teens' needs should be understood as distinctive and addressed.[53] Attention to the sex information needs of adolescents with disabilities is undertaken by Verhoef et al., who conclude that teens with spina bifida feel under-informed in specific aspects of their sexual health[54] (in this, these teens echo the sentiments of the adolescent population as a whole).[55] Additional studies of the reproductive health concerns of adolescents with disabilities have been undertaken.[56] The information issues attributed to adolescents with special needs who are involved in intimate relationships indicate that scholarly, empirical understanding of adolescent health information needs remains underdeveloped. Examination of the concerns of teens who, for any reason, fall outside the generally perceived norms of the sexually interested or active adolescent, warrant further research.

These studies examining adolescent attitudes toward and knowledge of sexual health conclude that, in many respects, teens possess information deficits. These studies also demonstrate that teens simply may not understand that information is needed or available. Sexual activity is prevalent, even among some teens who describe themselves as abstinent, a state of affairs that effectively deters these youth from seeking sexual health information. Even among youth who acknowledge their sexual activities, numerous conditions, ranging from peers as information sources to broadly held cultural attitudes, influence information seeking regarding sexual health matters. For example, both mass media and peers may deflect adolescents' willingness to locate information about sexual health. Key difficulties related to adolescent sexual health information needs, then, can be linked to the communities in which they function, as well as to individual decisions.

BARRIERS TO INFORMATION SEEKING, CONSIDERED AND RECONSIDERED

Medical researchers and those working in related fields have identified internal and external barriers to teens' efforts to obtain sexual health information. Chief among these obstacles are adolescent concerns about confidentiality. To state the research conclusions generally, lack of confidentiality deters teens from seeking reproductive health information in many environments. At the same time that researchers are increasingly able to demonstrate the strong value that adolescents place on confidentiality, laws and policies at both state and federal levels are being changed or scrutinized; the effect of most alterations is to reduce teens' abilities to obtain medical care and health information related to reproduction. An alternative to face-to-face consultations is to seek information via the Web; teens who use publicly funded computers in schools or libraries may be denied full access to electronic information sources by filtering. Filtering is generally presumed to have a dampening effect on information access, but there are some mixed results in this area.

The published research in this area repeatedly finds that "Teenagers are more likely to use health services when they are guaranteed confidentiality."[57] This is generally held to be true of their information seeking with regard to health information as well. Global studies as well as local ones report these concerns for both sexes.[58] Indications are that this desire to evade scrutiny is particularly strong in adolescents living in rural communities and smaller towns. Sexual activity is listed as an area for which rural youth have not sought medical advice, and fear of being stigmatized is one reason.[59] Recently developed guidelines for pediatricians treating gay, lesbian, or bisexual adolescents also encourage attention to confidentiality issues.[60] These findings have implications for teens' access to health information. Repeatedly, studies find that efforts to provide young adults with reproductive health information are "slight and slowed by controversy."[61] A combination of teens' own fears and social attitudes means their needs for health information are often underserved.

A strong motivation for adolescent use of Web-based health information is the privacy theoretically available to the searcher. Multiple studies have documented that young adults are among those who use the Web to obtain consumer health information. Yet the Web is not a panacea: teens' information skills as well as policy matters impede their access to Web-based health information.

Just as some studies in library and information science have found that young adults' Web surfing skills are not as sophisticated as popular perceptions would suggest,[62] research in the health sciences finds that youths' search skills impede their access to using online information sources. One such observational study determined that while the majority of the time—69 percent of the queries studied by researchers were answered correctly—teens could answer health questions using the World Wide Web, reasons for failed efforts included spelling errors, poor or inappropriate selection of search terms, and inadequate evaluation of retrieved Web pages.[63] Of interest to researchers in library and information science are recommendations emerging from this study, which include instructing adolescents in order to improve their online search skills; this may be because this article results from a research partnership between medical and information science researchers.

Also significant are factors found not to constitute barriers to information access. Much has been made of the impact of Internet filters on access to health information, and studies that have attracted attention in the library and information science community cite the restrictions imposed by filters.[64] Those in LIS emphasize barriers to information created by filtering, even when researchers note those findings are conditional.[65] One major filtering study has received little scrutiny in library and information science publications, and its findings conflict with common notions about limitations that result from filtering. Conducted with awareness of adolescent use of the World Wide Web to obtain sensitive information about sexual health, research assessed the effect of restrictions imposed by filtering software set with varying levels of restrictiveness. Researchers searched some one hundred terms, including *safe sex, condoms, breast cancer, rape,* and *gay* and *lesbian.* It was concluded that

> At their least restrictive settings, overblocking of health information poses a relatively minor impediment. However, searches on some terms related to sexuality led to substantially more health information blocking. More restrictive configurations blocked pornography only slightly more, but substantially increased blocking of health sites.[66]

The researchers note that under some conditions, blocking certain search terms still leaves reasonable amounts of relevant information available to searchers. These findings confirm and extend the conclusions of previous research that indicates moderate filtering does not necessarily constitute an absolute barrier to information about sexual and reproductive health information. Sexual health information, though, is an area researchers determined to be most affected by restrictive filtering software.

Barriers to teens' access to sexual and reproductive health information may take many forms, including adolescents' own search skills. Filtered Internet access and limited confidentiality protections are two barriers with consequences for adolescent health information seekers; these matters are established as concerns within both the health sciences and information sciences literatures. Although there are exceptions,[67] much that has been published in both fields critiques filtering as an impediment to information access. It is worth noting that some studies indicate youth will be able to access at least some reproductive health information even when filters are in place.

With regard to confidentiality, a distinctive disciplinary difference emerges because of laws requiring parental involvement in children's medical care. While the culture of library and information science, encoded in statements of professional ethics adopted by the American Library Association and other professional groups, has come to favor access to information, those in the health sciences may be restricted in their interactions with adolescents by laws that vary from state to state.[68] Different assessments of teens' reproductive health information needs may emerge from these variances in professional ethical and legal cultures.

PLUSSES AND MINUSES OF USING THE WORLD WIDE WEB AS A HEALTH INFORMATION RESOURCE

The research literature is nearly unanimous in acknowledging the prevalence of the Web as an information resource, especially for adolescents and particularly in the realm of sexual health information. While this chapter has already called attention to research that highlights the use of the Web to obtain reproductive health information, three studies warrant further scrutiny. Borzekowski and Rickert provide compelling evidence that the Web is the preferred venue for sexual health information seeking for teens, who describe the information they find there as satisfactory and valuable.[69] In other words, as has been established in other contexts, adolescents accept information found on the Web, rather than expressing concerns about the accuracy or authenticity of its information content.

Health sciences researchers have begun to explore the role of Web-based health information in adolescents' lives. These studies suggest that information use trends established in other contexts also hold true for adolescent information seeking for sexual and reproductive health information. Research by Skinner et al. notes the role of adolescents as "early adopters of new technologies" thereby requiring medical professionals to understand and to evaluate the health information available through technology-based resources such as the Web. This study describes websites as "the first places that study participants looked for health information" but associates lack of access to information technologies with participants from rural rather than urban areas.[70] Another study confirms that whether access is through home or public institutions including schools, youth who live in urban environments regularly use the World Wide Web for a range of online activities, including obtaining health information.[71] Although neither study is comprehensive, the results are congruent with national LIS research identifying the same kind of information technology disparities between urban and rural locations.[72] This finding modifies numerous other reports that describe inequity of access for urban information seekers in more absolute terms. Bleakley et al.'s results are also noteworthy in suggesting that the patterns of information seeking prevalent among adult Web searchers, in which women, who often bear responsibility for reproductive health care, are more likely to engage in searches for this kind of information than men, may be seen in this younger cohort. Thus, three further conclusions emerge from the general observation of use of the Web to obtain reproductive health information: first, that health information providers must know Web content on reproductive health; next, that adolescents in rural locations are less able to counter barriers to access than their urban peers, and finally, that even in adolescence, females bear more responsibility than males for obtaining reproductive health information.

These findings, though, are not unqualified. Ackard and Neumark-Sztainer present data in some degree of conflict with the patterns suggested by the Skinner and Bleakley research teams and identify Web-based information as among the least used information resources.[73]

Ackard and Neumark-Sztainer indicate male and female teens have different preferences for information sources, whether Web-based tools or face-to-face communication. While reporting that adolescents regard queries related to sex as embarrassing and therefore more difficult to satisfy, the researchers do not indicate whether teens opt for different information sources to combat feelings of embarrassment or privacy concerns. These findings, then, raise questions but do not strongly counter the prevailing research that shows teens commonly use the Web to access sexual and reproductive health information.

The prevalence of teen use of the Web as an information resource raises questions about the nature of the health information available in cyberspace. The reliability and readability of sexual health information presented via World Wide Web sites has not yet been fully assessed in the scholarly literature; the initial studies indicate some issues with regard to adolescent information seeking. Michaud and Colom report that many major and frequently linked sites, such as www.goaskalice.edu, have not been evaluated.[74] Assessment of this and forty other sexual health websites for adolescent audiences led researchers to conclude that while it is relatively easy to locate information about a specific sexual health problem or condition, such as symptoms of a disease or strategies to improve sexual satisfaction, it is more difficult to obtain general sexual health information, such as how the human reproductive system works, via the Web. Researchers also noted the prevalence of myths and false information about sexuality on what might appear to be authoritative sites.[75] A subsequent study with a narrower focus evaluates the American Social Health Association's www.iwannaknow.org site, whose designated purpose is providing "answers to your questions about teen sexual health and sexually transmitted diseases."[76] Findings from this study offer potential benchmarking data by identifying most frequently sought types of information and establishing the fact that teens constitute a minority of those using this site.[77] Because of findings like these and other sociocultural dimensions of adolescent behavior, Montgomery calls for further research into information dissemination via new media as it affects youth, with the objective of developing effective and meaningful policies.[78] Bay-Cheng has argued that websites providing sexual health information are particularly inadequate for the needs of gay and lesbian teens.[79] The small body of research on specific reproductive health websites suggests a need for further review of information disseminated via the Web, considering both content and use.

Given these findings, it should not be surprising that the need to teach adolescents Web evaluation skills is a recurring theme in these articles. Some researchers observe that multiple aspects of teens' information retrieval activities—from determining search terms to manipulation of site content—appear weak. This dimension of adolescents' activities as consumer health information seekers would seem to be a natural entry point for library and information science researchers.

CONCLUSION

There is a vast and multidimensional literature in the health sciences on teen sexual health. This literature review calls attention to selected recent work that engages issues paralleling those in library and information science research on adolescents' information-seeking behaviors. Overall, the findings point to significant gaps in adolescents' understanding of sexual and reproductive health information, coupled with barriers to information access. Health practitioners and policy makers interested in public health have concluded that "many adolescents do not have accurate information about sexual development or the risks or consequences of early and unprotected sexual activity."[80] These knowledge deficits are characterized more specifically by the head of adolescent health for the World Health Organization, who writes

> Adolescents in most of the world lack adequate knowledge about sexual maturation and the relationship between sexual practices and pregnancy or STD; they lack information about what services exist and how to use them; . . . they fear the consequences of disclosing their sexual behaviour to adults . . . ; and they find it difficult to communicate with each other about the subject.[81]

Where gains or improved health outcomes have been seen, Feldmann and Middleman observe, "it is disheartening that . . . declines are among the lowest risk groups, effectively widening the gap of health disparities between white and minority teenagers."[82] In the health sciences, these issues are a concern because lacking information, in turn, has been connected to poorer health and well-being outcomes. Yet the fundamental problems encountered in this health sciences research—

determining information needs, overcoming obstacles to information access, and discovering and evaluating sources of information—are the province of library and information science research as well. This congruence suggests the potential for library and information science researchers to learn from and to extend the existing literature on adolescent sexual health information needs.

Further investigation or research partnerships to study adolescent sexual health information seeking must acknowledge different research cultures and intellectual traditions. These differences pertain to matters ranging from the role of theory to ethical frameworks. Expectations regarding data sources and sample sizes may also differ.

Much library and information science work in adolescent information seeking depends on relatively small sample sizes. While case studies and focus groups are also used in health sciences research, these researchers more often use larger samples. Long-term national surveys provide big-picture assessments of youth sexual health. One is known as the Add Health survey, which aims to obtain not only descriptive information about youth sexual activity but to understand sociocultural factors that contribute to health-enhancing or risky decisions.[83] Another is the federal Youth Risk Behavior Surveillance System (YRBSS), which focuses on identifying and representing risky behavior in a range of areas, including sexual activity.[84] These two recently developed studies provide national statistics with attention to variances according to age, ethnic or racial background, and urban and rural environments. Some of the health sciences literature results from secondary analyses of these complex data sets.

Some information science research treats information acquisition as a proposed or theoretical factor in making life choices, while the health professions literature often posits that information interventions do in fact affect health positively. This may be seen, for example, in the difference between how information use is discussed by Todd and Edwards, who talk in terms of shifting and as yet tenuous theories of "information utilization,"[85] and by Grizzard et al., who document an intervention understood to have demonstrated potential to alter poor reproductive health outcomes for adolescents.[86] Thus, while library and information science researchers continue to investigate whether information makes a difference in daily life, there is a research tradition in the health sciences affirming, at least conditionally, that information helps to secure health improvements. In reproductive health, these findings date to the Progressive Era.[87] These assumptions do not presume that information provision alone prevents health problems, only that it is integral to promoting positive health choices.

A key effort of health sciences research is not only to determine effective practice but also to formulate policy. While professional associations in library and information science endorse freedom of information and nonjudgmental service, research leads clinical researchers to argue for the provision of unbiased information and, at the same time, to make judgments about health messages and about adolescent behavior. For example, based on findings that have determined adolescents are at increased risk from sexual activity, the Academy of American Pediatricians has advised physicians to counsel adolescents to delay sexual activity until closer to adulthood.[88] Other health science researchers have called for efforts to counter popular culture representations of sexuality that are harmful or encourage risky behaviors. These avenues of professional activity may seem alien in library and information science, where major professional associations value intellectual freedom in absolute terms and protest almost any threatened infringement on First Amendment freedoms for youth. In other words, where library and information science practitioners provide information but do not presume to advise young people's behavior, health sciences practitioners do assume roles as guides and advocates with regard to life choices.

Different research cultures aside, the existing literature suggests the potential for library and information science researchers to clarify and to improve what is known about adolescent sexual and reproductive health information seeking. Specific research issues include young adults' ability to locate information and to evaluate its accuracy and authority. Determining whether effective interventions can be made in young adults' search behaviors to improve their search skills is a related matter, and these topics are being actively explored in the health sciences.[89] Further, the information content of sexual health websites, which are increasingly provided as links from public library Web pages for young adults, also needs more assessment. It is in these and related areas that library and information science research can contribute to understanding youth needs and uses of sexual health information.

NOTES

1. "Neighborhood Matters: Selected Findings from the Project on Human Development in Chicago Neighborhoods," The Project on Human Development in Human Neighborhoods, www.hms.harvard.edu/chase/projects/chicago/news/annual/MA41_Neighbor_Matte rs.pdf (accessed December 6, 2005).

2. Catherine Cubbin, John Santelli, Claire D. Brindis, and Paula Braveman, "Neighborhood Context and Sexual Behaviors Among Adolescents: Findings from the National Longitudinal Study of Adolescent Health," *Perspectives on Sexual and Reproductive Health* 37, no. 3 (September 2005): 125–34.

3. Sexuality Education and Information Council of the United States National Guidelines Task Force, *Guidelines for Comprehensive Sexuality Education: Kindergarten Through 12th Grade*, 3rd ed. (New York: Fulton Press, 2004).

4. For instances of this interconnectedness, see Ruth Dixon-Mueller, "The Sexuality Connection in Reproductive Health," *Studies in Family Planning* 24, no. 5 (September/October 1993): 269–82; see also the analysis of the relationship of psychosocial factors influencing the age of first sexual intercourse for adolescent girls in Susan L. Rosenthal et al., "Sexual Initiation: Predictors and Developmental Trends," *Sexually Transmitted Disease* 28, no. 9 (September 2001): 527–32; and Jennifer Feldmann and Amy B. Middleman, "Adolescent Sexuality and Sexual Behavior," *Current Opinions in Obstetrics and Gynecology* 14 (2002): 489–93. The latter explicitly mention the SIECUS guidelines as a framework.

5. Dixon-Mueller, "The Sexuality Connection in Reproductive Health," 269–82.

6. Susheela Singh et al. *Adding It Up: The Benefits of Investigating Sexual and Reproductive Health Care* (New York: Alan Guttmacher Institute, 2003), 5, www.guttmacher.org/pubs/addingitup.pdf (accessed December 5, 2005).

7. Christina Bethell, Jonathan Klein, and Colleen Peck, "Assessing Health System Provision of Adolescent Preventative Services: The Young Adult Health Care Survey," *Medical Care* 39, no. 5 (2001): 478–90.

8. Michael I. Cohen, quoted in Morris Green and Judith S. Palfrey, eds., *Bright Futures: Guidelines for Health Supervision of Infants, Children, and Adolescents*, 2nd ed. (Arlington, VA: National Center for Maternal and Child Health, 2000, 231).

9. "Risk," *Medline Plus/Merriam-Webster Medical Dictionary*, www2.merriam-webster.com/cgi-bin/mwmednlm (accessed November 8, 2005).

10. Claire Brindis, "Advancing the Adolescent Reproductive Health Policy Agenda: Issues for the Coming Decade," *Journal of Adolescent Health* 31 (2002): 299.

11. Sexual Behaviors, "Healthy Youth! National Center for Chronic Disease Prevention and Health Promotion, Centers for Disease Control," www.cdc.gov/HealthyYouth/sexualbehaviors/ (accessed September 5, 2005).

12. K. A. Moore and J. F. Zaff, "Building a Better Teenager: A Summary of

'What Works' in Adolescent Development" (Washington, DC: ChildTrends, 2002), www.childtrends.org/Files/K7Brief.pdf (accessed September 7, 2005).

13. "Appendix L: Sexually Transmitted Disease Prevention and Screening," in Green and Palfrey, *Bright Futures*, 319. Also "Population Reports: Meeting the Needs of Young Adults" *Family Planning Programs*, Series J, no. 41 (October 1995): 1.

14. See, for example, Healthy People 2010, which includes Responsible Sexual Behavior among the Leading Health Indicators (LHI) for public health goals, www.healthypeople.gov/LHI/lhiwhat.htm (accessed November 13, 2005).

15. Paula Duncan, Rebecca R. Dixon, and Jennifer Carlson, "Childhood and Adolescent Sexuality," *The Pediatric Clinics of North America* 50 (2003): 765.

16. Gail Hornor, "Sexual Behavior in Children: Normal or Not?" *Journal of Pediatric Health Care* 18, no. 2 (March/April 2004): 57–64.

17. Patrick Jones, *Connecting Young Adults and Libraries: A How-To-Do-It Manual* (New York: Neal-Schuman Publishers, Inc., 1998).

18. "Adolescence," in Green and Palfrey, *Bright Futures*, 231.

19. W. B. Lukenbill, "Research in Young Adult Literature and Services," in *Libraries and Young Adults: Media, Services, and Librarianship*, ed. J. V. Rogers, 192–215 (Littleton, CO: Libraries Unlimited).

20. Patricia J. Campbell, *Sex Guides: Books and Films About Sexuality for Young Adults* (New York: Garland Publishing, 1986).

21. Melissa Gross, "Library Service to Pregnant Teens: How Can We Help?" *School Library Journal* 43, no. 6 (June 1997): 36–37.

22. Bernard Morrissey, "SexAndHealthForTeens.com," *e-VOYA*, 28, no. 5 (December 2005): web1–web4; Barbara D. Clapp and Barbara N. Lindsley, "The Health Information Project: Involving Teens in Lifestyle Issues in the Library," *VOYA* 28, no. 5 (December 2005): 374–75.

23. Ross J. Todd and Susan Edwards, "Adolescents' Information Seeking and Utilization in Relation to Drugs," in *Youth Information-Seeking Behavior: Theories, Models, and Issues*, ed. Mary K. Chelton and Colleen Cool, 535–86 (Lanham, MD: Scarecrow Press, 2004); Judah S. Hamer, "Coming-Out: Gay Males' Information Seeking," *School Libraries Worldwide* 9, no. 2 (July 2003): 73–89. See also, Ann Curry, "If I Ask, Will They Answer? Evaluating Public Library Reference Service to Gay and Lesbian Youth," *Reference & User Services Quarterly* 45, no.1 (Fall 2005): 65–75.

24. Virginia A. Walter, "The Information Needs of Children," *Advances in Librarianship* 18 (1999): 120–21.

25. Jennifer Burek Pierce, "Picking the Flowers in the Fair Garden: The Circulation, Non-Circulation, and Disappearance of Young Adult Nonfiction Materials," *School Libraries Worldwide* 9, no. 2 (July 2003): 62–72.

26. Donald O. Case, *Looking for Information: A Survey of Research on Information Seeking, Needs, and Behavior* (San Diego, CA: Academic Press, 2002), 270–72.

27. Kaiser Family Foundation, "Generation Rx.com: How Young People Use the Internet for Health Information," 2001, www.kff.org/entmedia/loader.cfm?url = / commonspot/security/getfile.cfm&PageID = 13719 (accessed September 3, 2005); Azy Barak and William Fisher, "Toward an Internet-Driven Theoretically-Based, Innovative Approach to Sex Education," *Journal of Sex Research* 38, no. 4 (November 2001): 324–32.

28. Andrew Large, "Children, Teenagers, and the Web," *Annual Review of Information Science and Technology* 39 (2005): 347–92.

29. Kristine M. Alpi, "State Health Department Web Sites: Rich Resources for Consumer Health Information," *Journal of Consumer Health Information on the Internet* 9, no. 1 (2005): 36.

30. Eliza T. Dresang, "More Research Needed: Informal Information Seeking Behavior of youth on the Internet," *JASIS* 50, no. 12 (October 1999): 1123–24.

31. As noted by Advocates for Youth (AFY), "In 1996, Congress signed into law the Personal Responsibility and Work Opportunities Reconciliation Act, or 'welfare reform.' Attached was the provision, later set out in Section 510(b) of Title V of the Social Security Act, appropriating $250 million dollars over five years for state initiatives promoting sexual abstinence outside of marriage as the only acceptable standard of behavior for young people." See Debra Hauser, "Introduction," in *Five Years of Abstinence-only-Until-Marriage Education: Assessing the Impact* (Washington, DC: Advocates for Youth, 2004). With education funding tied to an abstinence-based sex education programs, states have adopted education programs that neither mandate nor encourage fuller knowledge of reproductive health. The identifiable consequences of this, including knowledge deficits, are expanded upon in the AFY report. Compelling evidence of the lack of programmatic sex education is further provided by Brindis who observes that "As of July 2000, only 18 states and the District of Columbia require that schools provide any sexuality education at all" (p. 298). Elsewhere, as in the "Population Reports," it has been observed that young people confront sexual health with "too little factual information" and numerous barriers to obtaining it (p. 1).

32. Mary K. Chelton, "Future Direction and Bibliography," in *Youth Information-Seeking Behavior: Theories, Models, and Issues*, ed. Mary K. Chelton and Colleen Cool, 390 (Lanham, MD: Scarecrow Press, 2004).

33. Brindis, "Advancing the Adolescent Reproductive Health Policy Agenda," 297.

34. Cheryl R. Merzel et al., "Attitudinal and Contextual Factors Associated with Discussion of Sexual Issues During Adolescent Health Visits," *Journal of Adolescent Health* 35, no. 2 (August 2004): 108–15.

35. "Population Reports," 3.

36. Laura Sessions Stepp, "The Buddy System/Sex in High School and College: What's Love Got to Do with It?" *Washington Post,* 19 January 2003, F1.

37. Sharon Jayson, " 'Technical Virginity' Becomes Part of Teens' Equation,"

USA Today, 19 October 2005, www.usatoday.com/news/health/2005-10-19-teens-technical-virginity_x.htm (accessed December 1, 2005).

38. The National Campaign to Prevent Teen Pregnancy, "Teens and Oral Sex," *Putting What Works to Work: Science Says* 17 (September 2005): 5, www.teen pregnancy.org/works/pdf/ScienceSays_17_OralSex.pdf (accessed December 6, 2005).

39. Kristin Haglund, "Sexually Abstinent African American Adolescent Females' Descriptions of Abstinence," *Journal of Nursing Scholarship* 35, no. 3 (September 2003): 231–36.

40. Bonnie L. Halpern-Felsher et al., "Oral Versus Vaginal Sex Among Adolescents: Perceptions, Attitudes, and Behavior," *Pediatrics* 115, no. 4 (April 2005): 845–51.

41. The National Campaign to Prevent Teen Pregnancy, "Teens and Oral Sex," 5.

42. Teresa Metcalfe, "Sexual Health: Meeting Adolescents' Needs," *Nursing Standard* 18, no. 46 (2004): 40–43.

43. Alan Guttmacher Institute, "Teenage Sexual and Reproductive Behavior in Developed Countries: Can More Progress Be Made?" 2001, www.guttmacher.org/pubs/summeries/euroteens_summ.pdf (accessed December 1, 2005).

44. I. T. Zwane, P. T. Mngadi, and M. P. Nxumalo, "Adolescents' Views on Decision-Making Regarding Risky Sexual Behavior," *International Nursing Review* 51, no. 1 (March 2004): 15–22.

45. Research by neuropsychologist Jay Giedd and others offers a window into the issues involved in adolescent reasoning and decision making, revealing, among other findings, that the part of the brain governing rational thought is still developing in adolescence. An accessible overview of this work is available; see Sarah Spinks, "Adolescent Brains Are Works in Progress," *Frontline: Inside the Teenage Brain,* http://www.pbs.org/wgbh/pages/frontline/shows/teenbrain/work/adolescent .html (accessed December 6, 2005).

46. Liana R. Clark, "Will the Pill Make Me Sterile? Addressing Reproductive Health Concerns and Strategies to Improve Adherence to Hormonal Contraceptive Regimens in Adolescent Girls," *Journal of Pediatric and Adolescent Gynecology* 14 (2001): 153–62.

47. Brindis, "Advancing the Adolescent Health Policy Agenda," 298–99.

48. Sarah N. Keller and Jane D. Brown, "Media Interventions to Promote Responsible Sexual Behavior," *Journal of Sex Research* 39, no. 1 (February 2002): 67–74.

49. Laura Kann et al., "Youth Risk Behavior Surveillance—United States, 1997," *Journal of School Health* 68, no. 9 (November 1998): 355–70.

50. Jo Anne Grunbaum et al., "Youth Risk Behavior Surveillance—United States, 2003," *Morbidity and Mortality Weekly Report* 53, no. 1 (May 2004): 1–96.

51. Noting that too little data exists to draw firm conclusions, Elster et al. tentatively conclude that minority adolescents may be better served in the area of repro-

ductive health than their white peers; this is an exception to the general pattern of health care disparities according to race and socioeconomic status. Arthur Elster et al., "Racial and Ethnic Disparities in Health Care for Adolescents: A Systematic Review of the Literature," *Archives of Pediatric and Adolescent Medicine* 157 (September 2003): 867–74.

52. Shiprah A. Williams-Evans and Joy Sher'ron Myers, "Adolescent Dating Violence," *Association of Black Nursing Faculty Journal* 15, no. 2 (March 2004): 35–37.

53. "Population Reports," 17; Lori Kowaleski-Jones and Frank L. Mott, "Sex, Contraception and Childbearing Among High-Risk Youth: Do Different Factors Influence Males and Females?" *Family Planning Perspectives* 30, no. 4 (July/ August 1998): 163–69; Claire Brindis et al., "A Profile of the Male Family Planning Client," *Family Planning Perspectives* 30, no. 2 (March/April 1998): 63–67; Brindis, "Advancing the Adolescent Reproductive Health Policy Agenda," 303–4; Linda Juszczak and Kathleen Cooper, "Improving the Health and Well-Being of Adolescent Boys," *The Nursing Clinics of North America* 37 (2002): 433–42.

54. Marjolein Verhoef, "Sex Education, Relationships, and Sexuality in Young Adults with Spina Bifida," *Archives of Physical Medicine and Rehabilitation* 86 (May 2005): 979–87.

55. Brindis, "Advancing the Adolescent Reproductive Health Policy Agenda," 298.

56. Donald E. Greydanus, Mary Ellen Rimza, and Patricia E. Newhouse, "Adolescent Sexuality and Disability," *Adolescent Medicine: State of the Art Reviews* 13, no. 2 (June 2002): 223–45.

57. Katy Yanda, "Teenagers Educating Teenagers About Reproductive Health and Their Rights to Confidential Care," *Family Planning Perspectives* 32, no. 5 (October 2000): 256–57; Rachel K. Jones and Heather Boonstra, "Confidential Reproductive Health Services for Minors: The Potential Impact of Mandated Parental Involvement for Contraception," *Perspectives on Sexual and Reproductive Health* 36, no. 5 (2004): 182–91.

58. "Population Reports," 17.

59. Barbara A. Elliott and Jean T. Larsen, "Adolescents in Mid-Sized and Rural Communities: Forgone Care, Perceived Barriers, and Risk Factors," *Journal of Adolescent Health* 35, no. 4 (October 2004): 303–9.

60. Barbara L. Frankowski and the Committee on Adolescence, "Sexual Orientation and Adolescents," *Pediatrics* 113, no. 6 (June 2004): 1827–32.

61. "Population Reports," 1.

62. Andrew K. Shenton and Pat Dixon, "Issues Arising from Youngsters' Information-Seeking Behavior," *Library & Information Science Research* 26, no. 2 (Spring 2004): 177–200.

63. Derek L. Hansen et al., "Adolescents Searching for Health Information on the Internet: An Observational Study," *Journal of Medical Information on the*

Internet 5, no. 4 (October 2003), http://www.jmir.org/2003/4/e25/ (accessed September 6, 2005).

64. Literature oriented to practitioners includes press releases, websites, and other articles. For examples, see Amy Stone, "ACLU Reports on Use of Filters in R.I. Libraries," *American Libraries* 36, no. 6 (June/July 2005): 18; Walter Minkel, "Filters Block Needed Health Facts," *School Library Journal* 49, no. 1 (January 2003): 18; Pamela A. Goodes, "Kaiser Study: Filters Impede Health Research," *American Libraries* 34, no. 1 (January 2003): 20; ALA links to numerous studies that demonstrate the impact of filtering upon younger audiences, including "New Study Confirms Internet Filters Fail to Block Much Pornography, Deny Important Health Information to the Public," http://www.ala.org/Template.cfm?Section = issuesrelated links&Template = /ContentManagement/ContentDisplay.cfm&ContentID = 78096 (accessed December 5, 2005); Electronic Privacy Information Center, "Faulty Filters: How Content Filters Block Access to Kid-Friendly Information on the Internet," December 1997, www2.epic.org/reports/filter-report.html (accessed November 22, 2005). The report does not assess the information provided via sites not impacted by filtering software but provides statistics on the relative percentages of hits returned by Alta Vista and Net Shepherd Family Search. It concludes that upwards of 95 percent of content "that might be of interest to young people" (Summary, para. 1) including terms like *puberty* and *teen pregnancy* (Table of Results: Miscellaneous Concepts or Entities) were blocked. The ALA listing of filtering-related reports, titled ALA, CIPA and Libraries is available at http://www.ala.org/ ala/washoff/WOissues/civilliberties/cipaweb/newsarticles/articles.htm (accessed November 22, 2005).

65. Note the difference in the language of the ALA press release on the Kaiser study versus that in the executive summary of the study, which states that "Internet filters most frequently used by schools and libraries can effectively block pornography *without significantly impeding access to online health information*—but only if they aren't set at their most restrictive levels." "See No Evil: How Internet Filters Affect the Search for Online Health Information," www.kff.org/entmedia/3294-index.cfm (accessed November 22, 2005), (emphasis added).

66. Caroline R. Richardson et al. "Does Pornography-Blocking Software Block Access to Health Information on the Internet?" *JAMA* 288, no. 22 (December 2002): 2887–94.

67. Coverage of a court case on the legality of the Children's Internet Protection Act, *American Library Association and American Civil Liberties Union, Plaintiffs v. United States of America, Defendants*, encapsulates the divergence of opinion within the LIS community in this regard; the reporting, however, focuses on access to pornography over other controversial material like sexual and reproductive health information. Iver Peterson, "Access to Pornography on the Net Is at Center of Library Fight," *New York Times*, March 29, 2002.

68. For a discussion of the evolving legal context regarding adolescent health,

see Abigail English, "Reproductive Health Services for Adolescents: Critical Legal Issues," *Obstetrics and Gynecology Clinics* 27, no. 1 (March 2000): 196–211.

69. Dina L. G. Borzekowski and Vaughn I. Rickert, "Adolescent Cybersurfing for Health Information: A New Resource That Crosses Barriers," *Archives of Pediatric and Adolescent Medicine* 155, no. 7 (July 2001): 813–17.

70. Harvey Skinner et al., "How Adolescents Use Technology for Health Information: Implications for Health Professionals from Focus Group Studies," *Journal of Medical Internet Research* 5, no. 4 (October 2003), http://www.jmir.org/2003/4/e32/ (accessed August 31, 2005).

71. Amy Bleakley et al., "Computer Access and Internet Use Among Urban Youths," *American Journal of Public Health* 94, no. 5 (May 2004): 744–46.

72. John Carlo Bertot, Charles R. McClure, and Paul T. Jaeger, "Public Libraries Struggle to Meet Internet Demand," *American Libraries* 36, no. 7 (August 2005): 78–79.

73. Diann M. Ackard and Dianne Neumark-Sztainer, "Health Care Information Sources for Adolescents: Age and Gender Differences on Use, Concerns, and Needs," *Journal of Adolescent Health* 29, no. 3 (September 2001): 170–76.

74. Pierre-André Michaud and P. Colom, "Implementation and Evaluation of an Internet Site for Adolescents in Switzerland," *Journal of Adolescent Health* 33, no. 4 (October 2003): 287–290.

75. Meghan Smith, "The Content and Accessibility of Sex Education Information on the Internet," *Health Information and Behavior* 27, no. 6 (December 2000): 684–94.

76. American Social Health Association, www.iwannaknow.org (accessed November 22, 2005).

77. Lisa K. Gilbert, Julie Rae E. Temby, and Sarah E. Rogers. "Evaluating a Teen STD Prevention Web Site," *Journal of Adolescent Health* 37, no. 3 (September 2005): 236–242.

78. Kathryn Montgomery, "Youth and Digital Media: A Policy Research Agenda," *Journal of Adolescent Health* 27, no. 2, suppl. 1 (August 2000): 61–68.

79. Laina Bay-Cheng, "SexEd.com: Values and Norms in Web-Based Sexuality Education," *Journal of Sex Research* 38, no. 3 (August 2001): 241–51.

80. "Adolescence," in Green and Palfrey, *Bright Futures*, 243.

81. Herbert L. Friedman, "Reproductive Health in Adolescence," *World Health Statistics Quarterly* 47 (1994), 31–35.

82. Feldmann and Middleman, "Adolescent Sexuality and Sexual Behavior," 492.

83. Heather Boonstra, "The 'Add Health' Survey: Origins, Purposes, and Design," *The Guttmacher Report on Public Policy* 4, no. 3 (June 2001) www.guttmacher.org/pubs/tgr/04/3/gr040310.html (accessed November 24, 2005).

84. "Healthy Youth! Data and Statistics." YRBSS: Youth Risk Behavior Surveillance System. National Center for Chronic Disease Prevention and Health Pro-

motion. Centers for Disease Control. www.cdc.gov/HealthyYouth/yrbs/index.htm (accessed November 24, 2005).

85. Ross J. Todd and Susan Edwards, "Adolescent Information Seeking in Relation to Drugs," in *Youth Information-Seeking Behavior: Theories, Models, and Issues*, ed. Mary K. Chelton and Colleen Cool, 354–55 (Lanham, MD: Scarecrow Press, 2004).

86. Tarayn Grizzard et al., "Innovations in Adolescent Reproductive and Sexual Health Education in Santiago de Chile: Effects of Physician Leadership and Direct Service," *Journal of the American Medical Women's Association* 59, no. 3 (2004): 207–9.

87. Jennifer Burek Pierce, "'Newly Invited . . . Into Government': Origins of Federal Government Information on Maternal and Child Health," *Journal of Government Information* 30 (2004): 648–657.

88. American Academy of Pediatrics, Jonathan D. Klein, and the Committee on Adolescence, "Adolescent Pregnancy: Current Trends and Issues," *Pediatrics* 116, no. 1 (July 2005): 281–86.

89. Nicola J. Gray, Jonathan D. Klein, Peter R. Noyce, Tracy S. Sesselberg, and Judith A. Cantrill, "The Internet: A Window on Adolescent Health Literacy," *Journal of Adolescent Health* 37, no. 3 (September 2005): 243.e1–243.e7.

4

Process of Information Seeking during "Queer" Youth Coming-Out Experiences

Bharat Mehra and Donna Braquet

The *Time* cover story in the October 2005 issue entitled "The Battle Over Gay Teens" discusses contemporary changes in the front lines of America's culture war since the 1990s that reflect a surge of openly gay youth who are coming out in hundreds of thousands and "disclosing their homosexuality with unprecedented regularity."[1] Coming out for homosexual people, according to recent research, defines the process as a lifelong journey for "queer" individuals as "simply about being true to yourself" in "identifying as gay, lesbian, bisexual, or transgender" and disclosing this to other people.[2] What is quite astonishing is that according to *The New Gay Teenager*, a recent publication from the Harvard University Press, contemporary youngsters are coming out at a much younger age[3]—the book cites a Pennsylvania State study of 350 youth from various local gay social networks that found the mean age at which lesbians first have sexual contact with other girls is sixteen; its just fourteen for gay boys.[4] Such changes in coming-out dynamics reported of homosexual youth today are partly a result of recent and closer attention to a range of associated behaviors that include: first sex experiences,[5] same-sex attractions,[6] and homosexual identity formation,[7] among others, which were not traditionally studied in prior research on young people's sexuality.[8] Other reasons for study of new domains in youth sexuality and increasing numbers of younger "queer" youth are attributed to changing mores and acceptance in the social and cultural climate,[9] greater media attention and awareness of homosexual issues,[10] and more visible "queer" role models,[11] to name a few.

This chapter recognizes and acknowledges the reading of a gay-themed cover story in a popular magazine today and the current scholarly attention to youth sexuality, as a progressive sign of changing times. However, it also raises a cautionary voice against the tendency to make sweeping statements and generalizations that reflect all-encompassing trends in youth sexuality conditions, both in terms of psychological development and prevailing social and cultural environments. For the wave of optimism and perceived acceptance for "queer" youth seems quite misplaced, when one turns attention to the nation-wide tangible and intangible policies of bigotry and discrimination set in motion against "queers" by actions supported by legislature, fundamental religious groups, local businesses and multinational corporations, faith-based community organizations, media and newspapers, and specific individuals.[12] We also see the affects of homophobia and prejudice in K–12 school and college campuses that give expression to a range of hateful activities from ridiculing graffiti targeted against gay youth scribbled on library carrels and toilet walls to the purposeful exclusion of "queer" issues in classroom lectures.[13] A recent Climate Survey in 2003 by the National Gay and Lesbian Task Force (NGLTF) reported that 43 percent rated overall campus climate as homophobic; 20 percent feared for their physical safety; 51 percent concealed their sexual orientation or gender identity to avoid intimidation, and 41 percent felt that their college/university was not addressing issues related to sexual orientation and gender identity.[14]

What is important to note is that research findings documenting progressive social climates for "queer" youth are based on select sample participants in academic environments located in cosmopolitan and urban places in Maryland, Vermont, New York, and California, which does not necessarily mean that they are representative of the social and cultural climate in all parts of the country.[15] Additionally, what is missing in current debates about youth sexuality and homosexual coming-out experiences is that there is no consolidated picture of the kinds of information sources that young people use during different times. Nor is there an adequate understanding of their information-seeking behaviors that may provide tangible directions for improvements in existing information support services. A lack of a systematic and comprehensive picture of the information seeking of "queer" youth thus leads to a reliance on anecdotal and fragmentary evidence. Also, recent research addresses the coming-out process of adults and youth broadly in terms of its general stages and characteristics.[16] What is missing in such studies is a detailed mapping of the information usage and information-seeking patterns of "queer" youth during different times.[17] Based on narratives of coming-out experiences in a representative Southern state located in the heart of the "Bible belt," this chapter fills these gaps in its presentation of a holistic model for understanding "queer" youth experiences and its identification of concrete directions for improvements in effective information support service development for youth during their coming-out process. The model records and draws connections between the following three domains of knowledge related to coming-out experiences during different times: types of information sources and their role in coming out, information-seeking process based on individual attributes, and ideal information support services needed.

By drawing connections between these three constructs that have been researched in an isolated manner in past work, this model helps better understand the information seeking of "queer" youth in terms of existing information sources, usage and determinants, characteristics, and potential application toward supportive initiatives that libraries and information professionals can take to provide more appropriate information support services for the marginalized "queer" youth of today. Mapping the information-seeking behaviors during coming-out experiences in terms of the feelings (affective), thoughts (cognitive), and actions (physical) during various times, leads to more culturally appropriate and concrete efforts that make idealized information support services a tangible reality. The assumption is that the classic trinity of feelings, thoughts, and actions provide a holistic understanding of information-seeking behavior and are interrelated in any sense-making and coping mechanism for an individual.[18] An extended role of libraries and information professionals is discussed toward making more socially proactive efforts in partnering with other social agencies and reaching out into the community, while, at the same time, proposing improvements in design of their traditional information support systems, services, collections, and institutional policies in order to create greater support to youth in their coming-out process.

"QUEER" CONSTRUCTIONS
AND COMING OUT

Contemporary scholars studying sexuality document homosexual youth behavior and practices that challenge cultural understandings that continually limit within traditional heterosexual/homosexual binary in the service of "queer youth"; these call for a wider recognition of how "queer" youth are "increasingly redefining and renegotiating their sexuality in ways that make the use of words such as "gay," "lesbian," or "bisexual," identity-meanings associated with the words, quite meaningless. Such work raises awareness of the limitations in the use of stereotyping labels, constructs, and behaviors in human sexuality, especially in the context of ambiguities and degrees of variation observed in definitions related to sexuality for today's young people in terms of orientation, behavior, and identity. As an acknowledgement of these disparate and varied representations of gay youth sexuality, the authors use the word "queer" to include diverse expressions and manifestations that are not heterosexual and include gay, lesbian, bisexual, transgender, and questioning youth. We recognize "queer" to be most inclusive to represent sexual minorities since it covers all individuals who do not identify with or are not recognized as part of a heterosexual majority. Following the work of Foucault, [19] this chapter follows the contemporary use of the abusive word "queer" by advocate groups as a mark or ownership, empowerment, and appropriation that ironically self-consciously historicizes and marks the repressive character of social discourses surrounding sexuality.[20] Quotation marks are used with the word "queer" in this chapter to recognize the history of abuse, ridicule, discrimination, and violence projected against "queer" people and calls for a need to reexamine the past and turn the table around via building a more progressive and accepting cultural environment.

Adolescence is a time in which individuals explore and integrate their sexual identity into their personal identity[21] and the role in identity formation of "queer" youth is greatly impacted by the process of coming out.[22] Researchers now recognize that coming out is not an "all or nothing" occurrence, but rather a continual process.[23] That being said, a chief concern of "queer" individuals is the constant negotiation of self-identification as "queer," as well as obtaining the strategies and resilience to manage social and family situations that arise as a result of disclosure.[24] One such strategy may be that "queer" youth lead "double lives"[25] until appropriate resources, networks, and support can be secured. Lasser and Tharinger[26] propose the term "visibility management," which refers to the continual decision making process that "queer" youth use to determine whether to disclose, to whom, and how to disclose their sexual orientation, making the distinction between "coming out," which they call an "event," and visibility management, which "better captures the complexity of the strategic and continuous process." Though "queer" youth, with each decision to make their identity known, run the risk of rejection and alienation by family, friends, classmates, and teachers; verbal and emotional abuse; and physical violence,[27] the benefits can outweigh the costs by bringing about "catharsis,"[28] an enhanced sense of self-acceptance and self-esteem, and a decrease in overall stress.[29]

Five main phases of the coming-out process were detailed by Cass, and by George and Behrendt,[30] these include the following: self-recognition of being different; sharing with other "queer" people in order to become part of a "queer" social network and community; telling close friends, relatives, and coworkers; development of a positive self-identification; integration into all parts of one's life and acceptance of being "queer." In later years Cass[31] focuses on one's internal awareness, rather than disclosure to others in six phases of coming out, which include: identity confusion, identity comparison, identity tolerance, identity acceptance, identity pride, and identity synthesis. Researchers have argued over what the authors consider minor points of contention, such as whether disclosure to the "other" implies other heterosexual or "queer" people[32] and whether self-identification is a stage within or distinct from coming out.[33] These overarching theories provide a sound base in understanding the coming-out process, but fail to acknowledge the complexities and uniqueness of the process as it pertains to individuals; nor do these researchers recognize that their linguistic and symbolic descriptions are mere constructions of communication and definition that reality of multiplicity in experiences transcend. For the purpose of this research, the aforementioned "controversy" is insignificant.

Coming out is considered a process, "a journey, not a destination," and three significant issues related to coming out are:[34] (1) Although coming out is a beneficial experience for most "queer" youth, confusion about identity during the process can affect an individual's self-esteem, school work, and social relationships (both negatively and positively). In fact, health professionals compare the coming-out process to the stages in grieving in terms of: denial, anger, bargaining, depression, and acceptance.[35] Further, Temes [36] identifies the stages of grief in terms of numbness, disorganization, and reorganization, and varied degrees of these are expressed during different "queer" youth's coming-out process based on individual experiences, sociocultural expectations, and perceived hostility or acceptance; (2) While deciding who to tell about their sexuality, young "queer" people have well-founded fears of negative reactions and rejection or causing distress to the person they are telling; (3) A nonjudgmental and supportive environment, guarantees of safety, availability of secure and confidential contacts to reduce anxiety and overcome isolation, presence of role models, and positive treatment to feel confident about their future are some positive directions of support for youth during coming out. In 1982, Coleman stated that American society's homophobic nature causes people with same-sex attractions to develop negative conceptions of themselves,[37] and sadly this statement rings true over twenty years later. Society's lack of progress over the years makes it imperative that positive and accurate information is available to youth, especially considering the difference could mean life or death for a "queer" youth who may be driven to taking his or her life.

The implications of a homophobic society on "queer" youth are truly devastating. Recent research reveals the following frightening and striking findings: (1) Sexual minority youth are among the most likely to report suicidality (suicidal thoughts, plans, and attempts);[38] (2) during the past decade, there has been marked shifts in "queer" male initial suicide attempts that occurred at a younger age for those who reached the age of twenty-five years after 1990, even though prevalence of attempted suicide had remained constant across birth cohorts;[39] and (3) What leads these youth to a suicidal path is not their sexuality but the stigma and discrimination that they encounter in a heterosexual world.[40]

The connection between these suicidal trends and information seeking is reflected in findings elicited through interviews with thousands of young "queer" individuals who indicate that accurate and supportive information would have made their experiences related to sexual identity and orientation easier and less painful, not only at a personal level, but also at the level of social acceptance.[41] Thus, the need for adequate information support services for "queer" youth[42] is more important than ever, especially considering the common public perception that a recognizable increase in political and religious intolerance has occurred in recent years for sexual minorities and is exemplified by President George W. Bush's reelection to the White House for a second consecutive term in which gay people were used as a wedge issue.[43]

LITERATURE REVIEW

This section synthesizes what is known through existing research about "queer" information seeking, and what is known through existing research about the provision of information sources and services to this group. Current research in both areas shows wide gaps between the information-seeking preferences of youth and the library and information resources designed specifically for them.[44] Deficiencies that exist for youth in general greatly impact the lives of "queer" youth as well, though often in worse ways.[45] For example, young people's lack of access to relevant information has a rather a more poignant significance in the light of contemporary studies that identify greater risks and higher rates of suicide among "queer" young Americans today.[46] A minimal involvement of youth in a study of their information-seeking behaviors[47] plays itself out in the context of research on information provision to young "queer" people that derives from identity politics of "queer" communities, without understanding "queer" information behavior.[48] Additionally, a focus of existing research on youth information seeking in digital environments, at the cost of ignoring connections to real-life social experiences [49] results in poor and inadequate information support services during life-threatening situations during "queer" youth coming-out experiences.[50]

In order to better understand information seeking during youth coming-out experiences, a discussion of characteristics and factors that shape their information-seeking motivations and needs during these self-struggling and socially unaccepting times is important. The following is a brief summary of key aspects in coming out that strongly determine the nature of information seeking in these experiences.

The Role of Heterosexist Social and Cultural Environment

To provide any understanding of information seeking of "queer" youth, it is important to acknowledge the symbolic and directive role of the external social and cultural environment in response to which "queer" youth come out of the proverbial closet and reveal to friends, family, and strangers, the true nature of their attraction to people of the same sex.[51] Just as some members of society face societal oppression and its stifling impact on their identity development based on ethno-racial classifications, similarly, in order to address the needs of "queer" youth it becomes significant to understand how the group "views the world as a function of its experiences with social injustice and the influence of cultural orientation."[52] Prevailing heterosexual social and cultural assumptions and norms, reinstated via family, schooling practices, media, and the surrounding environment create internal fear, stress, and anxiety in the "queer" self.[53] Social acknowledgement of "queer" disclosure is made extremely difficult especially in American schools and colleges, where heterosexual socialization practices, roles, and goals are ingrained in students to mold behavior;[54] heterosexual adult role models and assertions via formal and informal curriculum render "queer" existence as "invisible" in American history and culture;[55] negative portrayals and stereotyping images of "queer" people marginalize and accentuate stigma;[56] ignoring or turning a blind eye to "queer" verbal harassment and physical abuse of homosexuals further perpetuates such behavior;[57] and "queer" people are made the focus of hatred, fear, or a central theme in campus humor.[58]

Such socially sanctioned and culturally acceptable practices of heterosexism, homophobia, and "homohatred"[59] and the historical and contemporary social, political, legal, and cultural reality, at the national, state, and local levels, of intolerance have had a strong influence upon "queer" youth information seeking[60] during the coming-out process. For example, the larger social, cultural, and political environment shapes the nature and lack of information support services that "queer" youth encounter in their coming-out experiences[61] since existing resources are geared toward providing service based on heterosexual assumptions and biases.[62] Additionally, "queer" youth are hesitant and self-consciously aware of "feeling different"[63] and alienated,[64] which shapes their information-seeking abilities during the coming out process due to the lack of supportive environment and lack of access to "identity-affirming resources."[65]

Nonsequential Continuous Phases of Coming Out (Instead of Stages)

The coming-out process is not a set of discrete stages that is progressed through sequentially, but rather a process that differs from person to person depending on many factors including: (1) age at which "feeling different" or same-sex attraction occurred;[66] (2) rejection, fear of physical violence, verbal or emotional abuse, and being kicked out of the home;[67] (3) being a member of a group that is particularly homophobic, whether it be racial, ethnic, religious, or occupational;[68] (4) extent of positive social and family support.[69] This has an impact upon information seeking that also becomes a process that is based on an intersection of various variables during coming-out experiences.[70] Library and information services will be more effective in their support to "queer" youth if they recognize this reality and create flexibility and variation in choices to negotiate the impact of these factors on information seeking during coming out experiences.[71]

"Queer" individuals are a "hidden minority." Unlike other minorities (racial, ethnic, persons with disabilities), sexual minorities have to reveal their minority status by disclosing themselves as being "queer."[72] American society assumes that everyone is heterosexual, unless refuted. Having to disclose one's sexual identity makes the coming-out process of "queer" youth (as perceived by them) a life-long process, in which each new situation requires a weighed decision on whether or not to "come out."[73] Depending on an individual's progress toward integration of being "queer" into their self-concept and identity, some believe that their process will change and evolve over time.[74] Staging models[75] have provided greatly needed information about a "generic" coming-out experience, though contemporary research calls for their recognition as "just models" and it is more likely that coming out is a combination of phases that can be reordered, reencountered, or absent altogether.[76] Moreover, a linear unidirectional "stage theory" should not attempt to explain the complexity of issues involved in entire human sexuality, and subsequently, information seeking over a lifetime of coming out needs information support services that are more varied and diverse in their forms, representations, kinds of providers, nature of content, and degrees of user involvement required.[77]

Intersection of Multiple Factors Shape Variation in Information-Seeking Behaviors

A related characteristic of the coming-out process for "queer" youth is the intersection of multiple factors associated with the individual, other people, and context that determines the information-seeking processes. Individual and social factors include: (1) thought-related factors such as cognitions (perceptions, coding, memory, judgments), personality types, and learning styles; (2) behavior-related factors include communication and language skills and social interaction abilities; and (3) demographic factors include natural (sex, age, sexual orientation), cultural (gender, sexual orientation, race, ethnicity, country of origin, family status, habitation status), and conditional factors. In addition, context-driven factors are related to growing-up experiences in specific urban, semiurban, rural, or other environments. Researchers have recorded personal narratives of coming-out experiences that expose the process not as "a uniform, ahistorical, stage-driven process," but as a socially and historically constructed process that cannot be used to represent same-sex attraction in all spatial, temporal, and cultural situations.[78] Information seeking too is a reflection of these complexities in "queer" youth coming-out experiences, and information support services will need to become individually responsive and outcome-driven to respond to these variations. For example, Alex Carballo-Diéguez[79] recognizes the role of religion and folk beliefs in shaping information seeking during coming-out experiences of Hispanic "queer" youth, who encounter much conservatism and an environment limited in terms of availability of modern information resources owing to it being steeped in traditional values, that act as barriers to an open gay lifestyle.

Importance of Both Broad Knowledge and Specific Information

Homosexual people have to experience a change in the meaning of the cognitive category "homosexual" before they begin to place themselves in that category. Dank stresses the role of knowledge in the process of information seeking during coming out by stating: "The change of self-identity in homosexual is intimately related to the access of knowledge and information concerning homosexuals and homosexuality."[80] On one hand, "queer" youth's need for acquisition of broad knowledge during coming out helps in the formation and concretization of their identity for "integration and meaning-making between different, often contradictory sets of knowledges."[81] This understanding rejects "dichotomous (or linear) notions of how power is exerted in society" and allows "for a complex analysis of how transgressive, often covert paths of resistance are formed by those excluded from mainstream privilege and authority."[82] The role of broad and holistic knowledge during such times supports ambiguity and contradictions that the word *information* does not represent. This chapter recognizes the concept of knowledge in information seeking that relates to a broader meaning of knowledge as reflected in its root verb "to know," where it gets defined as the meanings individuals, groups of people, society, and communities, consciously or unconsciously, become aware of in order to internalize, negotiate, and reject (or accept) socially constructed perceptions, values, and behaviors. "Information support services" is used in this chapter to represent these mechanisms and avenues and symbolize a broader sense of understanding and reality in the coming out process.

Having made that point, it is also important to mention that "queer" youth do have a need for specific, targeted information (that they seek), in addition to broad knowledge, during coming-out experiences. Unique disadvantages that "queer" youth face during the coming-out process are attributed to how, unlike racial minorities dealing with discrimination and intolerance, they cannot rely on parents for such information.[83] In addition, unlike other minorities, "queer" individuals may be the only minority whose own families consistently reject them.[84] In such situations, perceiving the existence of positive climates (and finding them) during information seeking[85] as well as locating specific information that indicates cultural appropriateness, visibility, and "queer" affirming stories[86] is important, for example, to facilitate disclosure during coming out to families and friends who feel shock, disappointment, shame, isolation, or grief[87] after their loved ones reveal their sexual orientations/gender identities to them. During such times, it is important not only for "queer" youth to gain broad knowledge and specific information for themselves; in addition, they must access accurate information sources about "queer" issues, to share with close family and friends, since the more these other people find out about such issues, the better the adjustment will be during coming out.[88]

"Queer" youth have been one group that has slipped through the gaps in the ability of traditional library and information support services to meet their needs and expectations.[89] Additionally, since these youth have few social and political advocates, and very few places that provide relevant information accessible to them, agencies such as libraries, universities, high schools, health clinics, and community organizations must play a more proactive role in providing positive outlets for them and doing aggressive advertising of their appropriate services. However, in recent years homophobia's resurgence can be tracked to the pervasiveness of "moral values" rhetoric that smothers all forms of expression except those of the so-called norm, thus shutting out any expression of alternative sexualities, and this has also resulted in the existence of very slowly emerging "queer" youth information support services in the present-day library and information-related context. Hence, over the years, both public and academic libraries have considered "queer" youth low on their priorities, and few advances have been made to address equal representation of their issues in services, collections, and policies.[90] "Queer" patrons consider libraries the last places to seek information, and the major barriers in library use include misinformation and prejudice, lack of availability of materials, censorship, and lack of bibliographic access (for patrons who do not wish to ask librarians for assistance).[91] Even during the past few years, there has not been much progress in effective library service to "queer" clientele: "Although many public and academic libraries are engaged in developing their collections, compiling pathfinders and guides, and offering other types of services, LBGTQ users are still vastly underserved and library collections vastly underdeveloped."[92]

This need for libraries to become more user-friendly to "queer" patrons by preparing, collecting, and maintaining collections of specific interest to them and the need to make people aware of these materials have been documented for over a decade.[93] However, what concrete efforts have been made by libraries since is quite debatable. Libraries' advocacy for "queer" support is not uniformly practiced all over in the country,[94] if at all in some locations. In fact, a recent library literature review recognizes homophobic librarians, fear of homophobic reactions from librarians, absence of appropriate materials, lack of display or promotion of such items, and lack of relevant subject headings as blocks to the provision of adequate information and services to the "queer" community.[95] Owing to limitations in space, it is beyond the scope of this chapter to examine in more detail the advances and limitations in information support services provided by libraries to address "queer" issues. It is sufficient to say that provision of adequate and appropriate information support services for "queer" youth is one area highly conspicuous by its absence in priorities of libraries.[96]

One thing that is missing in past work on "queer" youth information seeking about coming-out experiences and provision of library and information services during these times is the lack of application to needs in the coming-out process. The current research provides an approach to address the gap via a proposed model that connects existing types of information and their roles in coming-out experiences, information-seeking behaviors, and the ideal information support services desired to provide better support during the coming-out process at different times. Types of information and their roles reveal the underlying need; the information-seeking process is represented through a holistic approach that recognizes the importance of cognitive, affective, and physical dimensions; while idealized information support services present a direction that library and information professionals should be heading toward via design of library information support systems, services, collections, and institutional policies.

RESEARCH METHODS

Qualitative research methods used in this study included in-depth narrative interviews and informal discussions that provided detailed feedback about youth experiences of coming out with twenty-one "queer" participants self-identified as gay, lesbian, bisexual, transgender, or questioning from a representative Southern city in the United States. There were two lesbians, twelve gay men, six bisexuals (four women and two men) and one heterosexual transgender (female-to-male) individual who self-identified in terms of these categorizations. There was much variation in participant experiences based upon their identification and perceptions as gay, lesbian, bisexual, or transgender. The purpose in this research is not to minimize these differences, and owing to a lack of significant numbers to represent the different groups, future research will correlate these sexual identity-related labels with participant response patterns. Having stated that point, research findings also show an underlying shared sense of being "marginalized" as sexual minorities that was reflected in the youth experiences, and it established a common platform encompassing the various demarcating labels of difference.[97] It is important to recognize both differences and the shared sense of marginalization in the individual experiences; based on the understanding, this chapter calls for the provision of information support services in libraries during various coming-out phases that acknowledges variations and common points of intersections that go beyond broad generalizations.

The individual narrative interviews and informal discussions took place in private meeting rooms at the local academic library in order to maintain anonymity of the participants. Participation was elicited via personal contacts and through local "queer"-related agencies and organizations on the university campus and in the community such as The Lambda Student Union and local electronic mailing lists. Flyers were also posted at popular places such as libraries, student union, and local cafes and "queer" events organized by students. Methods of snowballing sampling proved significant in getting participants for later interviews, where initial interviewees recommended others from their social networks to participate in this study. Participants signed a consent form indicating their voluntary participation in the research and each participant was given a $20 gift certificate as a token of appreciation for his/ her efforts.

Narrative interviews with participants lasted from one to two and a half hours each, during which participants were asked questions on coming-out experiences; types of information sources sought and its role in coming out; information-seeking behaviors in terms of thoughts, feelings, and actions; and ideal information support services sought during different coming-out phases. A postinterview questionnaire provided demographic characteristics and contextual instrumentals about the case participants.

Grounded theory principles were used to analyze the extensive notes that were taken during narrative interviews and interview transcriptions to generate themes and patterns[98] that helped produce socially relevant understanding based on participants' narratives of occurring social phenomena.[99] Narrative interviews provided an apt hermeneutic method in this research since they were applied without any preconceived theoretical framework beyond trying to broadly understand the concerns of the participants during their coming-out process and explore possible library interventions in the process. During the narrative interviews, participants told "little stories" about their coming-out experiences that provided a rich source for developing scenarios. Scenarios were pieces of personal narratives, connected together, and used in data presentation and analysis to reflect participants' perspectives as well as identify idealized information support services (see examples of scenarios in the section on findings).

The process of coding interview data in this research involved socially grounded elements: seeking multiple perspectives as a part of the research inquiry; adopting triangulation strategies that verified specific information from multiple sources; following systematic and rigorous procedures for understanding social processes and phenomena that case participants spoke about; and employing techniques of induction, deduction, and verification to develop theory based on constant comparative analysis.[100] Coding practices incorporated grounded theory techniques of open coding that accounted for concepts (named activities, processes, events, moments of awareness) that emerged from the interview data; axial coding in relating categories and subcategories to each other, and selective coding that helped integrate them to the interview questions and to the broader coming-out experiences and perspectives of participants. The following scenario of one participant makes clear the process of coding procedures that were adopted and how such "stories of experience" shared by participants became tools for presenting and pulling together, piece by piece, various aspects related to the "queer" youth coming-out experiences.

First was curiosity [1a] and like I found myself wanting to go into the bathroom when my mom's boyfriend was in there [1b], just to see what men were like, this was when I was around eleven [q.5]. So, it started with curiosity [9.q4.1.p5]. . . . And then I went through a big denial phase [2a], almost all the way through high school [2b]. I got really involved in church [2c], really involved with my small group of friends, and really trying hard to find girls to date [2d] because I didn't want to admit, even to myself [2e], that I was gay [9.q.4.2.p6]. . . . Then toward the end of high school there was a questioning phase [3a]. It wasn't quite experimental yet, it was just opening up to the possibilities [3b]. Admitting to small groups of friends, small details [3c], like I wouldn't even say "I'm gay" or anything, I would just say, "What do you think about that guy? [q.7]. Maybe he's cute. I can like that even though I am straight" [3d]. I was still in denial [3e] [9.q.4.3.p7]. . . . Then there was the coming out phase [4a], and I guess mine was kind of twisted because I got a job at a doctor's office and the manager told me that he was a counselor for gay and lesbian teens and if I ever needed to talk to somebody, I'm here for you [4b]. Well, it was a lie. He would come back after everyone left and try to show me pornography on the Internet, really manipulating me. So, that pushed me back a long way as far as coming out [4c]. This is why I find a real strong need to focus on "queer" youth [4d], because if there is not a positive influence, there will be a negative influence [9.q4.4.p9].

Each scenario that is presented in this research is composed of spoken statements of only one person. In other words, statements of different case participants haven't been put together in one scenario. This procedure is adopted in order to maintain simplicity as much as possible, avoid clouding issues, and retain clarity in terms of identifying the main issues that each person was sharing. The above scenario is composed from four pieces of narratives that were separated by additional sentences that have not been presented for purposes of their irrelevance or brevity. This is indicated by the presence of the ellipses that point out that the narratives are disjointed in their occurrence in the transcription. In different instances, the underlying thread connecting two or more disjointed narratives is that either they are in response to the same question or refer to issues that are tied together.

For coding the data, an initial step involved numbering the interviews in sequence. In the identification code, this appears at the very start of each tag. For example, in the above scenario all the tags begin with "9," which indicates that the scenario is taken from the ninth interview as sequenced by the authors. The following step for coding involved sequencing the questions broadly in terms of how they were enacted during the actual interviews. Since there was much variation during the interviews owing to situational dynamics of interaction, the sequencing only broadly reflects the interview process enactment. This is indicated by portions of the tag such as "q.4.1," "q.4.2," "q.4.3," and "q.4.4." These indicate that the scenario is a response to question four (as sequenced by the authors) which was: "Think back when you came out or perhaps a friend's experiences of coming out. What were the different times in the coming-out process that were meaningful to you or your friend?" The numbers (1 through 4 as in "q.4.1") following the decimal in the tags indicate that there were four main points of consideration in that response of that case participant to the question of meaningful times during the "queer" youth coming-out process. These included times of curiosity ("q.4.1"), experiences of denial ("q.4.2"), questioning phase ("q.4.3"), and coming-out element in disclosing one's sexuality to others ("q.4.4"). The use of these tags also indicates open coding since important concepts associated with that question are identified. The last part in each tag indicates the page number on the transcribed copy of the interview where the particular narrative occurs ("p1," "p2," "p3," "p4," and "p5"). Also, there have been additional tags used throughout the scenario text ("3a," "3b," "3c," "3d," and "3e") that indicate various dimensions associated with point "4.3" in the narrative. In this instance, "4.3" refers to the "questioning phase" in response to the particular question, and the tags "3a," "3b," "3c," "3d," and "3e" used throughout the scenario refer to its identification (namely, that it is identified by the participant as the "questioning phase"), participant's significance of this phase, actions participant took during this phase (admission to friends, perceived subtle verbal disclosure), and the characteristic of denial respectively. These tags also show use of axial coding, where different categories and subcategories are related to each other. This scenario explores issues such as the need for broad information, role models, specific information, confusion, coming out to other gays, coming out to relatives/friends, denial, trying to act straight, stereotypes, geographic, age, nonsequential phases, and probably more. In this chapter, only limited coding is shown in order to maintain simplicity in presentation and explanation.

The above example shows how open, axial, and selective coding practices were followed in this research to identify categories of information, establish relationships between subcategories, and relate them to the other questions and to broader research questions, in terms of understanding coming-out behaviors and participant perspectives. Additionally, use of other question numbers ("q5") indicated how that point was related to the case participant's response to another question asked earlier or later in the interview. For example, in the above scenario, noting "q5" refers to the question "What was it like for you during your initial coming-out times?" while the tag "q7" refers to the question "What was it like for you when you started coming out to family/friends?" Connecting the details of what case participants said to their demographic characteristics, progress in coming out, and temporal and structural stage (as indicated by the interview number, as in "4" in the context of the above scenario) represents the practice of selective coding. This is because such strategies allowed us to place the sharing of specifics connected to case participant experiences in relation to where they were in terms of general phases in their "queer" youth coming-out experiences.

As the research progressed, constant comparing and tracking overlaps, intersections, and variations from other interviews helped refine and make clearer the various dimensions in the different phases of the "queer" youth coming-out experiences of case participants. Both the authors were involved in coding practices. A limitation of this study is that only some participants identified themselves as youth (twenty-three years or below), while others shared their youth experiences about coming out. In this research, this limitation was faced owing to difficulties in getting access to younger youth and obtaining necessary human subjects permissions for conducting research with children. Future research will address this limitation and get more youth involved in such work.

FINDINGS AND DISCUSSION

The following section presents findings related to the three significant elements in the information-seeking model of "queer" youth coming-out experiences, namely: types of information sources and their role in coming out; information-seeking behaviors in terms of thoughts, feelings, and actions; and ideal information support services sought during different coming-out phases. Scenarios or personal narratives of participants provide richness to the discussion by incorporating direct evidence of participant voices to support the claims.

Types of Information Sources Sought and Their Role in "Queer" Youth Experiences

Table 4.1 presents the most significant information sources that participants sought during their coming-out experiences when they experienced self-recognition as "queer." Information sources ranged from online resources like "queer" chat rooms and message boards to offline spaces like "queer" collections in bookstores and flyers on "queer" events in coffee shop and store bulletin boards. Recognition and identification with popular and famous openly "queer" role models (such as Ellen DeGeneres, Lance Bass, Rosie O'Donnell, Rupert Everett, and Melissa Etheridge, to name a few) was an important information source during this coming-out phase, though participants revealed a need for greater visibility of local "queer" community members. During this phase in coming out, participants sought information sources

Table 4.1. Types of Information Sources Sought and Their Role during the Phase of Self-Recognition as "Queer"

Types of Information Sources Sought	Role of Information Sources
Message Boards and Chat rooms (Yahoo! Chat, Gay.com, Technodyke.com)	Provide information about what it is like to be "queer" and how a person knows if he or she is "queer"
Coming-out stories (bookstores, websites)	Give some understanding about what to expect during coming out and provide advice on how to come out
"Queer" bookstores	Recommend resources on being "queer" and what to do if you are questioning (play an information provider role)
Role models (openly "queer" actors, musicians, politicians, teachers, etc.)	Give concrete examples that show "normal" and "positive" "queer" life is possible

that provided an understanding about sexuality in general, definitions, categorizations, and meanings associated with being "queer"; expected and experienced behaviors during coming out; and examples of real people who were openly "queer." For example, as one participant reported:

> I actually started [coming out] by joining an online discussion forum called Technodyke.com. Basically it is about 13,000 lesbian, bisexual, or transgender women who talk about everything and everything. It was a great information source, not necessarily for accurate information, because there is a lot of opinion on there. But it is an excellent source of honest information, very blunt, open information.

Table 4.2 identifies key information sources that participants sought during their coming-out experiences when they disclosed their queerness to other "queer" people. Most common information source avenues were those that provided information about local "queer" people and groups, for participants felt an urgent need to meet and interact with others in their community. An interesting point that was observed is related to the fact that during earlier times in their process of coming out, participants had explored online avenues for disclosure to other "queer" people; during this phase they wanted to socially interact with others in face-to-face situations. One participant said:

> The Internet was huge, I used it quite a bit to find out what is going on, were there any groups that meet, was there anything I wasn't aware of. I now mostly look for social groups and community things to do, and meet others. Like there was a big dance that was held every month and all sorts of stuff like that, I mainly found online. Sometimes there were posters and flyers, but I am pretty spoiled with the Internet to show me where to go in my area to connect with others.

Table 4.3 presents common information sources that participants sought during their coming out experiences when they disclosed their queerness to their family/friends. The information sources sought during these different times were those that fulfilled either of two kinds of expectations: provided institutional and authoritative legitimacy and support to "queer" representation via sharing their meanings and interpretations about issues; and, presented simple, clear, and easy to understand explanations and descriptions, without theoretical or jargon

Table 4.2. Types of Information Sources Sought and Their Role during the Phase of Disclosure to Other "Queers"

Types of Information Sources Sought	Role of Information Sources
Listing of local groups and clubs	Provide avenues to meet other "queers" in person to make friendships and for sexual encounters
Groups recognized or perceived by participants to have membership of other "queer" people (men's choirs, theatre, women's sports)	Allow ways to meet "queer" people in places "safer" and other than the bars
Symbolic merchandise (rainbow bumper stickers, "queer" symbol key chains, etc.)	Provide a mechanism to develop and express a "queer" identity (with pride) and connect with others in the "queer" community
Student organizations (Lambda student group, gay-straight alliances, etc.)	Make connections on campus; gain leadership skills and raise awareness on campus
"Queer" bookstores	Employees provide mentoring and "protection" during coming out; they become a safe space, a social alternative to meeting in bars
"Closeted" groups	Provide ways to meet "queer" people, but remain "closeted" in professional and broader personal life
Dating websites (PlanetOut.com. Gay.com)	Provide ways to meet potential partners

language, that lay people could easily understand. As one participant spoke:

> I was seeking websites that would help explain what it was to my family who are not that educated, that it is not a disease, that it can't be changed, that it is not a choice. So I ended up at the APA, American Psychological Association website, and P-FLAG that had brochures that you could print out. . . . The owners of the bookstore showed me various books on how to come out and I bought that book Now That You Know. They were very influential in my coming-out process because they shared how to approach my family and how not to be defensive in coming out.

Table 4.3.   Types of Information Sources Sought and Their Role during the Phase of Disclosure to Family/Friends

Types of Information Sources Sought	Role of Information Sources
Professional associations (American Psychological Association)	Provide a formal and institutional mechanism of support for "queer" representation; provide authoritative explanations for reasons/causes of being "queer" (not a disease, not a choice)
Reputed organizations (Parents and Friends of Lesbians and Gays [PFLAG])	Provide firsthand accounts about what it is like to have "queer" family members and friends
Books (Titles like *Now That You Know; Prayers For Bobby; Beyond Gay*)	Become a "trigger" that motivates to come out to family/friends and books are shared with them to provide knowledge
Queer bookstores	Recommend resources for coming out to family/friends (play an information provider role)

Table 4.4 lists participant feedback about important information sources and their roles during the positive self-identification phase in their coming out experiences. Information sources were sought that provided information about ways to achieve political, legal, civil, social, and individual equality and fairness in "queer" concerns. Participants also sought those information sources that shared positive stories about progressive efforts from larger cosmopolitan areas in the country and the world at large. One participant said:

> We would go to Atlanta on the weekends and pick up all sorts of magazines and newspapers from there because they actually had print material available. We would get it back here and share them in all the coffee shops and bookstores because there was no stuff like that printed here.

Table 4.5 provides examples of information sources that play a key role in the integration and acceptance phase in coming-out experiences. These include those information sources that play a role in relating "queer" interests and representation of issues in all areas of everyday life such as recreation and tourism, professional and workplace envi-

Table 4.4. Types of Information Sources Sought and Their Role during the Phase of Positive Self-Identification

Types of Information Sources Sought	Role of Information Sources
"Queer" advocacy organizations (Human Rights Campaign website)	Help understand health-related, legal, and political dimensions; provide access to politicians and decision makers on civil rights issues
Films and music with "queer" themes by "queer" actors/musicians or individuals	Help recognize legitimization in society; provide mirror where they see themselves reflected in the lives of celebrities; make people feel less isolated
"Queer" magazines and newspapers	Learn about "queer" culture, news, events, and venues from large cities

Table 4.5. Types of Information Sources Sought and Their Role during the Phase of Integration and Acceptance

Types of Information Sources Sought	Role of Information Sources
Self-help books	Provide information about "queer" relationships and coping
"Queer" travel websites	Give information about places and venues to visit that are "gay friendly"
"Queer" legal websites	Provide information for legal equality and addressing homophobia in the workplace; Provide avenues for writing letters to the editors of magazines/journals
Anti-"queer" websites and e-mail lists	Provide information on anti-"queer" rhetoric as a way to "know your enemy"
Keyword alerts from Google	Help spread the word and support others to learn about issues by posting information to/from "queer" lists

ronments, advocacy and political action, and networking and education. For example, one participant reported:

> I've got Google set up to send me news on various news and I probably get thirty to forty articles per day off of these automatic searches and I post them to a Yahoo! Group. I get to know gay things and I post things from all over the world, not just local or U.S., just trying to get a grip of what is going on in the world.

Information-Seeking Behaviors in "Queer" Youth Coming-Out Experiences

Table 4.6 summarizes the information-seeking behavior during coming-out experiences in terms of thoughts, feelings, and actions that participants communicated about during various times. During the phase of self-recognition as "queer" in the coming-out experiences, participants spoke about the prevailing heterosexual assumptions and expectations in society as one of the main reasons that created fear, anguish, and denial to accept their queerness. Repression of feelings and attempts to psychologically "distract" via alternative avenues of psychic concentration (such as religion) were "compensatory" actions that participants took to overcome guilt, fear, and perception of social isolation. In this context, there is a potential role for library and information professionals of providing safe space programs to remove ignorance and fear and openly addressing "queer" topics and issues. Of this phase of self-recognition one participant said:

> From eight to nineteen I didn't deal with coming out, I hid it. I didn't mention it to even a single person, not a soul. I didn't say a word, because I lived in such a small community and I was so scared. When I was eight I didn't know what gay meant, I just knew I liked being around my friends who were girls. I really didn't have a clue, but I also knew it was wrong somehow. The religious part was so bred into me and so dictated to me, that I knew, "Oh goodness, don't say anything different." That is the world I grew in.

During the phase of disclosure to other "queers," several participants shared how they found it very difficult to find and interact with them. In this context, there is definitely a much-needed role for libraries and information professionals to collect and advertise local information about all aspects related to "queer" issues, including events, people and

Table 4.6. Information-Seeking Behaviors in "Queer" Youth Coming-Out Experiences

Coming Out Phase	Thoughts	Feelings	Actions
Self recognition as "queer"	New consciousness awareness and acknowledgment of attraction to members of the same sex	Confusion, denial, anxiety	Repression of feelings; trying to "pass" as straight; seeking counseling; compensatory actions (religious commitment to "overcome sexuality")
Disclosure to other "queers"	Fear of being identified; don't know where to find "queer" individuals and social groups and how to interact with them	Partial self-acceptance of oneself as "queer"; loss of traditional "heterosexual life"; feel less or more isolated	Seeking local and dispersed "queer" information and social support avenues
Disclosure to family/friends	Need to reveal to someone from inner social network to overcome "double-life guilt"	Fear of being rejected; loss of closeness	Sharing knowledge of queerness with close family/friends; dealing with disappointment or isolation as a result of revelation to loved one(s)
Positive self-identification	Positive sense of self; feeling good about oneself for coming out	Pride; need to know about "queer" role models; feeling satisfied and fulfilled	Seek external environment of acceptance, validation, and support; seek positive relationships with other "queer" people
Integration and acceptance	Openness	Nondefensiveness about one's sexual orientation	Out and available for support to others; couples live a comfortable life together and generally seek out other couples

groups, support services, and resources available in the community. Participants also spoke about the fact that they were always fearful of being found out when they interacted with other "queers" and often felt as if they were leading double lives and committing a crime that they did not want people who knew them to find out. One participant stated:

> I use the Internet and magazines a lot and I have now made a lot of gay friends. I have a bunch of friends in _____ [name of big city], it is a lot larger and they have a much bigger gay community and the best thing is that no one knows me there. They are much more politically progressive than here and I visit them once or twice a month. I had friends that lived here and moved there and then I just met more people but none of my straight friends know, so I live in two worlds—gay and straight (or don't know I am gay). Its more accepting there, they have huge events every couple of months, the community is aware.

During the phase of disclosure to family/friends, the fear of rejection, anger, and being disowned by those whom they shared their secret with were chief in the minds of participants. Several participants also talked about how it was definitely worthwhile to have gotten the burden off their shoulders since, even if they lost some people whom they cared for in the process, they definitely felt positive and true to themselves. One participant observed:

> A more formal group for support to my family would have been better, maybe a local organization; here they don't really have one or at least I didn't know about it. And my parents could have used some help, they just started going to therapy and they don't approve. I think more exposure to gay issues has to be the way to make people get used to the idea. I just think they didn't have any exposure to gay culture and gay people. They totally didn't understand it. I am not sure if there was something more informal to ease them into it. Maybe other parents of gay children could have talked to them, because I don't think any of their friends had gay children.

Such experiences identify an urgent need for the potential role of library and information professionals to address issues of visibility for "queer" topics and concerns, provide adequate collections and infor-mation support services, act as referral to community information resources for "queer" people, address ignorance and homophobia, and do greater proactive marketing and networking to address equality in other community avenues such as schools and colleges, and churches and religious institutions.

During the phases of positive self-identification and integration and acceptance in the coming-out experiences, participants sought to achieve internal individual peace about their "queerness" as well as social support in their professional lives. For example, one participant said:

> I am completely out now. My family and my work people know about it and have accepted it. I think the first are those that you are most intimate with, your closest friends. I think you let some people who you are comfortable with and slowly you keep letting people into that group. Soon it doesn't matter and if the situation comes up, you just mention it as if you are telling someone you went to the market. And if they are offended, it is their problem.

Types of Information Support Services Ideally Needed during "Queer" Youth Coming-Out Experiences

Based on participant feedback, table 4.7 presents a summary of the kinds of information support services that would have ideally eased some of their painful experiences during coming out. These provide ample directions for libraries and information professionals to work for "queer" youth and expand their existing traditional functions associated with provision of collections, systems, and services connected to information creation, organization, and dissemination processes. Also, there is potential for libraries and information professionals to extend their traditional roles to engage in newer roles of greater proactive involvement in community dynamics to bring about change in support of "queer" youth during their coming-out experiences. During the phase of self-recognition as "queer" in coming-out experiences, the main focus is on providing information support services that help in self-understanding and self-awareness, acceptance and support for the individual as they cope with coming out. As one participant stated:

> For me I think I always kind of knew, but I really didn't know how to define it. And it started in high school, lots of friends would joke with me and it hurt because they made fun and I didn't know how to respond. Though I would not disagree since you know what they were talking about but it only made it

Table 4.7.   Types of Information Support Services Ideally Needed During "Queer" Youth Coming-Out Experiences

Coming Out Phase	Information Support Services Ideally Needed
Self recognition as "queer"	Counseling services; information related to self-labeling; information about understanding sexualities, formation of "queer" identity, and positive consequences for self-acceptance as "queer"; sex education, sexuality information, and information about safe practices, health, and diseases (including HIV/AIDS)
Disclosure to other "queers"	Information about other "queer" individuals and social and cultural groups; "queer" social interaction resources on "queer" norms of behavior, how to be comfortable with "queer" people, and resources for confidence building and developing "queer" friendship circles
Disclosure to family/friends	Resources on how to come out and/or discuss "queer" issues with family/friends
Positive self-identification	Learning about "queer" culture and its history, "queer" role models, and how to play an active role in "queer" empowerment and community building (political/social activism)
Integration and acceptance	Resources to help live as an out "queer" based on equality, pride, and respect; legal rights, partner benefits, nondiscrimination policies, etc.

worse. One friend helped me a lot and I used to go with her to the bookstores to get information. That was my main source of literature.

During the phase of disclosure to other "queers," the focused dimensions of idealized information support services during coming-out experiences shifts from creating individual acceptance to addressing issues in the social context, where provision of information about social and community resources becomes one goal. For example, a participant noted:

If there would have been a resource center to visit and talk to other gays, and to get information and know that it was ok and that you were not alone, that would have been great. I think a resource center is very important because if you do not have a friendship network or are not "in the know" about community events then you are at a loss. And you need a safe place. There were no gay organizations, you just had to keep your ears open and try to find them. I put myself in situations where I could try to seek out gay people or at least people that would be comfortable with me being gay.

During the phase of disclosure to family/friends in the coming-out experiences, resources on how to come out to loved ones in a way that helps to strengthen those relationships should be an important component of an ideal information support service during this time. One participant observed:

I don't know if telling the family is ever going to be easy. From all of the stories I have heard, it is forced upon you. A sibling or someone gets mad, or they confront you and it is usually a very negative thing. For me, it was horrible. It was the most wretched thing ever. I have also lost dear friends, especially Christians that were very conservative. I keep losing friends. Just in the last year I have had to let go of a friend because of her closeness to her religion—every time she was around me she would cry because she was sad that I was gay because its wrong.

During phases of positive self-identification and integration and acceptance in the coming-out process, learning about "queer" history, culture, and individuals and getting information about social, legal, and political equality are important ingredients in the design of ideal information support services for "queer" youth. During these phases, most participants acquired skills and became their own ideal information support service since society and the local community was not able to provide adequate resources or knowledge of what was available. One participant said:

For finding information I have joined a couple of listservs and some chat rooms where I find information. And now I use the Internet for more than answering questions of curiosity. I am actually finding useful information, seeking out certain things on my own. For instance, the Southern Comfort Conference, I want to go there, so I google it, find it, find out when it is, what I need to do to get involved. Now I know where to go and how to find what I am looking for. Before I might have just typed in "gay bookstore."

CONCLUSION: IMPLICATIONS
FOR LIBRARY SUPPORT

This chapter presents an information-seeking model of coming-out experiences in response to past limited research that provided incomplete understanding of "queer" youth information seeking and searching processes. Making connections between the types of information sources and their role in the coming-out experiences, information-seeking behaviors during various coming-out phases, and idealized information support services desired during those times, provides a more holistic understanding about the experiences of "queer" youth during coming out. This also helps draw meaningful and concrete intersections between theoretical understandings of information seeking and tangible efforts that may lead to progressive change. The model of information seeking during "queer" youth coming out experiences is an implicational model that emerges from reflection on research findings and interview data. Hence, it is a hypothetical model that will be tested in future studies with other "queer" participants.

Findings in this research show an urgent need for stronger involvement and proactive efforts on the part of libraries and information professionals in advocacy and support of "queer" youth during their coming-out process. The following are future roles and activities that libraries and information professionals should pursue in order to make them more supportive and useful in coming-out experiences:

- Expand access to different kinds of "queer" materials as a part of their collections;
- Promote advertising and marketing of available "queer" information support services;
- Develop their services and referral on community information resources on "queer" concerns;
- Develop the physical library and information center as a safe space for "queer" youth via promoting workshops, lectures, book talks, and other programs on "queer" topics and issues;
- Build collaborations and partnerships with community agencies (school, churches, businesses) to address abuse, homophobia, and hate crimes;

- Identify local, regional, national, and international "queer" networks and information support services;
- Use the media to market the library as a supporter of empowerment of "queer" youth;
- Address "queer" issues via education and community action.

Based on some of the above identified strategies, libraries and information professionals may be able to salvage their discredited reputation based on such findings as in the above study, where libraries were identified as one of the last places where participants sought information support services during coming-out experiences. Library and information professionals were quite conspicuous by their absence in any list that participants identified of supporting agencies where they were able to seek information, advice, support, or comfort during their coming-out process. By applying the information-seeking model of "queer" youth coming-out experiences to better understand the use of existing information sources by this underserved group, librarians and informational professionals may be able to identify more appropriate interventions of support.

NOTES

1. John Cloud, "The Battle Over Gay Teens," *Time*, October 10, 2005: 42–51.

2. Human Rights Campaign (HRCF), *Resource Guide to Coming Out for Gay, Lesbian, Bisexual and Transgender Americans* (Washington, DC: HRCF, 2004), www.hrc.org/Template.cfm?Section = Resources2&Template = /ContentManagement/ContentDisplay.cfm&ContentID = 22631 (accessed July 15, 2005).

3. Ritch C. Savin-Williams, *The New Gay Teenager* (Cambridge, MA: Harvard University Press, 2005).

4. Anthony R. D'Augelli, "Victimization History and Mental Health among Lesbian, Gay, and Bisexual Youths" (paper presented at the biennial meetings of the Society for Research on Adolescence, San Diego, CA, February 1998).

5. IngBeth Larsson and Carl G. Svedin, "Sexual Experiences in Childhood: Young Adults' Recollections," *Archives of Sexual Behavior* 31 (2002): 263–73; Bruce Rind, "Gay and Bisexual Adolescent Boys' Sexual Experiences with Men: An Empirical Examination of Psychological Correlates in a Nonclinical Sample," *Archives of Sexual Behavior* 30 (2001): 345–68; Ritch C. Savin-Williams and Lisa M. Diamond, "Sex," in *Handbook of Adolescent Psychology*, ed. Richard M. Lerner and Laurence Steinberg, 189–231 (New York: John Wiley and Sons, 2004).

6. Judith Levine, *Harmful to Minors: The Perils of Protecting Children from Sex* (Minneapolis: University of Minnesota Press, 2002); Roy F. Baumeister, "Gender Differences in Erotic Plasticity: The Female Sex Drive as Socially Flexible and Responsive," *Psychological Bulletin* 126, no. 3 (2000): 3247–374.

7. Lisa M. Diamond, "Was It a Phrase? Young Women's Relinquishment of Lesbian/Bisexual Identities over a Five-Year Period," *Journal of Personality and Social Psychology* 84 (2003): 352–64; Paula C. Rust, "Two Many and Not Enough: The Meanings of Bisexual Identities, *Journal of Bisexuality* 1, no. 1 (2001): 31–68.

8. Robert Garofalo, R. Cameron Wolf, Laurence S. Wissow, Elizabeth R. Woods, and Elizabeth Goodman, "Sexual Orientation and Risk of Suicide Attempts among a Representative Sample of Youth, *Archives of Pediatric Adolescent Medicine* 153, no. 5 (1999): 487–93.

9. Ritch C. Savin-Williams, *And Then I Became Gay: Young Men's Stories"* (New York: Routledge, 1998); Kevin Jennings, *Telling Tales Out of School: Lesbian, Gay, and Bisexual People Remember Their School Years* (New York: Alyson, 1998).

10. John D'Emilio, William B. Turner, and Urvashi Vaid, *Creating Change: Sexuality, Public Policy, and Civil Rights* (New York: National Gay and Lesbian Task Force, 2000); Eric Marcus, *Making Gay History: The Half Century Fight for Lesbian and Gay Equal Rights* (New York: HarperCollins Publishers, 2002).

11. Ann Wells, "Thoughts from a Gay Teacher in a Catholic School: A Junior High Teacher Yearns to Be a Positive Gay Role Model in Her Catholic School. But She Wonders, 'Does the Church Love Me as Much as I Love It?'" *U.S. Catholic* 67, no. 1 (January 2002): 38–39; Michael T. Ford, *Outspoken: Role Models from the Lesbian and Gay Community* (New York: HarperCollins Publishers, 1998).

12. Larry Gross and James D. Woods, *The Columbia Reader on Lesbians and Gay Men in Media, Society, and Politics* (New York: Columbia University Press, 1999).

13. Janet H. Fontaine, "The Sound of Silence: Public School Response to the Needs of Gay and Lesbian Youth," in *School Experiences of Gay and Lesbian Youth: The Invisible Minority*, ed. Mary B. Harris, 101–10 (New York: Harrington Park Press, 1997); Ian Rivers, "Violence Against Lesbian and Gay Youth and Its Impact," in *Pride & Prejudice: Working with Lesbian, Gay and Bisexual Youth*, ed. Margaret S. Schneider, 31–47 (Toronto: Central Toronto Youth Services, 1997).

14. Susan R. Rankin, *Campus Climate: For Gay, Lesbian, Bisexual, and Transgender People: A National Perspective* (New York: The Gay and Lesbian Task Force Policy Institute, 2003), http://www.thetaskforce.org/downloads/Campus Climate.pdf (accessed July 15, 2005).

15. Carolyn A. Guenther-Grey, Sherri Varnell, Jennifer I. Weiser, Robin M. Mathy, Lydia O'Donnell, Ann Stueve, Gary Remafedi, and the Community Intervention Trial for Youth (CITY) Study Team, "Trends in Sexual Risk-Taking among Urban Young Men Who Have Sex with Men, 1999–2002," *Journal of the National Medical Association* 97, no. 7 (July 2005): 38S–43S.

16. Gershem Kaufman and Lev Raphael, *Coming Out of Shame: Transforming Gay and Lesbian Lives* (New York: Random House, 1996).

17. Judith S. Hamer, "Coming-Out: Gay Males' Information Seeking," *School Libraries Worldwide* 9, no. 2 (July 2003): 73–89.

18. Carol C. Kuhlthau, *Seeking Meaning: A Process Approach to Library and Information Services*, 2nd ed. (Westport, CT: Libraries Unlimited, 2004).

19. Michel Foucault, *The History of Sexuality: Volume 1* (New York: Vintage Books, 1980).

20. Mark Blasius, *Sexual Identities, Queer Politics* (Princeton: Princeton University Press, 2001); Marjorie Garber, *Vice Versa: Bisexuality and the Eroticism of Everyday Life* (New York: Routledge, 1995).

21. Erik H. Erikson, *Childhood and Society* (New York: Norton 1950); Erik H. Erikson, *Identity: Youth and Crisis* (New York: Norton, 1958); Margaret Roario, Joyce Hunter, Shira Maguen, Marya Gwadz, and Raymond Smith, "The Coming-Out Process and Its Adaptational and Health-Related Associations Among Gay, Lesbian, and Bisexual Youths: Stipulation and Exploration of a Model," *American Journal of Community Psychology* 29, no. 1 (2001): 133–60.

22. Tanis L. Stenback and Alvin M. Schrader, "Venturing from the Closet: A Qualitative Study of the Information Needs of Lesbians," *Public Library Quarterly* 17, no. 3 (1999): 37–50.

23. Adrian Coyle and M. Daniels, "Psychological Well-Being and Gay Identity: Some Suggestions for Promoting Mental Health among Gay Men," in *Promotion of Mental Health*, Volume 2, ed. Denise R. Trent and Colin Reed, 189–207 (Aldershot, England: Avebury Press, 1992).

24. Ruth K. Westheimer, *Sex for Dummies* (Foster City, CA: IDG Books, 1995).

25. Mary J. Rotheram-Borus and Isabel Fernandez, "Sexual Orientation and Developmental Challenges Experienced by Gay and Lesbian Youths," *Suicide and Life Threatening Behavior* 25 (supplement) (1995): 26–34.

26. Jon Lasser and Deborah Tharinger, "Visibility Management in School and Beyond: A Qualitative Study of Gay, Lesbian, Bisexual Youth," *Journal of Adolescence* 26, no. 2 (April 2003): 233–44.

27. Ruth Fassinger and Brett A. Miller, "Validation of an Inclusive Model of Sexual Minority Identity Formation on a Sample of Gay Men," *Journal of Homosexuality* 32, no. 2 (1996): 53–78; Elizabeth J. Rankow, "Lesbian Health Issues for the Primary Care Provider," *Journal of Family Practice* 40, no. 5 (May 1995): 486–93; K. E. Gillow and L. L. Davis, "Lesbian Stress and Coping Methods," *Journal of Psychosocial Nursing* 23, no. 1 (1987): 26–34; Joyce Hunter, "Violence against Lesbian and Gay Male Youths," *Journal of Interpersonal Violence* 5, no. 3 (1990): 295–300.

28. William B. Stiles, "'I Have to Talk to Somebody.' A Fever Model of Disclosure," in *Self-Disclosure: Theory, Research, and Therapy*, ed. Valerian J. Derlega and John H. Berg, 257–79 (New York: Plenum Press, 1987).

29. Scott L. Hershberger and Anthony R. D'Augelli, "The Impact of Victimization on the Mental Health and Suicidality of Lesbian, Gay, and Bisexual Youths," *Developmental Psychology* 31, no. 1 (1995): 65–74; Ritch Savin-Williams, *Gay and Lesbian Youth: Expressions of Identity* (New York: Hemisphere, 1990).

30. Vivienne C. Cass, "Homosexual Identity Development: A Theoretical Mode," *Journal of Homosexuality* 4, no. 4 (1979): 219–35.; Kenneth D. George and Andrew E. Behrendt, "Therapy for Male Couples Experiencing Relationship Problems and Sexual Problems," *Journal of Homosexuality* 17 (1987): 77–88.

31. Vivienne C. Cass, "Homosexual Identity Formation: Testing a Theoretical Model," *Journal of Sex Research* 20, no. 2 (1984): 143–67.

32. Eli Coleman, "Developmental Stages of the Coming-Out Process," in *Homosexuality: Social, Psychological and Biological Issues*, ed. William Paul, James D Weinrich, John C. Gonsioreck, and Mary E. Hotvedt, 149–58 (Beverly Hills, CA: Sage, 1982).

33. John A. Lee, "Going Public: A Study in the Sociology of Homosexual Liberation," *Journal of Homosexuality* 3, no.1 (1977): 49–78; Evelyn Hooker, "Male Homosexuals and Their World," in *Sexual Inversion: The Multiple Roots of Homosexuality,* ed. Judd Marmor, 83–107 (New York: Basic Books, 1965).

34. AIDS Education and Research Trust (AVERT), "Talking About Homosexuality in the Secondary School," 1997, http://www.avert.org/media/pdfs/homosexualityinschool.pdf (accessed July 15, 2005).

35. Elisabeth Kubler-Ross, *On Death and Dying* (New York: Collier Books, 1993).

36. Robert Temes, *Living with an Empty Chair: A Guide Through Grief* (New York: Irvington Publishers, 1980).

37. Coleman, "Developmental Stages of the Coming-Out Process."

38. Stephen R. Russell, "Sexual Minority Youth and Suicide Risk," *The American Behavioral Scientist* 46, no. 9 (2003): 1241–57.

39. Jay Paul, Joseph Catania, Lance Pollack, Judith Moskowitz, Jesse Canchola, Thomas Mills, Diane Binson, and Ron Stall, "Suicide Attempts among Gay and Bisexual Men: Lifetime Prevalence and Antecedents," *American Journal of Public Health* 92, no. 8 (August 2002): 1338–45.

40. Ellen C. Perrin, Kenneth M. Cohen, Melanie Gold, Caitlin Ryan, Ritch C. Savin-Williams, and Cindy M. Schorzman, "Gay and Lesbian Issues in Pediatric Health Care," *Current Problems in Pediatric Adolescent Health Care* 34, no.10 (November–December 2004): 355–98.

41. Steve L. Joyce, "Lesbian, Gay and Bisexual Library Service: A Review of the Literature," *Public Libraries* 39, no. 5 (2000): 270–79; Connexions, "Information and Guidance on Engaging Young Lesbian, Gay and Bisexual People," 2002/ 2003, www.connexions.gov.uk/partnerships/publications/uploads/cp/LGBreprint final03.0 4.pdf (accessed July 15, 2005).

42. Charles R. Fikar and Mary Koslap-Petraco, "Pediatric Forum: What about Gay Teenagers?" *American Journal of Diseases of Children* 145, no. 3 (1991): 252.

43. Glenn H. Utter and James L. True, *Conservative Christians and Political Participation: A Reference Handbook* (Santa Barbara, CA: ABC-CLIO, 2004).

44. Yasmin Kafai and Marcia J. Bates, "Internet Web-Searching Instruction in the Elementary Classroom: Building a Foundation for Information Literacy," *School Library Media Quarterly* 25 (1997): 103–11; Mark S. Wolcott, "Information Seeking and the World Wide Web: A Qualitative Study of Seventh-Grade Students' Search Behavior during an Inquiry Activity" (PhD dissertation, University of San Francisco, 1998); Denise E. Agosto, "Bounded Rationality and Satisficing in Young People's Web-based Decision Making," *Journal of the American Society for the Information Science and Technology* 53, no. 1 (2002): 16–27.

45. Peter Gibson, "Gay Male and Lesbian Youth Suicide," in *Report of the Secretary's Task Force on Youth Suicide*, ed. Marcia Feinleib, 110–42 (Washington, DC: Department of Health and Human Services, 1989); A. Damien Martin, "Learning to Hide: The Socialization of the Gay Adolescent," in *Adolescent Psychiatry: Developmental and Clinical Issues*, ed. Sherman C. Feinstein, John G. Looney, Allan Z. Schwarzenberg, and Arthur D. Sorosky, 52–65 (Chicago: University of Chicago Press, 1982).

46. Peter LaBarbera, "The Gay Youth Suicide Myth," Leadership U, 1996, www.leaderu.com/jhs/labarbera.html (accessed July 15, 2005); Michel Dorais and Simon L. Lajeunesse, *Dead Boys Can't Dance: Sexual Orientation, Masculinity, and Suicide*, trans. Pierre Tremblay (Montreal: McGill-Queen's University Press 2003).

47. Allison Druin, *The Role of Children in the Design of New Technology* (College Park: University of Maryland Human/Computer Interaction Laboratory, 1999); Brenda Laurel, "Introduction," in *The Art of Human-Computer Interface Design*, ed. B. Laurel, 1–12 (Reading, MA: Addison-Wesley, 1990).

48. Janet A. Creelman and Roma M. Harris, "Coming Out: The Information Needs of Lesbians," *Collection Building* 10, nos. 3–4 (1990): 37–41; M. Garner, "Changing Times: Information Destinations of the Lesbian, Gay, Bisexual, and Transgendered Community in Denver, Colorado," *Information for Social Change* 12, www.libr.org/ISC/TOC.com (accessed March 1, 2003).

49. Dania Bilal, "Children's Use of the Yahooligans! Web Search Engine: III. Cognitive and Physical Behaviors on Fully Self-Generated Tasks," *Journal of the American Society for Information Science & Technology* 53, no. 13 (May 2000): 1170–83; Francis F. Jacobson and Emily N. Ignacio, "Teaching Reflection: Information Seeking and Evaluation in a Digital Library Environment," *Library Trends* 45, no. 4 (1997): 771–802; Leslie Miller, Melissa Chaika and Laura Groppe, "Girls' Preferences in Software Design: Insights from a Focus Group," *Interpersonal Computing and Technology: An Electronic Journal for the 21st Century* 4, no. 2 (1996): 27–36; Delia B. Neuman, "Designing Databases as Tools for Higher-Level Learning: Insights from Instructional Systems Design," *Educational Technology Research and Development* 41, no. 4 (1993): 25–46.

50. Henry Minton and Gary McDonald, "Homosexual Identity Formation as a Developmental Process," *Journal of Homosexuality* 9, nos. 2–3 (1984): 91–104.

51. Adrian G. Coyle, "The Construction of Gay Identity," Volumes I and II, (PhD thesis, University of Surrey, UK, 1991).

52. Rita Hardiman and Bailey W. Jackson, "Racial Identity Development: Understanding Racial Dynamics in College Classrooms and on Campus," in *Promoting Diversity in College Classrooms and on Campus*, ed. M. Adams, 21–37 (San Francisco: Jossey-Bass, 1992).

53. Edward Laumann, John H. Gagnon, Robert T. Michael, and Stuart Michaels, *Sex in America: A Definitive Survey* (Boston: Little, Brown and Co.,1994).

54. Sandra Huges-Hassell and Alissa Hinkley, "Reaching Out to Lesbian, Gay, Bisexual, and Transgender Youth," *Journal of Youth Services in Libraries* 15, no. 1 (Fall 2001): 69–41.

55. P. C. Rust, "Coming Out in the Age of Sexual Constructionism: Sexual Identity Formation among Lesbians and Bisexual Women," *Gender and Society* 7 (1993): 50–77.

56. A. McKee, "Images of Gay Men in the Media and the Development of Self-Esteem," *Australian Journal of Communication* 27, no. 2 (2000): 80–98.

57. Abby Abinati, "Legal Challenges Facing Gay and Lesbian Youth," *Journal of Gay & Lesbian Social Services: Issues in Practice, Policy, and Research* 1, nos. 3/4 (1994): 149–69.

58. Virginia Uribe and Karen M. Harbeck, "Addressing the Needs of Lesbian, Gay, and Bisexual Youth: The Origins of Project 10 and School-Based Intervention," *Journal of Homosexuality* 22, nos. 3/4 (1991): 9–28.

59. George A. Appleby and Jeane W. Anastas, *Not Just a Passing Phase: Social Work With Gay, Lesbian, and Bisexual People* (New York: Columbia University Press, 1998).

60. Frederick R. Lynch, "Nonghetto Gays: An Ethnography of Suburban Homosexuals," in *Gay Culture in America: Essays from the Field*, ed. Gilbert Herdt, 165–201 (Boston: Beacon Press, 1992).

61. Joseph Carrier, *De los Otros: Homosexual Desire among Mexican Men* (New York: Columbia University Press, 1995).

62. R. B. Hays, *What Are Young Gay Men's HIV Prevention Needs?* AIDS Research Institute: Center for AIDS Prevention Studies, 1996, http://www.caps.ucsf.edu/YGMtext.html (accessed September 5, 2003).

63. Gilbert Herdt, "Gay and Lesbian Youth," *Journal of Homosexuality* 17, nos. 1–2 (1989): 1–42; Richard R. Troiden, "Becoming Homosexual: A Model of Homosexual Identity Acquisition," *Psychiatry* 42, no. 4 (November 1979): 363–73.

64. Martin, "Learning to Hide."

65. Anthony R. D'Augelli, "Lesbian and Gay Male Development: Steps toward an Analysis of Lesbians' and Gay Men's Lives," in *Psychological Perspectives on Lesbian and Gay Issues, Volume 1: Lesbian and Gay Psychology: Theory,*

Research, and Clinical Applications, ed. Beverly Greene and Gregory M. Herek, 118–32 (Thousand Oaks, CA: Sage, 1994).

66. Bertram Cohler and Robert Galatzer-Levy, *The Course of Gay and Lesbian Lives: Social and Psychoanalytic Perspectives* (Chicago: University of Chicago Press, 2000).

67. Kenneth M. Cohen and Ritch C. Savin-Williams, "Developmental Perspectives on Coming Out to Self and Others," in *The Lives of Lesbians, Gays, and Bisexuals: Children to Adults*, ed. Kenneth Cohen and Ritch C. Savin-Williams, 113–51 (Fort Worth, TX: Harcourt Brace, 1996).

68. Ruth E. Fassinger, "The Hidden Minority: Issues and Challenges in Working with Lesbian Women and Gay Men," *The Counseling Psychologist* 19 (1991): 157–76; Fassinger and Miller, "Validation of an Inclusive Model"; Linda D. Garnets and Douglas C. Kimmel, "Cultural Diversity among Lesbians and Gay Men," in *Psychological Perspectives on Lesbian and Gay Male Experiences*, ed. Linda D. Garnets and Douglas C. Kimmel, 331–37 (New York: Columbia University Press, 1993); Craig O'Neill and Kathleen Ritter, *Coming Out Within: Stages of Spiritual Awakening for Lesbians and Gay Men* (San Francisco: HarperSanFrancisco, 1992).

69. Victor G. Carrion and James Lock, "The Coming Out Process: Developmental Stages for Sexual Minority Youth," *Clinical Child Psychology and Psychiatry* 2, no. 3 (1997): 369–77.

70. C. Kitzinger and S. Wilkinson, "Transitions from Heterosexuality to Lesbianism: The Discursive Production of Lesbian Identities," *Developmental Psychology* 31 (1995): 95–104.

71. Bharat Mehra and Donna Braquet, "A 'Queer' Manifesto of Interventions for Libraries to Come Out of the Closet! A Study of 'Queer' Youth Experiences during the Coming Out Process," *Library and Information Science Research Electronic Journal* 16, no. 1 (March 2006), http://libres.curtin.edu.au/libres16n1/ (accessed November 2, 2006).

72. Jessica F. Morris, "Lesbian Coming Out as a Multidimensional Process," *Journal of Homosexuality* 33, no. 2 (1997): 1–22; Roy Cain, "Relational Contexts and Information Management among Gay Men," *Families in Society: The Journal of Contemporary Human Services* 72 (1991): 344–52.

73. Morris, "Lesbian Coming Out as a Multidimensional Process."

74. Joy S. Whitman, Sherry Cormier, and Cynthia J. Boyd, "Lesbian Identity Management at Various Stages of the Coming Out Process: A Qualitative Study," *International Journal of Sexuality and Gender Studies* 5, no. 1 (2000): 3–18.

75. Cass, "Homosexual Identity Development"; Coleman, "Developmental Stages of the Coming-Out Process"; Barry M. Dank, "Coming Out in the Gay World," *Psychiatry* 34 (1971): 180–97; Lee, "Going Public"; Kenneth Plummer, *Sexual Stigma: An Interactionist Account* (London: Routledge, 1975); Troiden, "Becoming Homosexual."

76. David Scasta, "Issues in Helping People Come Out," *Journal of the Gay & Lesbian Psychotherapy* 2, no. 4 (1998): 87–98.

77. Bharat Mehra and Donna Braquet, "Will the Library Please Come Out," *Library and Information Science Research Electronic Journal* 16, no. 1 (March 2006), http://libres.curtin.edu.au/libres16n1/ (accessed November 2, 2006).

78. Gilbert Herdt and Andrew Boxer, *Children of Horizons: How Gay and Lesbian Teens Are Leading a New Way Out of the Closet* (Boston: Beacon Press, 1993), 33.

79. Alex Carballo-Diéguez, "Hispanic Culture, Gay Male Culture, and AIDS," *Journal of Counseling and Development* 68 (1989, September/October): 26–30.

80. Dank, "Coming Out in the Gay World."

81. John P. Egan, "Not Str8: The Construction of Queer Male Identity in Sydney, Australia," in *Adult Education for Democracy, Social Justice and a Culture of Peace*, proceedings of the Joint International Conference of the Adult Education Research Conference (AERC) (45th National Conference) and the Canadian Association for the Study of Adult Education (CASAE), l'Association Canadienne pour l'etude de education des adultes (ACEEA) (23rd National Conference), ed. Darlene E. Clover, Julia Shinaba and Catherine Etmanski, 125–30 (Victoria, Canada: National Library of Canada Cataloging in Publication, 2004).

82. Egan, "Not Str8," 182.

83. Lou A. Lewis, "The Coming Out Process for Lesbians: Integrating a Stable Identity," *Journal of the National Association of Social Workers* 29, no. 5 (1984): 464–69.

84. G. B. MacDonald, "Exploring Sexual Identity: Gay People and Their Families," *Sex Education Coalition News* 5, no.1 (1983): 4.

85. Lisa K. Waldner and Brian Magruder, "Coming Out to Parents: Perceived Resources and Identity Expression as Predictors of Identity Disclosure for Gay and Lesbian Adolescents," *Journal of Homosexuality* 37, no. 2 (1999): 83–100.

86. Anthony R. D'Augelli, "Lesbian and Gay Male Development."

87. Michael C. LaSala, "Lesbians, Gay Men, and Their Parents: Family Therapy for the Coming-Out Crisis," *Family Process* 39, no. 1 (2000): 67–81.

88. Adial Ben-Ari, "The Discovery That an Offspring Is Gay: Parents', Gay Men's and Lesbians' Perspectives," *Journal of Homosexuality* 30, no. 1 (1995): 89–112.

89. Jason Cianciotto and Sean Cahill, *Education Policy: Issues Affecting Lesbian, Gay, Bisexual, and Transgender Youth* (New York: The National Gay and Lesbian Task Force Policy Institute, 2003).

90. Helma Hawkins, "Opening the Closet Door: Public Library Services for Gay, Lesbian, and Bisexual Teens," *Colorado Libraries* 20, no. 1 (1994): 28–31.

91. Ellen Greenblatt and Cal Gough, "Gay and Lesbian Library Users: Overcoming Barriers to Service," in *Diversity and Multiculturalism in Libraries*, ed. Katerine H. Hill, 227–33 (New York: JAI Press, 1994).

92. Ellen Greenblatt, "Barriers to GLBT Library Service in the Electronic Age," *Information for Social Change* 2001, www.libr.org/ISC/articles/12-Green blatt.html (accessed July 15, 2005).

93. Cal Gough, "Making the Library More User-Friendly for Gay and Lesbian Patrons," in *Gay and Lesbian Library Service*, ed. Cal Gough and Ellen Greenblatt, 109–39 (Jefferson, NC: McFarland, 1990); Heike Seidel, "The 'Invisibles': Lesbian Women as Library Users," *Progressive Librarian*, no. 14 (Spring 1998): 34–40.

94. Suzy Taraba, "Collecting Gay and Lesbian Materials in an Academic Library," in *Gay and Lesbian Library Service*, ed. Cal Gough and Ellen Greenblatt, 25–37 (Jefferson, NC: McFarland, 1990).

95. Joyce, "Lesbian, Gay and Bisexual Library Service"; C. J. Bott, "Fighting the Silence: How to Support Your Gay and Straight Students," *Voice Youth Advocates* 23, no. 1 (2000): 22–26.

96. Julie Carter, *United States: Reaching Out with Library Services for GLBTQ Teens* (Buffalo, NY: Hawthorn Press, Inc., 2005).

97. Cal Gough and Ellen Greenblatt, *Gay and Lesbian Library Service* (Jefferson, NC: McFarland, 1990).

98. B. G. Glaser and A. L. Strauss, *The Discovery of Grounded Theory: Strategies for Qualitative Research* (Chicago: Aldine, 1967).

99. T. A. Schwandt, "Constuctivist, Interpretivist Approaches in Qualitative Research," in *The Handbook of Qualitative Research*, ed. N. Denzin and Y. Lincoln, 118–37 (Thousand Oaks, CA: Sage, 1994).

100. A. Strauss and J. Corbin, "Grounded Theory Methodology," in *The Handbook of Qualitative Research*, ed. N. Denzin and Y. Lincoln, 273–85 (Thousand Oaks, CA: Sage, 1994).

5

Teens and Pleasure Reading: A Critical Assessment from Nova Scotia

Vivian Howard and Shan Jin

BACKGROUND

A 1995 survey by the National Center for Educational Statistics in the United States, "Services and Resources for Children and Young Adults," concluded that almost 25 percent of public library users are teenagers; in other words, one out of every four individuals entering a public library is between the ages of twelve and eighteen (National Center for Educational Statistics 1995). Clearly, teens are an important public library user group, with needs and concerns very distinct from those of either children or adult users. However, as Virginia Walter (2003) very effectively demonstrates in her recent article "Public Library Service to Children and Teens: A Research Agenda," the research community has spent little time investigating either the information needs or the information-seeking behavior of teens. This gap is certainly as true for Canadian teens as it is for their American counterparts. There are currently 4.4 million teens in Canada, making them the second-largest demographic group in the country. However, the reading habits and public library use of Canadian young adults are not well understood. While this topic was the subject of several quantitative studies in the

1970s, it has not been investigated in the new social and technological context of the twenty-first century.

Today, it is apparent that the Canadian social situation is significantly different from the 1970s. In many jurisdictions, funding for school and public libraries has declined dramatically while at the same time the discretionary spending power of teens has undergone an equally dramatic increase. Both libraries and independent booksellers are besieged by the "big box" chain bookstores. Furthermore, twenty-first-century teens have a wealth of previously unknown multimedia options available to them. Time formerly spent reading a book or magazine can now be spent playing a computer game, surfing the net, or interacting with friends in an online chat room. What impact have these factors had upon teens' public library use and leisure reading habits?

PURPOSE

This chapter reports on the first phase of a two-part research study into the role of recreational or pleasure reading in the lives of Nova Scotia teenagers. Phase one, a quantitative survey, analyzes whether there is a significant relationship between age, gender, and level of parental education and teenagers' reading, book purchasing, and library usage patterns in the province of Nova Scotia. Findings are discussed in the context of similar studies by a range of Canadian and international researchers from the 1970s to the present day. The specific survey described in this chapter explores a wide range of issues of relevance to an understanding of the information-seeking behavior of teens in their selection of pleasure reading materials and provides essential background context for the second phase of this study, which will provide a detailed and critical exploration of teen information-seeking behavior for a wide range of pleasure reading materials. Phase two, currently under way, uses qualitative methodology (focus groups and interviews) to illuminate and enrich the findings from the preliminary survey research.

LITERATURE REVIEW

In the late 1970s and early 1980s, in the early years of the phenomenon known as young adult literature, several researchers (Amey 1981; Burdenuk 1979; Landy 1977; Lewis 1976) undertook studies of Canadian young adult reading habits. These studies reached several important conclusions:

- Girls read more than boys
- Television, sports, movies, and radio are all more popular than reading
- TV or movie tie-ins can dramatically increase a book's popularity
- Friends are very influential in determining teens' reading choices
- Librarians, both school and public, exert very little influence on teens' reading choices

However, despite teens' perception that they were little influenced by librarians in their reading choices, most teens during this period used both the school and the public library as their primary sources of leisure reading material and did not commonly purchase their own books.

The General Social Survey (GSS) conducted by Statistics Canada is a useful tool for tracking Canadians' leisure time use and participation in cultural activities such as reading and visiting the public library. Cycle 12 of this survey, conducted in 1998, gathered data from all individuals aged fifteen and over living in a private household in one of the ten provinces. This survey confirms that Canadian teens use the public library significantly more than their adult counterparts. This survey also notes that teens tend to read slightly more books and magazines than adults, though both adults and teens appear to be reading less than they were in 1992, when the GSS on Time Use (Cycle 7) was previously conducted.

A more recent study of the reading, media, and public library use by 3,486 children in grades four to six in six Canadian cities (Halifax, Hamilton, Montreal, Regina, Toronto, and Vancouver) was conducted by a research team led by Fasick, Gagnon, Howarth, and Setterington. Follow-up focus groups were conducted with children in each of the six cities. The objectives of this national study were to discover children's attitudes to the public library and to reading and to make recommendations on policies, collections, services, and programs to help libraries respond to the needs of children aged ten to twelve. The results of this study were published in 2005 under the title "Opening Doors to Children."

Another key study, "Reading and Buying Books for Pleasure" (Createc 2005), was conducted by the department of Canadian Heritage in January 2005. This study was the first major national survey of Canadian reading and book-purchasing habits since the 1991 survey "Reading in Canada." In this national telephone survey, 1,963 Canadians aged sixteen and over were asked about their reading behaviors and preferences, their reading skills, their attitudes toward reading, their use of the public library, and their book-buying habits. In contrast to the 2004 National Endowment for the Arts (NEA) poll of Americans and their reading habits ("Reading at Risk: A Survey of Literary Reading in America") discussed below, this survey concluded that reading for pleasure in Canada is a "solidly established and widespread habit with little or no change over the last 15 years." Eighty-seven percent of Canadians read at least occasionally (in contrast to only 47.6 percent of Americans) and 54 percent of Canadians read every day. Only 13 percent of Canadians self-identify as nonreaders, the same percentage as in 1991, in contrast to the 43 percent of Americans who self-identify as nonreaders according to the NEA poll. Canadians appear to be distinctly different from their American counterparts, over half of whom read an average of less than one book per year and whose reading rate has substantially decreased over the past twenty years, particularly among those in the eighteen-to-twenty-four-year-old age group. The only significant decline in reading was found to be in the number of books read per year: in 1991, Canadians reported reading an average of twenty-four books per year and this number has fallen to seventeen books per year in this latest survey. The specific reasons for this decline are not known, but the report writers speculate that increased time reading on the Internet may be a contributing factor.

Although "Reading and Buying Books for Pleasure" presents a generally positive view of the leisure reading habits of adult Canadians, the report does not examine the reading habits of children or younger teens and includes a call for further research on these groups: "More in-depth research on very young Canadians [i.e., those aged less than sixteen] would certainly add to and enhance our current knowledge about the adult population" (Createc 2005, 2).

Some studies from outside Canada provide further relevant background for this research. A 1996 survey of American attitudes toward libraries entitled "Buildings, Books and Bytes: Libraries and Communities in the Digital Age," revealed that eighteen-to-twenty-four-year-olds (the youngest age group to be surveyed) also had the most negative attitudes toward libraries and strongly expressed the opinion that libraries would have a diminished role in a digital future. These findings are echoed by the previously cited 2004 poll conducted by the NEA, which tracked a steady decline in book reading by adult Americans over the past twenty years, with the steepest decline among the youngest age group surveyed, those eighteen to twenty-four years old. The number of Americans who read literature has declined from 56.9 percent in 1982 to 47.6 percent in 2002, leading the investigators to conclude that the decline in reading correlates with increased use of the Internet, DVDs, videogames, and portable digital devices: "Literature now competes with an enormous array of electronic media. While no single activity is responsible for the decline in reading, the cumulative presence and availability of these alternatives have increasingly drawn Americans away from reading."

A large-scale survey of the leisure reading habits of 9,000 ten-to-fourteen-year-olds in the United Kingdom (Hall & Coles 1999) revealed a preference for buying reading material rather than for borrowing it from the library and further supported the positive influence of friends and peers on reading choices. In Australia, Nieuwenhuizen conducted a 2001 study of the reading habits of ten-to-eighteen-year-olds. The goals of this study were to understand teens' attitudes to reading, to assess teens' current reading behavior in relation to other leisure activities, and to identify the main barriers and influences to reading. Quantitative data were obtained through a phone survey of 801 ten-to-eighteen-year-olds and 626 adults aged eighteen-plus; qualitative data was generated through a series of interviews and focus group discussions with young people from English-speaking and non-English-speaking backgrounds, parents of young people, journalists, booksellers, and school and public librarians.

FINDINGS OF PREVIOUS STUDIES

Most previous studies of reading habits have found that reading increases until age ten to twelve and then begins to decline at age thirteen to fourteen. The Canadian "Opening Doors" study reports that respondents in grade four are significantly more enthusiastic about reading than respondents in grade seven. Nieuwenhuizen's 2001 study reports parallel findings: "Enjoyment of reading for pleasure drops dramatically in teenagers, with 45 percent of primary students saying they really like reading for pleasure, down to 24 percent amongst secondary school students. None of the other pleasure activities register such a decrease in enjoyment post-puberty. Clearly, something happens to the reading experience of young people to make it seem a lot less enjoyable when they reach secondary school than it was in primary school" (19).

In all the studies of reading habits cited here, gender is found to be a significant factor in the reading habits of children and teens: from age six onward, girls read more frequently than boys, they read a greater quantity than boys, and fewer girls are nonreaders. A national survey by the British Office for Standards in Education (OFSTED) found that boys tend to have a more negative view of reading and of libraries than girls (OFSTED 1996, 1998). This finding was replicated by Nieuwenhuizen's 2001 study of Australian teens, in which she found that girls are more likely to see reading as easy, fun, and something their friends do than are boys; in contrast, boys are more likely to see reading as boring and nerdy (20). Similarly, the Canadian "Opening Doors" study finds that girls read more often and visit the public library more frequently than do boys.

Furthermore, in England, the United States, Australia, and Canada, girls outperform boys in standardized tests of reading literacy. In the Atlantic Provinces of Canada, more girls are graduating, male students are taking longer to move through high schools, grade-eight female students are "overwhelmingly more positive than males about all aspects of their school life . . . and more female than male graduates are enrolling in university" (Atlantic Province Education Foundation 1996, 7). The Canadian Council of Ministers of Education report on reading achievement of thirteen- and sixteen-year-olds in Canada noted that girls enjoy reading more than boys and are more confident readers than boys at age thirteen; after age thirteen, they continue to develop that confidence, becoming even more sure of their reading abilities by age sixteen. In contrast, boys appear arrested in attitude and behavior from age thirteen to sixteen: neither their reading skills nor their reading confidence appears to change during this period and in many boys their attitude toward reading actually deteriorates. Thus, in Canada, the gender gap in reading skills widens during the critical age from thirteen to sixteen.

Previous studies confirm that boys and girls have different reading preferences: girls tend to prefer reading fiction while many boys prefer information books. When they read fiction, boys prefer mysteries, humor, fantasy, and adventure stories. Some researchers have pointed out a dramatic contrast between school reading and recreational (or "life") reading: in his study of boys in grades six to twelve, Wilhelm found that "school reading was assigned, unconnected to their interests, too long and hard; life reading was freely chosen, built on their interests, and was usually short texts they felt competent to read" (quoted in Cox & Collins 2003). In SmartGirl.com's Web-based reading survey (1999), half of the 1,246 boys aged eleven to eighteen who responded said that they read video magazines in contrast to only 7 percent of the girls; 64 percent of boys indicated that they read sports magazines, and 50 percent indicated that they read computer and music magazines. Hobby-related magazines are clearly an important reading resource for male teen readers. The 2002 OECD (Bussiere et al. 2001) reading literacy report found that magazines are the number one reading choice for both genders, with comics ranked second by boys.

Relatively few studies of reading habits have examined factors of multiculturalism or ethnicity in influencing reading habits. Those studies that have examined these factors have conflicting findings: some studies have identified a positive relationship between membership in an ethnic community and amount of reading while other researchers have found the opposite relationship. In their analysis of the reading motivation of urban fifth and sixth graders in the United States, Baker and Wigfield (1999) found that African American students reported more positive reading motivation and higher levels of reading than their white counterparts. These findings are consistent with those of Stevenson et al. (1990), who found that African American fifth graders liked reading more and had more positive views of their own reading ability than did white fifth graders. In a national poll of twelve-to-eighteen-year-olds conducted in 2001 by Peter D. Hart Research Associates for the National Education Association in the United States, "The Reading Habits of Adolescents Survey," teens rated reading as the most important skill for future success. Interestingly, minority teens reported the most prolific reading habits. When asked to rate their enjoyment of

reading on a five-point Likert scale, 47 percent of white teens, 51 percent of black teens, and 56 percent of Hispanic teens chose a score of
4–5. Half of all black teens, 40 percent of all Hispanic teens, and 37
percent of white teens reported reading fifteen or more books in the past
year and 52 percent of black teens, 47 percent of Hispanic teens and 43
percent of white teens said that their parents actively encouraged them
to read.

In contrast, the recent national survey of adult Canadians, "Reading
and Buying Books for Pleasure," found a negative correlation between
visible minority membership and recreational reading: "Respondents
who stated that they are part of a visible minority are substantially less
likely to read regularly (46 percent) or to read mainly literary materials
(32 percent) than other respondents (56 percent and 46 percent, respectively)" (Createc 2005, 58). This study also found that Francophones
have lower reader rates than Anglophones: the reading rates for Francophones are similar to those with a foreign first language. Fifty-nine percent of Anglophones reported reading regularly in contrast to 45
percent of Francophones and 44 percent of those whose first language
is neither French nor English. Francophones reported reading 13.9
books per year in contrast with the 17.6 books reported by Anglophones. When provincial reading rates are compared, the largely fran-
cophone province of Quebec has the lowest rate in the country and the
lowest rate of literary readers. The "Opening Doors" study also found
some significant differences between respondents in the French-speak-
ing city of Montreal and in the other five cities surveyed; in every city
but Montreal, most children surveyed reported that reading was one of
their favorite leisure activities. Children in Montreal were markedly less
enthusiastic about leisure reading.

Only a few studies have examined the impact of rural and urban locations on reading habits. The recent national survey of "Reading and
Buying Books for Pleasure" found no correlation between reading and
rural/urban setting. However, a 2002 study, "Understanding the Rural-
Urban Reading Gap" (Cartwright & Allen 2002), conducted for Statistics Canada, found that rural children and teens read significantly less
than their urban counterparts, regardless of their parents' level of educational achievement.

THE NOVA SCOTIA STUDY

Context

Nova Scotia, located on the Atlantic coast of Canada, is one of the Atlantic or Maritime Provinces. It is almost an island, attached to the mainland of Canada by a narrow strip of land, and the Nova Scotian economy has traditionally relied upon resource-based industries such as mining and fishing, currently in global decline. As a result, the provincial economy is increasingly dependent upon the retail sector, manufacturing, and tourism. The average provincial family income is approximately twelve thousand dollars less than the national average. The population of the province hovers at just under a million (908,007 according to the 2001 census); the capital city of Halifax, with a population of 360,000, is the sole major urban center.[1]

True to its name ("New Scotland"), most Nova Scotians claim English or Scottish descent, and English is the first language of 96 percent of the province's residents, in contrast to 59 percent of the Canadian population as a whole. Only 4 percent of the provincial population claim visible minority status, in contrast to 13 percent of the overall Canadian population, and the largest single visible minority group are African Nova Scotians, whose ancestors settled in the province in the mid-eighteenth century. Most immigrants to the province are from the United Kingdom or the United States, although there is a small population of Lebanese, South Asian, and Chinese immigrants, most of whom live in the metro Halifax region. Overall, Nova Scotia has a very small immigrant population: only 5 percent of the province's residents are immigrants in contrast to 18 percent of the overall Canadian population. Two percent of Nova Scotians claim aboriginal identity. Thus, in summary, with the exception of the city of Halifax, Nova Scotia is a largely rural region, with a relatively homogenous, English-speaking population. It is far less multicultural than other regions of Canada and the multicultural population of the province is largely centered in Halifax.

Procedures

This study, funded by a grant from the Research Development Fund, Faculty of Graduate Studies, Dalhousie University, Halifax, Nova Scotia, ran from November 2002 to June 2003, and consisted of a mail-out survey to 500 teenagers from throughout the province of Nova Scotia. The objective of the survey was to obtain a provincial overview of current reading habits and preferences from the perspective of teenagers themselves. Using the Nova Scotia Department of Education's projected enrolments by school board district for 2002–2003, a proportional sample of students from each school board was selected. Equal numbers of male and female and of junior high (grade eight) and high school (grade eleven) students were surveyed, and the sample was stratified to ensure representation from regions and urban and rural settings.[2] Anonymity and confidentiality of respondents was assured. Names of individual students, schools, or school districts were not identified on the survey instrument itself.

Overall, 159 usable surveys were returned, for a response rate of 32 percent. Gender and grade distribution were quite evenly balanced: 49 percent of respondents were male and 52 percent were female; 56 percent were in grade eight and 44 percent were in grade eleven. Unfortunately, the rural/urban distribution was quite unbalanced: only 21 percent of respondents were from the urban Halifax area, making it difficult to draw any firm conclusions about rural/urban differences in reading habits and public library use patterns, though some tentative trends can be very cautiously identified. Further study is definitely needed to examine rural/urban patterns in more detail before any firm conclusions can be drawn.

It is important to note that the current study is primarily exploratory, asking a wide range of questions to a limited number of respondents in a fairly restricted geographic area. The objectives of the current study are to identify general trends in teen reading habits and public library use, and to point the way to further areas of more specific research. A second phase of this study is currently under way which will use qualitative methodology (focus groups and interviews) to investigate the significance of reading for pleasure in the lives of teens as well as specific information-seeking behavior for pleasure reading materials.

Results

1. Book Reading

Teens in Nova Scotia *are* reading books. In fact, this survey suggests that Nova Scotia teens read more than the amount reported for teens nationally in the 1998 General Social Survey: 84 percent of respondents indicated that they read at least a book a year for pleasure, in contrast with the 71.4 percent of all Canadian teens reported by the national survey (see figure 5.1).

Reading appears to decline with age. Grade eight students are reading more than their grade eleven counterparts. This finding is quite predictable, as grade eleven students are often juggling school and part-time jobs and have less leisure time for reading (see figure 5.2).

Female students read more than male students and the reading gap between the genders appears to be widening: 59 percent of girls but only 23.7 percent of boys consider themselves to be relatively avid readers, reading at least a book a month for pleasure. In contrast, 26 percent of boys consider themselves to be nonreaders in comparison with only 6 percent of girls (see figure 5.3).

Rural teens are more likely to be nonreaders than their urban counterparts. Nine percent of all urban respondents indicated that they are nonreaders in contrast with 18 percent of all rural respondents. Level of parental education appears to have little or no influence on the amount of books read.

2. *Preferred Fiction Genres*

In the survey, teens were asked to rank their frequency of reading of 14 fiction genres. The same genre categories were used as were

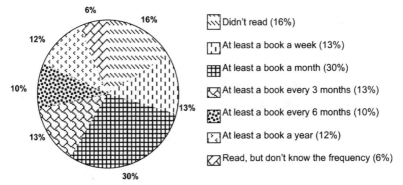

Figure 5.1.   Number of Books Read

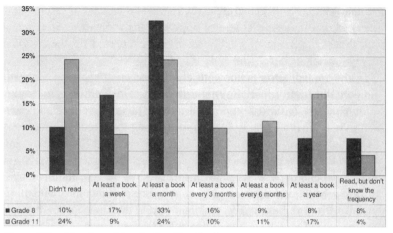

	Didn't read	At least a book a week	At least a book a month	At least a book every 3 months	At least a book every 6 months	At least a book a year	Read, but don't know the frequency
■ Grade 8	10%	17%	33%	16%	9%	8%	8%
▣ Grade 11	24%	9%	24%	10%	11%	17%	4%

Figure 5.2. Number of Books Read by Grade

employed by Burdenuk in his 1979 survey, to permit comparison of results. In the current survey as in Burdenuk's study, mysteries were the most popular fiction genre among all teens surveyed and overall genre preferences seem remarkably unchanged in the past twenty-five years (see figure 5.4).

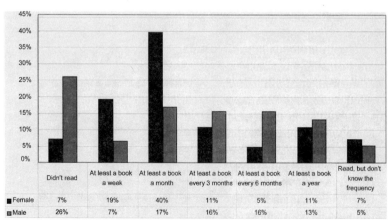

	Didn't read	At least a book a week	At least a book a month	At least a book every 3 months	At least a book every 6 months	At least a book a year	Read, but don't know the frequency
■ Female	7%	19%	40%	11%	5%	11%	7%
▣ Male	26%	7%	17%	16%	16%	13%	5%

Figure 5.3. Number of Books Read by Gender

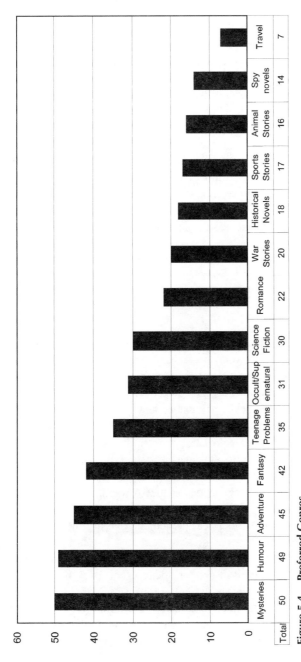

	Mysteries	Humour	Adventure	Fantasy	Teenage Problems	Occult/Supernatural	Science Fiction	Romance	War Stories	Historical Novels	Sports Stories	Animal Stories	Spy novels	Travel
Total	50	49	45	42	35	31	30	22	20	18	17	16	14	7

Figure 5.4. Preferred Genres

Grade eight students rated humor as their preferred fiction genre, but generally showed strong preferences for humor, mysteries, adventure stories, and fantasy. Grade eleven students showed less strongly polarized genre preferences (see figure 5.5).

Interesting gender differences were also apparent in fiction genre preferences: all teens surveyed appear to favor mysteries, humor, and fantasy, but boys appeared to like adventure stories much more than girls (37 percent to 20 percent) and girls preferred problem novels very much more than did boys (34 percent to 9 percent). Teenage male genre preferences remain almost identical to those identified by Burdenuk in 1979, but female preferences show a slight decline in the popularity of romance (rated the second most popular fiction genre by female respondents in 1979, but tied for fifth place in the current study; see figure. 5.6).

Parental education and location appear to have no significant impact on fiction genre preferences.

3. Newspaper Reading

This study suggests that newspaper reading is declining among teens in Nova Scotia. Twenty years ago, Amey (1981) found that 96 percent of the urban Ontario tenth-grade students responding to his survey considered themselves regular newspaper readers. The 1998 GSS tracks a modest decline of 11 percent in newspaper readership since 1992 for both the overall Canadian population and for teens. According to the 1998 GSS, 62 percent of the general Canadian population and 51 percent of teens read the newspaper at least three times per week.

In the current survey, however, only 29 percent of respondents consider themselves regular newspaper readers, reading the newspaper as a leisure activity at least three times per week or more in either print or online format. An identical percentage classify themselves as nonreaders of the newspaper, indicating that they had not read a newspaper as a leisure activity in the past twelve months. Newspaper reading habits show no difference in gender, location, or level of parental education, although grade eleven students reported reading the newspaper more often than did grade eight students (see figure 5.7).

These results are consistent with observations made by Canadian historian Robert Wright about young readers and newspapers. In his book

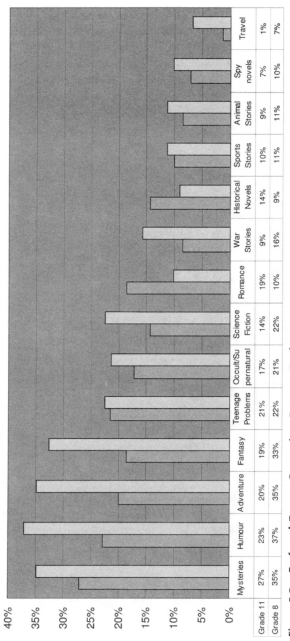

	Mysteries	Humour	Adventure	Fantasy	Teenage Problems	Occult/Supernatural	Science Fiction	Romance	War Stories	Historical Novels	Sports Stories	Animal Stories	Spy novels	Travel
Grade 11	27%	23%	20%	19%	21%	17%	14%	19%	9%	14%	10%	9%	7%	1%
Grade 8	35%	37%	35%	33%	22%	21%	22%	10%	16%	9%	11%	11%	10%	7%

Figure 5.5. Preferred Genres, Comparison Between Grades

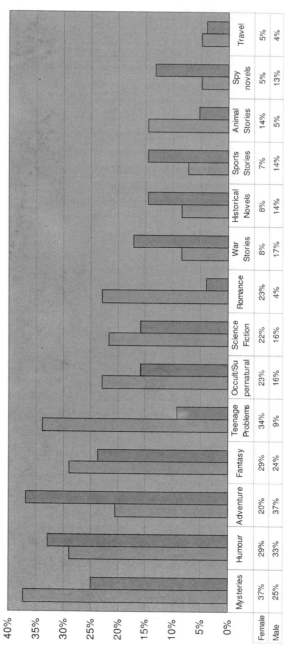

	Mysteries	Humour	Adventure	Fantasy	Teenage Problems	Occult/Supernatural	Science Fiction	Romance	War Stories	Historical Novels	Sports Stories	Animal Stories	Spy novels	Travel
Female	37%	29%	20%	29%	34%	23%	22%	23%	8%	8%	7%	14%	5%	5%
Male	25%	33%	37%	24%	9%	16%	16%	4%	17%	14%	14%	5%	13%	4%

Figure 5.6. Preferred Genres, Comparison Between Genders

Hip and Trivial: Youth Culture, Book Publishing, and the Greying of Canadian Nationalism (2001), he notes that the current "Internet generation" has never developed the newspaper habit and newspaper publishers around the world, seriously concerned about declining subscription rates and loss of readership, are courting teens with various youth-oriented innovations.

4. Magazine Reading

This survey suggests that magazines are an important source of leisure reading for teens. Thirty-nine percent of respondents indicated that they read magazines for pleasure on a weekly basis, while a further 30 percent do so monthly. Therefore, 69 percent of Nova Scotia teens read magazines regularly for pleasure. Only 13 percent classify themselves as nonreaders of magazines. Neither age, gender, location, or parental education appears to have an impact on magazine reading habits; magazine reading, unlike the reading of books, does not appear to decline with age or to be a primarily female habit (see figure 5.8).

5. Teens and Public Libraries

The findings in this survey indicate that teens in Nova Scotia are relatively frequent users of the public library. Overall, 61 percent of Nova Scotia teens surveyed reported that they had visited the public library during the past twelve months. Although these findings indicate a

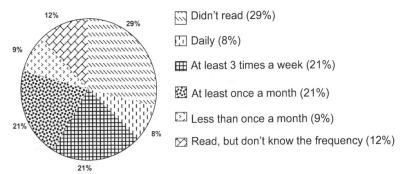

Figure 5.7. Number of Newspapers Read

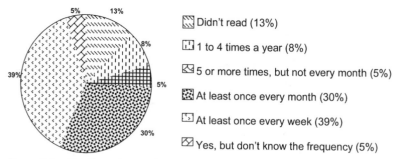

Figure 5.8. **Number of Magazines Read**

decline in teen library use in the years since Amey (1981) conducted his study of urban Ontario grade 10 students and found that 85 percent of respondents visited the public library at least once a year, ten years after Amey's study, the 1992 GSS found that only 59 percent of teens (and 32 percent of the overall Canadian population) used the public library annually. These statistics dropped to 45 percent for teens and 28 percent for the overall Canadian population in the 1998 GSS. Clearly, teens in Nova Scotia appear to be using the public library somewhat more than the national average, and their amount of library use does not appear to be influenced by location or level of parental education. This finding is also in contrast to the national survey, "Reading and Buying Books for Pleasure" (Createc 2005), which found that 56 percent of Canadians aged sixteen-plus have a public library card and 40 percent have borrowed a book in the past year. However, this national study found that public library use in Canada follows a geographic continuum and declines from west to east. Forty-nine percent of those surveyed in the western province of British Columbia had borrowed a book in the past year in comparison to only 30 percent of those surveyed in the Atlantic Provinces (see figure 5.9).

Respondents indicated they used the public library primarily to do research, to use the computers or to borrow books. Rural teens are more likely to visit the library to use computers. This finding is in contrast with the 1998 GSS, which found that teens primarily used the library to borrow books and much less often visited the library for Internet access. It is likely that the lack of home computers and/or the lack of

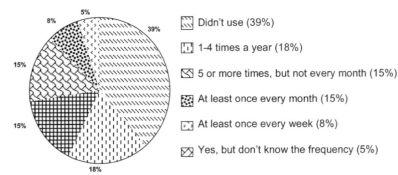

Didn't use (39%)

1-4 times a year (18%)

5 or more times, but not every month (15%)

At least once every month (15%)

At least once every week (8%)

Yes, but don't know the frequency (5%)

Figure 5.9.   Amount of Public Library Use

quality Internet connections make public library computers an important resource for Nova Scotia teens.[3]

Age has only a slight impact on amount of library use: grade eight students reported visiting the public library slightly more often than grade eleven students. Gender has the most significant impact on library use: 67 percent of girls but only 54 percent of boys surveyed considered themselves users of the public library (see figure 5.10).

Library programming for teens in Nova Scotia appears to be either unsuccessful or nonexistent. Only two respondents indicated that they

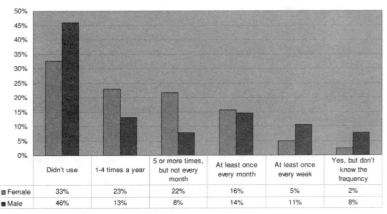

	Didn't use	1-4 times a year	5 or more times, but not every month	At least once every month	At least once every week	Yes, but don't know the frequency
Female	33%	23%	22%	16%	5%	2%
Male	46%	13%	8%	14%	11%	8%

Figure 5.10.   Amount of Public Library Use by Gender

had visited the public library to attend a program during the previous twelve months.

6. Where Teens Obtain Their Leisure Reading Material

When asked where they usually obtain the books they read for leisure, respondents showed a strong preference for buying books rather than for borrowing them from the library. Twenty-two percent of respondents stated that they buy new books themselves while a further 31 percent indicated that they prefer to read books that are already in their home book collection. Only 14 percent usually borrow their leisure reading material from the public library and only 13 percent usually borrow books from the school library (see figure 5.11).

Eleventh-grade students, with a larger discretionary income, are more likely to purchase books themselves than are eighth-grade students. However, this survey revealed no gender differences in book purchasing patterns.

Parental education does appear to influence where teens obtain their leisure reading. The following trends are suggested by this survey:

- Respondents with the most highly educated parents (those with an undergraduate or graduate university degree) are the most likely to

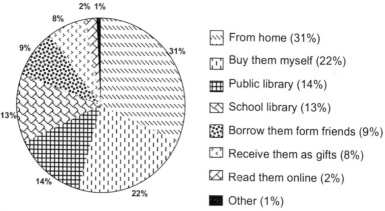

Figure 5.11. Where Teens Obtain Books for Leisure Reading

buy books for themselves. This group is also the least likely to borrow leisure reading material from the school library.

- Respondents with moderately well-educated parents (those with some college or university training, but not necessarily a degree) are the most likely to borrow leisure reading material from the public library.

7. Where Teens Purchase Their Leisure Reading Material

When asked where they usually purchased their leisure reading materials, the 100 respondents who had purchased books in the previous twelve months indicated a strong preference for chain bookstores. Age or level of parental education does not have an impact on this finding. Rural respondents were more likely to shop at independent bookstores, but some respondents commented that while there is no chain bookstore in their community, they try to visit a major chain bookstore whenever they can get a ride to the city. Interestingly, few respondents make use of online bookstores, probably because they do not yet have credit cards necessary for online purchases (see figure 5.12).

8. Factors Influencing Leisure Reading Choices

Respondents indicated that the major factor influencing their decision to read a book is their personal interest in the subject. The second most

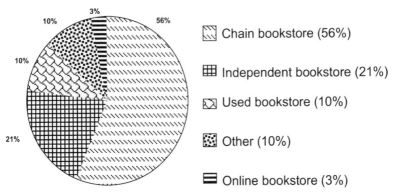

Figure 5.12. Where Teens Buy Books for Leisure Reading

important factor is hearing a personal recommendation from a friend or peer. In contrast to findings from the 1970s, movie or television tie-ins and cover art seem to exert relatively minor influence. Only very few respondents (3 percent) indicated that book talks by teachers or librarians influence their reading choices. Location and level of parental education had no impact on these findings (see figure 5.13).

9. Personal Influences on Leisure Reading Choices

When asked "Who influences you in your choice of books?" 24 percent respondents chose "no one," indicating that they perceive themselves to be highly independent in their choice of leisure reading material. The second most popular choice overall was "friends," at 22 percent. Public and school librarians were rated as very insignificant influences.[4] Neither location or level of parental education had an impact on this finding (see figure 5.14).

Some significant differences appear when results are analyzed by grade. Eighth graders rate friends as the most important influence, whereas eleventh graders are more likely to state that no one influences them in their leisure reading choices. Teachers have almost equal influence on students from both grades. Interestingly and somewhat surpris-

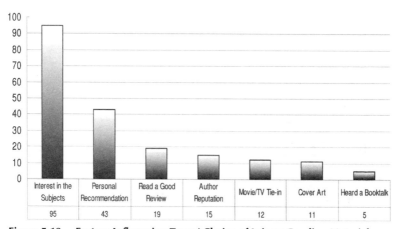

Figure 5.13. Factors Influencing Teens' Choice of Leisure Reading Materials

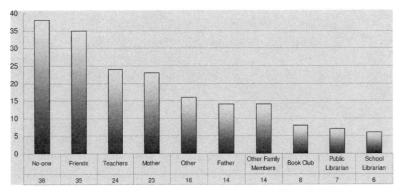

Figure 5.14. Personal Influences on Teens' Leisure Reading Choices

ingly, 9 percent of grade eleven students state that school librarians had an important influence on their reading choices in contrast with 0 percent of grade eight students. This finding could reflect the fact that in Nova Scotia, many school libraries, particularly at the elementary and junior high school levels, are not staffed by professional teacher librarians (Doiron 2003). (See figure 5.15.)

Discussion

1. Teens in Nova Scotia appear to be reading more books than the amount reported for teens nationally in the 1998 GSS. Eighty-four percent of Nova Scotia teens, in contrast with 71.4 percent of teens nationally, read at least a book a year for pleasure. Nova Scotia teens also appear to be avid magazine readers, although newspaper reading is declining.
2. The book reading gap between the genders appears to be widening and teenage girls in Nova Scotia read significantly more fiction books than their male counterparts. Boys are much more likely to be nonreaders of fiction books than girls. This gender gap is not apparent for newspapers or magazines.
3. Teens in Nova Scotia use public libraries for research, for computer access, and to borrow books. They do not visit the public library to attend programs.

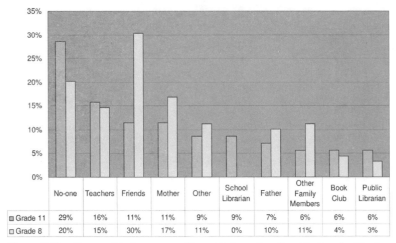

	No-one	Teachers	Friends	Mother	Other	School Librarian	Father	Other Family Members	Book Club	Public Librarian
▣ Grade 11	29%	16%	11%	11%	9%	9%	7%	6%	6%	6%
▢ Grade 8	20%	15%	30%	17%	11%	0%	10%	11%	4%	3%

Figure 5.15. Personal Influences on Teens' Leisure Reading Choices by Grade

4. Chain bookstores are rapidly gaining popularity with teens and are the preferred source of pleasure reading material.
5. Teens in Nova Scotia perceive themselves to be quite independent in their reading choices, although friends and peers are perceived to be influential, especially by younger teens
6. Level of parental education does not seem to influence teens in the amount they read or in their genre preferences. Level of parental education does appear to influence teens' preferred sources of leisure reading materials.
7. Teens do not perceive that librarians influence their reading choices.

It is important to note that the current study is primarily exploratory, asking a wide range of questions to a limited number of respondents in a fairly restricted geographic area. The objectives of the current study were to identify general trends in teen reading habits and public library use, and to point the way to further areas of more specific research. In particular, the current study focused primarily upon teens' reading of fiction books; future studies should be undertaken to address teens' nonfiction recreational reading interests as well as their interest in magazines, graphic novels, and other formats (such as zines), topics not considered by the current study.

While some of the findings of this study are encouraging, other results should give public librarians food for thought. Many of the findings of this study echo findings from the 1970s and early 1980s, cited earlier. However, there are some important distinctions. Even though teens in the 1970s stated that they did not perceive librarians to influence their reading choices, teens in this period relied almost exclusively upon libraries, both school and public, for their leisure reading materials. Teens did not typically report purchasing books to read for pleasure. In contrast, the twenty-first-century teens who participated in this survey reported a strong preference for purchasing books as opposed to borrowing them from the library, making their perception of librarian influence somewhat more ominous. Although teens may not recognize the influence of librarians on their reading choices, any teen who uses the public library for leisure reading material is, of course, being influenced indirectly by book displays, book lists, and the very collection itself—all of which reflect the professional activity and selection decisions made by librarians. However, this study suggests that teens increasingly view the public library as a place to complete homework assignments and to access the Internet, but not necessarily as a source of appealing leisure reading materials, preferring to purchase their pleasure reading at chain bookstores. The preference for chain bookstores transcends gender, age, location, and parental education.

How can public libraries respond to this preference? Of particular relevance are the findings of Cook, Parker, and Pettijohn's 2005 survey of 616 grade six, seven, and eight students in Springfield, Missouri, which noted that the overall image of the public library declined steadily with age of respondent, and stressed the importance of responding to the needs of young teens in order to encourage them to maintain the library habit throughout their teen years. Many teens in this survey had a positive attitude to the public library, although 40 percent rarely visited the library because they simply did not think about it. Very few teens (only 8.6 percent) had ever attended a teen activity or program at the library, but almost 35 percent reported that they would attend if they knew about upcoming events. This study noted that, from the library's perspective, "one surmountable challenge entails placing libraries in the teen market's . . . top-of-mind awareness" (161). This awareness could be achieved by reaching young teens electronically, via e-mail and compelling library websites, as well as by using teen opinion leaders to provide peer group influence. Promoting library programs to parents was also recommended, since young teens are still "very affected by family influence" (161).

The "Opening Doors" study (2005) also found that lack of promotion was a major problem: preteen respondents were frequently unaware of library services, collections and programs. This study advocated making the library website more engaging and youth-friendly and using the website to promote programs and services. School/library collaboration could also be enhanced to publicize these features. This study noted that their preteen respondents make daily use of e-mail and recommended using e-mail to announce upcoming library programs and events. The "Opening Doors" study established that their respondents appreciate reader's advisory and recommended providing booklists in both print format and on the library website, and further suggested fostering reading through book displays, book clubs, and book reviews posted on the library website. It recommends that libraries should solicit preteens' opinions about library services and collections through focus groups, an advisory board, or ideas team and website surveys/polls.

Book buying, as opposed to book borrowing, appears to be the preference in Nova Scotia as elsewhere. In the United States, Bhatia (2001) reports that, according to surveys conducted in 2001, consumers under that age of twenty-five are buying books at three times the overall market and bookstores report a 20 to 75 percent jump in young buyers over the past three years. One-quarter of survey respondents under the age of twenty-five say that reading is their favorite pastime, up 10 percent from the previous year. This growth in youthful consumers has had a huge impact on book publishing, making books more glamorous and celebrity-centered. A *Publishers Weekly*/Book Expo America poll of 100 teens aged twelve to seventeen revealed that, on average, teens spent 10 percent of their income on books. This poll revealed that teens surveyed had a strong preference for buying at chain stores: 76 percent of teens surveyed bought books at chain stores in contrast to 51 percent of adults. Maughan (2002), also writing in *Publishers Weekly*, reports on the huge growth of the tween book market in the United States. Tweens, aged ten to twelve, make up a mere 8 percent of the U.S. population but these 30 million tweens make direct purchases of $10 billion annually. Publishing for the tween market is very successful, with tweens spending an average of nine dollars per week on reading material (books, magazines, comic books).

According to Hill Strategies' detailed report on book buying in Canada, based on Statistics Canada's 2001 Survey of Household Spending as well as personal interviews with almost 17,000 Canadian households, in 2001, Canadians spent $1.1 billion on books, an average of $95 for each of the 11.9 million households. Overall book spending in Canada increased by 23 percent from 1997 to 2001. In contrast to the previously cited reports from the United States, this study found that those under 25 have the smallest overall share of book spending, 2 percent, for total book expenditures of $18 million per year. Canadians aged forty-five to fifty-four, in contrast, are the heaviest book buyers at 32 percent, with total book expenditures of $359 million. However, those in the youngest and oldest age groups spend the most on books as a percentage of total income. There are also some interesting regional differences in book purchasing patterns: spending on books is highest in the Prairies, with 53 percent of households reporting book purchases, in BC (52 percent) and in Ontario (50 percent). In contrast, residents of Quebec and the Atlantic provinces are the least likely to buy books, with 41 percent and 45 percent of households, respectively, reporting some spending on books. The Atlantic Provinces, with $64 million in annual book purchases, represent the smallest share of the regional Canadian book market at 6 percent.

Should the apparent trend toward book buying be a concern for public libraries? Several researchers have found an overall symbiosis between book borrowing and book buying: those who borrow the most also buy the most. Heavy book borrowers/buyers are also more likely to spend more time reading, to have more books at home and to have enjoyed reading as children. England (1994) reports: "Heavy buyers tend even more to be women, and to be rather younger. . . . Library use is something people grow into after they have developed their purchasing habits. If this is true, then being a heavy buyer but a non-library user is part of a progression of interest in books" (30). The 2000 survey "Reading the Situation" also found that individuals who borrow from the public library are more likely to buy books than those who do not;

thus partnerships between libraries and bookstores can potentially increase markets for both buying and borrowing.

Also of concern is the apparent gender gap in both reading and library use. Several previous researchers have examined this issue and have posited possible explanations. Hall and Coles (1997) and Millard (1997) note that the school curriculum privileges narrative fiction, which is the preferred genre for girls whereas boys prefer to read other types of materials such as comics and hobby magazines, often seen as unsuitable for school reading. A similar problem arises in the public and school library, as American youth services specialist Jones et al. (2003) point out: "Most YA sections in public libraries are filled with fiction; there is very little recreational non-fiction. If there is . . . it is more likely to be self-help, health-related, about teen issues, or pop-star biographies. There might be magazines, but the chances are they are aimed more at girls than boys. Comic books are more than likely not to be there, and graphic novels, if collected, are not featured. There probably isn't a newspaper lying around" (10).

In short, many boys who self-identify as nonreaders or reluctant readers may, in practice, be readers, but they read materials such as magazines, comics, or websites, which they have been taught not to consider as actual reading. Parents similarly often privilege print-based reading, particularly novels, rather than electronic forms and may even limit their sons' access to competing leisure pursuits such as computers and magazines.

This preliminary survey clearly demonstrates the need for a larger-scale study of teens, their reading habits, their relationship with libraries, and their information-seeking behavior for pleasure reading materials. Further research is definitely needed to determine the specific needs and interests of teens, especially if public libraries are committed to serving the educational, informational, and recreational needs of teen patrons and to retaining their patronage after they leave high school and become members of the community's adult population. What is the significance of pleasure reading in the lives of twenty-first-century teens? How do they select their pleasure reading materials? How can the public library best serve teens' pleasure reading needs? These are all fascinating questions, which will be investigated in the second phase of this ongoing research study.

NOTES

1. All statistics are taken from the 2001 Census Profile of Nova Scotia. Accessed 15 September 2005 at http://www.bcstats.gov.bc.ca.

2. According to the Nova Scotia Department of Education Statistical Summary 2002–2003, 12,164 students were enrolled in grade eight in Nova Scotia and a further 12,413 were enrolled in grade eleven. Thus approximately 2 percent of Nova Scotia students in grade eight and eleven received the survey.

3. Looker and Thiessen's 2003 analysis of access to information technology in Canadian schools found that while equal proportions of rural and urban Canadian youth use computers, rural households are less likely to have a home computer. As a result, rural youth report more computer use in libraries and at school than do their urban counterparts. Furthermore, Looker and Thiessen noted significant discrepancies in access to quality Internet connections in rural areas. These findings are echoed by Rideout's examination of digital inequalities in Eastern Canada (2003).

4. Overall, this finding is consistent with Burdenuk's 1979 study. Clearly, librarians in Nova Scotia have not been successful in raising their profile or increasing their influence with teens in the twenty-five years since Burdenuk's survey of Ontario teens.

REFERENCES

Amey, Larry. 1981. Information-seeking activities of adolescents of different socioeconomic classes in a Canadian urban centre. PhD dissertation. University of Toronto.

Atlantic Provinces Education Foundation. 1996. *Education indicators for Atlantic Canada.* Halifax: Atlantic Provinces Education Foundation.

Baker, L., and A. Wigfield. 1999. Dimensions of children's motivation for reading and their relations to reading activity and reading achievement. *Reading Research Quarterly* 34(4): 452–77.

Bhatia, B. P. 2001. Books: Look who's reading—under-25 crowd is purchasing books in record numbers; Faulkner as fashion statement. *Wall Street Journal,* November 9, W1.

Burdenuk, Gene. 1979. Adolescents and recreational reading. *Children's Book News*: 7–18.

Bussiere, P., F. Cartwright, R. Crocker, X. Ma, J. Oderkirk, and Y. Zhang. 2001. *Measuring up: The performance of Canada's youth in reading, mathematics and science; OECD PISA study-first results for Canadians aged 15.* Ottawa: Statistics Canada.

Cartwright, Fernando, and Mary K. Allen. 2002. Understanding the rural-urban reading gap. Ottawa: Statistics Canada.

Cook, S. J., R. S. Parker, and C. E. Pettijohn. 2005. The public library: An early teen's perspective. *Public Libraries* 44(3): 157–61.

Council of Ministers of Education, Canada. 1999. *School achievement indicators program: Reading and writing II assessment.* Toronto: Council of Ministers of Education, Canada.

Cox, R. E., and C. Collins. 2003. From boys' life to thrasher: Boys and magazines. *Teacher Librarian* 30(3): 25.

Createc. 2005. *Reading and buying books for pleasure: 2005 national survey.* Ottawa: Canadian Heritage.

Doiron, Ray. 2003. *Forging a future for Nova Scotia school libraries: A research report prepared for the Nova Scotia Teachers Union and the ad hoc Committee on Teacher-Librarian Services.* http://www.upei.ca/~raydoiro/html/publica tions.html (accessed May 16, 2005).

England, L. 1994. *The library users: The reading habits and attitudes of public library users in Great Britain.* London: The British Library Board.

Fasick, A., A. Gagnon, L. Howarth, and K. Setterington. 2005. *Opening doors to children: Reading, media and public library use by children in six Canadian cities.* Regina, Canada: Regina Public Library.

Hall, Christine, and Martin Coles. 1999. Children's reading choices. London and New York: Routledge.

Hill Strategies Research, Inc. 2005. *Who buys books in Canada? A statistical analysis based on household spending data.* Ottawa: Canada Council for the Arts.

Jones, P., D. C. Fiorelli, and M. H. Bowen. 2003. Overcoming the obstacle course: Teenage boys and reading. *Teacher Librarian* 30(3): 9.

Landy, Sarah. 1977. Reading as an expression of uniqueness. *Emergency Librarian* 5: 3–5.

Lewis, Holly. 1976. Reading habits of grade nines in Nova Scotia. *Atlantic Provinces Library Association Bulletin* 40: 33–47.

Looker, Dianne, and Victor Thiessen. 2003. *The digital divide in Canadian schools: Factors affecting student access to and use of information technology.* Ottawa: Statistics Canada.

Maughan, S. 2002. Betwixt and be'tween: How publishers are reaching out to a vast demographic of eight-to-fourteen-year-olds. *Publishers Weekly* 245(45): 32–36.

Millard, E. 1997. Differently literate: Gender identity and the construction of the developing reader. *Gender and Education* 9(1): 31–48.

National Center for Educational Statistics. 1995. *Services and resources for children and young adults in public libraries.* U.S. Department of Education, Office of Educational Research and Improvement, Report NCES 95-357. Washington, DC: U.S. Department of Education.

National Endowment for the Arts. 2004. *Reading at risk: A survey of literary reading in America.* http://www.nea.gov/pub/ReadingAtRisk/pdf (accessed May 27, 2005).

Nieuwenhuizen, A. 2001. *Young Australians reading: From keen to reluctant read-*

ers. http://www.slv.vic.gov.au/about/information/publications/policies_reports/reading.html (accessed May 12, 2005).

OFSTED. 1996. *The gender divide: Performance differences between boys and girls at school*. London: FSTED.

OFSTED. 1998. *Recent research on gender and educational performance*. London: OFSTED.

Peter D. Hart Research Associates. 2001. *The reading habits of adolescents survey*. Washington, DC: National Education Association.

Rideout, Vanda. 2002/2003. Digital inequalities in Eastern Canada. *Canadian Journal of Information and Library Science* 27: 3–31.

Statistics Canada. 1996. *Reading the future: A portrait of literacy in Canada*. Ottawa: Statistics Canada.

———. 1998. General Social Survey, cycle 12: time use (1998). Public (2) use microdata file. Ottawa: Statistics Canada.

Stevenson, H. W., C. Chen, and D. H. Uttal. 1990. Beliefs and achievement: A study of black, white and Hispanic children. *Child Development* 61(4): 508–23.

Walter, Virginia A. 2003. Public library service to children and teens: A research agenda. *Library Trends* 51: 571–83.

Wright, Robert. 2001. *Hip and trivial: Youth culture, book publishing, and the greying of Canadian nationalism*. Toronto: Canadian Scholars' Press.

6

Online Information Seeking and Higher Education Students

Manjeet K. Dhillon

THE AIM OF THE STUDY

This research will aim to identify and analyze the information-seeking behavior of third-year leisure, tourism, and adventure tourism students studying at Birmingham College of Food, Tourism and Creative Studies (BCFTCS) based in the United Kingdom, in relation to online databases. A select number of databases were considered within this study which largely relate to the students' courses.

BACKGROUND

Information seeking is no longer the sole domain of the student researching for academic purposes. As the World Wide Web continues to grow and information becomes more easily accessible, so the general public wish to exploit the Internet for knowledge on a vast number of subjects, as observed by Chew, "To become informed, the public needs many types of information."[1] However, in order to become adept at utilizing this information source, the public will need the necessary skills to retrieve this information, "Information literacy, the ability to access, evaluate and use information skills . . . is central to successful learning and living."[2] There is a need for information literacy in order for the public to locate the information they need as proficiently as possible.

Information seeking itself can be studied in a number of fields, whether it is for health information or food additives, for goods purchases or travel destinations. There has been research conducted in most of the aforementioned areas and particularly with respect to seeking information in health, from authors such as Moorman and Matulich,[3] Harris,[4] and Kassulke et al.[5] There is in contrast a considerable gap in the literature with regards to student perceptions toward electronic information. As Brace-Govan and Clulow observe, there is a "paucity of studies about how students actually experience online learning."[6]

Students are growing up accustomed to the technology around them and information skills are essential in order to use online resources for coursework. However, online information seeking can be daunting to the new searcher, "The vast quantity of information available on almost any subject can be absolutely staggering to an undergraduate attempting to do research."[7] Therefore, effective skills are required in order to manage this amount of information. A study by Brown[8] demonstrates that a number of skills, particularly computing skills, are required to enhance a student's ability to learn and achieve in higher education and personal career development. It is the learning process in order to gain these skills that will be investigated within this project.

Academic libraries have developed to encompass the growth of the new information age, and many institutions have spent vast sums, usually many thousands of pounds, on acquiring new online resources for the benefit of their students. Purchasing online technologies are costly and as technology becomes ever more advanced, academic libraries appear to be spending much more on electronic resources; as Kyrillidou's research indicates, "data collected by ARL libraries over the last decade indicate that the portion of library materials budget that is spent on electronic resources is indeed growing rapidly."[9]

As journals and books become more widely available online, the argument continues as to whether or not online journals and books will eventually replace print versions. As collections grow, the main benefit to this will be that library space can be freed by having online versions; space can be an issue in this respect for many academic libraries. However, at present the condition with many journals is that online access is available subject to having the print subscription. In either case, it is clear that enabling students to fully utilize the online databases subscribed to by educational institutions for the purpose of research, has to be a priority for all academic libraries, as the amount spent on databases needs to be justified.

The introduction of Joint Academic NETwork (JANET)[10] into UK colleges and universities has provided students with free access at the point of use to the Internet as well as a number of online services provided through Joint Information Systems Committee (JISC),[11] for students and academic staff. These services include Mailbase which offers information sharing via e-mail lists; Bulletin Board for Libraries (BUBL) offers descriptions of Internet resources and a current awareness service; National Information Services (NISS) is a core of information resources accessible to research communities worldwide and UK Office of Library Networking (UKOLN) provides current information on online technological advances concerning libraries. JANET also allows access to the OPACs (Online Public Access Catalogues) of many UK universities as well as special collections. SuperJANET is the powerful core of JANET that provides fast access to all JANET organizations and ensures they can successfully communicate.

There are now many other databases available to students according to what their individual academic institution has subscribed to; these can include databases such as Emerald, Infotrac, and Mintel. Through these, students are able to access abstracts and full-text documents and articles from a diverse range of sources such as journals, newspapers, and market research reports. Students in many cases may also access databases remotely off-campus to view and print articles from home using individual passwords, for example, through Athens authentication. Recently, BCFTCS has introduced Devolved Authentication, a new system of accessing Athens. Students and staff are now also able to access Athens via Blackboard (a Virtual Learning Environment, or VLE). The advantages of this have been numerous. Firstly, it has taken away the need for the administration involved, as staff and students are no longer required to complete forms in order for accounts to be set up manually by library staff; the highest demand for these would peak in September and October, the busiest months of the year for academic librarians at the college. Secondly, with the new system, it is possible for any announcements regarding Athens (for example, if it is temporarily down), to be easily executed and displayed within Blackboard, thus warning students beforehand, which in turn eliminates unnecessary student enquiries. Thirdly, Blackboard requires one set of passwords, which would consist of the student's usual college computer login. Once logged into Blackboard, there is no further need to log in into any of the Athens databases; and finally, placing access to Athens within Blackboard has served the double purpose of raising awareness of Blackboard itself.

PREVIOUS STUDIES

Studies into information-seeking behavior of electronic sources have increased since the 1990s, in relation to the increase of electronic information. However, according to Day and Ray, "little is known about student attitudes towards this form of information provision and without a better understanding, it is difficult to know if [educational institutions] are meeting the needs of students effectively."[12] Although surveys do exist, particularly in the use of the CD-ROM, there is little regarding other technologies,[13] and according to Brittain, "most user studies have looked at the situation through the eyes of the information professional rather than the user."[14]

Previous studies that do exist include JUBILEE and JUSTEIS,[15] which were both undertaken by JISC. Some of the main findings from the JUBILEE and JUSTEIS studies are as follows:

- Variance in research postgraduates' pattern of use to that of taught postgraduates.
- Undergraduate students use EIS (Electronic Information Services)
- Variance in patterns of EIS among disciplines.
- The influence of academic staff over student use of online information.

It is evident that usage of online information differs between groups of students. A study undertaken by Baruchson-Arbib and Shor[16] revealed that most of those using online information had a computer background and that in a previous study, students with prior knowledge of computers and who also received encouragement from their lecturers tended to make more use of online information. Similarly, Avigdori[17] proves that although there is no difference between different cultural backgrounds, there are disparities between students from various disciplines, with computer science students appearing most competent, followed by social science students and then humanities students; researchers who felt they were competent in using the Internet used online information resources more frequently.

Studies by Avigdori[18] also show younger people are more comfortable using CD-ROMs than older people (over thirty-six years old). However, it did not seem to matter whether users were male or female. There have been surveys done on usage of the World Wide Web. Spink et al.[19] and Ellis et al.[20] observed that the main reason for unsatisfactory results following the use of a search engine was mainly due to a user's lack of understanding of how a search engine interprets a query, of using *and* and *or* and expecting a search engine to recognize single terms and phrases. Koll described it as an attitude of "I'll know it when I see it"[21] by many users.

Systems designers also have a keen interest in how computers are used, particularly in relation to the interface, in order that navigating the system can become more effective. Veryard claimed this could be done quite simply, "Interview users . . . talk to the users at various levels, individually or collectively, to discover the decision-making and control processes they are responsible for, the performance measures they use, and the needs they have for information."[22] He goes on to suggest analyzing these information needs.

Dolan[23], Wanger,[24] and Hock[25] argue that apart from the skills that can be learned, there are several attributes to being a successful online searcher that are inherent—these are having subject knowledge; being people-oriented; being logical; and having analytical ability, self-confidence, enthusiasm, intelligence, and self-esteem. They further suggest that having an open-minded learning approach will produce better results, particularly when online searching is viewed as a problem-solving process. A searcher needs to have a willingness to "grow." Their advice is to "persevere, think flexibly and question constantly."[26]

Although there are several projects promoting online information and studies undertaken in information-seeking behavior, there appears to be little relating directly to the use of online databases. This may have been due to a lack of usage statistics; these are now becoming more widely available by database providers. They are also becoming more consistent as COUNTER (Counting Online Usage of Networked Electronic Resources)[27] takes a more prominent role as an authoritative benchmark for usage statistics; COUNTER is an international initiative intended to benefit librarians, publishers, and intermediaries by facilitating the recording and exchange of online usage statistics. Librarians will be able to compare usage statistics from different vendors and therefore make better-informed purchasing decisions. Publishers and intermediaries will be able to provide data to customers in a format they want, and learn more about genuine usage patterns. COUNTER mainly focuses on journals and databases, as these types of content are usually the largest purchases for most library material budgets.

However, although this is a leap forward in terms of recording online usage statistics, they cannot reveal the behavior of the user while searching online databases. Consequently, there appears to be a gap in the literature in this subject area. Although previous studies exist on the usage of the Internet and CD-ROMs, such as the JUBILEE and JUSTEIS studies, there are not any specifically relating to databases within the scope of leisure and tourism. This study focuses specifically on BCFTCS and the usage of subscription databases by leisure, tourism, and adventure tourism students at the college. There have been a few surveys, particularly with regard to CD-ROMs (for example, the study by Day and Ray);[28] however, the views of users have not been widely sought.

Databases

Databases have been defined by Harter as "a file of individual records in machine-readable form."[29] Databases may consist of information in many different forms—bibliographic, citations, abstracts, figures, tables, and charts. Rowley clarifies, "A file is a collection of similar records with relationships defined between these records. A database system may comprise a number of linked files."[30] To access this information is known as online information retrieval.

Databases may be accessed locally within an organization for the retrieval of transactions and financial records or connect a group of organizations. An example of this is the union catalog of the consortium of university research libraries (COPAC),[31] which contains the merged library catalogs of a number of universities in the United Kingdom and the British Library; this is a free service accessible to the public. COPAC is available remotely and includes monographs of books, reports, periodicals, and conferences. There are also records of printed and recorded music, videos, and electronic materials. Details of journal titles and holdings for these have been made available.

Source databases are those containing statistics, full-text and multimedia, such as Mintel. There is usually no need to refer to anything further than the information contained in this type of database.

Information-Seeking Behavior

Studies undertaken regarding information-seeking behavior in general, are plentiful, particularly in the field of health.[32] T. D. Wilson is responsible for extensive projects relating to information seeking and has created models to this affect. Wilson's model illustrates the various elements found in "information behavior" research; these include information need, information exchange, and use.[33]

Wilson has illustrated there must first exist a need to seek information. The individual will then set about finding this information, either through various manual or online systems or through interaction with other people. He also shows that information found through other sources will be used and then satisfaction or nonsatisfaction can be registered, with the latter leading back to a need. Wilson does not separate these factors and suggests that once an information need has been satisfied, the searcher may not need to seek any further information. A second model has been developed by Wilson that includes Ellis's[34] work on information seeking. It seeks to acknowledge the elements that shape the environment in which the need for information arises. This second model shows the barriers that may hinder the search for information; for example, there could be a personal barrier to a person seeking information, such as the avoidance of a news story due to its distressing content. An example of an environmental barrier could be seen as the physical environment, such as the World Wide Web not being available to everybody around the world, and therefore this may form a potential barrier to information.

The Search Process

Search engines are now becoming much more user-friendly and are moving toward introducing search features that respond to the ways in which users prefer to search these. However, more advanced features do not necessarily mean users want to use them. This was shown to be the case from the study DEVISE,[35] where efficiency was classed as the most important factor to users, followed by effectiveness, utility, and interaction as least important. Similarly, Jansen[36] commented following analysis of transaction logs by users of Excite that users do not feel comfortable with Boolean operators and other advanced features and found that many users do not usually look beyond the first page of results. Navarro-Prieto's study of a group of students found that none of the students understood how search engines used their queries to produce results. From this research, Navarro-Prieto et al. identified three different models of searching:

- Top-down strategy—participants undertook a *general search* and then narrowed this down by following links until they found a satisfactory result.
- Bottom-up strategy—participants used a *specific keyword* and then scrolled through results for the information required. It was mainly experienced searchers who used this strategy.
- Mixed strategies—the group used *both of the above* simultaneously. This again was only used by more experienced searchers.[37]

Furthermore, most of the group could not remember searches undertaken and ignored search engines and queries that gave poorer results. The majority of students were fairly satisfied with the results given. The meaning of "satisfactory" in terms of results found by users will hold a different meaning from one person to another as Allen[38] found following a number of studies involving use of CD-ROMs by students. Similarly, Day et al.[39] established that a high percentage of respondents found results to be satisfactory, and the question was then posed as to whether respondents were satisfied with a high number of results rather than relevant results.

Academia and Online Technology

At BCFTCS, there generally appears to be good collaboration between academic librarians (also referred to as subject or faculty librarians) and academic staff; there are a number of lecturers who make regular use of the library and its resources. Since the introduction of Athens at the college in 2001, there seems to have been a surge of interest in online resources, as a number of lecturers informed their colleagues of the benefits of having an Athens account, which motivated other staff into applying for accounts. This "word-of-mouth" communication appeared to be more effective than announcements by library staff in newsletters and program boards. As a result, Athens has become much more popular among staff than was predicted; this could perhaps be due to the fact that most subscription databases can now be accessed from one point, and even more simply since Devolved Authentication was introduced. The academic librarians arranged refresher sessions at the beginning of the academic year for lecturing staff, and it was ascertained that most of those who came along for the training did so at the recommendation of their line managers. Even so, turnout was less than expected, and it is perhaps due to most academic staff being accustomed to searching for online information, hence there were few requests from lecturers for formal training in the use of databases. From feedback, it was found that those who did attend these sessions found them very useful; new staff are particularly interested and appear to view online training as an essential part of their introduction to college facilities.

Academic Librarians

The function of the academic library has evolved with the growth of information literacy. Herrington believes that "the academic library has arrived at the threshold of a new mission. It . . . moves the academic library from a custodial role into a direct educational one."[40] Academic libraries must now see teaching as one of their core roles; as Owusu-Ansah observes, "These libraries must no longer just acquire, organize, disseminate and preserve information, but they must also instruct in the strategies for retrieving, evaluating and using information."[41]

The role of the academic librarian has been defined by the Chartered

Institute of Library and Information Professionals (CILIP) as, "Information professional, educationalist and manager of resources."[42] Adams and McElroy[43] go on to suggest qualities that are desirable in an academic librarian during a time of constant change—confidence is required in order to work closely with staff at all levels, a user-oriented approach, open-minded to change, tenacity, and good interpersonal skills. Rudge and Wilson also suggest a number of skills that academic librarians need to develop within their new roles; one of these is to "train and empower library users in the interpretation and evaluation of electronic information."[44]

However, Adams and McElroy state that there are librarians "who are content to administer the library . . . embrace all forms of information . . . and yet fail to see their role extending beyond the library's doors"[45] and therefore will be unsuccessful in interacting with academic staff. Nevertheless, there appears to have been an increase in the demand for academic librarians over recent years; as Raspa and Ward[46] acknowledge and as Rudge and Wilson point out, "User education has been an important element of most academic librarian's roles since the 1960's,"[47] and they believe that there has been the pressure to teach users more recently, "with the development and implementation of electronic information resources."[48] Owusu-Ansah agrees, "They (academic librarians) cannot be deterred by the structural changes the new responsibilities may entail."[49] Doyle states that, "Information literacy . . . skills at the very core of library instruction, is central to successful learning and living."[50] Isaacson supports this, "One of the most valuable services of the academic librarian is instruction."[51]

However, as highlighted by Davidson[52] in her research, many librarians feel unprepared for the responsibility of teaching. There were found to be many reasons for this; "a major area of concern was the lack of understanding of teaching and learning methods."[53] Davidson reached the conclusion that this was partly due to very few library school courses available that train librarians to teach information skills. Baruchson-Arbib and Shor suggest that schools of library and information science (LIS) should "emphasize the teaching role in their curriculum to help ensure that future librarians are good teachers."[54] In order to suitably fulfill this role, academic librarians need to be properly equipped with the skills required to teach.

Another aspect is the possibility of conflicting views as academic librarians move from a supporting role to one of teacher—do they receive the same respect from students as other lecturers are shown, as well as respect from other lecturers? Blake points out that faculty regard librarians "overwhelmingly . . . as skilled professionals . . . but never as peers."[55] There are also those with strong views such as Bessler who feels that, "service, not instruction, should be the hallmark of the profession."[56]

Nevertheless, in the current climate, the responsibility of the academic librarian is to fulfill the need of educational institutions to train and produce students "capable of dealing with the realities of the societies they are destined to face and operate in."[57] For the future, Wolff offers his opinion that, "Far more then an archivist or support worker, the librarian of the future will play a critical role as a teacher."[58]

Teaching online information literacy was previously undertaken in an ad hoc fashion at BCFTCS, usually upon the request of lecturers. However, this situation has changed as proactive lecturers and academic librarians have established a fundamental need for information-skills training sessions to become compulsory. These were introduced in Autumn 2002 as part of a new module, Research Skills and IT, which requires academic librarians to teach all first-year degree-level students in how to utilize online databases effectively. This is increasingly becoming the case in a number of higher education institutions throughout the United Kingdom, which have launched similar courses.

METHODOLOGY

Questionnaires were used for this study to gain an insight into how subscription databases are being utilized and also to determine specific problems that students may have when using these. It was a useful means of highlighting the numbers of students experiencing similar problems when using databases, and this in turn would help formulate solutions and recommendations. Although a focus group had originally been planned to provide qualitative research, this idea was abandoned due to a poor response from students; as a result, a quantitative method was relied upon.

Questionnaires are a means of gaining quantitative data that consist of numerical information. This can be simple counts or frequency of occurrences; these type of data need to be analyzed and interpreted, and to assist in this, tables and diagrams can be used. Qualitative research uses words instead of numbers and can be much more difficult to analyze compared to quantitative research, hence the data collected will need to be classified into categories before analysis. Whereas quantitative data is analyzed through the use of diagrams and statistics, qualitative data needs to be evaluated through the use of conceptualization.

A case study approach has been taken in this research. A case study can be defined as a method used to investigate a case, such as an individual or an institution, to answer specific research questions. In order to achieve this, the researcher needs to extract and collate evidence that already exists in the case setting. Multiple sources of evidence may be used for the research.[59]

For the purpose of this research, a survey sample was selected from the population that consisted of third-year students at BCFTCS, and from these, a sampling frame was drawn that consisted of leisure, tourism, and adventure tourism students. A particular subgroup had been selected, therefore taking a purposive approach by choosing a sample of people who were of interest. Purposive (nonjudgmental) sampling is a technique usually used in case studies, as this enables the researcher to use their discretion in selecting suitable cases to answer research questions. This is the technique employed for this particular case study. One problem, however, with this type of selection is that it may not be representative of the rest of the population at the college.

THE QUESTIONNAIRE

In designing the questionnaire used for the purpose of this research, many factors had to be considered. Wording, for example, can have a major effect on answers—the respondent may have literacy problems for a number of reasons and therefore find the questionnaire a daunting task. An answer to this may be interviews; as Gillham[60] notes, some people talk more easily than they write; however, interviews or focus groups may in fact be deemed as intrusive in some cases. Interviews and focus groups were considered and may have been a valuable addition to the research; however, due to the busy time of year at college, it proved difficult to gather suitable numbers of students for a focus group. Therefore questionnaires were solely relied upon for this study.

It is also imperative that respondents are informed as to why the information is being gathered and for what purpose the data will be used; for this reason, a brief statement of the purpose was included at the start of the questionnaire. As Robson[61] observes, questionnaires are a structured method of gathering information for research purposes. The researcher determines the questions to be asked and, depending on how structured the questionnaire, will receive a series of *yes* and *no*, *agree* and *disagree* answers, which will be relatively straightforward to analyze, and the researcher may have an idea on the type of responses to expect. However, this amount of structuring can render the data received somewhat superficial—the researcher is not able to gather data on what respondents are thinking.

Therefore, the questionnaire used for this survey included a variety of different types of questions. Included were those requiring simple *yes* and *no* answers; grid questions with a choice of answers ranging in strength of emotion (e.g., *strongly agree* and *disagree*), allowing the researcher to gain a degree of qualitative indication from the questionnaire by ascertaining strength of feeling; questions that required one answer only as well as list questions where all answers that applied needed to be shaded; a ranking question asking for a first, second, and third choice; and two scale questions to compare students' perception of the importance of databases when compared to the Internet. Respondents were also encouraged to add their own comments to several of the questions; this does not always guarantee a response, but those received proved to be constructive.

There were also other issues to consider. Coming toward the end of first semester meant that both lecturers and students had increased workloads; some lecturers and students may have been away from college for various reasons when questionnaires were being distributed. It could also have been the case the students would object to completing questionnaires unrelated to their courses. According to Saunders et al., it is important to have "as high a response rate as possible to ensure that your sample is representative."[62] In order to ensure this, permission was gained from lecturers and the survey took place at the end of lectures, gaining a captive audience and resulting in a 100 percent response rate (i.e., 127 questionnaires were distributed and the same number collected in 2003 and similarly, 139 in 2005). A "captive" group caught in a lecture theatre or during a meeting will provide a response rate of 100 percent, although there may be students who are not present at the time.

FINDINGS

The following charts have been used to illustrate the findings of the questionnaires. These have been included followed with an analysis.

Have you heard of Athens relating to databases?

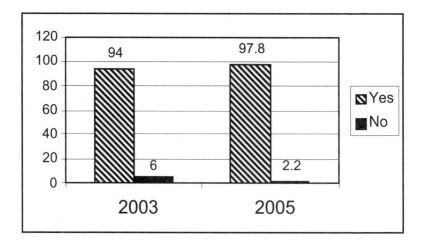

It was reassuring to see that the number of students who had heard of Athens had risen since 2003. The academic librarians have tried to promote Athens as widely and comprehensively as possible—through inductions, tutorials, workshops, via student queries and at meetings; various print guides have been produced to support students' use of Athens.

Which of the following databases have you used?

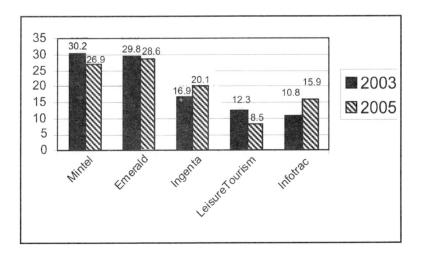

Not all databases available to students at the college were used within this research; those included were as follows:

- Ingenta (previously Catchword)—social science journals database.
- Infotrac (Thomson Gale)—includes newspaper, journals, and reference databases.
- Mintel—contains market research reports.
- Leisuretourism—includes leisure and tourism journal abstracts.
- Emerald—includes full-text management journal articles and abstracts.

This illustration indicates that use of Emerald has remained fairly consistent while use of Ingenta and Infotrac has risen considerably. Infotrac was a fairly recent acquisition in 2003, and also at this time, Ingenta changed its name from Catchword. It takes a certain amount of time to become accustomed to new resources and familiar with the contents of these; this may pose an even greater challenge to students who have many other new resources to discover. Infotrac includes both a journals and a newspaper database; these each have large volumes of full-text articles from a wide variety of sources across numerous subject areas that would appeal to students from all disciplines at the college.

An interesting observation was the slight drop in usage of Mintel in 2005; this is a database containing market research reports with in-depth analysis on various markets and industries, containing company overviews and statistics; however, by their third year at college, students are expected to mainly be focusing their research in academic journals—Mintel would be used for factual information with statistics while journal articles are more likely to supply theory required for an academic piece of work. The corresponding rise in full-text databases containing journal articles (Ingenta and Infotrac) would support this assumption. Usage of Mintel would be expected to be considerably higher for first- and second-year students.

Use of Leisuretourism has also dropped in 2005. This is a database not accessible via Athens but from the Internet, with a separate username and password. Leisuretourism offers abstracts rather than the full-text of articles. If students are embarking on their search in Athens and finding sufficient data in full-text for their purpose, Leisuretourism could well be overlooked, giving the indication that students are automatically exposed to all subscription databases when they log into Athens and perhaps more likely to discover these first. A solution to this are that print guides are provided, which offer information regarding all Athens as well as non-Athens databases.

How did you first hear of these databases?

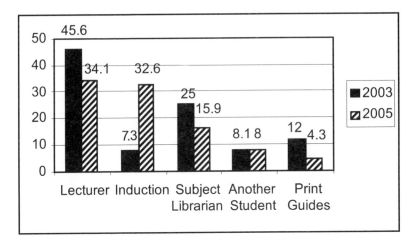

This question had been included to find out how well the databases had been individually promoted by various sources; it also provides an indication as to the most effective method of promoting online resources.

The lead taken by the choice of lecturer is unchanged in 2005, although there is a considerable drop in this figure compared to 2003. There has been a conscious effort in the promotion of databases through inductions, hence this has been reflected in the numbers. Inductions are preparatory sessions for new and existing students at the start of the academic year in which students are also introduced to their academic librarian and informed of library facilities, services, and any changes. Academic librarians usually have a "library slot" in the induction process, where databases will also be discussed with supporting guides provided. Although the figure for academic librarians has dropped, the cumulative figure for inductions/academic librarians is higher than in 2003. Inductions also appear to be a more effective form of raising awareness than print guides, and this is encouraging, as learning about databases from print guides would indicate that students only find out about these at the point of use without any prior knowledge. The figure for hearing of databases from other students is identical for both surveys.

This overall result indicated that lecturers have the strongest impact on students for promotion of databases.

How often do you search using each of the following databases?

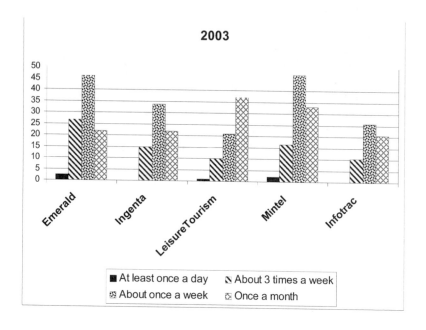

2003

At least once a day   About 3 times a week
About once a week   Once a month

2005

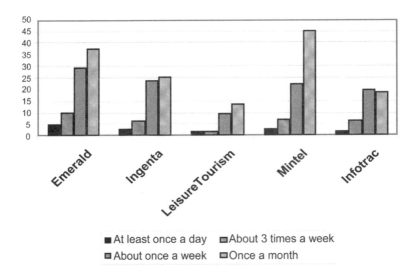

■ At least once a day ▣ About 3 times a week
▣ About once a week ▢ Once a month

Despite a slight drop in usage, Mintel was the most popular database, being used once a week by 47 percent of students in 2003, closely followed by 46 percent of students using Emerald just as frequently. In 2005, Mintel is still the most popular, followed again by Emerald with most respondents admitting to using these at least once a month.

There has been a shift in 2005 to many students appearing to be using databases less frequently, once a month, whereas once a week usage dominated the results in 2003. It can also be seen that usage of once a day and three times a week has also dropped considerably. It is hoped that this has resulted from increased teaching in the use of databases and the searches that have taken place are fewer but more successful and therefore a lesser need to search more frequently.

How would you describe databases?

This question consisted of a number of statements that were put to the students to ascertain feelings and thoughts toward the use of databases; the first statement was as follows:

I find databases enjoyable to use

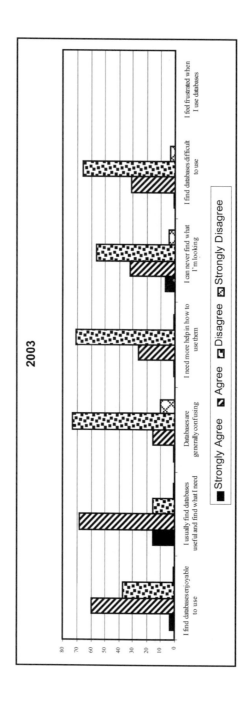

2003

Legend: ■ Strongly Agree ▨ Agree ▣ Disagree ⊠ Strongly Disagree

Categories (x-axis): I find databases enjoyable to use; I usually find databases useful and find what I need; Databases are generally confusing; I need more help in how to use them; I can never find what I'm looking; I find databases difficult to use; I feel frustrated when I use databases

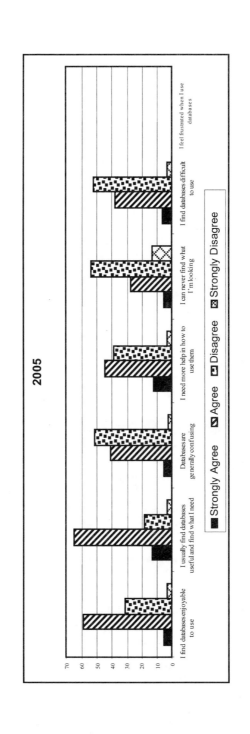

2005

The research revealed that very similar numbers of students found databases enjoyable to use. For those who did not, this may be due to problems experienced while searching in databases. "Enjoyment" may also have been seen as meaning "fun" and students may view databases simply as resources to exploit for information and may not be seen in the same context, for example, as the Internet, which may be used for more leisurely pursuits. The JUBILEE and JUSTEIS studies also found that undergraduate students use electronic sources mainly for academic purposes. Compared to the Internet, databases require a more refined search strategy, unlike a search in Google, for example. Students may perhaps be expecting and are accustomed to the type of results achievable through a search engine—a journals database would produce a set of results that include in-depth, specialist articles, whereas results from a search engine will be much more vast and far-ranging, from various sources, some of which may be questionable. The interface in some of the databases may seem to be intimidating to students who have become familiar with searching on the Internet.

I usually find databases useful and find what I need/ I can never find what I'm looking for

It was found that 83 percent (2003) of respondents either agreed or strongly agreed with this statement. This was a pleasing result and would indicate competency in using databases by most students. The result for 2005 was very similar, but it had been hoped that this figure would have been higher; however it is difficult to assess what the expectations of students are from a set of search results. As expected, this result corresponds with similar numbers, who indicated they disagreed with the statement that they could never find what they needed.

I feel frustrated when I use databases
Databases are generally confusing

A pattern was now emerging as proportionately comparable results were seen for these two statements. An average of 64 percent of respondents disagreed with these comments while a quarter agreed. The results found were similar to those results from the previous statement where 37 percent of students did not find databases enjoyable.

In 2005, a higher percentage of students found databases confusing. This could be a cause for concern, as all first year students receive training as part of a compulsory module, therefore these third-year students should have the necessary skills to utilize these databases to a satisfactory standard. Similarly about 6 percent more students felt frustrated with using databases; again it is questionable what students' expectations are of databases and whether they are aware of sources of help.

I find databases difficult to use—I need to learn more about how to use them

For both surveys, on average 64 percent of respondents disagreed with these statements and 35 percent of students agreed with them and felt they needed further assistance in the use of online resources. This again can be compared to the number of students who did not enjoy using databases. This further supports the theory that a considerable proportion of students require additional support and training in effectively utilizing databases, over and above the formal training received in their first year. Results in 2005 show a larger percentage of students who are admitting to finding databases difficult to use. This rise in students finding databases difficult to use could perhaps be due to their reluctance to seek help when needed. As well as the formal training that has been introduced on all first-year courses, the academic librarians offer several workshops a week to reinforce this teaching, where students are welcome to discuss any problems they are experiencing while searching online.

Previous to the workshops, academic librarians offered support to students on an appointment basis with students receiving instruction at the academic librarians' desks. This resulted in insufficient time to see as many students, however, it appears students seemed to prefer this method as there have been fewer students attending workshops than previous numbers that have booked individual appointments. On this basis, one-to-one appointments are still offered to students who may wish to receive individual training, although students are guided to workshops in the first instance. The advantage is that the workshops take place in computer rooms, giving students the opportunity to demonstrate where they are experiencing particular problems and continue researching, with support on hand if required.

What help do you think you need with regards to databases?

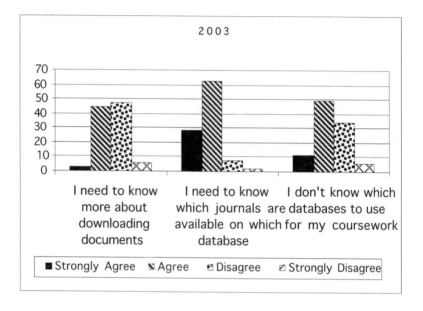

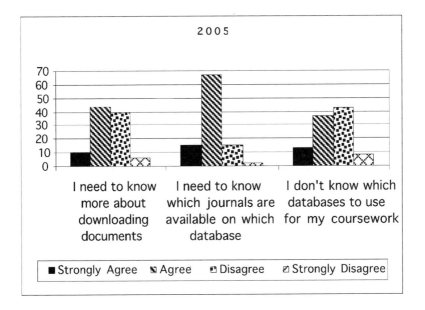

In order to answer this question, statements were posed for the students to respond to. This helped the researcher to ascertain the extent of respondents' experiences of databases.

I need to know more about downloading documents

Although 70 percent (2003) of respondents had previously stated that they usually find databases useful and find what they need, in contrast 47 percent of students were unsure of how to download documents. For those who are uncertain of downloading documents, this would indicate a need for further training. The trend in 2005 appears to be almost identical to 2003, with slightly more students wanting to know more about document downloading. During the two-hour teaching session delivered by the academic librarians, the main points are attempted to be included on all aspects of online researching, downloading, and printing. However, in this amount of time it is not possible to train on all databases in depth; they all differ slightly, including the ways in which documents are downloaded; hence print guides are provided to answer technical queries on all databases.

I need to know which journals are available on which database

This statement was included as many students have frequently queried this with the academic librarians at the college. A high number (91 percent in 2003) of respondents agreed with this statement, and this was not unexpected. The academic librarians had been considering this issue and have consequently produced a revised Guide to Journals that not only indicates titles held in print at the library but also whether these are available online and in which database. These have been made widely available with a print copy to all new students during the teaching sessions; all students are now also able to access this document online via Blackboard (the VLE). This seems to have translated into the recent slightly better result of 85 percent. However, this still appears to be an unnecessarily high figure and may indicate a reluctance to view the online version of the Guide to Journals by third-year students.

I don't know which databases to use for my coursework

It was found that 40 percent (2003) of students felt they knew which databases they needed to access for their coursework with 60 percent stating that they did not know; the gap seems to be closing in 2005, with a 50-50 split. Print guides indicating which databases would be useful for different subject areas have been produced, and the academic librarians focus their training session around databases appropriate to the group they are teaching. Print copies of everything covered are handed out, materials are also placed on Blackboard following the training. There would be a problem if students had not attended this session for some reason; if this is the case, then there is a need for students to become more active in seeking the information they need.

Please state from which of the following you prefer to learn about databases

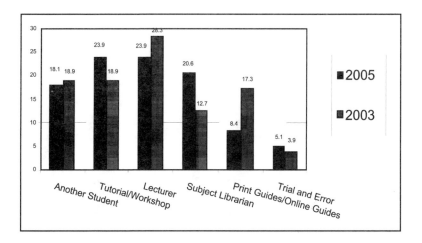

The results were fairly evenly distributed; the highest result was 28 percent of students in 2003 who preferred to learn from their lecturer in class. This result also relates to the findings of the JUBILEE and JUS-TEIS studies, which show that academic staff have more influence over students' use of online resources than library staff and that friends are also influential. In 2005 this has dropped slightly, while workshops and academic librarians have become a more popular source of training. It must also be remembered that academic librarians would be considered in the capacity of a lecturer when they deliver training on the Research Skills and IT module. Although a higher number of students preferred to use print guides than ask an academic librarian in 2003, approaching an academic librarian became more popular in 2005. The use of print guides has dropped considerably; these results would indicate that students do prefer to be taught in class rather than be self-taught.

The results in 2003 signify that students are familiar with their lecturers and trust them to give appropriate information, over and above friends and their academic librarian; this could also be a case of accessibility—the lecturers are already close by in class for queries to be answered. However, this dropped by 4 percent in 2005 and 8 percent more would seek support from an academic librarian.

If you experienced problems in using a database, what would you do? (please state your 1st, 2nd and 3rd choice)

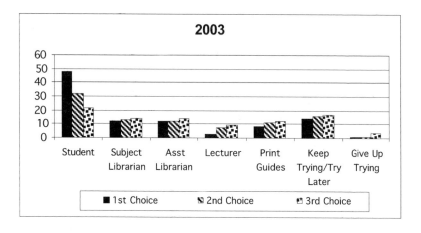

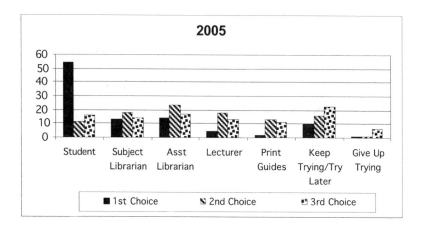

It was interesting to learn of the behavior of students once they experienced problems with using a database and the outcome of this. The overwhelming result for first choice was 48 percent (2003) of respondents and 54 percent (2005) who would ask a friend or another student. This may have been a predictable result, as students tend to sit with friends at computers and it would be a natural reaction for them to turn for help from their peers first. Other first choices were to "ask a subject librarian" (13 percent) and "ask an assistant librarian" (12 percent) with respective figures in 2005 of 13 percent and 14.5 percent. The main differentiation between an assistant librarian and an academic librarian (or subject librarian) is that an assistant librarian is usually based at the issue desk and will have a broad role in the library such as dealing with general enquiries whereas an academic librarian will normally be qualified to postgraduate level and have a subject-specialist role, therefore dealing with more complex student enquiries, liaising with academics regarding purchasing resources, producing user materials, delivering inductions ,and in many cases being involved with lecturing.

Although the most popular second choice in 2003 was to "ask an assistant librarian," in 2005 students would be even more likely to make this choice. The issue desk is very accessible to the computers in the library, and therefore the assistant librarians would be a first port of call for many students. In contrast, the academic librarians are seated on the upper floor of the library away from the computers on the lower floor, therefore making them perhaps a little less accessible when problems arise.

For third choice, the most popular option for students would be to ask fellow students for help in 2003, secondly to ask an assistant librarian, and the third most popular option was to ask an academic librarian. However, 2005 saw students more likely to keep trying before turning to a friend for help. Failing this, they would try asking an assistant librarian and then an academic librarian. One remarkable outcome was that although many had indicated they preferred to learn about databases from lecturers, the same number would not seek help from their lecturers when experiencing problems while online; this appears to be another indication of a tendency to seek help from within the direct environment and students would perhaps not wander far, even if it were for more expert help.

What other resources do you use for assignments or your dissertation?

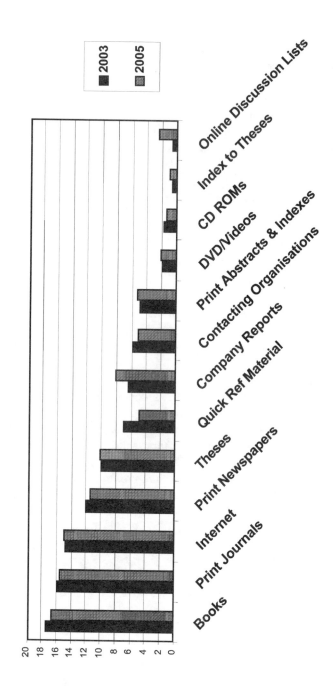

This question was asked to ascertain which other resources were popular with students other than online databases. Books, journals, and the Internet were the most popular sources of information during both surveys. Almost 2 percent of students indicated they used CD-ROMs in both surveys; this would relate to the general decrease in the popularity of CD-ROMs, with databases largely replacing these and the increasing demand for information to be accessible effortlessly via the Internet. Day and Ray's[63] study shows that 80.7 percent of students used CD-ROMs, alongside the Internet in 1996. There is a significant difference between this figure and the small percentage of respondents using CD-ROMs in this particular case; in 2005 this figure has decreased even further. This acts as a guide to the popularity of CD-ROMs in 1996 and technological advances since that time.

How often do you use Athens databases at home?

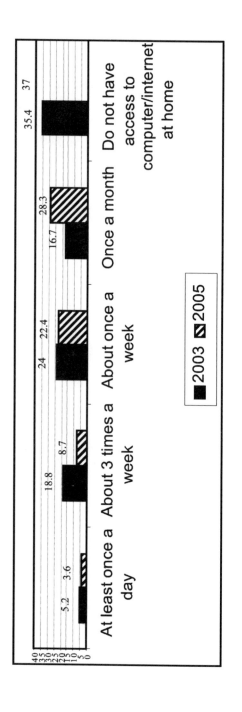

It was found that those students who had Internet access at home, searched in Athens on a fairly regular basis.

It was surprising to see that about the same number of students did not have a computer/Internet access at home in 2003 as in 2005. However, it could be the case that many students do not wish to work at home and prefer to carry out their research at college, where they can have access to the Internet late into most evenings and weekends. It does seem highly likely that students are probably making more use of the facilities available at the college as this has been reflected in the fact that the demand for computer bookings in the library have also risen significantly since 2003. Again, this result correlates with the earlier seen usage of databases dropping from more frequent use to monthly use becoming more popular.

How important are databases and the Internet to you for coursework?

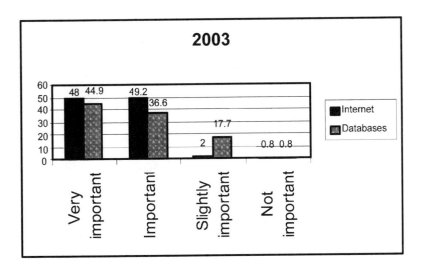

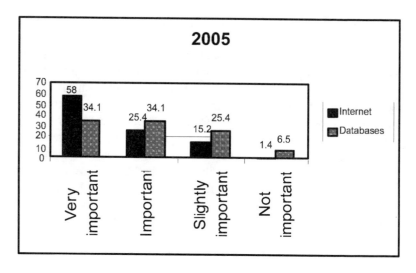

This question was posed in the form of a scale ranging from "very important" to "not important." Respondents were asked to mark their preference along a scale to indicate how important each of these online resources is to them. Results for both resources were similar, with a very slightly higher percentage indicating a preference for the Internet and a more pronounced preference in 2005 toward the Internet. This result could be a reflection of the recent advances in the number of scholarly articles and documents now available directly from the Internet. It could also mean that students are perhaps not so discerning when searching for resources. This is a cause for concern as it is essential that students are taking full advantage of the invaluable sources of information available from subscription databases. With the slightly higher number of students in 2005 seeming to experience difficulties in using databases, this could also indicate a possible correlation in those feeling the Internet is more accessible, perhaps in terms of ease of use.

Please score on the scale how satisfied you are with using online databases?

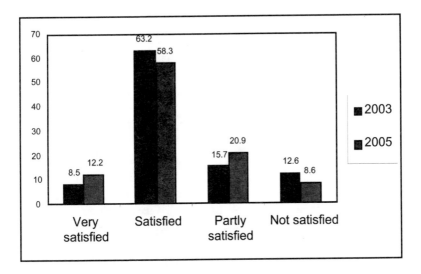

The majority of respondents (71 percent in 2003) were satisfied, mostly satisfied, or very satisfied with using databases, with almost the same number in 2005. This is inconsistent with the results from previous questions indicating students experienced frustration with online databases. It could be that students are mostly satisfied with the results from successful searches they have found. Day and Ray's study in 1996 also showed a high number of respondents who were "satisfied" with the outcome of searching; however, they were concerned that students were "interested in high recall rather than high precision."[64] Culbertson found in an earlier study that although "end users could obtain and print results, few used refining techniques."[65] What was promising with the current study was that the number not satisfied in 2003 had dropped and those who were mostly satisfied had risen in 2005.

CONCLUSIONS

This research was designed to investigate the online information-seeking behavior of students at Birmingham College of Food, Tourism and

Creative Studies, to identify databases utilized and to establish whether any alterations to the training of these was necessary in order to support students further. A survey was undertaken in order to ascertain the behavior including the thoughts and feelings of students toward usage of online databases. A response rate of 100 percent was achieved as students were approached during lectures. The research was set against a background that is seeing an influx of online databases into higher education institutions along with an increase in student numbers. In conjunction with this, there is the raised profile of the academic librarian and the teaching role undertaken within this position and the challenges this may bring.

The amount of students' usage of the databases was analyzed and the results revealed that some databases were utilized much more than others. Emerald and Mintel were found to be very popular, and this related to feedback from academic staff training that usage of these databases was high among lecturers and they were actively promoting these to students. The survey revealed that although academic librarians at the college were actively promoting and training students and academia on various databases, academic staff had the greatest influence on students in terms of promoting resources. Leisuretourism had become less popular, and this may be due to it offering abstracts of articles only.

The survey consisted of full-time students only and did not consider the needs of part-time students. Mature and other part-time students are more likely to be at a disadvantage, particularly with regard to online resources, as they may spend less time at college than full-time students; therefore it is essential to introduce this group to online databases at induction. Athens will help, as this allows access from home; however, it is vital that this group of students are also given support as needed. One method of support is that of academic librarians providing e-mail addresses in order for students to send enquiries when they are off campus.

The questionnaire used in this study provided quantitative data; however, many of the questions helped to reveal students' perceptions at a deeper level. For example, a set of statements were used for students to respond to by indicating whether they agreed or disagreed. To a small extent, this provided the researcher with valuable qualitative data, although it was not as informative as a focus group may have been. A few comments were made by students in a number of the questionnaires that gave another dimension to the survey, hence it was found that a certain amount of qualitative data could be extracted from question- naires if the questions are designed with this factor in mind. Timing is not a straightforward element in the distribution of questionnaires. Equally, it can be difficult to anticipate an appropriate time particularly in an educational setting, where the workload for students and lecturers is generally intense throughout the academic year. In this case, it would be more advantageous to distribute the questionnaires over a longer period of time.

Even though the survey carried out was not on a large scale, a number of key observations were gained:

- The majority of students used two databases, Emerald and Mintel, much more frequently than other databases.
- Emerald and Mintel are also very popular among lecturing staff.
- Although students showed a preference for learning about online databases from lecturers, students will seek help from the person in their direct vicinity when encountering difficulties; therefore, they are more likely to turn to fellow students for help than a lec- turer or a librarian, in the first instance.
- Students saw Athens passwords as an important resource; how- ever, 60 percent admitted being unsure which of the databases to use for their coursework, and nearly 50 percent had difficulty downloading documents.

These points together with additional comments made by some respondents highlighted a need for further information-skills training for students. In the past, students have been supported by academic librarians who have offered appointments to see students individually for database training at their desks. Students seem to prefer individual appointments with academic librarians; the main challenge is for aca- demic librarians to encourage students to attend the workshops as addi- tional training in a supportive environment. This is likely to continue to be an ongoing process.

The compulsory training sessions for first-year students has helped both students and the academic librarians—the librarians are able to teach groups in one session; therefore, this has proved time-effective and students have the opportunity to learn at individual computers. The survey revealed that there is a need for further support following formal teaching sessions, and although emphasis has been placed on students to attend additional workshops, these have yet only been utilized by small numbers of students; it has been found at BCFTCS that the optional "drop-in" element of workshops is frequently thought of as less important than formal lectures, so one idea is to link a number of follow-up workshops directly to the formal training session, giving students the opportunity to carry out research with expert help on hand from an academic librarian. Another idea is to receive feedback on aspects of the session that students would like to learn more about or did not understand fully. It may also prove beneficial to have a trial with academic librarians sitting at the enquiry desk based close to the computers in the library for a few hours a week, therefore becoming more accessible to students seeking help; this would also assist in establishing particular problems encountered by students while researching. However, this would only prove successful if students were to actively come and seek help.

This research was undertaken to find out how students behaved during the process of searching for information using online databases. In this context, although this was a relatively small study and therefore cannot be generalized to other educational institutions, it could form a basis for a further long-term project in this topic area.

NOTES

1. F. Chew, "The Relationship of Information Needs to Issue Relevance and Media Use," *Journalism Quarterly* 71, no. 3 (Autumn 1994): 676–88.

2. C. S. Doyle, "Information Literacy in an Information Society," *Emergency Librarian* 22 (March/April 1995): 30–32.

3. C. Moorman and E. Matulich, "A Model of Consumer's Preventative Health Behaviours: The Role of Health Motivation and Health Ability," *Journal of Consumer Research* 20 (September 1993): 208–28.

4. J. Harris, "You Can't Ask If You Don't Know What to Ask: A Survey of the Information Needs and Resources of Hospital Outpatients," *New Zealand Medical Journal* 105 (27 May 1992): 199–202.

5. D. Kassulke, K. Stenner-Day, M. Coory, and I. Ring, "Information-Seeking Behaviour and Sources of Health Information: Associations with Risk Factor Status in an Analysis of Three Queensland Electorates," *Australian Journal of Public Health* 17, no.1 (1993): 51–57.

6. J. Brace-Govan and V. Clulow, "Varying Expectations of Online Students and the Implications for Teachers: Findings from a Journal Study," *Distance Education* 21, no. 1 (2000): 118–35.

7. D. Raspa and D. Ward, *The Collaborative Imperative: Librarians and Faculty Working Together in the Information Universe* (Chicago: American Library Association, 2000), 21.

8. J. Brown, *Embedding Graduateness and Demonstrating Standards*, Internal Research Paper Series, Centre for Business and Management (Lancashire: Edge Hill, 1999).

9. M. Kyrillidou, "Research Library Spending on Electronic Scholarly Information Is on the Rise," *Journal of Library Administration* 35, no. 4 (2001): 89–91.

10. Joint Academic NETwork (JANET), www.ja.net.

11. Joint Information Systems Committee (JISC), www.jisc.ac.uk (accessed January 5, 2005).

12. J. Day and K. Ray, "Student Attitudes Towards Electronic Information Resources" (dissertation Department of Information and Library Management, University of Northumbria, UK, 1996), http://informationr.net/ir/4-2/paper54.html (accessed April, 14 2005).

13. J. M. Brittain, "Information-Specialists—New Directions for Education and Training," *Journal of Information Science* 13, no. 6 (1987): 321–26. Cited in D. Bawden, *User-Oriented Evaluation of Information Systems and Services* (Aldershot: Gower, 1990).

14. Brittain, "Information-Specialists."

15. J. R. Griffiths and P. Brophy, "Student Searching Behaviour in the JISC Information Environment," *Ariadne* 33 (October 2002), www.ariadne.ac.uk/issue33/edner/intro.html (accessed March 18, 2005).

16. S. Baruchson-Arbib and F. Shor, "The Use of Electronic Information Sources by Israeli College Students," *The Journal of Academic Librarianship* 28, no. 4 (July–August 2002): 255–57.

17. D. Avigdori, "Use Patterns of Databases in a Heterogonous Population" (master's thesis, Ramal Gan, Israel: Bar-Ilan University, 2000).

18. Avigdori, "Use Patterns."

19. A. Spink, T. Wilson, D. Ellis, and N. Ford, "Modelling Users' Successive Searches in Digital Environments," *D-Lib Magazine*, April 1998, www.dlib.org/dlib/april98/o4spink.html (accessed February 27, 2005).

20. D. Ellis, N. Ford, and J. Furner, "In Search of the Unknown User: Indexing and Hypertext on the World Wide Web," *Journal of Documentation* 54, no.1 (1998): 28–47.

21. M. Koll, *Automatic Relevance Ranking: A Searcher's Complement to Indexing*, proceedings of the 25th annual meeting of the American Society of Indexers (Port Arkansas, TX: American Society of Indexers, 1993), 55–60.

22. R. Veryard, "Modelling of Information Needs," *Information and Software Technology* 30 (1988): 571–78.

23. D. R. Dolan, "The Quality Control of Search Analysts," *Online* 3 (April 1979): 8–16.

24. J. Wanger, "Multiple Database Use," *Online* 1 (October 1977): 35–41.

25. R. E. Hock, "Who Should Search? The Attitudes of a Good Searcher," in *Online Searching Technique and Management*, ed. James J. Maloney, 83–88 (Chicago: American Library Association, 1983).

26. Dolan, "Quality Control"; Wanger "Multiple Database Use"; Hock "Who Should Search?"

27. COUNTER, www.projectcounter.org (accessed December 12, 2004).

28. Day and Ray, "Student Attitudes."

29. S. P. Harter, *Online Information Retrieval: Concepts, Principles, Techniques* (London: Academic Press Inc., 1986).

30. J. Rowley, *The Electronic Library* (London: Facet Publishing, 2002), 102.

31. COPAC, www.copac.ac.uk (accessed January 7, 2005).

32. G. Hammerschlag, "Using Electronic Journals in Medicine," *Information and Librarianship* 23, no. 2 (1998): 5–16.

33. T. D. Wilson, "Information Needs and Uses: Fifty Years of Progress," in *Fifty Years of Information Progress: A Journal of Documentation Review*, ed. B. C. Vickery, 15–51 (London: Aslib).

34. D. Ellis, "A Behavioural Approach to Information Retrieval System Design," *Journal of Documentation* 45, no. 3 (1989): 171–212.

35. F. Johnson, J. R. Griffiths, and R. J. Hartley, "DEVISE: A Framework for the Evaluation of Internet Search Engines," Resource Report 100, www.cerlim.ac.uk/projects/devise.htm (accessed June 15, 2005).

36. B. J. Jansen, "Real Life, Real Users and Real Needs: A Study and Analysis of User Queries on the Web," *Information Processing and Management* 36, no. 2 (July 2003): 207–27, www.ariadne.ac.uk/issue33/edner/ (accessed January 27, 2005).

37. R. Navarro-Prieto et al., "Cognitive Strategies in Web Searching," 1999, cited in G. Allen, "Patron Response to Bibliographic Databases on CD-ROM," *RQ* 29, no.1 (1989): 103–10.

38. Allen, "Patron Response."

39. J. Day, C. Edwards, G. Walton, S. Curry, M. Bent, and M. Jackson, "Higher Education, Teaching, Learning and the Electronic Library: A Review of the Literature for the IMPEL2 Project: Maintaining Organisational and Cultural Change," *New Review of Academic Librarianship* 2 (1996): 131–204.

40. V. J. Herrington, "Way Beyond BI: A Look to the Future," *Journal of Academic Librarianship* 24 (September 1998): 381–86.

41. E. K. Owusu-Ansah, "The Academic Library in the Enterprise of Colleges and Universities: Toward a New Paradigm," *Journal of Academic Librarianship* 27, no. 4 (July 2001): 282–94.

42. CoFHE Group, "Survey of FE College Libraries in England, 1992, cited in

Marie Adams and Rennie McElroy, eds., *Colleges, Libraries and Access to Learning* (London: Library Association Publishing, 1994): 16.

43. Adams and McElroy, *Colleges, Libraries and Access to Learning*, 16.

44. S. Rudge, and I. Wilson, "Electronic Information Delivery: Joint Working at UCE," *Vine* 122 (March 2001): 41–47.

45. Adams, and McElroy, *Colleges, Libraries and Access to Learning*, 35.

46. Raspa, and Ward, *The Collaborative Imperative*.

47. Rudge, and Wilson, "Electronic Information Delivery."

48. CoFHE Group, "Survey of FE College Libraries in England," 16.

49. Owusu-Ansah, "The Academic Library in the Enterprise of Colleges and Universities."

50. Doyle, "Information Literacy in an Information Society."

51. D. Isaacson, "An Educationally and Professionally Appropriate Service," *Journal of Academic Librarianship* 16 (May 1990): 80–81.

52. S. A. Davidson, "Training Librarians to Teach" (master's dissertation, University of Central England, UK, 1998).

53. Raspa and Ward, *The Collaborative Imperative*.

54. Baruchson-Arbib and Shor, "The Use of Electronic Information Sources by Israeli College Students." ·

55. V. L. P. Blake, "Library School Educators and Academic Librarians: A Symbiotic Relationship," *Public & Access Services Quarterly* 1, no. 2 (1995): 11–31.

56. J. Bessler, "Do Library Patrons Know What's Good for Them?" *Journal of Academic Librarianship* 16 (May 1990): 76–77.

57. H. Johnson, "Information Skills in UK Higher Education: The SCONUL Task Force on Information Skills" (SCONUL briefing paper, 1999), www.sconul .ac.uk/Conference/springconf02/Johnson.ppt (accessed May 5, 2004).

58. R. A. Wolff, "Using the Accreditation Process to Transform the Mission of the Library," *New Directions for Higher Education* 90 (Summer 1995): 77–91.

59. B. Gillham, *Case Study Research Methods* (London: Continuum, 2000).

60. B. Gillham, *Developing a Questionnaire* (London: Continuum, 2000).

61. C. Robson, *Real World Research*, 2nd ed. (Oxford: Blackwell, 2002).

62. M Saunders, P. Lewis, and A. Thornhill, *Research Methods for Business Students*, 2nd ed. (Essex: Pearson Education Ltd., 2000).

63. Day and Ray, "Student Attitudes."

64. Day and Ray, "Student Attitudes."

65. M. Culbertson, "Analysis of Searches by End-Users of Science and Engineering CD-ROM Databases in an Academic Library," *CD-ROM Professional* 5, no. 2 (1992): 76–79.

7

"It'd Be Really Dumb Not to Use It": Virtual Libraries and High School Students' Information Seeking and Use—a Focus Group Investigation

Joyce Kasman Valenza

BACKGROUND

The effective virtual school library offers 24/7 accessibility, just-in-time/just-for-me learning opportunities, and customized resources, as learners navigate the often overwhelming processes of accessing and using information. Virtual libraries allow teacher-librarians to apply their traditional skills for collection development, collaboration, reference, and instruction in powerful new ways in highly populated, new information landscapes. They allow learners independence as they allow teacher/librarians opportunities for intervention. As scalable strategies, virtual libraries allow librarians and educators to guide unlimited numbers of students—onsite, at home, or otherwise distant. Through their virtual libraries, teacher librarians can extend their three roles as defined in *Information Power* (AASL & AECT 1998) Learning and Teaching, Information Access and Delivery, and Program Administration.

School virtual libraries have powerful potential, perhaps beyond the potential of academic and public libraries. In addition to a clear mission set out by *Information Power*, teacher-librarians serve generally smaller, more homogeneous populations. Effective teacher-librarians regularly collaborate with teachers. They have clear understandings of the curriculum for the grade levels and content areas that are within the sphere of a limited learning community. School virtual libraries have the potential to provide extraordinary opportunities for customized online instruction and guidance.

Though studies of secondary students' use of the Internet largely examine the behaviors of novice information seekers, those without the benefit of the online presence of a librarian, few studies address the influence of teacher-librarian guidance through the framework of a learner-centered virtual library interface. While studies of the effectiveness of online interfaces exist for public and academic library environments, little serious research examines the effectiveness of *school* library service online, student response to online service, and specific criteria for evaluation of school virtual library interfaces.

RESEARCH QUESTIONS

Clearly, the hundreds of school virtual library efforts, compiled by such sources as SchoolLibrary.NET (Milbury, Woolls, & Loertscher 2005), are not equally effective. These professional efforts, range from single-page *library brochures* to dynamic, multipage learning environments. The disparity of these efforts, compounded by students' growing need for online intervention, suggests critical research questions:

- How do virtual libraries affect student information-seeking habits? How do they respond to virtual access to resources and guidance?
- To what extent are these interfaces effective environments for information access and for learning?
- In a Google-reliant world, would students be motivated to begin their searches in an alternate interface, even if that interface was customized to meet their specific information needs?

After nearly nine years of maintaining a school library site, six of these years at Springfield Township High School, I wondered how my own online efforts affected student research and about student users' perceptions and appreciation of the library site. I asked the following questions in the focus group interviews:

Q1. When do you use online school library services?
Q2. What prompts you to use the school Virtual Library?
Q3. Is it is usually the first place you go or your last resort?
Q4. Can you describe the last success you had with the interface?
Q5. What features of the school library website do you most value?
Q6. How have those features helped you with your research? Your understanding of the scope of online resources?
Q7. Does the librarian's influence appear to be present in the site?
Q8. What problems or flaws do you encounter with the interface?
Q9. What improvements or additional features students would like to see in the website?
Q10. Do you feel the school library website helped you prepare for college or real-life research?

(Question numbers throughout this report refer to student responses to the above questions.)

High school seniors were selected for their long-term use, familiarity, and experience with a library interface. Because of the broad range of academic abilities across any high school community, I wanted to examine students of varying achievement levels to determine if students involved in advanced placement classes would approach the website in ways different from general academic students. This study reports the findings of focus group interviews with four groups of Springfield Township High School seniors and is a pilot for a larger study of school library websites identified as examples of best practice. The full study, including student responses in a fourteen-school Web-based survey, will be described in my upcoming dissertation.

LITERATURE REVIEW

What Are Virtual Libraries?

The terms virtual library, digital library, electronic library, cyberlibrary, and library website are used in the literature of information science and education to describe such dissimilar efforts as: national libraries; the archives of major organizations; the specialized digitized text, image, and media archives of museums and universities; aggregated commercial databases; as well as the focus of this study—library websites developed by teacher-librarians to serve their own user groups who are predominantly learners.

Virtual school libraries generally extend their services beyond the creation of an online information delivery structure in their attempts to implement instructional missions. Distinguished from sites that merely house archives or collect bookmarks, virtual libraries in educational institutions can reach beyond intellectual access, utilizing the professional skills of the librarian to offer instruction in information literacy, as outlined in *Information Power: Building Partnerships for Learning* (AASL & AECT 1998). Marchionini and Maurer (1995a, paragraph 6) describe such efforts as "building intellectual infrastructures" and point to their potential for creating communities of learners. Neuman (1997) cites several studies that point to virtual libraries as venues for higher level thinking and learning. Marchionini, Plaisant, and Komlodi (1998) echo Neuman's conclusions. "Digital libraries are the logical extensions and augmentations of physical libraries" and in addition to amplifying existing resources, "they enable new kinds of human problem solving and expression" (536).

Though researchers continue to disagree over terminology, this study will use the term *virtual library* to describe a customized, structured online learning environment/community, developed by a teacher-librarian to improve and extend the services and mission of the library program to the learning community.

Students and Their Information Habits

No longer limited to the traditional collections physically available in their school libraries, or the content of their textbooks, today's student researchers confront an explosion of information choices. High school students, who have literally grown up on the Web, prefer it as a primary information outlet (Levin et al. 2002; Jones & Madden 2002; Tenopir 2003). They have high expectations for information speed and convenience and high expectations for library service (Abram & Luther 2004).

A Pew Internet and American Life study, *The Digital Disconnect: The Widening Gap Between Internet-Savvy Students and Their Schools* (Levin et al. 2002) finds that most students (78 percent) prefer to use the Internet for research and homework. Tenopir (2003) notes high school and college students use the Internet more than their libraries. But she warns that their quality judgments about Internet materials "may not exactly match faculty criteria" (32).

College students, just one year beyond our high school seniors, may not be prepared to recognize quality or to realize their broader search options. According to the Pew study *The Internet Goes to College* (Jones & Madden 2002), nearly three quarters of students (73 percent) report that they use the Internet more than the library. When they are using the Internet for research, they make use of commercial search engines and generally ignore their library's rich online resources because they don't know how to find them.

The Pew Internet & American Life Study, *Teens and Technology: Youth Are Leading the Transition to a Fully Wired and Mobile Nation* (Lenhart, Madden, and Hitlin 2005) reports that nearly nine in ten teens are Internet users and that half have broadband connections. The survey concludes that "teens are enveloped in a wired world" (20), using technology for communicating, shopping, game playing, and information seeking. Interestingly, although the study noted that teens increasingly use the Internet at their libraries, stating that "more than half (54%) of all online teens say they have gone online from a library, up from a little more than a third of teens (36%) who reported utilizing library internet resources in 2000" (14), the report seems to equate library resources with library hardware. The word *database* does not even appear in the study.

Students and Their Information Issues

Despite our students' comfort and familiarity with things digital, researchers point to their need for more instruction, as well as the support of improved interface design, if they are to become effective seekers and users of information. Virtual libraries address young users' needs on both fronts.

It is natural for students to face challenges finding, evaluating, and using information. They confront a trillion-page Web—a Web created primarily for adults. It is natural for users of any age to be baffled by the multiplicity of search choices offered by the Web—the commercial search engines, the subject directories, the portals. And then there are the millions of pages that comprise what we call the Invisible Web, most notably the subscription databases in which libraries invest so heavily.

While popular media attribute near guru status to young adults (Prensky 1998; Tapscott 1997), our own literature, the literature of library and information science, documents students' feelings of confusion and frustration and less-than-effective approaches when interacting with information technologies. The research reveals troubling data relating to students' searching capabilities, their abilities to navigate the Web to find the resources they need for academic research, and their understandings of search environments, despite common feelings of self-efficacy.

Students have trouble naming their information needs. Limited vocabulary and the inability to predict category patterns are prevalent cognitive issues. Brown (1995) found that 65–80 percent of subject search terms used by students from third grade through college fail to match the subject headings of electronic search tools. Shenton and Dixon (2004) observed similar naming problems with students representing their information needs in search terms. Large and Beheshti (2000) observed that sixth-grade students had trouble selecting appropriate search terms and that the problem was compounded when they had to search multiterm concepts.

In addition to their own developmental learning issues, young people come face-to-face with information glut as they confront hundreds of choices for any information task. Which search tools should they use for a particular information task—search engines, subject directories, subject portals, subscription databases? Which search strategies should they employ within each chosen search tool? How should they evaluate their overwhelming lists of results? What does quality look like? How should they document the sources they select? Agosto (2002) notes that students experience cognitive constraints in the form of information overload both within individual sites and with the Web as a whole. She describes students' overwhelming choice of websites as *outcome overload* and discusses the negative impact of this overload on student decision making, applying Simon's (1955) behavioral decision-making models of bounded rationality and "satisficing" to young adult information seeking, *Satisficing* is selecting decision outcomes that are good enough to suit decision maker's purposes, though not necessarily optimal—a blend of *sufficing* and *satisfying*. Student participants often stop searching before they reach a satisficing choice and select disappointing sources. For some students, the major decision making *stop rule*, is the first acceptable option they come across. Reminiscent of Gross (1999), Agosto's students describe a dichotomy of tasks—the imposed query, as when there is a teacher-designed task and deadline for a school project, and the self-generated search.

The *2003 OCLC Environmental Scan* (De Rosa et al. 2003) identifies major trends and patterns of change in the information landscape and its users. The report points to three changes among all information consumers. In terms of *service*, users are moving to self-sufficiency. Users see their worlds as *seamless*; they view their academic, leisure, and work worlds as fused. And echoing Agosto's findings relating to satisficing, in terms of *satisfaction*, information consumers are largely satisfied with the quality of the information they find, even though information professionals might not deem those materials satisfactory.

A Pew Internet & American Life Project study, *Search Engine Users: Internet Searchers Are Confident, Satisfied and Trusting—But They Are Also Unaware and Naïve* (Fallows 2005), looks at the public's trust in free Web search engines. Most users, especially young people, "paint a very rosy picture of their online search experiences" (2). Users are in control and feel confident. They are satisfied with their results. They see their favorite search engines as fair and unbiased sources of information and are largely unaware of alternative search tools.

Fidel et al. (1999) point to high school students' difficulties using the Web, the need for training, and the need for improved system design informed by examination of users' seeking and searching behaviors. The Fidel study notes that students know little about the various search choices available to them and are glad to be told where they might start. The research team observed significant student inefficiency and frustration, and conclude that training is needed and that search environments can be much improved.

Neuman (1997) describes high school students as novices in terms of their understanding of the research process. Students often chose inappropriate databases, had naïve and inflexible conceptions of how information is organized, and often misunderstood the structures of the electronic information resources they use.

The Importance of Mental Models and Navigation Aids

School virtual libraries attempt to organize the Web and other information sources for students through their use of image maps and other types of visual and text-based structures. Research points to a strong need for this type of guidance. Pitts (1995), Marchionini (1989), Neuman (1997), and Slone (2002) conclude that students have limited mental models for information seeking and lack the necessary framework for understanding information organization and the types of information available to them. Marchionini and Teague (1987) and Liebscher and Marchionini (1988) point to the need to create mental models to help users better understand information structures and navigate electronic environments. Large, Beheshti, Nesset, and Bowler (2004) conclude that student searching is improved when they are navigating venues that offer clues in a variety of media. In their study of adolescents' use of the *Science Library Catalog*, Borgman, Hirsh, Walter, and Gallagher (1995) explore and confirm the importance of hierarchal subject categories as recognition devices to aid in searching. Neuman's (1993, 1995, 1997) studies of high school students' interactions with online information resources reveals that students' compelling misunderstandings of database structures sabotage their independent use of these resources.

Nilan (1995) notes that navigational metaphors make particular sense when groups of users have some shared sense of the meaning of the metaphor. In the case of school virtual libraries, the in-person instruction of the teacher-librarian helps to reinforce the meaning of a common metaphor or structure for a student population who also use the site remotely.

Barker (1998) emphasizes the importance of mental models in the design of educational interfaces as cognitive structures. According to Barker, virtual libraries are themselves navigational metaphors that facilitate knowledge transfer between domains of knowledge and enable users to find their way around computer-based systems. Barker concludes, "the design of effective and efficient end-user interfaces that are able to stimulate the development of rich mental models will be of vital importance to the successful use of digital libraries as a teaching and learning tool" (6).

Fidel et al. (1999) note that students seek landmarks or graphical clues as they navigate the Web. Comparing the Web to a shopping mall where store windows must visually attract visitors, the researchers recommend that system designers recognize the importance of graphical guides for searchers.

Marchionini, Plaisant, and Komlodi (1998) identify principles to consider in the design of digital libraries. Among the design goals they point to are minimizing "disorientation by reducing navigation," "anchoring users in a consistent context" and supporting "rapid relevance decisions through overviews and previews" (535).

Park and Hannafin (1993) identify twenty empirically based principles relating to the organization of information. Among the most relevant of the principles for virtual libraries is that knowledge should be organized to reflect the learner's familiarity with the content, the nature of the learning task, and assumptions about the structure of knowledge. The researchers also note the importance of providing concept maps to indicate relationships among concepts and providing hypermaps to visually guide learners to relevant instructional tools.

Marchionini and Maurer (1995a) argue that virtual library interfaces play central roles in guiding learners through the research process both in the library and remotely: "At the nexus of physical and intellectual infrastructure is the interface to the digital library. . . . Good interfaces will allow learners to take advantage of digital resources equally well in classrooms, homes, and offices" (paragraph 8).

Online Interventions and Emerging Instructional Roles for Librarians

School libraries share specific missions different from those of special, academic, and public libraries. According to *Information Power: Building Partnerships for Learning* (AASL & AECT 1998), the mission of the school library is, "to ensure that students and staff are effective users of ideas and information" (6). The document explains that this mission is accomplished through seven goals. By organizing collections of information in a single interface to serve the *curricular mission* of the school, as well as the *learning missions* of the school library program, school virtual libraries can clearly translate and serve and extend at least four of *Information Power's* established goals:

- to provide intellectual access to information through learning activities
- to provide physical access to information through a carefully selected and systematically organized local collection of diverse learning resources
- to provide learning experiences that encourage students and others to become discriminating consumers and skilled creators of information
- to provide a program that functions as the information center of the school (6–7).

Wang (2003) suggests that virtual libraries "should provide the infrastructure for supporting the creation, assimilation and leverage of knowledge" (113) and ought to be constructed by examining the needs of learners, their learning priorities, and the mission of the organization.

Kuhlthau (1997) describes virtual libraries as offering new zones of intervention for librarians and encourages librarians to design such systems through which they can accommodate, guide, and coach learners. Kuhlthau sees virtual libraries as constructivist learning environments and argues that when virtual libraries are truly user-centered, learners' goals shift from merely accessing information to gaining new understandings of the learning process. Kuhlthau (1999) notes that when librarians intervene to create customized virtual libraries to meet the needs of specific learners, students are less likely to be overwhelmed by irrelevant information options. Clyde (1997) contends that a home page moves a school library "from being a user of online information to being an online information provider" (see "Rationale: Why have a home page?" section, paragraph 1). Clyde sees the virtual library's primary purpose as instructional—the delivery of "information skills that will be the essential life skills of the information age" (Introduction, paragraph 1).

Neuman (1997) recognizes the value of virtual libraries in gathering the specific information resources students need and sees the virtual library as "an essential venue for learning the concepts and skills necessary for conducting research and handling information in an information age" (79). Neuman also notes that teacher-librarians who study use, can improve their online instructional practice.

Virtual libraries offer opportunities for what constructivist educator Margaret Riel (1998) labels *just-in-time learning*—learning that is both time and place independent. Jasinski (1998) echoes Riel and notes that well-designed, customized online instructional environments can significantly improve learning, by providing opportunities for improved access and "just-in-time, just-enough and where-I-am learning" ("Individual learning model" section, paragraph 4).

Marchionini and Maurer (1995b) describe and predict the future of the virtual library medium in the school environment. They point to the ability of virtual libraries to break down physical barriers and facilitate communication "outside the formal learning environment" (paragraph 9).

Jenny Levine (2004), well known as the Web's Shifted Librarian, describes major differences in our students' approach to information use and the need for librarians to intervene on *their* turf, and to make their professional intervention portable. Levine suggests, "librarians have to start adjusting now. I call that adjustment 'shifting' because I think you have to start meeting these kids' information needs in their world, not yours. The library has to become more portable or 'shifted'" (paragraphs 7 and 8).

Roes (2001) argues that online intervention is a critical role for librarians in educational settings—there is no excuse for librarians "to wait and see." The role of the librarian off- and online is to "to support teaching and learning, and to develop relationships with faculty further and in the direction of supporting their teaching." Roes believes librarians must develop their "unique skills to support educational innovation" and function as role models for their institutions.

Evaluation of Virtual Libraries

Little research exists on evaluating school virtual libraries. Bruce and Leander (1997) note that research is heavy in virtual libraries for specialized workplaces, but see an unrealized potential for the development of educational digital libraries. They argue for the evaluation of school virtual libraries by observing their use in the context of their individual educational goals and their use of current technologies. In terms of design, the researchers suggest that to be most effective, virtual libraries should be customized and that the librarians who create them must examine their use by students and educators as searchers—"who they are, what their practices and needs are, and what we expect them to know."

Saracevic and Covi (2000) conclude that evaluation of digital libraries "has yet to penetrate research, practice, or even debate" and advocate evaluation efforts that may lead to improved access and use "across the landscape of digital libraries" (11). They admit that it is too early to set standards that might "freeze innovation," but note that it is not too early to urge professionals to consider evaluation as a critical part of digital library evolution. Saracevic (2000) both asks and partially answers the ultimate question: "How are digital libraries transforming research, education, learning, and living? At this stage we don't have the answers, but we have indications that significant transformations are indeed taking place" (368). Wang (2003) notes that educational virtual libraries should be maintained and modified according to user feedback, specifically relating to success and failure navigating the interface and unanticipated results.

Clyde's (1997, 2000) research centers specifically on the evolution and the evaluation of school virtual libraries. Clyde's compelling rationale for creating school library websites includes:

- demonstrating the role of librarian in information skills development;
- contributing to the development of a school information center on the Web;
- seizing a critical opportunity to promote the school library and the information technology skills of its staff;
- promoting collections, activities, and services; and
- offering guides to information sources in such forms as pathfinders, style sheets, tutorials; and making the library catalog widely available.

Clyde's rationale offers a base for evaluation efforts. Regrettably, while in 1997 Clyde saw endless possibilities, her early, small-scale content analysis revealed that most existing sites lacked purpose and made little effort to identify their users' needs. Clyde's (1999) longitudinal analysis of school library websites attempted to identify the most popular pages and features, to point to effective design models, and to develop *quality indicators* observed in the current state-of-the-art.

METHODOLOGY

Four focus group interviews with high school seniors were conducted in an attempt to gain a clearer sense of *why* and *how* students use a virtual library site. I sought to get a snapshot of the environment, to better understand students' experiences and behaviors using or not using the site for school research.

Focus groups were used to gain deeper insights into attitudes, opinions, experiences, needs, and concerns. This method was selected in the belief that the reflections of learners are critical in understanding use and information-seeking behaviors, and in planning and improving instruction and service. Focus group interactions also allow researchers to observe levels of consensus and disagreement in both words and body language.

Students were asked to reflect on their long-term experience using Springfield's Virtual Library interface. Specific questions addressed patterns of use—the *whys* and *whens*, the features students most value, how those features help them with their research, what problems and flaws students encounter with the interface, and improvements or additional features students would like to see. A full list of questions is appended.

After being granted approval for all components of the study from the Institutional Review Board at the University of North Texas, I videotaped and transcribed the discussions. The transcribed discussions, as well as qualitative data gathered from a Web-based survey, were coded using WEFT QDA 9.6. These four focus group interviews are one component of a larger mixed-method study that includes a Web-based survey of 1,257 high school seniors in fourteen schools with websites identified as *best practice* and a content analysis of those websites. The results of the larger study will be described in my dissertation. Three open-ended questions from the Web-based survey are analyzed in this chapter to validate the focus group responses.

Students were purposively selected as peer groups to inspire relaxed and easy discussion in the hope that individuals who shared commonalities would more likely share information with others like them. Volunteer students were selected from both Advanced Placement and regular academic classes to compare student responses in homogenous peer groups. Would honor students be more serious users of the Virtual Library? Would they employ more sophisticated information behaviors? Or was the influence of the Virtual Library broader, more universal, influencing the larger school population?

Volunteers were solicited from groups of Springfield Township High School students participating in the Web-based student survey also conducted during the first week of May 2005. Two of the groups were pulled from one Advanced Placement English class. The other two groups were pulled from two Global Studies classes scheduled for library research. I selected the first students willing to volunteer from each of the classes. The first group was girls only; the other three groups were mixed gender. The groups were ethnically mixed, and roughly reflected the 20 percent minority (predominantly African American) population of the school. The four groups were composed as follows:

- Group 1: Seven girls from AP English
- Group 2: Six students—four girls, two boys—from AP English
- Group 3: Seven students—four girls, three boys—from regular academic Global Studies
- Group 4: Six students—three girls, three boys—from regular academic Global Studies

Students eighteen years old and over signed a consent form prior to the discussions. Students younger than eighteen submitted signed parent consent forms. Students appeared eager to participate. Following certain housekeeping details—adjusting the camera, ensuring that students were comfortably seated, and collecting consent forms, the purpose of the study was explained and I assured students that their responses would be anonymous and that I sought their honest responses and was sincerely interested in learning from their experiences. Students sat in a semicircle in the library office in comfortable, upholstered chairs. They were offered refreshments. Each of the four discussions lasted approximately thirty minutes. The groups were sensitized to the focus group discussion questions, having first participated in the Web-based survey about the library website.

BACKGROUND: ABOUT THE
VIRTUAL LIBRARY

The Virtual Library has been in existence at Springfield Township since the current librarian arrived in September 1998. In 2001 the site won the IASL/Concord School Library Website of the Year Award (IASL 2003). According to Web counting software, over the course of the last school year, the site hosted 15,142 visitors per month. Students use the website when they are not at school. Though the counter software used does not allow differentiation of Springfield Township student users from nonstudent users, approximately 15 percent of total website use occurs on Saturdays and Sundays and 38 percent of usage occurs during the hours after school.

The homepage is an image map, a metaphor representing a physical library. The image of the librarian invites e-mail help. Among other features, the homepage leads to:

- *Catalogs and Databases*, which displays icons for the library's own subscription databases, those funded by the state of Pennsylvania, the library's online catalog, e-books collections, the state-wide interlibrary loan catalog and the online catalogs of the local public library and two nearby universities. The library staff regularly updates and distributes a list of passwords for the databases for students' home use.
- *Online Lessons*, which links students to an archive of many of the lessons, handouts, and assessment tools developed by teachers in collaboration with the librarian.
- *Research Guide*, formerly a lengthy print document, it describes school expectations and presents models for preparing formal papers and projects.
- *Reference Desk*, which leads students to free online almanacs, dictionaries, encyclopedias.
- *MLA Style Sheet*, which leads students to documentation advice

and models. At the request of the Science Department, the librarian recently added APA examples to this page.

- *Pathfinders*, a collection of librarian-created guides to resources supporting major student projects and types of projects. Pathfinders include: Social Issues, Literary Criticism, Primary Sources, Nations and Travel, Doing the Decades, Elizabethan/Shakespeare, the Middle Ages, Health and Diseases, College Search, and Streaming Video Resources.
- *Search Tools*, which lists and categorizes a wide variety of search tool choices for the free Web.
- Students also have one-click access to the Noodle Tools citation generator and to Turnitin.com, used for checking drafts of their work for originality.

BACKGROUND: ABOUT THE SCHOOL

Springfield Township is a suburban high school located just outside the Philadelphia city border. The student population of 900 students includes grades eight through twelve. The school community is experiencing growth as families from the city seek to move to the suburbs for the reputation of the small suburban district. The 2005 senior class consisted of 132 students. A total of 78 percent of them planned to continue to higher education, with 67 percent attending four-year colleges and 11 percent attending two-year colleges.

The school offers include seven Advanced Placement courses (English, U.S. history, calculus, physics, statistics, computer science, and environmental science). Honors courses are also offered in English, Social Studies, Mathematics, and Science.

As a culminating graduation requirement, twelfth-grade students complete Senior Seminar, a course that requires students to create an independent project based upon an area of interest. In addition to the project, students prepare a thesis-based research paper and incorporate technology in a formal presentation to faculty and peers. The course assesses students' grasp of information and communication fluencies learned over their high school careers.

ASSUMPTIONS

It was assumed that Springfield Township seniors were not novice information seekers. Springfield students are consistently involved in research projects for the five years of their high school careers. For the past four years, Springfield Township has focused efforts on improving student research. Courses and units examine essential questions. Student projects are inquiry and thesis driven. The principal requires one of each of the teachers' annual professional goals to address improving student research skills. Most of the seniors interviewed in the focus groups experienced four or five years of Virtual Library use, a hybrid experience involving both independent use and instruction occurring as students visited with their classes. Password lists are regularly distributed to students visiting individually and with their classes promoting the use of subscription databases at home. A schoolwide Research Integrity Policy (http://mciu.org/~spjvweb/acadintegrity.html) defines plagiarism and lists its potential consequences.

Students are encouraged to reflect on the effectiveness of their research. Teachers are expected to reflect on their own practice. Focus groups are part of the larger school culture. Over the past two years I and other members of the school faculty have conducted focus groups with students to explore such issues as student motivation, diversity, and effectiveness of rubrics as tools to guide learners. For the past five years I have been conducting exit interviews with seniors to better understand their learning relating to research and information fluency skills.

LIMITATIONS OF THE STUDY

Students in the four groups knew me as their librarian. Finding a qualified, trained moderator presented a challenge with time running out before seniors left school for their internships, the LEAP Program, in mid-May. I therefore opted to function as moderator because of my unique understanding of the interface and because of my connections with the students. The existing relationships with the students allowed a relaxed, informal atmosphere that encouraged the students to freely express opinions. Indeed, the students appeared comfortable and participated with enthusiasm and energy. Their honesty was confirmed by the more anonymous Web-based survey in which student responses to three qualitative items mirrored the responses of the students in the focus groups. Though the twenty-six students in the discussions also completed the Web-based survey, creating overlap, an additional thirty students (a total of fifty-six) provided remarkably resonant responses.

Though it is possible the students wanted to please me, due to long-established relationships, students were encouraged to respond honestly and were assured their anonymity would be respected. I was mindful of maintaining a climate in which students were comfortable in expressing their feelings freely. Students interviewed were merely three weeks away from graduation and felt little academic pressure to respond in a positive manner.

Like other students in schools with virtual libraries, Springfield students live in a hybrid environment. Though Springfield's Virtual Library exists in cyberspace, it also *lives* in the students' physical learning space. It is part of the school culture. The librarian and the faculty use it as an instructional tool. Teachers contribute to its growth and rely on it in their classes for reinforcing learning. It houses an archive of collaborative lessons, handouts, and student tools. Students use the site independently when they are in school and when they are home or otherwise remote. Findings relating to student use of the website naturally relate to its interconnected influence within the school culture of teaching and learning.

The four focus groups displayed strong group-to-group validation. In fact, the degree of consensus within and across the groups was extraordinary. Although it might be expected that honors or Advanced Placement students would approach the discussion or their work more seriously than general academic classes, each of the groups responded thoughtfully and discussed their research experiences with evident pride. Each described similar satisfaction and similar issues with the interface.

In each group, students were classmates and appeared comfortable and secure in their peer groups. The groups shared common research assignments and experiences and, in discussions, built on each others' comments, both positive and negative. The interaction among the participants was synergistic and spontaneous.

The degree of emotional engagement, as evidenced by the students' body language, animation, and frequent "chiming in" to agree was impressive, especially when it is noted that these are students discussing subjects that traditionally move librarians only. All students responded that they used the site. Several responded that they "love it." Nearly all agreed it was the first place they went when they started a research project (Q3). All students responded that they used it when they were not at school (Q1). Many noted that it was bookmarked on their home computers. Some said they had made it the homepage on their home computer. All were enthusiastic about the guidance offered by the Virtual Library over the course of their high school years. All noted that they relied on it heavily for school projects, most recently their Senior Seminar, English, and Global Studies classes (Q2 and Q6). They understood that the site was designed for them, that specific pages were created and maintained to meet the needs of specific Springfield assignments and specific Springfield teachers (Q7). Students understood the structure of the site. They knew the categories and why each was useful. Some commented that they liked the little pictures and found the site "pretty" (Q6).

Students spoke predominantly of their school research needs, queries inspired or imposed by their assignments and their teachers, although a few also described searches relating to personal information needs—for instance, the search for college information or for suggestions for books to read for leisure reading either from the Web-based OPAC or the linked reading lists (Q2).

RESULTS: GENERAL FOCUS
GROUP OBSERVATIONS

The most common reasons students listed for accessing the site were to use the subscription databases, to check documentation styles, to find quality resources and primary sources, and to use curricular tools developed collaboratively by their teachers and the librarian (Q2).

In each of the four groups, the favorite or most used area of the site was Catalogs and Databases, where students had access to subscription databases, the OPAC, and the catalogs of other libraries for interlibrary loan. Students described their favorite databases as if they were *fans*, as they might describe their favorite actors or musicians. "I love GaleNet." "I am obsessed with ABC-CLIO." When students suggested site improvements, their improvements focused heavily on improving their access to databases (Q5).

Students appeared to have understanding that Google was a wonderful search engine, but that it was not the best strategy for beginning academic research tasks. In fact, it made their academic research harder to manage. They relied on the school library website as a quality filter (Q6).

Students described their thoughtfulness in selecting quality information. They used the word *scholarly* thirteen times. Use of this word is likely connected to Springfield teachers' requirement that upperclassmen cite content from peer-reviewed journals in their projects. The website is part of the larger school culture that values high-quality resources and is dependent on the site to guide students to quality (Q4 and Q6).

Second to the Catalogs and Databases area in student preference in all four groups, was the MLA Style Sheet and assistance with documentation. Students universally noted appreciation that the sources they were looking for were used as examples. They clearly appreciated customized documentation advice available whenever they needed it (Q7). Many expressed enthusiasm for NoodleBib, a citation generator added to the site late last school year. Students noted that their teachers were serious about documentation. Their grades were related to their ability to document accurately. The format listed on the website was the format their teachers required (Q2, Q5, and Q6).

Students were eager to compare their experiences to those of their peers who do not have access to library websites. They displayed serious pride about their abilities and their knowledge of their Web options compared to their friends' in other schools (Q6).

Student responses are listed verbatim to illustrate the ranges and richness of responses. Grammar has not been corrected. Group numbers are included to illustrate the significant resonance of the responses across student ability levels.

"It'd be really dumb not to use it. Everything there's laid out for you." Reasons for Use (Q1, Q2, and Q5)

Students offered several reasons why they use the library site. Recurring concepts included:

- that the site is customized to their needs
- that it makes research expedient
- that the site functions as a quality filter
- that their teachers trust and recommend its resources

In all the groups, students noted that they used the site "whenever we have projects to do." Interestingly, only two students discussed searching for information when the search task was not imposed. They described personal searches for college information facilitated by the College and Career Pathfinder. In a school where research is regularly assigned, students themselves limited the conversation to information needs that addressed school research.

Among the academic reasons listed for use were:

A: If you need help with citing, you go and it has everything basically that you'll ever need.

A: Primary sources are a big one that it's really hard to find if not using the website, so we also go to that. (Group 1)

A: I'm trying to find like literary criticism or scholarly articles, I always go there first. But sometimes I'll type the Google search in first to give me like a general idea of what I should be looking for, and then I'll go there. But I pretty much always use it.

A: I love the pathfinders. I make good use of them. Extremely specific. You just go "doot" and then you're there. (Group 2)

A: It's usually the first place I go to primary search anything.

A: When I do a research paper, like a lot of MLA styles to make sure I'm doing the citations right. Databases too, like you want some scholarly articles you can go on, Bigchalk like one of those big databases that can really be helpful. (Group 4)

Many students felt the site offered them expedience in the research process:

A: It makes it a lot quicker to do research, whereas otherwise you'd have to go through like pages and pages of useless stuff, but it's a lot quicker and it's a lot more consistent. (Group 1)

A: And it also makes the research process less time-consuming, so if you have a project you're going to go to that because it's easy to use and it's fast, and it gets you right to where you need to be. (Group 2)

Students understand that the site is dynamic—that this page and others is responsive to new resources (Q7).

> A: I use it every year. You see it changes every year. And it keeps it updated so I know it's still there, reliable resources.

"They say you need scholarly things." Influence of Teachers in Encouraging Site Use (Q2, Q3, and Q5)

Students noted that they used the site because their teachers recommend it. They notice their teachers' roles in developing the online lessons, handouts, and pathfinders. Students from both regular academic and honors classes perceived that the site allowed them to meet their teachers' requirements for using *scholarly* sources.

> A: The teachers, you know, when they say you need scholarly things. (Group 1)
> A: And also teachers lead us towards the website for different classes. They have like their own little section set up so I use it then. (Group 2)
> A: Yeah, many of them just place emphasis on using the website for primary sources, and literary reviews, so in English and history, the more social type classes use it quite often. And also for like biology because you have like databases and pathfinders that you can use. (Group 2)
> A: I like it because they give you scholarly articles and most teachers require that, so it's a good place to start. (Group 3)
> A: And a lot of the teachers will have a place on the library's website where you can go to find assignments if you've missed any, which is another useful amenity. (Group 4)

Some students said that their teachers recommended it, but they would use the site even it that were not the case.

> A: I find myself going to it not just because the teachers wanted us to but because it was a good resource.
> A: Well, over the years I've found it useful.
> A: Yeah.
> A: Yeah.
> A: It's never like a last resort, because it'll be easier just to go straight there and see if it has it, because it usually does, and then do Google. (Group 2)

When do students use the site? Students clearly use the site at home, in the evenings, and on the weekends. In each group students noted that the site was either bookmarked at home or was their homepage on their home computer (Q1, Q2, and Q3).

> A: If I have a project, I'll use it at home to work on the projects. So I do use it at night and on the weekends sometimes.
>
> A: Basically whenever I have to research for a project, I use it, whether that's at home and on the weekends or at school, it'll be the first stop. (Group 2)
>
> A: And it's easier to use than, like if I'm at home I can use it instead of just having to go to the (public) library and hoping that the library has what I need, and sometimes it doesn't, so . . .
>
> JV: So do you guys use it at home, evenings, weekends?
>
> All: Yes.
>
> JV: You all use it at home.
>
> All: Yes.
>
> JV: Is it bookmarked?
>
> All: Yes. (Group 3)
>
> JV: Is it usually the first place you go or the last resort, or somewhere in between?
>
> A: Usually the first place.
>
> A: Yeah, the first.
>
> A: Yeah.
>
> A: It's my home page at home, so it's the first place I go. (Laughter) (Group 4)

"There's a database for everything." Virtual Library as Quality Filter (Q5 and Q6)

Students spoke often about the importance of discerning quality information, the importance of being able to locate primary and scholarly sources. They valued pathfinders as a way to quickly get to resources for specific assignments and to quickly access particular information formats. But perhaps the biggest revelation from the groups was the enormous appreciation students felt for access to online databases. Student voices gushed as they easily listed and described their favorites. GaleNet, especially its Opposing Viewpoints database, was universally acclaimed. A kind of "me too" syndrome emerged in each group as they discussed their most-loved databases. Though students had their favorites, they recognized that they each had particular strengths and choosing the right one for a particular information task was important. Some displayed surprising understanding of which database was provided by which vendor. (In a perfect virtual library world, that concept would be transparent to the user.)

A: I like e-library.

A: Me too.

A: I like GaleNet.

A: I love GaleNet.

A: I love EBSCOhost.

JV: Why do you like the databases?

A: Because they really give you good essays and good material. Like you're not getting little flimsy thingies from Google, you're getting good solid essays.

JV: So databases seem to be like the primary value.

All: Yes. (Heads nodding in agreement) (Group 1)

JV: What features of the library website do you value the most?

A: Catalogs and Databases. (Yes, all, laughter)

JV: It seems like that's a value for everyone?

All: Yeah. (All responding at the same time) GaleNet—yes, GaleNet! EBSCOhost, I like e-library. e-library is the best for Global.

JV: It's interesting to see that it is such consensus over the databases. Why is that, do you think?

A: 'Cause they have everything. It links you to the whole world.

A: There's a database for everything. Like if you need newspaper articles, there's one for that. If you need like scholarly sources, there's one for that too. If you need like pictures or reviews, there's stuff for them too. (Group 2)

A: I use it when—actually, I'm a dork. I use it when I don't know anything about that particular issue just to read up on it, or also if we have debates like the UN model that we did in one of our classes, I wanted to know a lot about my position that I was given, so I used Opposing Viewpoints and Research Gold (Student Resource Center Gold) which actually really helped me to get in-depth what I needed to learn.

A: I like how there's like a myriad of different databases in there, because if I'm in GaleNet's Opposing Viewpoints and I type in my topic and I only get three articles, I go search at e-Library and I find 20 articles. (Group 3)

Why the universal acclaim for databases? They give students efficient access to the materials their teachers value and those they have come to value themselves. Students noted that databases offered greater searching flexibility and more options than free Web search tools. They knew that databases offered opportunities to filter for peer-reviewed materials and to search by media or document type.

A: And also because you can be really clear about what you're searching for, and you can say like peer-reviewed or only magazines or only video pictures, primary sources. Just the options make it valuable. (Group 1)

And students appreciate the portability of their database options.

JV: So you appreciate search options in databases.

All: Yes.

A: A lot. And I also use them at home too since we have the passwords. And I usually go back and research further at home on the databases on my own computer. (Group1)

Students explained that their strategies for evaluation extend to examining database result lists. In Group 3, one young man brought up a selection process that moves well beyond satisficing. He described the importance of the critical evaluation of results even when they appear in already filtered databases.

A: The other thing is the ability to differentiate. I mean, yes, you have something like GaleNet and Opposing Viewpoints. But even Opposing Viewpoints might have articles that don't hold up to par as some others might, and you learn to look at those with a critical eye, learn to differentiate between good articles. I mean, it's not like looking at Google and GaleNet. You're looking at something that's very good and then deciding between great and better. (Group 3)

"I really don't have to Google things anymore, to aimlessly research." Comparing Google to the Databases and Virtual Library Resources (Q6 and Q10)

Convincing students to look beyond the free Web and commercial search engines has been described by many researchers as an uphill battle. (De Rosa, Dempsey, and Wilson 2003; Fallows 2005; Griffiths and Brophy 2005; Mann 2005). In fact, the OCLC Environmental Scan quotes one content vendor saying, "Google is disintermediating the library" (De Rosa, Dempsey, and Wilson 2003, introduction, paragraph 2). For the students in the focus groups, there are times to use Google, and there are clearly times when Google does not quickly get them what they need. A student in Group 1 expressed an understanding of

Google's limits, noting, "Apparently there's an invisible Web that I didn't even know about."

When searching options are no more than an extra click away, and when use of those options are highly valued by their teachers, the slope to develop a richer searching tool kit does not seem as steep. Without prompting, nearly all the students were eager to compare their experiences with the world's most popular search engine to their experiences with the Virtual Library for academic research. Students compared their lack of success with Google to their positive experiences with the website twenty-three times.

While students continue to use Google's significant information reach for other information tasks, their academic behaviors and attitudes fly in the face of the Pew findings relating to college students who ignore their university's resources. The Pew researchers observed "students who were using the computer lab to do academic-related work made use of commercial search engines rather than university and library Web sites" (Jones and Madden 2002). Each focus group repeatedly expressed the belief that their school library's customized interface was better able to give them what they needed, as well as what their teachers hoped they would find. Google didn't "cut it" for their school projects. It wasn't efficient for their information needs; it didn't filter for quality. It didn't have the type of search features they found in their favorite databases.

> A: When you research at the Virtual Library, you know that you're getting like correct information and stuff. Like going to Google and getting someone's like crap. Or a student project. (Group 3)
> A: If you end up going to Google, you have all sorts, you have all this huge pile to sift through, but the library's already sifted through all of those. (Group 4)

Students often compared Google to subscription databases. Though Google may have quality materials, students generally felt it would be more expedient to use databases. (Interestingly, these same students are linked on the Virtual Library to Google Scholar, Google Print, and Google's Advanced search screens. In the short answer items of the Web-based survey, students noted appreciation for being introduced to these extended Google tools.) The focus group students appear to understand the difference between general free Web search tools and databases.

> A: Google doesn't really come up with . . .
>
> A: Scholarly articles. That's how the Virtual Library helps us out. (Group 1)
>
> A: I think I understand more about like general Google searches versus the databases, like how they're separate and how they each kind of do different things for you. (Group 2)
>
> A: To me a good researcher is someone who doesn't try to find the easiest way out. I mean, it can take you, yeah, ten seconds, whereas ten minutes you can find twice amount of articles, journals, scholarly articles than you could have found on Google or Jeeves. I mean, they're search engines, and that's what they're specified for, search engines. They're not in-depth scholarly articles. You're not going to find Harvard Journal . . . and if you do, maybe Google's stepping up their game. (Group 3)
>
> A: I know that like before my boyfriend got into a different private school, the teachers don't even know what a database is. They are just like go on Google or something. . . . And then I compare it to students at this school, and it's like this is real information, I see that it's from a scholarly article rather than like someone's website project or something. (Group 3)
>
> A: I think it's a waste to go on Google, because like five articles from Google equal one from GaleNet. (Group 3)

Group 4 noted that other school websites may have limited resources and they feature prominent links to Google. The group laughed and wondered why a library would bother to link students to create such a link.

> A: I went to sites from a different high school and they had like a website but it didn't have any databases, good ones, they had maybe like two, it was like Ask Jeeves and Google. (All laugh)
>
> A: A link to Google. (Laughter)
>
> JV: Why do you laugh when you hear that?
>
> A: 'Cause it's so . . .
>
> A: It's like a joke to us.
>
> A: Cause now we have all these resources.
>
> A: All we go to Google is for pictures now.
>
> A: When we started out to research, every time we'd go to the library to research, we hear, now don't just go to Google." And other schools are like, "Hey, go to Google."
>
> A: In eighth grade they used to tell us all Google, and sites like Dogpile.

A: And now when I go to Google and I actually read stuff, I'm like, did a 12-year-old write this?

A: And they're just like weak. (Group 4)

Students sensed that the sources found using databases would be preferred by their teachers. Although the search engine would not likely be visible in the URL in a standard citation, the here student refers to the general quality of the choices (Q4):

A: Well, the other thing is when your teacher looks at your citations he or she is not going to see Google, Google, Google, Google, Google, Ask Jeeves. It's personally embarrassing for me to have that, so having something like New York University Medical Journal . . . that's a very good thing to have. And the teacher says okay, this person took time to do it. (Group 3)

"And I always know to like click on the desk if I want help." Instruction and Intervention (Q7)

Students noted with laughter that the Virtual Library continually expresses the librarian's voice and reinforces face-to-face instruction. Students' appreciation of this type of online intervention echoes Kuhlthau's (1997) descriptions of students' affective response to school research and the importance of adult intervention at critical points in the process, as well as the growing potential for intervention online. Students view the website as a hybrid experience. Instruction they receive formally or informally from their teachers and librarian during school hours is continued after school or when they are in school but not in direct contact with faculty.

Students understand the e-mail button is really their librarian and that she understands their information needs. Some students noted that they made use of e-mail help.

A: I know I can click on the desk if I need help. (Group 1)

Students as a group have come to understand that the sites preferred by their librarian, and their teachers are noted and might be worth visiting first. Formal lessons and over-the-shoulder instruction appear to resonate during students' independent use of the site.

A: I see like a lot of the databases and like how things are set up, it's like what you teach us to go to, and I can see how you're trying to get us to access those things that you tell us are useful for us.

A: And I think there's a lot of instructions on the page that kind of mimic your voice. It says I know when you come to like the classrooms telling us what to do, like if you look at the website, look at like what you have to do in the pathfinders or if you're going to a certain type of website, then like your voice is there because you're leading us towards it without you actually being there. (Group 2)

A: It's there. Yes.

JV: In what way do you hear my voice when you're at home?

A: When you research, you're like, when you're typing in the key words . . .

A: To rephrase it.

A: Yeah, to rephrase it if you don't . . .

A: To not just give up, not just give up if you don't get a match right away.

A: Keep doing all kinds of . . .

A: And to use different databases.

All: Yeah. (Group 4)

Although students in Group 1 didn't recognize they were using what the librarian called "Pathfinders," they later described these customized instructional tools as very useful. One young woman in Group 2, raved about their ease of use for specific projects:

A: "You just go 'doot' and there you are." (Group 2)

A: I think that's the main thing for me. And they give you so many options to choose from. It's like a win-win situation that you don't really lose from it. (Group 4)

"And it's pretty, so you don't think about having to do research." Schema and Organization as Implicit Instruction (Q6, Q4 and Q7)

The organization of the Virtual Library is designed to be implicitly instructional, with search choices and other resources categorized around an image map, guiding students to both Web and school-specific resources. Students felt that the scaffolding of choices reduced their cognitive load and made research more enjoyable.

A: I think it's cute. It's like a graphic organizer with pictures you can find. And it's pretty, so you don't think about having to do research. So it makes it easier. It makes it happier.

JV: In terms of the organization, does it help you?
All: Yes. (Group 1)

A number of instructional tools were developed for and are archived in this central location in order to facilitate access and reinforce instruction. Students understand that many teachers had favorite places on the site and places they themselves helped to develop—that their teachers' voices, as well as their librarian's, are present. For instance, as a school devoted to inquiry, the faculty offers supports to help students develop thesis statements.

> A: We definitely use the thesis test just about every time. That's helpful just because you have the five questions to check yourself with.
> A: I know in Senior Sem our teacher printed out a few of the resources I haven't seen. Some are on like more than just the thesis generator. There was one that was like different ways to word your thesis. You can use like comparisons, or like most people think this but in truth it's this. And I actually hadn't seen those before so it was really helpful.
> A: There is like a list of good introductory phrases that help in generating a thesis. (Group 1)

"Every citation on every paper." Documentation Help and Information Ethics (Q4 and Q5)

Second to databases, students noted the most useful feature of the Virtual Library was its guidance in documentation. Students appreciated the customization of the examples.

> JV: After databases, what do you like?
> A: Citations.
> A: Noodletools and the MLA style sheet. (All nodding heads)
> A: They have the like style sheet. I use it for every paper. (Group 1)
> JV: What other features do you use?
> All: Definitely. The style guide. Yeah! (Nodding heads, enthusiasm) (Group 3)
> A: The other thing is every time a teacher says you have this paper to do, oh and by the way, you have to do the MLA citations and works cited, so it's perfect to print it out and have it. (Group 3)
> A: I would do it like at nights to make sure that I have good sources, I'll go over and recheck them on the websites, and the MLA really helps you a lot, because there's a lot of different, there's a lot of different little stuff

that you can miss if you don't look at it correctly, and it gives you an example, which is always good.

A: Even doing works cited since you were in middle school, but I still, every time I do works cited, I still need to glance at the home page just to make sure everything's right, just periods and everything like that. (Group 4)

This year students were offered a citation generator as well as the style guide. Though they were always linked to free citation generators, NoodleBib is full-featured and includes specific guidance for citing all the school's databases services.

A: I like the citation generator this year as well.

A: Yes.

A: Yes

A: I use that quite often, especially when I've done a paper and it's all done and I've done my research and everything, and it's like the day that it's due and I'm like, oh no, I didn't do my works cited, I have to run up to the library and do that, and I just use the generator.

JV: NoodleBib works pretty well for you?

All: Yeah. (Group 3)

A: NoodleBib's amazing.

A: I like it because all you have to do is like enter in the information.

A: It's basically a template of all the information that you want to, what you'd add in for a works cited, and it just does it for you. (Group 4)

"So are you talking about interlibrary loan? A: Yes, that's it." Interlibrary Loan (Q4 and Q5)

Though no one could actually name the service, several students raved about the statewide interlibrary loan system. In an age of immediacy, where alternate information is likely available via e-books, websites, and full-text databases, this particular move away from satisficing speaks to student willingness to plan and to wait a couple of days, or even a couple of weeks, to get preferable information sources. It also speaks to student willingness to use print. Through the discussions, students revealed their understandings that libraries are networked environments and that university and public libraries generally have collections different from, and often larger than, school library collections. I attribute this willingness and these understandings to instruction in interlibrary loan use for major projects; the efficiency of the state-

wide catalog system, Access PA; the accessibility of local online university OPACs; and the ease of access to these services from the
Catalogs and Database page.

> \: I was looking for information about films that weren't just reviews of
> films, and I found a lot of stuff through the library website that were actu-
> ally through other universities and things like that.
>
> JV: Are you talking about interlibrary loan, the university catalogs?
>
> A: That too, but also using other schools' catalogs and things that we might
> not have here but we have connections to get to them, so that was very
> helpful. (Group 1)
>
> A: And like my senior project, I got to order those books from other libraries,
> the local libraries don't have them, and that really helped, especially when
> you don't really have access to things that you need for your projects.
> (Group 2)
>
> A: Also the Pennsylvania—my personal favorite is, next to GaleNet and
> e-Library, next is the Pennsylvania exchanges.
>
> JV: Do you mean interlibrary loan?
>
> A: Yeah, interlibrary loan, and you get it within two days, it's perfect, espe-
> cially when you're on a deadline. It's the best. (Group 3)
>
> A: Via PA Electronic Library or whatever, where all the libraries in PA are
> connected, so if our library doesn't have a book, it'll tell you where you
> can get it.
>
> JV: So are you talking about interlibrary loan?
>
> A: Yes, that's it. (Group 4)

"Much better. So much better. We have a lot of advanced programs here." Compared to Other Schools (Q4, Q5 and Q10)

Students spoke of their research skills with confidence and were eager
to compare their experiences to those of their friends in schools without
the guidance of virtual libraries. In fact, this comparison sparked animated conversation and agreement in all four groups. Students noted
that other high schools do not focus on student research. They suggested that teachers in other schools may not know what a database is.
The students expressed gratitude for the resources to which they had
access and clearly realized that not all their peers had access to online
guidance, customized curricular resources, and easy access to databases
to support their academic projects. These students regularly guide stu-

dents in other schools—high school students as well as students in higher education—to the Springfield Township site.

One senior who transferred to Springfield as a sophomore, made this comparison to her former school, which had a limited website.

> A: Not many libraries have set up what we have because other schools websites that I went to. And they might give you links to stuff that's going on in the library, but not Catalogs and Databases that we have available to us. They have like this online website and I wish in previous years back like I had access to it and knew about it, because it makes things so much easier with researching. (Group 1)

Another student noted that the site was important because it matched the strong research focus of the school. She suggested that students in other schools, with lower expectations for research, may not have the need for an extensive site.

> A: I know that I talk to a friend who goes to a Catholic school, a couple of schools, and they said that they really didn't write long papers, they usually write five-paragraph expository essays and that they only wrote a couple long papers in their high school career, and I feel like we are a lot more research-driven in that we write a lot more longer papers with scholarly articles cited, so I feel that we've been research-driven pretty much, and the website has helped with that. (Group 2)

Students spoke with evident pride of helping friends whose school libraries did not maintain extensive sites.

> A: And I know that friends, some of my friends from other schools, they always ask me where did you go to find the research for the information, or ask me to help them with their research because I know I can just go to the school website and then it'll be just that simple. (Group 2)

Students in Group 3 compared their experiences to their friends', admitting that they "illegally" shared their licensed database passwords. They were proud to be able to display their abilities to efficiently access quality material for school research.

> JV: Can you compare your research experience with those of your friends in other schools?

A: Better.

A: Much better. So much better.

A: A lot better. (Nods, agreement)

A: My friend was doing a senior project the same time I was, and she was like I need some more sources, like I can't find anything on Google or Yahoo or anywhere else she was searching. So I had to give her like my list of passwords and like the sites that I use. I was like, oh, don't give this to anybody else. She's like thanks so much. And I like did some research for her because I had the access to it. It only took me like five minutes to find just like a packet of stuff just to give to her, and she's like this is more than what I've gotten by myself in like a month.

A: Yeah, I do the same thing. Like if my friends are in trouble and I'm just like, oh, here, let me show you a place to go, and I pull up GaleNet, and I pull up Opposing Viewpoints, and they're like oh my gosh, thank you so much, this is exactly what I need. But my school doesn't have this. (Group 3)

The comment and the general feeling, "We have a lot of advanced programs here," is a little surprising. Strangely the students compared their *privileged* experiences to students whose schools had, at very least, access to the statewide Access PA POWER Library databases, an extensive collection that includes the EBSCOhost suite of databases. These databases are available free to most students in the state through either their schools or public libraries. Participants perceive that they are uniquely gifted with many of these free databases through the Virtual Library. They believe that their friends' access to these resources is limited, possibly because of limited awareness of the site through which the resources are available.

A: I know we just have a lot of advanced programs here. Especially online, but also if I talk to people that go to [the local community college], they struggle with writing papers that we could have written in like eighth grade.

A: I don't know if other schools really have everything that we have.

A: Yeah, my friend from (a local high school) couldn't even write like a paper and have all the resources like us. It was like a joke paper to us.

A: I went to sites from a different high school, and I felt I really didn't have, they had like a web site but it didn't have any databases, good ones, they had maybe like two, it was like Ask Jeeves and Google. (All laugh) (Group 4)

"I plan to use it next year." College Research Readiness (Q4, Q6 and Q10)

Nearly all students spoke of their attachment to the site. And although they all expressed their feeling that the site helped them prepare for college research, some expressed concern about moving on to new and larger interfaces. "I think I am still confused. I am sheltered within the system," said one young woman in Group 2. "I don't know what I would do in researching without it." This particular young woman's comments were both reassuring and distressing. She spoke to the comfort level students felt with the interface, as well as a certain lack of confidence for moving on. She was not alone. Several students expressed the fear that their college might not have a website that would be as easy to use. After the student expressed that thought, others responded that they suspected university library sites had similar structures and they would likely to be able to transfer concepts and understandings to the more academic environment.

Though most students expressed their readiness for college and academic research, each group noted they would likely return to the high school site. Several students noted that older siblings, because they are so comfortable with the interface, continue to visit as alumni. They grow especially reliant of databases that proved successful to them in their high school years. Though the sharing of a database password violates the school license, students are obviously using these passwords well beyond their high school tenure.

For these students, the site seemed almost like the neighborhood candy or convenience store. They know where the candy bars are and they know the shopkeeper behind the counter. The word "pretty," used by a young woman in Group 1, is likely used to refer to the image map that has served as a consistent schema, or mental map, for students over the years.

A: I plan to use it next year.

A: Yeah.

A: We'll be coming back. (All)

A: Everyone who's graduated says that they get a password sheet and use it so you can use it in college. I know my sister asked me for a password to use it for a student in college, and it makes me nervous, I'm afraid I'm going to go to college and they're not going to have like all this stuff to use.

JV: It's funny, because they will have really much bigger databases there.
A: They might not be pretty. (Group 1)

Another student reassured his group that they should be able to transfer their knowledge of the types of resources available to the university interface.

A: I think that it will help us in college with our university web pages, because I know that there's other institutions that have web pages set up like ours, so I think it helps us navigate in those sorts of databases. (Group 2)

A young man echoed the feeling of comfort, predicted a similar desire to return, and expressed understanding that the university site would lead to even richer options.

A: At first, when I go to college I'll probably still want to come back and use these databases. There's liable to be a whole ton more there, but I know how to use these. I mean, they've been effective. When I need more, I'll go find more, but so far, most stuff I've gotten here in high school has been amazing. (Group 3)

A young woman described her experiences using the site to help her brother, a Springfield graduate who is currently an engineering student. Though his college library likely had more extensive resources, he felt more comfortable using the familiar environment of the high school site. His younger sister spoke with obvious pride of her ability to help him.

A: Like just over this weekend, my brother called me. He graduated three years ago. And he called me to get the list of passwords to our databases. He's like (sister's name), I really need this, I have a project. And I was like, why can't you use the information that your teachers gave you? He's like 'cause I know that the information on this virtual library will give me the correct things that I need. He said I need EBSCOhost but I don't have the password, and that's what my teachers asked for. I was like I have stuff here as a high school student that college students need, and I think that prepares me well for college because now I know where I have to go, what I need, and I already know this stuff before I even get there.
A: Mm-hmm. (All) (Group 3)

While each group responded that they felt the website "definitely" helped them prepare for next year's college research, Group 4 was emphatic, and felt that they understood the need for quality, expressed confidence in their abilities, as well as concern about losing access to their familiar databases.

> JV: Do you feel that the school library website helped prepare you for doing college or real-life research?
>
> Several: Yeah.
>
> A: Definitely.
>
> A: Because you know that there's going to always be a better research thing out there. You can always get better information if you're not satisfied with what you do have. Like in college it's not going to be laid out for us like this, but at least we know now—
>
> A: We can keep the passwords.
>
> A: Yes. I'm definitely keeping them.
>
> A: Can we get a printout?
>
> A: You don't change the passwords every year, do you?
>
> JV: In other words, you feel prepared.
>
> A: Yes, definitely. (Group 4)

These discussions about college readiness point to the need for potential lessons introducing university interfaces to college seniors, so that students might transfer their understandings of categories of resources available to a larger interface. If students saw familiar, if extended, resources on these larger sites, the transition might be far less intimidating.

IMPROVEMENTS (Q8 AND Q9)

Students thought seriously about potential site improvements and were quite frank about their suggestions, despite any perceived investment of the researcher/librarian. Five major themes emerged as students described strategies for improvement of the site.

"Big list of links." The Need to Weed and Annotate!

For some students dead links were a problem. While the Virtual Library has been gradually evolving from a focus on lists of links to annotated

Pathfinders, old pages remain to frustrate student users. Students noted that they read and rely on annotations as clues to relevance and they would like to see more of them.

> A: For some of the links, I know I've come up to pages where it's just like a big list of links, and it would be kind of be helpful I think if there was like just a little star or something that just describes what the site is or what it has, because some of them are broken and some of them aren't what you were looking for or whatever. (Group 1)
>
> A: For me, I think on some of the less-used links, like the links to quotes, links to books. Some of them are broken, and have been for a lot of years. (Group 1)

"There should be a topic list for the databases." Describe and Organize the Databases!

In each group students wanted more information upfront describing the databases. They knew they had many choices, but were not always sure where to begin. Students felt they missed some of the *good stuff* because they had trouble identifying the best database for a particular task. Though individual databases, like Gale's Biography Resource Center and EBSCOhost's Business Source Premier are separately identified in the Pathfinders as students work on individual projects, databases are arranged by vendor in the Catalogs and Database area. This organization is meaningless to the student user. Several students requested that we organize the individual databases by subject, or perhaps create topical pull-down lists of databases for various information needs or for commonly researched questions. Following the focus group discussions, the librarian responded by adding mouse-over descriptions for many of the databases and plans to create pull-down links organizing databases by subject.

> A: There's should be like a topic list for the databases, so that way like common questions that kids ask while they're on there, they could just have a list of databases that apply to each topic.
>
> A: If there was a description of like the databases underneath or somewhere near so you could find it, to help you like direct to where you should actually be looking for a topic. 'Cause a lot of times I would be looking in different databases and I'd ask somebody, the librarian would say no, you

should be looking here or here. If there was a description underneath the databases, that would help. (Group 3)

"I don't have those sheets." The Problem with Passwords

Each of the groups noted frustration with the experience of losing the database passwords when they need to work at home. They wanted to see better strategies than lists of dozens of passwords, different for each database. These issues seem worth investigating and are not unique to Springfield Township. Many universities allow students to log in to all their online resources with the same student number and password that they use for many other academic and campus life purposes. K–12 vendors do not seem to be promoting similar strategies. As a result of the focus group discussions, the librarian plans to negotiate with the vendors for more uniformity in remote passwords.

> A: Sometimes when I want to access it from home I don't have those sheets to use it or something, and maybe they could put them on the website instead.
> A: It might be good to have like a website that has all the different passwords but have only like one password that you need to access that website so that you don't have to remember as many passwords at a time, and you can just access that if you need it. (Group 2)
> A: I think something that would be really cool would be like, you know how there's like that password sheet that you said is also in the background somewhere, I think it would be helpful if you could log in as if you were, like kind of like remote accessing something, you could log in as your first—or your last name, first initial and your password that you use at school, and then so that at home you could just click on all the different databases and not have to put in the new codes. (Group 3)

"Because I pick the wrong words . . ." Trouble Naming the Need

In each group students discussed their difficulty in expressing searches. This is consistent with much of the research describing issues with expressing information needs as well as the many researchers who suggest the importance of supports to help students as they search (Brown 1995; Fidel et al. 1999; Large & Beheshti 2000; Neuman 1997; Shenton & Dixon 2004). It is impressive that the focus group students actually recognize their issues as relating to *their own* limitations. They recognize that poor searches get them fewer results or results of lesser quality. To a small degree, this issue may be addressed in Pathfinders for individual projects, but would it be far more effectively addressed if search tools more seriously considered the vocabulary limitations of children and young adults. Working independently, students need the support of thesauri and systems that make alternative descriptors and related words and phrases more evident.

A: I found even I'm using a database, sometimes I don't know exactly what to search under, and I try a bunch of things. Sometimes it helps, sometimes it doesn't. But if I had like a more direct purpose in my search terms, it would save a lot of extra searching that I have to do.

JV: You're talking about developing key words?

A: Yeah. (Group nodding heads) (Group 1)

A: I remember having to do an exposé on Chinese prisons and I kept writing China prisons, and it wouldn't give me anything, it kept saying specify, specify, and that's really hard to do because you don't know how more specific to make it. So you put it in quotations, you do italics, you don't know. (Group 3)

A: That would be cool if they had some feature where you could type in what you want to search for, but it comes up as like twenty different ways to say it, because I pick the wrong words and then—

A: Cause it matters how you word stuff, how much information you get. (Group 4)

"The more we can get similar to that, the better." More Databases, Please!

Despite the fact the library website displays a wide variety of database options, Springfield students know that university budgets provide for a far greater array of resources. They expressed their desire for even more resources.

A: Well, I've seen like some of those university websites and they just have so many databases on there, and I guess a lot of that is a money issue, but GaleNet and e-Library, like we find there are like some databases that are just really good, and the more that we can get similar to that, the better. (Group 2)

RESULTS FROM THE WEB-BASED SURVEY

As part of the larger study of fourteen schools, Springfield Township High School seniors participated in a Web-based survey prior to the focus group discussions. The open-ended responses of fifty-six Springfield Township seniors (42.4 percent of the class) who participated in a survey help to validate the data expressed in the focus groups. Though overlap exists—the twenty-six focus group participants were among the fifty-six responders—the Web-based survey includes thirty additional students from other visiting classes. Web survey participation was more anonymous. No librarian observed. No camera intruded. Students who might have easily opted to answer only the "less energetic," quantitative items, clearly spent time composing responses in three concluding qualitative questions. These open-ended items corresponded to questions asked in the focus groups. All but one student wrote several sentences of responses to the following items:

- Can you describe a successful experience you have had using the school library website (Q4)?
- What additional features or improvements would you like to see the librarian(s) make to the site (Q8 and Q9)?
- In your own words please describe the influence the school library website has had on your high school studies (Q6).

Responses to the Web-Based Survey Questions

Student responses to the Web survey questions echo the responses of the focus group participants. (The following discussion connects the focus group questions to the Web survey responses.) Common themes for the "successful experience" item included the students' appreciation of access to databases, citation advice, and easy access to interlibrary loan. Students used the word *scholarly* nine times (Q4 and Q6).

Again they compared the use of the site to their experiences with Google:

> It showed me different alternatives in researching other than going straight to Google.
> I have learned how to decide if a site is credible or not, and I have learned

how to find more information and better ways to finding it rather than Goo-
gling everything.

They noted their appreciation for access to databases and an understanding that they have both free and invisible Web options:

> The databases are essential to most school projects and provide a lot of qual-
> ity material that can't really be found on the free Web.
>   I have recently finished a paper and project about Africa and the majority
> of my resources for the paper came from links on the school library website,
> such as SIRS, EBSCO, and GaleNet sources.

Next to the databases, students commented that they appreciated advice
in documenting their sources:

> Recently, I had to use the MLA style citation guide for a annotated bibliogra-
> phy for my English class. Many of the sources I used, I had never really used
> before, and this site was helpful in demonstrating the proper way to cite them.

They expressed satisfaction with online library services and connected
its use to their academic achievement:

> I have used the library website for every major project at school. In my junior
> year, I did my end-of-the-year project worth 170 points using only the library
> resources and I got an A on my presentation which was graded by the one of
> the teachers that is an extremely hard grader.
>   I have used the school library website for almost every project I have done
> in High School. . . . This website has saved my life many times during school
> and I couldn't have done as well as I did in High School without it.
>   I used the website for help in all major papers when it came to research
> and citations so that I was not to plagiarize. I relied most in my high school
> career on the Library web page for help in researching my senior thesis paper
> and project. It has been a great help and I may have been lost with out the
> guidance of the web page.

Though more than half of the students said the site was just fine as
is, the Web responses relating to suggestions for improvements also
echoed those of the focus group participants. Students requested even
more databases, online password lists for easier access to databases at
home, and more annotations for the links. They wanted the dead links

fixed. And they wanted more support for searching vocabulary (Q8 and Q9):

> Sometimes I forget to take the sheets that the library provides for passwords to use when accessing the website features at home. Then I have no way to access the things I need.
>
> While I often have the search engines and databases I need to search with, the search terms I am using often don't come back with the results I am looking for.

One student apologetically suggested that the site should go beyond research needs and focus on students' leisure interests:

> Maybe there could just be a site to link up to popular interest sites so that it does not overwhelm students and so that the web page is not used strictly for work. If I missed a link that sends students to sites for leisure, I am sorry, just an idea.

Student responses to the item on the influence of the site on their high school career overlapped themes covered in the item on successful experiences. Among the typical responses were (Q6):

> The library website has broadened not only my knowledge in all research topics, but has also helped me to better understand where to find the best information on the Internet.
>
> It has completely changed the way I research for a project. I no longer Google everything. I am better able to find information, and I am able to find the information more quickly.
>
> It easily guides the student through the research process, allowing them the luxury to focus on the content, style, grammar, and mechanics of the project itself. It truly makes the research process less arduous and time-consuming.
>
> Every paper or research assignment that I have had throughout my high school career, I have used this site for just about all of my research. I show it to all of my other friends that don't have a virtual library and they love it. I couldn't live without it.

CONCLUSION

The focus groups sessions clearly demonstrated that these four groups of students valued the library website and relied upon it heavily. Springfield students' responses to the qualitative items on the Web-based survey resonated with the focus group responses. What was especially surprising was the degree of consensus, both within and across the four focus groups, as well as the survey questions.

Student use the site when they are at home—evenings and weekends—and when they are at school (Q1). For many, it is the starting point for academic research and it is bookmarked on their home computers. Students in each group appeared eager to share successes with the interface. They believe that over the course of their studies, the website not only guided them to useful resources, it guided them to better grades. The site helped them meet their teachers' expectations (Q1, Q3, Q4, and Q6).

These are not novice users. These students display sophistication in their information seeking and appear to have learned from the site over their five-year high school experience. Students were well aware that their information choices extended far beyond the result lists of commercial search engines. These students consistently move beyond satisficing. They voluntarily and energetically seek out the nonimmediate and nonelectronic, as demonstrated in their interest in interlibrary loan. They are serious about evaluation. While current studies (De Rosa et al. 2003; Fallows 2005; Griffiths & Brophy 2005; Mann 2005) note that the general public relies heavily, often exclusively on Google, students in the focus groups noted that they avoided Google for their academic assignments and relied on the other search tools, including databases they discovered on the library website and the multiple sources types they discovered in customized pathfinders (Q6). They universally appreciate access to databases and recognize even within databases there is good information and great information. These students understand the need to use information ethically and demonstrate pride as they discuss the care they take in documenting sources with the guidance of resources available on the interface (Q5 and Q6).

Feedback from the groups spotlighted problems students faced in deciding which databases to use for particular tasks and how to develop a good query. The discussion confirms the need for both instruction and for database and website support for students looking for keywords as they search. It also confirmed the need for improving website annotations and for a more user-centered access plan for remote database users (Q8 and Q9).

Clearly, it is not the website alone that is inspiring the serious research behaviors. Use of the site for these students is a hybrid experience. Springfield Township teachers are users and advocates of the site as well as contributors to the site. Students note that they hear the actual voice of the librarian, as they interact online. That voice reinforces advice they hear when they are in the physical library (Q2 and Q7). Students expressed a confidence in their research skills that they attribute to use of the Virtual Library. Though they expressed interest in continuing to visit the site after graduation, they also expressed the feeling that the site helped prepared them for the types of resources they would likely encounter in an online academic setting (Q6 and Q10).

While the results of these focus groups cannot be generalized, these students are likely representative of students in their classes and they provide encouraging feedback and thoughtful suggestions for improvement of online service and instruction and suggest the possibilities that students can be influenced by virtual libraries to move beyond novice use of information.

Clearly designers of school library websites cannot make assumptions that strategies that work in one culture will work in other school communities. Currently both qualitative and quantitative data from the larger study of fourteen schools identified as best practice in school library websites is being examined to extend the study. A content analysis of the sites will compare the features and services presented and a Web-based survey of nearly thirteen hundred high school seniors will offer a larger picture of the impact of virtual library service. Will the data from the other schools resonate with the data from Springfield Township? To what degree does library online instruction and guidance influence the information-seeking habits of young adults? What role does school culture play in use and effectiveness of these sites?

ACKNOWLEDGMENTS

I thank teachers Veronika Sweeny and Carol Rohrbach for allowing their students to participate in the focus groups and the students themselves for their honesty and their investment of time in helping to improve virtual library service to the students who follow them at Springfield.

REFERENCES

Abram, S., and J. Luther. 2004. Born with the chip: The next generation will profoundly impact both library service and the culture within the profession. *Library Journal* 129(8): 34–37.

Agosto, D. E. 2002. Bounded rationality and satisficing in young people's web-based decision making. *Journal of the American Society for Information Science and Technology* 53(1): 16–27.

American Association of School Librarians (AASL) and Association for Educational Communication & Technology (AECT). 1998. *Information power: Building partnerships for learning*. Chicago: American Library Association.

Barker, P. G. 1998. The role of digital libraries in future educational systems. http://www.philip-barker.demon.co.uk/online98.doc (accessed October 25, 2006).

Borgman, C. L., S. G. Hirsh, V. A. Walter, and A. L. Gallagher. 1995. Children's searching behavior on browsing and keyword online catalogs: The Science Library Catalog Project. *Journal of the American Society for Information Science* 46(9): 663–84.

Brown, M. E. 1995. By any other name: Accounting for failure in the naming of subject categories. *Library & Information Science Research* 17(4): 347–85.

Bruce, B. C., and K. M. Leander. 1997. Searching for digital libraries in education: Why computers cannot tell the story. *Library Trends* 45(4): 746–71.

Clyde, L. A. 1997. The school library as information provider. University of Iceland. School of Library and Information Science. http://www.hi.us/~anne/sl homepage.html (accessed October 18, 2004).

———. 1999. The school library Web site: On the information highway or stalled in the car park? In *Unleash the power! Knowledge, technology, diversity: Papers presented at the Third International Forum on Research in School Librarianship*, ed. L. Lighthall and E. Howe, 227–37. Seattle, WA: International Association of School Librarianship.

———. 2000. School library Web sites: The state of the art. University of Iceland, School of Library and Information Science. http://www.hi.is/~anne/isis2000.html (accessed October 18, 2004).

De Rosa, C., L. Dempsey, and A. Wilson. 2003. *2003 OCLC Environmental Scan: Pattern recognition*. http://www.oclc.org/membership/escan/introduction/default.htm (accessed October 1, 2004).

Fallows, D. 2005. *Search engine users: Internet searchers are confident, satisfied and trusting—but they are also unaware and naïve*. Pew Internet & American Life Project. http://www.pewinternet.org/PPF/r/146/report_display.asp (accessed July 24, 2005).

Fidel, R., R. K. Davies, M. H. Douglass, J. K. Holder, C. J. Hopkins, E. J. Kushner. 1999. A visit to the information mall: Web searching behavior of high school students. *Journal of the American Society for Information Science* 50(1): 24–37.

Griffiths, J. R., and P. Brophy. 2005. Student searching behavior and the Web: Use of academic resources and Google. *Library Trends* 53(4): 539–53.

Gross, M. 1999. Imposed queries in the school library media center: A descriptive study. *Library and Information Science Research* 21(4): 501–21.

International Association of School Librarians. 2003. IASL/Concord School Library Web Page Awards. http://www.iasl-slo.org/web_award.html (accessed November 1, 2004).

———. 2003. IASL/Concord School Library Web Page Awards: Selection criteria. http://iasl-slo.org/web_criteria.html (accessed November 20, 2004).

Jasinski, Marie. 1998. Pedagogical issues emerging from this project. In *Teaching and learning styles that facilitate online learning.* http://www.tafe.sa.edu.au/lsrsc/one/natproj/tal/pedissues/pedaiss.htm (accessed November 15, 2004).

Jones, S., and M. Madden. 2002. *The Internet goes to college: How students are living in the future with today's technology.* Pew Internet & American Life Project. http://www.pewinternet.org/report_display.asp?r = 71 (accessed September 20, 2004).

Kuhlthau, C. C. 1997. Learning in digital libraries: An information search process approach. *Library Trends* 45(4): 708–24.

———. 1999. Accommodating the user's ISP: Challenges for information retrieval systems designers. *Bulletin of the American Society for Information Science* 25(3): 1–7.

Large, A, and J. Beheshti. 2000. The Web as a classroom resource: reactions from users. *Journal of the American Society for Information Science* 51(12): 1069–80.

Large, A., J. Beheshti, V. Nesset, and L. Bowler. 2004. Designing Web portals in intergenerational teams: Two prototype portals for elementary school students. *Journal of the American Society for Information Science and Technology* 55(13): 1140–54.

Lenhart, A., M. Madden, and P. Hitlin. 2005. *Teens and technology: Youth are leading the transition to a fully wired nation.* Pew Internet & American Life Project. http://www.pewinternet.org/PPF/r/162/report_display.asp (accessed October 17, 2006).

Levin, D., S. Arafeh, A. Lenhart, and L. Rainie. 2002. *The digital disconnect: The widening gap between Internet-savvy students and their schools.* Pew Internet & American Life Project. http://207.21.232.103/PPF/r/67/report_display.asp (accessed September 30, 2004).

Levine, J. 2004. What is a shifted librarian? *The Shifted Librarian.* http://www.theshiftedlibrarian.com/stories/2002/01/19/whatIsAShiftedLibrarian.html (accessed July 5, 2005).

Liebscher, P., and G. Marchionini. 1988. Browse and analytical search strategies in a full-text CD-ROM encyclopedia. *School Library Media Quarterly* 16(4): 223–33.

Mann, T. 2005. Research at risk. *Library Journal* 120(12): 38–40.

Marchionini, G. 1989. Making the transition from print to electronic encyclopedias:

Adaptation of mental models. *International Journal of Man-Machine Studies* 30(6): 591–618.

Marchionini, G., and H. Maurer. 1995a. Digital libraries in education: promises, challenges and issues. In *The role of digital libraries in teaching and learning.* http://www.ils.unc.edu/~march/cacm95/sub8.html (accessed November 19, 2004).

———. 1995b. How do libraries support teaching and learning? In *The role of digital libraries in teaching and learning.* http://www.ils.unc.edu/~march/cacm95/mainbody.html (accessed November 19, 2004)

Marchionini, G., and J. Teague. 1987. Elementary students' use of electronic information services: An exploratory study. *Journal of Research on Computing in Education* 20(2): 139–55.

Marchionini, G., C. Plaisant, and A. Komlodi. 1998. Interfaces and tools for the Library of Congress National Digital Library Program. *Information Process & Management* 34(5): 535–55.

Milbury, P., B. Woolls, and D. Loertscher. 2005. *School libraries.Net: Peter Milbury's network of school librarian Web pages.* http://www.school-libraries.net (accessed November 2, 2004).

Neuman, D. 1993. High school students' use of databases: Results of a national Delphi study. *Library Trends* 45(4): 687–707.

———. 1995. High school students' use of databases: Results of a national Delphi study. *Journal of the American Society for Information Science* 46(4): 284–98.

———. 1997. Learning and the digital library. *Library Trends* 45(4): 687–707.

Nilan, M. S. 1995. Ease of user navigation through digital information spaces. *Sigois Bulletin* 16(2): 38–39.

Park, I., and M. J. Hannafin. 1993. Empirically based guidelines for the design of interactive multimedia. *Educational Technology Research and Development* 41(3): 63–85.

Pitts, J. M. 1995. Mental models of information: The 1993–94 AASL/Highsmith Research Award Study. *School Library Media Quarterly* 23(3): 177–84.

Prensky, M. 1998. *Twich speed: Keeping up with young workers.* http://www.twitchspeed.com/site/article.html (accessed October 15, 2004).

Riel, M. 1998. *Education in the 21st century: Just-in-time learning or learning communities.* Center for Collaborative Research in Education, University of California–Irvine. http://www.gse.uci.edu/vkiosk/faculty/riel/jit-learning/ (accessed October 20, 2004).

Roes, H. 2001. Digital libraries in education. *D-Lib Magazine.* http://www.dlib.org/dlib/july01/roes/07roes.html (accessed November 19, 2004).

Saracevic, T. 2000. Digital library evaluation: Toward an evolution of concepts. *Library Trends* 49(2): 350–70.

Saracevic, T., and L. Covi. 2000. Challenges for digital library evaluation. *Proceedings of the American Society for Information Science* 37: 341–50.

Shenton, A. K., and P. Dixon. 2004. Issues arising from youngsters' information-seeking behavior. *Library & Information Science Research* 26(3): 177–200.

Simon, H. A. 1955. A behavioral model of rational choice. *Quarterly Journal of Economics* 69: 99–118.

Slone, D. J. 2002. The influence of mental models and goals on search patterns during Web interaction. *Journal of the American Society for Information Science and Technology* 53(13): 1152–69.

Tapscott, D. 1997. *Growing up digital: The rise of the net generation.* New York: McGraw-Hill.

Tenopir, C. 2003. What user studies tell us. *Library Journal* 128(14): 32.

Wang, M. Y. 2003. The strategic role of digital libraries: Issues in e-learning environments. *Library Review* 52(3/4): 111–16.

8

Digital Reference Services: Recommendations for Supporting Children's Informal Learning

Joanne Silverstein

ABSTRACT

This chapter explores the use of formal digital reference services for supporting children's informal learning. First, a new model of question types is created to include digital reference questions that are informal, but submitted to formal online education services. Digital reference questions are defined as artifacts of informal learning, and digital reference services as conducive contexts for studying informal learning. Findings from a research study of children's "just curious" questions are reported and one finding is examined in detail: Temporally adaptive digital reference systems must be designed to allow automatic changes that reflect students' evolving information needs and practices. Three important components of temporally adaptive digital reference services are personal profiles of users, support for collaborative learning, and pedagogical agents. Examples of systems including these technologies are described, and topics for future reference suggested.

INTRODUCTION

Digital reference services offer rich venues in which to study the online, information-seeking behaviors of children. Most digital reference research investigates how children use tools to answer questions that arise in the classroom. An interesting and frequent phenomenon, however, children's use of digital references services to support informal learning, remains largely unexplored. As Riechel (1991) points out in a discussion of conventional libraries, there is "professional neglect in considering and supporting children's library use for self-generated needs." That neglect also applies to the study of children's use of digital libraries for self-generated needs. This is unfortunate because it indicates that digital reference services—a basic component of digital libraries—are unprepared for the nature and growing number of self-generated queries received from children. They may also be unaware of the potentially helpful role their services could play in supporting children's informal learning.

This chapter attempts to address the neglect by exploring children's use of formal digital reference services to support their informal learning. It proposes modifications to Bilal's (2002) Taxonomy of Tasks to include digital reference questions that are informal, but submitted to formal digital reference services. Also described are the findings from a recent research study, suggestions for software designers, and a topic for future research that will further support children's use of digital reference services for informal learning.

INFORMAL LEARNING AND
SELF GENERATED QUESTIONS

Informal learning is knowledge acquisition that occurs outside the formal classroom—often in museums, zoos, libraries, and at home. Because informal learning occupies a nexus of psychology, education, information science, and library science theory, it is described by many synonymous phrases. In the literatures of education and psychology, Oldfather and McCaughlin (1993) refer to it as "continuing impulse to learn," Kasworm (1983) as "self-directed learning," and Condry (1977) as "self-initiated learning."

In the motivation literature, Deci and Ryan (1985) link "intrinsic motivation" to informal learning. In a later discussion of self-determination theory (SDT), Deci and Ryan (2000) state that motivation to learn can be strengthened or weakened by external factors, but is intrinsic to human nature.

In the communications and new media literature, Sefton-Green (2004) links informal learning to life-long learning, stating:

> lifelong learning is a survival issue. . . . If knowledge, skills and learning abilities are not renewed, the capacity of individuals—and by extension, of communities or nations—to adapt to a new environment will be considerably reduced.

Within the domain of information science, Bilal (2002) writes about search tasks—a concept that is partially defined by the locus of the information need, saying:

> One may infer that when children generate their own topics, they may be more motivated, challenged, engaged and successful than when they pursue topics that are imposed or assigned.

The locus of information need is a defining characteristic of informal learning. It is this shared concept that compels a closer review of Bilal's Taxonomy of Tasks and its relationship to informal learning. Bilal defines a task as "an essential factor in the information seeking process. [The] type of task a user is given influences the user's information seeking, information use, and success." In her taxonomy (see figure 8.1), Bilal organizes tasks by type (open-ended versus closed), nature (complex versus simple), and administration (fully assigned, semi-assigned, and fully self-generated). Thus, a task may be:

Open-ended, complex: fully assigned, semi-assigned, or fully self-generated.

Closed, simple: fully assigned, semi assigned, or fully self-generated.

Open-ended, simple: fully assigned, semi-assigned or fully self-generated.

Closed, complex: fully assigned, semi assigned, or fully self-generated.

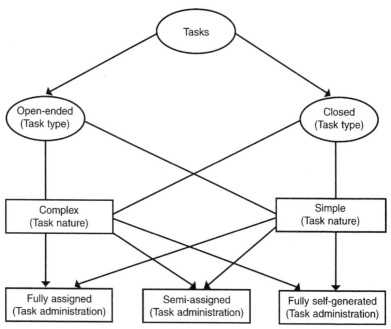

Figure 8.1. Bilal's Taxonomy of Tasks

The Taxonomy of Tasks is a useful construct and will be modified to support a model of question types later in this discussion.

Meanwhile, Bilal's "fully self-generated task," one component of the Taxonomy, is of specific interest here because it was based on a related concept, Gross's (1998) notion of the self-generated question. We may best comprehend the nature of the self-generated question by first understanding Gross's imposed query: a question that expresses an information need arising from an external source, e.g., homework, science fair, or preparing for a test. Conversely, a self-generated question is, "internally motivated in response to the context of an individual's life circumstance."

The self-generated question is an artifact of informal learning, and is the unit of study within the context of this chapter.

DIGITAL REFERENCE SERVICES AS CONTEXT
FOR STUDYING INFORMAL LEARNING

Digital reference services (also known as AskA services) are interactive communication technologies that provide outreach and human intermediation in response to users' e-mailed queries. An integral function to the digital library (Lankes 2002), their role correlates to the role of reference librarians in traditional libraries.

Digital reference services are a context for informal learning, as supported by the first two of Sefton-Green's (2004) informal learning contexts:

1. educational experiences provided to support curricula
2. educational experiences provided to support socially important, but not curriculum related learning
3. leisure activities outside the realm of socially valued educational experience

Digital reference services have become increasingly specialized to serve specific user populations, one of which is children, and those services are designed to support learning about school-related topics. "Ask an Astronomer" (http://curious.astro.cornell.edu/index.php) at Cornell University is one such service, and answers questions about astronomy, space-related careers, and space science. Other features of the site include searchable archives of previously asked-and-answered questions, essays and fact sheets, and links to other astronomy resources.

Another example of a digital reference service is AskNSDL, which responds to questions from users (students, parents, and teachers), who need information about the National Science Digital Library or its collections. The answers are provided by volunteers who possess wide ranges of expertise (http://nsdl.org/asknsdl/).

Digital reference services are conducive to studying the information-seeking behaviors of children for the same reasons that they are popular with the children who use them. First, the anonymity with which children may participate in digital references services provides them a sense of freedom to ask whatever they want. A result is that children use digital reference services for informal learning needs, not just formal learning needs. The inherent anonymity of digital reference services also enables researchers to gather data from children's searches, while protecting children's privacy. Second, children can easily participate in digital reference services: Use requires only basic typing skills, operation of the cursor, and access to the Web. Third, because digital reference questions are transmitted in electronic files, records can be easily captured, stored, analyzed, and presented, thus research data are easy to access.

For the purpose of this discussion, then, informal learning is operationalized as children's self-generated questions sent to digital reference services that were designed to support formal learning and imposed queries.

Having established digital reference services as a context for studying informal learning, all that remains before considering the data is to establish a model of question types that includes digital reference questions and shows their relation to other kinds of questions.

A MODEL OF QUESTION TYPES

Self-generated questions posed to digital reference services are not generally recognized in the literature. This section is intended to resolve that gap by (1) creating a model of question types that describes the kinds of digital reference questions possible, and (2) placing within that model questions asked in this study. The first task requires that we refer back to Bilal's taxonomy of tasks.

Bilal's tasks—online searches—are analogous to digital reference questions, and her taxonomy of tasks makes a good foundation for a model of question types. Let us start, then, by renaming "tasks" as "questions." Bilal organizes tasks by their type, nature, and administration, characteristics that can also be used to describe question types. Thus, this model of question types includes type, nature, and administration. To better describe the scope of questions and extend the question model's utility, let us add three categories.

The first additional category is "Intermediation" and it conveys whether a question was sent to a human-intermediated or non-human-intermediated information service. Non-human-intermediated resources include books, journals, websites, databases, and many others. Human-intermediated resources include, but are not restricted to, reference librarians, help desk personnel, and digital reference experts. The category entitled, "Intermediation," then, is added to the model, and its values can be Human or Non-Human.

Second—let us add "Venue," which describes whether the question is asked online or off-line. Books and journals are off-line resources, for example; and websites and databases are online resources. The category of "Venue," values for which include Off-line or Online, captures this dichotomy and is added to the model.

Finally, "Interaction" describes communication configurations and has values of Many-to-Many, One-to-Many, or One-to-One. A One-to-Many interaction would include, for example, a user posing a question to a listserv or blog community. A One-to-One interaction would include submittal of a user's question to an expert at a digital reference, or AskA service.

These six variables—"Type," "Nature," "Administration," "Intermediation," "Venue," and "Interaction"—comprise a model of question types, and a perspective for viewing digital reference questions examined in this research.

The questions examined in this study were self-generated, and asked in one-to-one interactions, of experts at human-intermediated, online digital reference services. Questions types included both open and closed, and task nature included both complex and simple. These questions are represented by the italic text in table 8.1, Model of Question Types.

Having established a context and a model that accommodates several

Table 8.1.   Model of Question Types

Type	Open	Close-ended	
Nature	Complex	Simple	
Administration	*Fully Assigned*	*Semi-Assigned*	Self-Generated
Intermediation	*Non-human*	Human	
Venue	*Off-line*	Online	
Interaction	*Many-to-Many*	*One-to-Many*	One-to-One

Note: The values in italics are not subjects of this study.

kinds of digital reference questions, we may consider their importance in better understanding children's online information seeking, and implications for the design of information systems that will support informal learning.

RESEARCH QUESTION(S)

Self-generated questions that were sent to digital reference services were the focus of a recent research study entitled Just Curious (Silverstein 2005). The research question of Just Curious was, "Do children use formal (curriculum reflective) digital references services to pursue informal learning?"

Findings from Just Curious showed that children make considerable use of digital reference services to obtain answers to their self-generated questions, and that they ask questions about specific non-school-related topics, the foci of which change as students get older. Further, the Just Curious study showed that digital reference services support the transfer of student motivation and curiosity from formal to informal learning.

Having established that children do make informal use of formal digital reference services, another question emerged: "What can we learn from these findings that could inform information system design to support children's online, informal learning?" This question led to a second review of the data, which was entitled Just Curious Second Analysis. The results of that research provide the focus of this chapter, and are discussed later. First, a brief review of the initial Just Curious study will provide the necessary background for discussing findings from the Just Curious Second Analysis.

METHODS AND FINDINGS FROM THE JUST CURIOUS STUDY

Children's questions for the Just Curious study were gathered in 2004 from two digital reference services, the Virtual Reference Desk's (VRD) Learning Center (http://vrd.askvrd.org/search.asp), and the ESTME Digital Reference Service—a digital reference service sponsored by the National Science Foundation during Excellence in Science, Technology, and Mathematics Education Week (ESTME).[1]

Data Processing for the Just Curious Study

Data processing included several steps: questions were consolidated in one database, and duplicate questions, defined as identically worded queries submitted almost simultaneously, were counted and then removed from the database.

Users submitting questions to these digital reference services were required to use a pull-down menu to describe a reason for wanting their information. They could select one from a total of twelve reasons, some of which were, "Homework," "Brief Research," "Essay," "Class Assignment," and "Just Curious." Only questions marked "Just Curious" were included in the study.

Users also had to identify their roles, and could choose from student, teacher, researcher and several other categories. Questions not labeled "Student" were removed.

In the case of some questions, roles were obviously mislabeled. For example, several questions were labeled as being asked by elementary school children, but the wording, ("My child wants to know . . .") showed that adults actually submitted the questions. Mislabeled questions were removed from the database.

The remaining questions were then grouped by "Elementary Student" (questions from students in grades K–5), "Middle School Student" (questions from students in grades 6–8), and "High School Student" (questions from students in grades 9–12).

One hundred fourteen e-mailed questions remained (thirty-five from the Learning Center and seventy-nine from the ESTME service) many of which contained several queries in one e-mail. These questions were labeled "Compound Question" and broken out into individual queries, after which there was a total of 150 queries.

Data Analysis for the Just Curious Study

Efforts to analyze the data began with a search for deductive methods that used existing question taxonomies. Deductive question taxonomies abound in the literature, but several shortcomings precluded their use in this study: They either categorize questions articulated by adults, (but children do not necessarily ask the same kinds of questions as adults); were imposed and based upon assigned readings (the questions in this study focus on students' self-generated questions); or simply didn't fit (an attempt to code according to the Graesser, Lang, and Horgan [1998] taxonomy failed because many of the children's questions fell into one and only one category, "concept completion"; this is useful information, but not sufficiently descriptive to support a deductive research method). Thus, deductive methods that use existing instruments or taxonomies were discarded in favor of inductive analysis.

Inductive analysis begins with data or answers, in the absence of an explanation. The researcher analyzes data not to compare them to existing rules, but to identify unexpected trends and patterns. This process usually leads to new research questions.

Inductive analysis of the data allowed identification of forty-three topics or code categories, some of which naturally clustered into supercategories. The supercategory entitled "Focus of Curiosity," for example, comprised six other categories, "My World," "My Stuff," "Other People," "The World," "The Universe," and "Abstract Thought." Forty-five percent of queries from elementary school students expressed interest about how the world works ("The World" and "The Universe"), while abstract or conceptual issues were of increasing interest to middle school students ("Abstract Thought"). Questions from high school students addressed mostly issues of their immediate circumstances ("My World" and "My Stuff"). These findings suggest that the topics about which a student is just curious may shift over time, from "how the world works" to "how my world works."

The code, "Curriculum-Related" describes queries that represent curiosity that has "carried over" from formal learning (extrinsic curiosity) to informal (intrinsic curiosity). One example is the following query, "I want to know about Hercules. It's not for school." A brief check of the curriculum for that student's grade level confirmed that this topic was part of the curriculum ("Ancient Worlds") for the student's school grade. The question was most likely stimulated by classroom work, but became the focus of intrinsic curiosity for the student. Nearly half of all queries from elementary school students were coded "Curriculum-Related" indicating that during the elementary school years, students' curiosity is more deeply influenced by school curricula than it will be in later years.

"Curriculum-Related" queries show that digital reference services can support informal learning by facilitating the transfer of curiosity from formal learning environments to informal learning.

Some questions seemed completely unrelated to classroom topics. Inductive methods do not allow dismissal of such questions as being out of scope, but require a way to explain them. These questions fall into code categories entitled "Career Planning," "Health and Welfare," and "Death and Anxiety."

Findings from the Initial Just Curious Study

A summary of findings from the initial Just Curious study, described in detail elsewhere, is reported as a brief list here:

- Students often use formal, curriculum-reflective digital reference services to pursue informal learning.
- Compound questions are a routine phenomenon in digital reference.
- Over the years during grades K–12, students' informal information seeking may shift in focus from a world perspective to a personal perspective.
- The use of children's digital reference services is high in elementary school and peaks in middle school.
- During the elementary school years, students' intrinsic curiosity is more deeply influenced by school curricula than it will be in later years.
- During the middle school years, use of digital reference services for informal learning about science is at a peak.
- High school students do not make great use of digital reference services.[2]
- Students used formal digital reference services frequently to pursue three topics of informal information seeking, Career Planning, Health and Welfare, and Death and Anxiety.

Methods and Findings from the Just Curious Second Analysis

Findings from the initial Just Curious study showed that children make informal use of formal digital reference services, and that there are patterns in that use. As is often the case with inductive analysis, these findings generated another research question, "What can we learn from patterns in the findings that could inform information system design to support children's online, informal learning?" This second research question required a second analysis of the data, which was entitled Just Curious Second Analysis. For the Just Curious Second Analysis, findings from the Just Curious study were reviewed, categorized, and compared to the literature.

Findings from the Just Curious Second Analysis led to six findings, five of which are described here only briefly. They are that digital references services should

1. broaden their topical domains to include non-academic topics of urgent concern to children
2. support efforts to interest children in science-related careers as early as fourth or fifth grade
3. be included in digital literacy training in elementary grades
4. investigate the reason for duplicate questions
5. accommodate compound queries

The sixth finding from the Just Curious Second Analysis pointed directly to a need for improving the design of digital reference systems, specifically the need for creating software that automatically and temporally supports users' changing needs and encourages informal learning. This finding is the focus of the remainder of the chapter.

IMPROVING THE DESIGN OF DIGITAL REFERENCE SYSTEMS

There is a small but growing literature in temporally based learning environments. Adams and Blandford (2005) observe that:

> the temporal elements of users' information requirements are a continually confounding aspect of digital library design. No sooner have users' needs been identified and supported than they change. . . . Ultimately, digital library designers need to identify not only the temporal aspects of the data stored within digital libraries but also the changing needs of the users interacting with those resources.

Adams and Blandford evaluated the temporally changing information requirements of several groups of users, and identified three temporal stages of an "information journey" that include:

- information initiation (how an information need arises and how existing tools support that early phase of information work)
- information facilitation (gathering)
- information interpretation (how people make sense of information)

They remark that the third stage—interpretation—is unsupported in digital library design and implementation:

> Having retrieved their information, users require different levels of support in its interpretation. . . . [T]his is a vital stage in the information journey that is largely unsupported by digital resources.

Digital reference services—an underutilized part of most digital libraries, do, however, support information interpretation. When children use digital reference services to ask Just Curious questions such as, "How can you know what's at the center of the Earth, if it's too hot to actually go there?" "Which came first, dinosaurs or God?" and "Was Nixon a *practicing* Quaker when he was in office?" they are seeking not only to obtain information (implementation), they are also attempting to make sense of it (interpretation).

Interpretation is an important component of informal learning, and often leads the user to ask new questions, and begin again on Adams and Blandford's information journey. Thus, digital reference services' capacities to support interpretation contribute to the usefulness of the digital libraries and learning environments in which they are employed.

Adams and Blandford address the temporal aspects of information searches that take place over a relatively short time, but lead us to ask: How we can improve digital reference services such that they would provide person-specific information that becomes more sophisticated over the years, along with their users? One answer is to create temporally adaptive systems. The term temporally adaptive systems originated in the field of computer science, but is used here to denote information systems that evolve automatically over time according to a user's changing needs.

In an investigation of how to implement mobile, life-long learning, Sharples (2000) created the HandLeR—a hand-held device for use by seven-to-eleven-year-old students. In preparation for the creation of HandLeR, Sharples gathered data requirements and reported that learning systems should include (but not be limited to):

1. a personal profile of the user
2. support for collaborative learning and links that connect users, resources and tools
3. pedagogical agents.[3]

These requirements for learning environments also apply to digital reference service environments, and are discussed in greater detail here.

1. Personal Profile of the User

Sharples advises that systems must be able to maintain profiles of learners that adapt to the learner's changing skills and knowledge:

> [Profiles] can determine the way in which the accumulated knowledge and learning material is stored and then presented back to the learner in new contexts. This presents a major research challenge. Most attempts at developing computer models of a learner's knowledge have concentrated on specific topic areas and learning over a short period of time.

This adaptation to learners' changing profiles, while a challenge to researchers, is less of a problem in commerce, where sophisticated, large-scale systems track users' predilections, paths and purchases. Two commercial techniques, for example, dynamic advertising reporting and behavioral targeting, are based on research and development in artificial intelligence and neural networks, and they allow online advertising agencies to control who sees an advertisement:[4]

> In behavioral targeting, the most important issue is starting with the right data . . . the 10 to 15 available data points . . . that can significantly impact the value of an audience member. The overriding and proven assumption here is that what pages Web site visitors click on and where they go from those pages indicates at least a presumptive interest in buying products related to the topics that they click on. For example, repeat visits to a Web page with reviews

of sport utility vehicles, coupled with a cruise to the automotive section of classified ads on a site, clearly indicate at least a curiosity about SUVs.[5]

This chapter is concerned with learners, not audience members, and with the desire to acquire knowledge rather than products. These technologies, however, could be employed to track users' changing information-seeking behaviors and the constantly evolving topics that they address. Such methods would be especially effective when combined with personal search agents and specialized search engines. Chau (2005) used machine learning and artificial intelligence to create personalized search agents that employed noun phrasing, text clustering, and multiagent technologies. The search agents were designed to satisfy users' information needs in different domains and contexts. Evaluation showed that the prototype systems performed better than or comparable to traditional search methods.

Another part of Chau's research investigated how artificial intelligence techniques could facilitate the development of specialized search engines. One specialized engine located URLs relevant to a given domain, and another, a feature-based text classifier was proposed to perform filtering on Web pages. Prototypes for both systems were evaluated and found to outperform traditional search approaches. Combined with the functionality of dynamic advertising reporting and behavioral targeting, personalized search agents and specialized search engines could provide user profiles that reflect individuals' information needs as they change over time.

2. Support for Collaborative Learning and Links That Connect Resources and Tools

By collaborative learning tools, Sharples means tools that conduct ongoing searches for other users who are performing similar tasks and who might engage the learner. Digital reference services are often asynchronous (e-mail-based) services that provide access to frequently or previously asked questions, allowing users to find out if others have asked their questions. The contributors of the original questions are anonymous, and because they are not concurrently online, cannot be contacted.

More recently, online chat is being used to connect question askers to experts, or question answerers. Thus far, however, digital library services use chat only to facilitate synchronous, one-to-one interactions. If users could "tune in" to topic-based channels, digital reference services could incorporate one-to-many, and many-to-many interactions, and provide support for collaborative learning. Once the desired collaborative resource is identified, the user would be offered links based on resource title, type, and keywords. After a student locates another user with a similar information need, for example, the system could bring up an image or the avatar of that user, with his or her instant message and/or e-mail information.

3. Pedagogical Agents

Pedagogical agents are online guides to resources and content. Most take the online forms of people or, for children's systems, animals. Sharples describes pedagogical agents for lifelong learning

> that might be embedded in everyday devices such as cameras, offering advice not just on how to operate the equipment, but also guidance on how to use it effectively or creatively (an agent embedded in a digital camera might suggest how a photograph might be improved, either by using a particular photograph as an example, or by referring to theories of composition or technical principles such as depth of field). The camera or other device acts as a tool to perform a task and also as a medium of instruction.

Pedagogical agents represent the information system and interact with users, guiding them through software and online processes. In a discussion of pedagogical agents for education, Johnson (2003) cites some ways in which they fail, and specifies many requirements for their success. Common failures include, repetitively criticizing the same mistake, and interrupting the learner after minor mistakes. Johnson's requirements list is too long to include here in its entirety, but some desired characteristics of pedagogical agents are that they should

- determine how and when to interact with the learner
- motivate the learner as needed
- assume the appropriate social stance toward the learner
- be sensitive to social relationship with the learner, and his or her cognitive states and characteristics

- select tasks
- include possible alternative courses of action
- evaluate actions for utility
- make action clear, understandable, and engaging
- avoid learner frustration
- assess learner engagement

Digital reference services would benefit by using pedagogical agents for familiarizing young students with the purposes and uses of the services, and supporting their changing informal learning needs and behaviors.

DISCUSSION

This study asked how research could inform information system design to support children's online, informal learning. One answer is to develop temporally adaptive digital reference systems that can integrate user profiles with personalized search engines and pedagogical agents. In an illustration of how these systems might work, let us observe their use by three fictional students, Kim, Pat, and Chris, who are in various stages of learning.

Kim is in the first grade and has logged on to ask. "Are all penguins black and white?" Kim's digital reference system checks the personal profile, and finds that Kim is seven years old, resides in Syracuse, New York, and lives in a Spanish-speaking home. Given this information, and the tools mentioned earlier, the digital reference service displays a cartoon-based interface and asks if Kim would like to work in English or Spanish. An expert at the AskAScientist service (http://www.ccmr-.cornell.edu/education/ask/?quid = 661/) has provided a Spanish-language answer to Kim's question; it is displayed in text, and an icon activates the spoken version of the answer. Kim's personalized search device retrieves information entitled, "Movies about Penguins"—and links to a spoken review of "The March of the Penguins," a documentary movie that has been rated as appropriate for seven-year-old children. In Spanish, the system asks if Kim would like to know the location of the closest library with copies available to lend. "No," says Kim, "Ya lo vi." ("I already saw it.") Another icon links Kim to the

Rosamund Gifford Zoo in Syracuse, and shows pictures of penguins in a newly created habitat. The system asks, "Would you like to see more pictures of penguins at the zoo?"

Pat is in the fifth grade and asks, "Are shooting stars really stars?" The personal profile reports that Pat is eleven years old, lives in Arizona and is a visual learner. Pat's interface is designed for a middle school student and is predominantly based on graphics, but subdued in color. Pat's question has received an answer from an astronomer at the Lowell Observatory in Flagstaff. Pat's personalized search engine has retrieved directions and visitor information for the Lowell Observatory in Flagstaff, Arizona; the Steward Observatory in Tucson; and the Kitt Peak National Observatory, located about an hour outside of Tucson. The personalized search engine also retrieved information from the National Science Digital Library (NSDL.org) about Telescopes in Education—a National Science Foundation project that lets qualified students remotely control the twenty-four-inch telescope at the Mount Wilson Observatory in California. When Pat clicks on the Telescopes in Action link, the system's pedagogical agent asks, "Lots of middle school students study astronomy for their science fair projects. Would you like information about how to participate in Telescopes in Action?"

Chris is in the tenth grade and asks, "How long can someone live with diabetes?" The personal profile shows that Chris is sixteen years old, is encountering difficulties in school, and lives in Bamberg, South Carolina. The answer to Chris's question is displayed in an interface that uses graphics and text appropriate for high school students. A health librarian who has provided a description of the disease, its symptoms, treatment, and outcomes, answered the question. He has included a live link to an online support group, Children with Diabetes, (www .childrenwithdiabetes.com) where Chris can meet and talk with people affected by diabetes. Also included is information about a clinic in a nearby town, where patients can undergo painless retinal scanning. Scan results are read by experts at the Columbia Eye Clinic who use a high-speed, satellite broadband service to link to diagnose remote patients (http://www.columbiaeyeclinic.com/research.htm). A pedagogical agent advises Chris to contact the family doctor to find out more about this service. Finally, an icon links to an academic mentoring site for teens who are dealing with family illnesses, and another pedagogical agent asks if Chris would like to visit that site.

FUTURE RESEARCH

Of the three requirements for temporally adaptive digital references, personal profiles are the most feasible, given current research. Existing technologies enable dynamic advertising reporting and behavioral targeting, personalized agents, and specialized search engines, and could provide the foundation for automated and temporally adaptive personal profiles.

Existing tools for collaboration, however, are rudimentary and much work remains to be done to implement fully automated and temporally adaptive collaborative learning tools.

The requirements for pedagogical agents are sufficiently daunting that designing even static systems is difficult. An important topic for future research, then, will be to create pedagogical agents that are temporally adaptive.

A CHALLENGE TO THE RESEARCH

Students who participated in this research comprised three grade level groups (elementary, middle school and high school), not a single population observed over time. A useful next step would be to observe the information-seeking behaviors and habits of one group of students, starting in early childhood, and continuing observation until at least post–college years.

CONCLUSION

In this chapter, digital reference questions were defined as artifacts of informal learning, and digital reference services as conducive environments for studying informal learning. A model of question types was presented that includes digital reference questions. Findings from the Just Curious Second Analysis were compared to the literature, and a conclusion reached: Digital reference services must be designed to allow temporal changes that reflect students' changing information needs and practices.

Temporally adaptive digital reference systems would accommodate personal and cognitive changes as students' foci move from how the world works, to abstract issues, and then back to the students' private world perspectives.

The three major components of temporally adaptive digital reference services are personal profiles of users, support for collaborative learning, and pedagogical agents. Examples of systems including these technologies were described, and topics for future reference suggested.

Not all of the required technology exists yet. When it becomes available, however, lifelong learners will be able to pursue informal learning using digital reference services that accommodate their personal information-seeking behaviors as they evolve over time.

NOTES

1. These services were administered by the Information Institute of Syracuse, a research center at Syracuse University's School of Information Studies (http://iis.syr.edu).

2. This finding is confirmed in Silverstein (2004).

3. This is a partial list, only, of Sharple's requirements for learning systems.

4. Hill and Hosein (1999).

5. Dave Morgan quoted by Russell Shaw (2004).

REFERENCES

Adams, A., and A. Blandford. 2005. Digital libraries' support for the user's "Information Journey." Preprint of paper to appear in *Proceedings of JCDL.* http://www.uclic.ucl.ac.uk/annb/docs/aaabJCDL05preprint.pdf (accessed September 1, 2005).

Bilal, D. 2002. Children's use of the Yahooligans! Web search engine. III. Cognitive and physical behaviors on fully self-generated search tasks. *Journal of the American Society for Information Science and Technology* 53(13): 1170–83.

Chau, M. 2005. Searching and mining the Web for personalized and specialized information. *ACM SIGIR Forum* 39(1): 57.

Condry, J. 1977. Enemies of exploration: Self-initiated versus other-initiated learning. *Journal of Personality and Social Psychology* 35(7): 459–77.

Deci, E. and R. Ryan. 1985. *Intrinsic motivation and self-determination in human behavior.* New York: Plenum.

———. 2000. The "what" and "why" of goal pursuits: Human needs and the self-determination of behavior. *Psychological Inquiry* 11(4): 227–68.

Graesser, A. C., K. Lang, and D. Horgan. 1998. A taxonomy for question generation. *Questioning Exchange* 2(1): 3–15.

Gross, M. 1998. The imposed query: Implications for library service evaluation. *Reference & User Services Quarterly* 37(3): 290–99.

Hill, A. and G. Hosein. 1999. *The privacy risks of public key infrastructures: Exposing the dangers that ubiquitous digital signatures and public key infrastructures pose to individual privacy, and exploring some possible solutions.* Montreal, Canada: Zero-Knowledge Systems, Inc. http://personal.lse.ac.uk/hos ein/pkirisks. (accessed August 17, 2005).

Johnson, L. 2003. *Social interaction with agents.* The Social Intelligence Project Center for Advanced Research in Technology for Education CARTE at USC, USC/Information Science Institute. http://www.isi.edu/isd/carte/proj_sia/So cial_Actors_AAMAS.ppt (accessed September 1, 2005).

Kasworm, C. 1983. Self-directed learning and lifespan development. *International Journal of Lifelong Education* 2(1): 29–45.

Lankes, R. D. 2002. Impact and opportunity of digital reference in primary and secondary education. White paper presented at the Digital Reference Research Symposium, Harvard University, Cambridge, MA.

Oldfather, P., and J. H. McCaughlin. 1993. Gaining and losing voice: A longitudinal study of students' continuing impulse to learn across elementary and middle level contexts. *Research in Middle Level Education* 3 (Fall): 1–25.

Riechel, R. 1991. *Reference services for children and young adults.* Hamden, CT: Library Professional Publications.

Sefton-Green, J. 2004. *Literature review in informal learning with technology outside school.* NESTA (National Endowment for Science Technology and the Arts) Future Lab Research Report 7. http://www.nestafuturelab.org/research/reviews/ 07_01.htm (accessed on August 16, 2005).

Sharples, M. 2000. The design of personal mobile technologies for lifelong learning. http://www.eee.bham.ac.uk/sharplem/Papers/handler%20comped.pdf (accessed August 24, 2005).

Shaw, Russell. 2004. *Behavioral targeting 101.* iMediaConnection. http:// www.imediaconnection.com/content/3297.asp (accessed August 21, 2005).

Silverstein, J. 2004. Next-generation children's digital reference services: A research agenda. In *Developing digital libraries for K-12 Education,* ed. M. Mardis, 141–58. Syracuse, NY: ERIC Clearinghouse on Information & Technology.

———. 2005. Just curious: Children's use of digital reference for unimposed queries, and its importance in informal education. *Library Trends* 54(2): 197–208.

9

Children's Web Portals: Can an Intergenerational Design Team Deliver the Goods?

Andrew Large, Jamshid Beheshti,
Valerie Nesset, and Leanne Bowler

The Web is now widely used by young students in elementary schools as a source of information for their class assignments.[1] Yet a growing body of research points to the difficulties that these students encounter in retrieving information that is appropriate for their needs. They find it difficult to formulate effective search strategies, use ill-defined queries, and in general do not find information seeking to be an intuitive activity.[2] These problems are exacerbated when they must use search engines designed primarily for adult users.[3]

One way to improve elementary school students' retrieval of information from the Web might be to design search engines especially for young users. In fact, a number of such search engines do exist but children appear to make little or no use of them. Large, Beheshti, and Rahman[4] conducted a series of focus groups with children aged ten to thirteen years in order to determine children's own opinions on these search engines and to identify design criteria that children might wish to see implemented in Web portals intended for their own use (we prefer the term *portal* to *search engine* as they typically offer capabilities other than searching, such as browsing mechanisms, access to games, etc.). Although all the child participants used "adult" portals to find information on the Web, they did not dismiss at all the concept of children's portals. But they did offer many criticisms of the four examples they evaluated in the focus groups: Ask Jeeves for Kids, KidsClick, Lycos Zone, and Yahooligans! Bilal[5] has explored with individual children in middle school (aged twelve to thirteen) the kinds of interfaces they would like to see designed for such portals. The research discussed in this chapter goes a step further by using two intergenerational teams including both elementary school students and the authors to design over several sessions two low-tech Web portal prototypes that have subsequently been built and evaluated by other students. At the heart of this research lies a new design method that emerged from the intergenerational teams and that the authors have termed "bonded design."

The chapter begins with a brief review of existing methods that have been used with children to design technologies. It then describes and discusses bonded design, and presents the main design and functional features of the two low-tech prototype portals that emerged from this process. Any assessment of the efficacy of bonded design depends upon the extent to which the portals could meet the needs of their clientele, and therefore the results from evaluations of the portals by elementary school students are next considered. The chapter ends with a discussion about the role of children in design and evaluation, and the consequences of this work for future developments in Web portals intended for young users.

CHILDREN AND THE DESIGN PROCESS

As a consequence of the emphasis on usability, user involvement in technology design is now commonplace. The critical role that users play in the design process has been accepted much more reluctantly, however, when those users happen to be children. Hanna, Risden, Alexander, and Czerwinski comment, "Usability research with children has often been considered either too difficult to carry out with unruly subjects or not necessary for an audience that is satisfied with gratuitous animations and funny noises."[6] Nevertheless, a number of design methodologies now find a place for young users.[7]

User-Centered Design

The first and most conventional form of design that includes users in the process is user-centered design. Some authors use this term to mean direct contact between users and designers throughout the design process.[8] However, in traditional user-centered design, the users are not introduced to the design process until the technology has already been developed and released onto the market. The main purpose of user-centered design is to identify and assess the end-users' goals and to ensure that the design has addressed them.[9] Thus, in user-centered design users are employed in the role of testers or evaluators[10] and the focus is on the impact of the technology on users,[11] enabling the development of future versions of the existing technology or the design of completely new technologies. The major drawback of this approach to design is that because the user is only involved after the technology has been designed, s/he has little or no control over the process. The user cannot initiate changes but only reveal any design shortcomings. The strengths of user-centered design lie in the ability of researchers to perform large, comprehensive studies with many users, as well as accomplish their work more quickly because they maintain control over the design process.[12] For example, Druin cites a study conducted with 1,300 children in 1991 at Vanderbilt University where children were watched and tested during the study but did not take part in the design process itself.[13]

Contextual Design/Inquiry

Contextual design is described by Beyer and Holtzblatt as "a state-of-the-art approach to designing products directly from a designer's understanding of how the customer works."[14] Its aims are to reveal the details and motivations of people's work, to make the customers and their work needs real to the designers, to use customer data as the basis of decision making, and to create a shared understanding of the data by researchers and users. Contextual design calls for researchers to collect data in the users' own environment by observing them performing typical activities. In the final stages, low-tech prototype mock-ups of the system are developed and tested with users. This allows for error detection and reparation even before any coding has begun. As explained by Beyer and

Holtzblatt, "Paper prototypes support continuous iteration of the new system, keeping it faithful to the users' needs. Refining the design with users gives designers a customer-centered way to resolve disagreements and work out the next layer of requirements."[15]

The use of low-tech paper prototypes, pictorial diagramming and concrete techniques lends itself to work with children. Although Contextual design does not involve users in all aspects of the design process, it does provide a framework for users' opinions and suggestions to be heard and considered by the designers. Contextual design's emphasis on a team approach and concrete methods of pictorial flowchart data analysis make it applicable and appropriate in a child-centered context.

Learner-Centered Design

Soloway, Guzdial, and Hay, expanding upon the idea that the long-term goal of computing is to make people smarter, decided that the HCI community needed to move from the traditional "user-centered" design to what they term learner-centered design.[16] This approach assumes that everyone is a learner, whether a professional or a student. In fact, Soloway and his colleagues describe professionals as "students who happen to learn outside of a classroom."[17] Therefore, the main focus of learner-centered design is to ensure that the technology is adapted to the interests, knowledge, and styles of the learners who use it. Whereas in user-centered design the emphasis is on tasks (what does it need to do?), tools (what tools are provided to handle these tasks?), and interfaces (what is the interface to these tools?), the issues at the heart of learner-centered design are understanding (how will the learner learn the practice?), motivation (how can software motivate a learner?), diversity (every learner is different—what can be developed that supports this?), and growth (the learner changes but the technology does not).

To address these learning issues Soloway et al. recommend using a "scaffolding technique" similar to that used in educational practices. In education, scaffolding is used to support learners while they are learning a new task. "Scaffolding, then, is provided to help a learner do a task that he or she can not [*sic*] do alone; as the learner develops the needed knowledge and skills, the scaffolding fades so that the learner is fully in control."[18] Kafai has adapted Soloway's approach for use with children by making them the actual software designers.[19] To do this, one must be aware of children's preconceived notions about software so that one has an idea of the limitations and/or benefits that might entail. In order to achieve success, she believes it is also necessary that the child learners be involved in the evaluation and testing of the software. Her research showed that young student designers are similar to professional designers in their concern for their users. They were conscious of, and tried to address such issues as content and user motivation, but they did not always fully grasp how to address their users' other needs. Kafai is convinced, however, that children have the ability to become more than just informants in the design; rather, they can become design process participants.

Participatory Design

The premise behind participatory design is that users are the best qualified to determine how to improve their work, and that their perceptions about technology are as important as technical specifications.[20] In a highly iterative approach, goals and the strategies for accomplishing them are continually refined. Participatory design looks to compromise rather than consensus as an end goal. According to Carmel, Whitaker, and George, there are two governing themes for the implementation of Participatory design principles. The first is called *mutual reciprocal learning*. In this form of participatory design, users and designers teach each other about work practices and technical possibilities through joint experiences. The second theme is called *design by doing*. This makes use of interactive experimentation, modeling and testing support, hands-on design, and learning by doing. It is a creative process using low-tech tools.[21]

Prototyping is integral to participatory design, since cooperative prototyping involves heightened user participation and "supports mutual learning by promoting cooperative communication."[22] Prototyping reinforces the iterative process of participatory design because designers collaborate as peers with the users in a mutual learning process. The principles of participatory design are very suitable for design projects involving children. Children's school or home environments substitute for the workplace, their creativity and enthusiasm thrive within a flexible structure, and educational techniques have long stressed the benefits of mutual learning.

Although widely adopted, participatory design faces challenges from some software design professionals because of its reliance on design input from ordinary users. Muller and Kuhn address this issue when they ask, "Can software professionals recognize and affirm the validity of perspectives other than their own, and value the expertise that comes from experience, not just the knowledge that is attested by academic credentials?"[23] Given this attitude regarding adult users' involvement in the design process, how much more reluctant would the designers be to accept children as their peers?

Informant Design

Developed by Scaife and his colleagues, informant design was introduced to address some of the perceived problems with user-centered and participatory design techniques when working with children.[24] In conventional user-centered design, users are involved only as evaluators or testers at the end of the design process and, therefore, their feedback is based on reaction rather than initiation. Furthermore, in user-centered design it is up to the designers to translate and interpret the users' reactions and this can be an inaccurate practice. The perceived problem with participatory design is its promotion of equality for all team members. Scaife and his colleagues consider this approach to be effective for a team comprised of adult users who can view each other as peers, but infeasible when dealing with children. They do not believe that children have the time, knowledge, or expertise to fully participate in the collaborative participatory design model.

For these reasons, Scaife et al. choose to take a position between the user-centered and participatory design perspectives, and he calls his participants (children and teachers) "native informants" because they "are aware of aspects of learning/teaching practices that we are not and which we need to be told of. . . . So, by 'informant design' we mean an interplay between privileged observations from potential users and ourselves with another set of skills."[25] In this approach, "each informant provides different inputs to the design at various phases of the project using different methods."

Informant design is an approach that attempts to maximize the input of the participants at various stages of the design process. Scaife and Rogers believe that informants can help the researchers "discover what we did not know rather than try to confirm what we thought we already knew."[26] Scaife and his team advocate the use of a diversity of informants (e.g., teachers and children) to maximize the variety of suggestions. The designer tries to elicit suggestions from the children and then lets them know if it is possible to incorporate them into the working design. Thus, in informant design, each informant shapes the design at different points and in different ways—at the beginning of the process to help "problematize the domain," in the middle to test and reflect upon the "cognitive and design assumptions, and at the end to evaluate the prototypes' 'real-world contexts.'"[27] Scaife and his colleagues consider informant design to be the best method "for the design of interactive software for non-typical users or those who cannot be equal partners (e.g., children)."[28] Its basic assumption is that in the design process, children are most helpful at suggesting ideas for motivational and fun aspects of educational software.

Cooperative Inquiry

Developed by Druin and her colleagues at the University of Maryland, cooperative inquiry is a combination of techniques from different design methodologies that have proven useful when working with children. It involves a multidisciplinary partnership with children, field research, and iterative low-tech and high-tech prototyping, and treats children as full design partners—equals to the professional adult designers on the team. Professional designers and users (children) of the technology are partnered in intergenerational design teams with the understanding that full participation of users requires training and active cooperation. According to Druin, cooperative design methods informed cooperative inquiry because of their attempt "to capture the complexity and somewhat 'messy' real-life world of the workplace."[29] It was found that many times sequential tasks were not accomplished by one person, but many tasks were done in parallel and in collaboration with others. Interestingly enough, this description could also easily refer to the complexity and "messiness" of a child's world."

Unlike contextual inquiry, with its minimal interaction between researcher and user, cooperative inquiry involves more than observation. Low-tech prototypes are developed by the entire intergenerational team in order to support the brainstorming and idea-generation stage of the design process. Low-tech prototyping (e.g., paper-based prototypes) because of the nature of the activity and the materials used, also provides an equal footing for children and adults.[30]

BONDED DESIGN: A NEW MODEL FOR WORKING WITH CHILDREN

Alongside these existing design methodologies has emerged a new approach. Bonded design was developed by Large and his colleagues in response to the need to design Web portals for elementary school students.[31] It is a means of bringing together for interface design purposes a team that unites in diversity. The children in the team play a full and active role in all aspects of the design process. It emphasizes, however, that there is a distinction between the roles of the adults and children: the adults are experts in interface design and the children are experts in being children. The name *bonding* refers to the fact that alone neither the adult members nor the child members could accomplish the design, but when bonded together in a team they are able to unite their separate strengths in a common endeavor. The team follows a planned course of action over a limited number of design sessions to create a low-tech prototype. It uses a variety of techniques such as brainstorming, viewing examples of related technologies, drawing mock-ups, and consensus building.

Bonded design draws upon ideas from the design methodologies described above. From conventional user-centered design it takes the most basic premise—involving users. From contextual design were borrowed the ideas of drawing paper prototypes and a similar process to what contextual design terms *work redesign* in the use of a white board to set out a map at the beginning of each session for what had already been accomplished and what remained to be done. Participatory design provided the concept of peer co-designers, drawings (low-tech prototyping), hands-on activities, and "learning by doing." Learner-centered design contributed the idea that all team members were learners. Informant design supported the approach of seeking new and creative ideas rather than merely confirming what the adults already knew. The researchers also shared some of the reservations voiced in informant design about the true equality of children alongside adults in a design team. Finally, cooperative inquiry was followed in the central focus upon intergenerational team design and the involvement of children from the start to finish of the design process. Essentially, then, bonded design is situated between cooperative inquiry and informant design. It shares the former's belief in the ability of children to work as partners in all aspects of the design process, but has reservations about the extent to which full and equal cooperation can occur across the generational divide, and in these respects, therefore, has similarities with the latter. Like cooperative inquiry, it emphasizes an intergenerational partnership in working toward a common goal. It also shares with it the idea that children should play an active role in design rather than merely being evaluators or testers at the end of the design process.

Bonded design shares aspects of learner-centered design in that it provides a learning environment for all team members—children and adults alike. Bonded design also shares some of the features of informant design in that it questions the extent of the cooperation between adults and children within the team. In this respect it shares some of Scaife and his colleagues' reservations concerning the extent to which true equality can exist within an intergenerational team.[32] At the same time, however, bonded design differs importantly from informant design in its inclusion of children throughout the design process and as full team members. It also rejects Scaife's view that children are most helpful at suggesting ideas only for motivational and fun aspects.

The intergenerational process used in bonded design can also be understood from another theoretical perspective—that of the Zone of Proximal Development (ZPD), a sociocultural approach to knowledge development.[33] This theory argues that when an appropriate structure (or scaffolding as Vygotsky calls it) is put in place, children are able to accomplish more complex tasks than if left to their own devices. In bonded design the design techniques represent this scaffolding, which supports collaboration among team members. The relationship between bonded design and ZPD is discussed further in Bowler, Large, Beheshti, and Nesset.[34]

Bonded design in its practical realization differs markedly from cooperative inquiry in three major respects. Using cooperative inquiry, Druin's intergenerational teams work together for multiple sessions extending over many months, whereas bonded design takes place over a limited number of sessions extending over several weeks. This difference is significant in that cooperative inquiry is only really feasible in an environment where both the adult and child team members are available on a long-term basis. Williamson, from his industry perspective, points to the problems in implementing cooperative inquiry: "Dedicating upwards of a year with intergenerational groups of children, researchers, artists and computer scientists is likely to be outside the bounds of most project budgets and schedules—regardless of whether they are commercial or experimental ventures." [35] Many researchers in other environments are likely to find it equally problematical to implement. The second difference relates to the ages of the child participants. In any particular bonded design team it is assumed that the children are of similar age, whereas in cooperative inquiry any one team might contain children spanning a range of years. This homogeneousness of age may be one reason why bonded design can work with many fewer design sessions in a compact time period. The bonded design model is shown in figure 9.1.

Since the primary distinguishing factor between the various design methodologies is the extent to which children are actively involved in the design process, it is helpful to situate bonded design on a continuum that reflects the degree of user involvement, moving rightward from a relatively low involvement to a high involvement (see figure 9.2).

BONDED DESIGN IN PRACTICE

Bonded design was applied by the authors in two intergenerational design teams comprising three researchers working alongside student

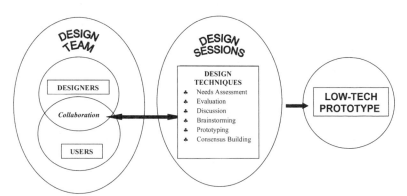

Figure 9.1. Bonded Design Model

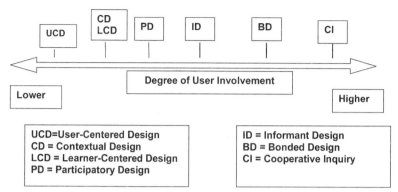

Figure 9.2. User Involvement in Design Continuum

volunteers. The teams' objectives were each to design a low-tech Web portal that could be used by elementary school students to find information on the Web about Canadian history. The first team with eight grade-six students and the three researchers designed a portal they named *History Trek*; the second team of six grade-three students and the same three researchers designed a portal they called *KidSearch Canada.*

The children were not selected for their computer expertise, although in practice all had used the Web for both entertainment and educational purposes. The only personal requirement to become a team member related to gender: both teams were to comprise equal numbers of girls and boys. The authors' earlier research as well as that of others suggests that gender can influence how children search for information on the Web and also how they respond to individual Web portals.[36] Children (and especially older ones such as the grade-six students) also seem to collaborate better and feel more at ease in a single-sex team. This was the main reason for the authors establishing single-sex focus groups in their earlier research where children were asked to evaluate children's Web portals.[37] It seemed unrealistic, however, to assume that in practice distinct Web portals would be built for boys and for girls. The researchers therefore abandoned gender-specific design teams. Nevertheless, it was considered appropriate to balance by gender the student representation in the teams so as to gain ideas from both girls and boys. In practice, gender appeared to have little significance for the workings of the grade-three team. In the case of the grade-six team, however, it was noticeable that unless deliberately arranged by the adult team members, the four boys always grouped themselves on one side of the table and the four girls on the other. In many respects there were two subgroups identified by gender within the team as a whole. This may not have affected the final design, but does give pause for thought as to whether the original notion of single-sex design teams would have been preferable.

Planning the Sessions

There is general agreement when working with children in focus groups that a session should not extend much beyond one hour.[38] In this case the design team sessions took place in the school's lunch break and lasted about seventy minutes, including time for lunches to be eaten. The grade-six students had no problems with this, but in the case of the grade-three children normally a few minutes were allocated at the end of the session for playing physical games. The sessions were held twice per week unless disrupted by holidays or school trips; competing lunchtime activities as well as the adults' schedules made more frequent meetings difficult, and less frequent meetings risked losing momentum, especially for the younger team.

The design teams met in the school's art room which was equipped with high-speed Internet access and where the sessions would be undisturbed. It has been argued by Large, Beheshti, and Rahman,[39] as well as others such as Krueger[40] that it is better to work with children off school premises; in the former's case the earlier focus groups, for example, were held either in students' homes or in one case at McGill University. The rationale behind this decision is to separate the sessions from regular school work, thereby emphasizing that the team comprises children and adults rather than students and teachers. However, in practice it is easier to gather a group of children on a regular basis within their school than to meet elsewhere, where safety and security issues as well as transportation might prove problematical. Despite the use of school premises for the sessions, there were no indications that the students felt intimidated or constrained in any way.

The Sessions

The content of the grade-six sessions was based on criteria adapted from an information architecture matrix constructed by Large, Beheshti, and Cole[41] for use in designing children's Web portals. These criteria formed a "topic timetable" for the sessions. A timetable was important if a portal design was to be completed within the number of sessions planned. At the same time, when working with children it is essential to maintain flexibility. In the case of the grade-three sessions it was more difficult to divide the sessions thematically; in practice any one session dealt with a variety of topics (for example, session two covered elements of retrieval, help, e-mail, and chat). A typical session involved some/all of the following: a quick résumé of the previous session (while the children ate their packed lunches), team discussion of portal features, brainstorming about portal design, viewing existing portals on the Web, individual drawing of portals, and consensus building. All the sessions were audio taped, and notes were also taken by one of the research assistants. All the drawings were copied for later analysis.

Team Building

Various techniques were employed to foster team spirit and to facilitate collaborative efforts toward a common goal—the design of a prototype Web portal. From the outset it was important to establish a group dynamic in which everyone, researcher or student, felt at ease. The researchers dressed casually and the children addressed them by their first names. All team members wore name badges (first names only). The students were actively discouraged from raising their hands when they wished to make a point as the sessions were not meant to replicate the teacher-student relationship. During the first session each team brainstormed ideas about an appropriate team name: the grade-six team opted for "The Web Wonders" and the grade-three team chose "The Web Wizards." Each team member then was supplied with a T-shirt with the team name printed on the front. Surprisingly, these seemingly innocuous decisions proved some of the most contentious; the grade-six team found it hard to agree upon the name, while the grade-three team argued at length over the color of the T-shirt. Despite these minor problems a strong team spirit was quickly established among both teams, so much so in fact that the presence of a fourth adult in two of the grade-six sessions later on in the process somewhat upset the normal routine.

Design Techniques

One of the first activities of the grade-six team was to conduct a user need assessment survey among the entire grade-six population (around sixty students) of the school concerning their Internet usage. The survey questionnaire provided factual data on which to base future design decisions (for example, the students' preference for fast response times had to be taken very seriously in any consideration of incorporating extensive animation into the portal) and also helped to promote from the outset a team spirit in the design team. This latter objective was achieved by delegating the administration of the questionnaire to the team's student members (although the questions had been formulated by the researchers). The team including grade-three students was not asked to conduct a similar needs assessment; the researchers (who had very little prior experience of working with such young children) assumed that grade-three students would be unable to answer such a questionnaire survey instrument. In fact, with the hindsight of working closely with grade-three students this now seems a dubious assumption and in future a needs assessment would be undertaken with them.

Throughout the sessions both viewing and critiquing adult and children's portals on the Web were integrated with other team activities such as brainstorming, drawing, and discussion. In most instances the viewing sessions were focused on specific portal aspects like retrieval capabilities, help facilities, and results display. Despite the researchers' best endeavors, a tension perhaps inevitably existed between a desire to inform the student team members through exemplars of Web portals and the desire to encourage these same students to think imaginatively and creatively from their own perspectives. The intermixing of viewing and critiquing along with encouraging the students to express their own ideas as exemplified particularly in their drawings was an attempt to resolve this tension as much as possible.

The major technique to encourage the students to express their portal design ideas was prototyping by means of regular drawing activities during the sessions. This has been used successfully by other researchers to extract design ideas from children.[42] Certainly, the students very much enjoyed this prototyping. In fact, the main problem encountered was a lack of time for them to complete their works to their satisfaction. These drawings provide a rich documentation of the evolution of the design process. In the case of the grade-six team the drawings were also found to be a valuable design tool. With the exception of the first drawing by the students (an overview of a Web portal interface) subsequent drawings focused on a particular aspect of a Web portal such as a hit display list. Although the grade-three students were equally enthusiastic about drawing, the technique was less productive for two main reasons: the students consumed much more time in completing their drawings; and they found it more difficult to undertake a drawing of just one specific aspect of a portal rather than an entire portal. This clashed with the researchers' intention to link the drawings to individual components within a portal, as described above in viewing and critiquing.

Brainstorming is often used as a technique in the business world to foster innovative and creative ideas. It plays an integral role in contextual inquiry as well as in other design theories such as participatory design and cooperative inquiry. Although in a brainstorming session all ideas are of equal merit, at some point these ideas must be evaluated and ranked by the team. In the case of the grade-six team brainstorming proved easy, and many ideas were generated on each occasion when it was employed. The grade-three students found brainstorming a more difficult exercise; also they tended to interpret things literally. For example, when asked to draw only a menu for a subject directory rather than an entire portal, one boy drew a flower stem with square menu boxes instead of petals. He had been influenced by what had been intended as a helpful analogy—imagine instead of an entire garden, only one flower within it. The analogy only served to confuse this student rather than clarify matters for him and points to the tendency of younger children to think in a concrete rather than abstract fashion. It also highlights the wide range of cognitive abilities that can be exhibited by young children, as several other student team members understood exactly the point of the analogy.

One approach tried with the grade-six team to foster brainstorming was small-group discussion. In two sessions the team was divided into two groups and each group was asked to brainstorm specific topics before reporting back to the team as a whole. Ironically, the small groups were more susceptible to domination by one team member than when the team met as a whole. Furthermore, the students themselves disliked breaking into small groups. Perhaps the exercise might have had more success if the groups had been divided along gender lines, because in the sessions the students naturally sat around the table in one group of boys and one group of girls. The researchers were reluctant, however, to encourage such a gender division and therefore never applied it when constituting the small groups.

The most difficult, though essential, technique to implement in both teams was consensus building. The students found it difficult to compromise on their own ideas, however impractical or unpopular with the team as a whole they might have been. In some cases the researchers had to point out that ideas, though intriguing, would be impossible in practice to realize (for example, the intelligent "help pal" who would instinctively know exactly what information the user was seeking and how to find it). In the case of the grade-three students, the first of these problems was by far the most prevalent, as each student member of the team wanted to see his or her own ideas implemented in the final portal. A good example is provided by one of the boys who was dismayed to find after one brainstorming session that none of his ideas had been incorporated into the emerging design. At the same time it was relatively easy to resolve such problems. In this case it was achieved by inserting into the design "back" and "forward" buttons of the kind that he advocated. Nevertheless, by dint of discussion and critical examination of the portal prototype (in the form of a composite drawing formed from the individual drawings completed by the team members) as it began to emerge, a consensus was reached. The final iterations of the prototypes from both teams were graphical representations of the interface on a computer screen, achieved with help from a professional artist. In the end all team members were very satisfied with their respective low-tech Web portal prototypes.

Students' Reactions to Bonded Design

A formally administered questionnaire that all design team students completed confirmed the adults' observations of the students during the sessions: they found the process very enjoyable and rewarding and would recommend their peers to volunteer for any future bonded design activities. Further details both on the bonded design methodology and the students' reactions to it can be found in Large, Nesset, Beheshti, and Bowler.[43]

THE WEB PORTALS

Both intergenerational teams successfully applied bonded design in order to produce two low-tech Web portal prototypes. A discussion of these two prototypes along with screen shots can be found in Large, Beheshti, Nesset, and Bowler.[44] These portals subsequently were converted into working, high-level prototypes that searched a database of hyperlinks to approximately two thousand three hundred Web pages in English and/or French dealing with Canadian history and whose content and language are appropriate for elementary-school students.[45]

The final versions of the high-tech portals differ to some degree from the low-tech prototypes designed by the two teams. In a few cases, features advocated by the design teams could not be realized; for example, the developers did not have the resources to build the e-mail and chat facilities nor to maintain their functionality. In other cases, modifications to the low-tech prototypes were made as a result of feedback from grade-three and grade-six students in preliminary testing of the high-tech prototypes.[46] The portals comprise multiple screens; for example, *History Trek* comprises approximately seventy-five screens, not counting the hit display screens that are dynamic in nature and constantly changing

History Trek

The opening screen of *History Trek* is shown in figure 9.3 (of course, color, though not reproduced here, plays an important role in the design). The design metaphor for this screen (and the subsequent screens) is the Canadian flag. Maple leaves (the national emblem appearing on the Canadian flag) provide the background motif, as well as appearing on each side of the portal name. The left and right side vertical borders are colored red, and the center section of the screen

Figure 9.3. Opening Screen of History Trek (Version 3.0)

white, reflecting the colors of the Canadian flag. The portal mascot, Willy the Web Wonder, prominently located in the center of the screen, is also based on the maple leaf. His flag is the only animated aspect within the portal—it waves back and forth.

The portal offers several approaches to information seeking: a keyword search box and a natural-language question search box in the top right, a topic menu on the left, an alphabetical browser, and a scrollable timeline. The portal also has a hyperlink to other Web portals (Google, MSN, and Yahoo, but not other "children's portals" like Yahooligans!) in case users wish to explore other options. The portal also has an advanced keyword search feature that allows phrase searching and keyword searching of the titles and subject fields. A scrolling timeline permits searching on particular dates. Words entered in the question or keyword search boxes are spell-checked whenever they fail to match with the database of Web page links.

Interface personalization is offered through the icon labeled "My

Site" on the left of the screen. This feature allows users to select different versions of the mascot, Willy the Web Wonder. The mascot is not simply decorative but serves the purpose of activating the help feature from any screen within the portal. Figure 9.4 shows one option within help—how to get suggestions on conducting a search.

In addition to the search features, the portal contains an icon linking to several Web-based quizzes on Canadian history. This is the only entertainment element available from the portal.

History Trek is fully operational in both English and French (although in this chapter all the examples are taken from the English-language version). The button labeled "EN FRANÇAIS" (and "in English" when the interface is displayed in French) toggles the interface between the two languages. When set to the English interface only English records are retrieved, and vice versa when it is set to the French-language interface.

A successful search on *History Trek* presents to the user information

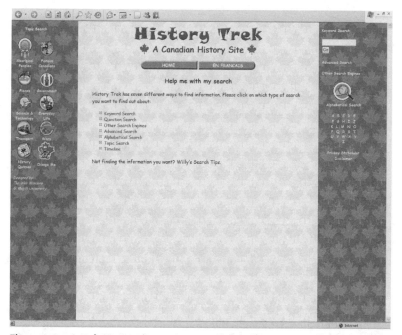

Figure 9.4. A Help Screen from History Trek (Version 3.0)

(records) about relevant websites together with hyperlinked access to the websites themselves ("Click here to see website"). The information for each site was compiled by the researchers and an example is shown in figure 9.5. More information about the database content can be found in Bowler, Nesset, Large, and Beheshti,[47] In each record one field is labeled "Topic" and another is labeled "Subjects" (see figure 9.5). Records are assigned to any one of six topics, as represented by the icons on the left-hand side of the screen in figure 9.3. Each topic is the highest level of indexing assigned to each website. Within each topic are up to three hierarchically subordinate subject levels. This indexing structure was specially developed by the researchers for both *History Trek* and *KidSearch Canada*.

KidSearch Canada

KidSearch Canada is designed around the metaphor of a student's desk (see figure 9.6). Sitting on the desk are a computer, a globe, a

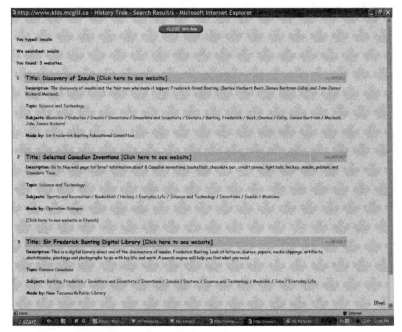

Figure 9.5.   Results Screen from History Trek (Version 3.0)

Figure 9.6. Opening Screen, KidSearch Canada (Version 3.0)

"Discman," a flowerpot, and a mouse holding a sign (this real mouse represents, of course, a computer mouse). Above the desk is a shelf of books, and attached to the wall on either side of the computer is a bulletin board holding several notes, and a poster. The design as a whole has a Canadian flavor, the computer's background screen represents the Canadian flag, and the surfing moose on the poster is an animal associated with Canada.

Despite the differing design metaphors, the functionality in *Kid-Search Canada* is not so very different from that of *History Trek*. The main distinction is that it offers only three approaches to information retrieval. Keywords can be entered in the search box on the computer's screen, the letters on the keyboard offer an alphabetic entry to searching ("Search by Letter"), and the books on the shelves present the topics.

The globe is used to switch interface languages between English and French, and will spin when clicked. The bulletin board provides access to help and personalization (labeled as "Colour Change"); this latter offers a choice between four screen savers available on the desktop computer (the default is the maple leaf shown in figure 9.6). The center of the flower provides access to a list of links to quizzes on Canadian history. The help features are accessed from the bulletin board, and in content are identical to those found on *History Trek* (though the screen designs are different). The database content, spell-checking, and the results screens are identical to those already described on *History Trek*.

HIGH-TECH PROTOTYPE EVALUATION

In order to determine whether bonded design really works it is necessary not only to establish that it can generate low-tech Web prototypes, but also that the high-tech versions of these prototypes can actually be used effectively by elementary-school students. Both portals therefore were evaluated by elementary school students from grades three and six using two methodologies: focus groups and operational studies.

Focus Group Evaluation

Twelve focus groups, each comprising four students, discussed both portals for around seventy minutes. For each focus group session a facilitator, a note-taker, and an observer were present, and the discussions were captured on audio tape. Six groups included students from grade three, and six from grade six; seven groups included females and five groups males; and eight groups came from an English elementary school and four groups from a French elementary school. The operational study involved two entire classes from grades three and six in one English school where the children used the portals over several weeks to find information for assigned class projects on Aboriginal Peoples in Canada. The grade-three class used *KidSearch Canada* (the portal designed by the intergenerational team including grade-three students) and the grade-six class used *History Trek* (designed by the grade-six team). The students were observed during a number of their search sessions in the school's computer lab, and at the end of the project most of the students were interviewed individually about their experience. What were their evaluations of the two portals?

The utilization of focus groups had several objectives. The first was to elucidate the students' first impressions of the design of the two portal interfaces. In any Web context first impressions really matter because it is so easy to move on to another site.[48] The second was to explore how students used the various retrieval features to answer four search questions. The third objective was to investigate the students' opinions on the results display. The final objective was to gain the students' overall evaluation of each portal as a means of finding information on the Web about Canadian history, to compare one portal with the other as a means of doing so, and to compare both portals with existing Web search engines (and especially Google, with which they were most familiar).

First impressions of *History Trek* were overwhelmingly positive regardless of the gender, grade level, or language of the student. The students liked Willy the mascot and appreciated the animation effect. They recognized the Canadian flag motif and liked the use of color. Overall, they found it "cool," "really attractive," and "funny." *KidSearch Canada* was well received by ten of the groups and was described in terms such as "cool," "I liked the mouse," and "c'est vraiment different [it is really different]." The only two groups of grade-six boys (one English and one French), however, were much less enthusiastic about *KidSearch Canada*, and their first impressions were muted. Interestingly, one group thought it was more appropriate for adults than children (even though it had been designed by the grade-three team) and that "the way to search doesn't stand out." The other group liked the colors but criticized the absence of animation, the smallness of the keyword search box, and the perceived clutter of the interface design. First impressions were based exclusively on the appearance of the portals' interfaces. At the end of each focus group, after the students had used the portals they were asked for their overall opinions. It is interesting to note that regarding appearance, their final impressions mirrored their first impressions.

In order to elicit searches the students in the focus groups were asked to find answers to four questions (it was emphasized to them that this was not a test!):

1. When did Jacques Cartier discover the St Lawrence River?
2. What can you find out about the everyday life of aboriginal peoples?

3. Which scientists invented insulin?
4. Find information about the fur trade in New France

Questions 1 and 3 were closed, while questions 2 and 4 were open. In any one focus group, the students tried two questions on *History Trek* and two on *KidSearch Canada*.

The retrieval features of both portals were very unevenly used by the students in answering the questions. Whenever possible on both *History Trek* and *KidSearch Canada* they opted for browsing rather than searching and tried to match terms in the question with terms in the topic search feature. For example, in question two about the everyday life of aboriginal peoples, they had no problem in identifying the topic "Aboriginal Peoples" as a good place to begin their search, and in almost every case did so. Likewise when answering question 3 they often succeeded in matching the search query with the "Science and Technology" topic. When a topic could not easily be identified from the question (and regardless of whether the question was open or closed) the English students on *History Trek* normally opted for "Question Search"; the French students used "Keyword Search." This was the case with question 4, where students were unsure about which topic to select (in fact, they could have tried either the "Place" topic or the "Everyday Life" topic). The explanation for this difference in approach between the students in the English and the French schools might be that the former were familiar with question-based searching on the "Ask Jeeves" Web search engine, which they were encouraged to use in their school, whereas the latter had never used such a search engine. On *KidSearch Canada*, of course, only keyword and not question searching was available. In terms of the Topic Search students tended to prefer the iconic representation of *History Trek* compared to the "book on shelf" approach adopted by *KidSearch Canada*.

Alphabetical searching was little used on either portal and, in fact, students often did not realize the need to search on a personal name under the first letter of the surname rather than the first name (e.g., *C* for Cartier rather than *J* for Jacques in answering question one); in one case a search for the St. Lawrence (question one) was undertaken under *L* rather than *S*. An additional problem, especially for the younger grade-three students, was created by the need to scroll down a long vertical list of terms beginning with any particular letter in order to identify the sought term in an alphabetical search. At least one student thought that the alphabetical search option on *KidSearch Canada* was a typing tutorial, whereas others thought that the letters were for typing in keywords in the search box above. No one on *History Trek* used the Advanced Search or tried the link to other Web-based search engines. The timeline was not used by anyone, but none of the questions required a specific date to be matched with an event. When asked to compare the two portals, the students were divided in their appreciation of the different retrieval features offered. A majority preferred the wider range of retrieval tools offered by *History Trek* compared with *Kid-Search Canada*, but a minority found the former's multiplicity of retrieval tools confusing and overwhelming.

Overall, the way in which retrieved hits are displayed to users was greeted positively. The focus group students, however, did encounter some problems. It was not always clear that the display screen does no more than present the results of a search, and that it is necessary to activate the hyperlink from the displayed title to open the Web page itself. This problem occurred despite the "Click here to see website" caption that followed the title (in the French-language interface the problem was exacerbated by using the translation "*Cliquer ici pour naviguer*," as many students were unfamiliar with the concept of navigating the Web and thought the verb *naviguer* referred in some way to traveling by boat). The students greatly appreciated the short but accurate descriptions of the websites and their use of language appropriate for young people. Ironically, the fact that the screen was clearly laid out and that the descriptions were user-friendly may have contributed to the students' misperception that there was nothing more to be found and hence their failure on occasion to go on to the actual website. There was little interest in who "made" the website, despite its importance as one means of verifying the authority of a site. The inclusion of "Topic" and "Subjects" fields served little purpose other than occasionally to divert the students from a relevant hit to other records perhaps of lower relevance—both topics and subjects were hyperlinked to retrieve other records that had been assigned the same Topic/Subject (as a means of broadening or reorienting a search). The focus groups held in the English school suggested that the font size used in the records be increased overall, and that additionally the font size used for the title should be bigger than that in the other fields; this was done by the time the French school's focus groups viewed the portals, though a few participants requested a yet larger font.

Do students prefer a portal that has been designed by a team including students from their own age group? The focus group evaluations suggest this not to be the case. No pattern can be discerned of the grade-three focus groups preferring *KidSearch Canada* and the grade-six focus groups opting for *History Trek*. One interesting observation, however, was that many of the students perceived *KidSearch Canada* to be more "adult" than *History Trek* and therefore less appropriate for elementary school students (it is hard to see why this should be so, though one explanation the students gave was that the topics were represented by pictures [icons] on *History Trek* but by books on *KidSearch Canada*). Nor can any difference in preference be attributed to the maternal language of the students in the focus groups. Neither language nor cultural differences were reflected in student evaluations. The only factor influencing evaluations seems to be gender. Overall, the boys, regardless of age or language, markedly preferred *History Trek*, and to a lesser extent the girls expressed themselves in favor of *KidSearch Canada*.

The students overall advocated specialized portals for particular subject areas. They appreciated the value of *History Trek* and *KidSearch Canada* in that they focused exclusively on one subject domain, Canadian history. They would prefer to use *History Trek* and/or *KidSearch Canada* rather than any "adult" (typically Google) Web search engine if searching for information on this subject. As expressed by themselves, compared with Google, *"C'est plus vite et puis c'est plus l'fun"* [It's faster and also more fun]. "Made for children, with words that they understand," and "It has all the stuff right there for you." Only one focus group—English grade-three boys—said they would prefer to use Google rather than either *KidSearch Canada* or *History Trek* "because you get to look at about a hundred million things."

Operational Evaluation

The operational evaluation took place only in an English elementary school (not the one used for the focus groups). Unlike in the focus groups where the students from any one grade looked at both portals, in the operational evaluation the grade-three students only used *KidSearch Canada* (the portal designed by the grade-three intergenerational team) and the grade-six students only used *History Trek*. Two classes from each grade (forty-three from grade three and forty from grade six) participated in the evaluation. In both cases they used the portal to find information for a project on aboriginal peoples in Canada. At the outset of each project, the students were required to use either *KidSearch Canada* or *History Trek*, but in the later stages could also use other existing Web portals if they wished. The grade-six students also were encouraged to exploit any relevant print resources. The computer lab sessions extended over four weeks and typically the classes met twice weekly. During most of these sessions the researchers were present in the lab to engage in participant observation. Shortly after their completion of the projects the students individually were interviewed using a semistructured approach and the interviews captured on audio tape.

Before the students began to actually use the portals they were given in the first lab session a brief introduction to the portals' retrieval capabilities, including a printout of an annotated screen that highlighted the various retrieval features. Participant observation confirmed that this brief training was sufficient for the students to competently use the portals to find information. In fact, most of the questions addressed to the researchers were about any technical difficulties experienced in attempting to connect to the Web via the school board's server. Although the students were able to review and print relevant websites, it was observed that they often skimmed the Web pages without truly comprehending their content. No students were observed getting lost within the portals, although for some students the use of some of the retrieval features was not straightforward. For example, in the topic search when a student clicked on "Aboriginal Peoples" the next screen gave a list of three categories: "Everyday Life," "Ancient Peoples," and "North American Peoples." It was not immediately apparent to some of the students what these categories represented and which one they should select.

The focus groups provided a snapshot of the students' reactions to *History Trek* and *KidSearch Canada*, but they could not reveal their evaluations after more extensive usage and when seeking information for a real class project. The operational study was a necessary compensation for this shortcoming. Here the portals were used during multiple sessions to find information for a project that would be assessed by the class teacher. Such more in-depth usage of the portals, however, only served to confirm the findings from the focus groups concerning each portal. Furthermore, their comparison of *History Trek* or *KidSearch Canada* with adult portals (again, almost always Google) was very similar to that of the focus groups. Of course, the focus groups had the opportunity to compare the two portals whereas in the operational study any individual participant only used one of the two portals.

The two class teachers were interviewed to gather their opinions on the two portals in general and the ways in which they might have helped their students find information for the class projects they had assigned them. Both teachers were really enthusiastic about the portals and felt that they had both helped the students and enriched the assignment. One reservation was expressed by the grade-three teacher; she thought that many of the websites accessible via the portal were too difficult in language and content for her young students to understand. In this she undoubtedly is correct, but unfortunately there are no other sites on Canadian history of a more appropriate nature—young users are not yet served well by websites that have a real informational value but are appropriate for their age group.

DISCUSSION

At every stage in the design, development, and evaluation of the two Web portals children were intimately involved. Bonded design, the methodology used to design the portals, requires the active participation of users alongside experts in a team approach where the users are experts in their own environments. In the case of the portal designs discussed in this chapter, the users in the two intergenerational teams were experts at thinking like children. Through a series of design sessions utilizing techniques such as viewing existing Web portals, discussing design attributes, drawing paper mock-ups, brainstorming, and consensus building, these two teams succeeded in producing two low-level Web portal prototypes. Furthermore, these designs were accomplished in a relatively short period of time by two small teams whose child members were randomly selected volunteers and who had not been screened for intellectual capabilities or Web experience.

The straightforward, if somewhat time-consuming, task of developing the low-tech prototypes into high-tech working prototypes was carried out by expert adults, but even at this development stage, children had a critical role to play. The two groups of children who tested the portals during this development process were an essential bridge between the design team and the completed working portals that were ready for evaluation. Their initial critiques of the portals at an intermediate development stage turned out to be as insightful as the conclusions that emerged from the subsequent evaluation provided by the more numerous focus groups and the operational study.

The formal evaluation of *History Trek* and *KidSearch Canada* relied entirely upon user reactions. The children involved in both evaluation phases overwhelmingly endorsed the work accomplished at the design and development stages. The elementary school students reacted positively and enthusiastically to all aspects of the portals. They found the designs to be attractive and appropriate for their user communities, they appreciated the retrieval facilities provided, especially by *History Trek*, and they endorsed the concept of Web portals for children. Furthermore, they responded positively to the concept of subject-specific Web portals as represented in the case of *History Trek* and *KidSearch Canada*, which focused on Canadian history.

In conclusion, bonded design offers an effective and feasible approach to technology design. Its application certainly is highly effective when involving children, but there is no inherent reason why it should not be applied with other user communities. The requests from many of the students in the two design teams, the twelve focus groups, and the two operational studies to have access to one or other of the portals after completion of the entire research project is a measure of the success attained by the bonded design methodology. In the spirit of bonded design there can be no stronger endorsement.

ACKNOWLEDGMENTS

The authors acknowledge the financial support from the Social Science and Humanities Research Council (Canada), which funded all stages of this research. To the many young Web users who participated in this research in various guises, the authors remain indebted.

NOTES

1. Andrew Large, "Children, Teens and the Web: Information, Education and Social Issues," in *Annual Review of Information Science and Technology*, vol. 39, ed. Blaise Cronin, 347–92 (Medford, NJ: Information Today, 2005).

2. Sandra G. Hirsh, "Children's Relevance Criteria and Information Seeking on Electronic Resources," *Journal of the American Society for Information Science* 50, no. 14 (1999): 1265–83; John Schacter, Gregory Chung, and Aimee Dorr, "Children's Internet Searching on Complex Problems: Performance and Process Analysis," *Journal of the American Society for Information Science* 49, no. 9 (1998): 840–49; Raven McCrory Wallace, Jeff Kupperman, Joseph Krajcik, and Elliot Solowa, "Science on the Web: Students Online in a Sixth-Grade Classroom," *The Journal of the Learning Sciences* 9, no. 1 (2000): 75–104.

3. Leanne Bowler, Andrew Large, and Gill Rejskind, "Primary School Students, Information Literacy and the Web," *Education for Information* 19 no. 3 (2001): 201–23; Wallace et al., "Science on the Web."

4. Andrew Large, Jamshid Beheshti, and Tarjin Rahman, "Design Criteria for Children's Web Portals: The Users Speak Out," *Journal of the American Society for Information Science and Technology* 53, no. 2 (2002): 79–94.

5. Dania Bilal, "Children Design Their Interfaces for Web Search Engines: A Participatory Approach," in *Proceedings of the 30th Annual Conference of the Canadian Association for Information Science*, ed. Lynne C. Howarth, Christopher Cronin, and Anna T. Slawek, 204–14 (Toronto: CAIS, 2002); Dania Bilal, "Draw and Tell: Children as Designers of Web Interfaces," in *Humanizing Information Technology: From Ideas to Bits and Back: Proceedings of the 66th Annual Meeting of the American Society for Information Science and Technology*, 135–41 (Medford, NJ: Information Today, 2003).

6. Libby Hanna, Kirsten Risden, Mary Czerwinski, and Kristin Alexander, "The Role of Usability Research in Designing Children's Computer Products," in *The Design of Children's Technology*, ed. Alison Druin, 3–26 (San Francisco: Morgan Kaufmann Publishers, 1999). Quote is on page 4.

7. Valerie Nesset and Andrew Large, "Children in the Information Technology Design Process: A Review of Theories and Their Applications," *Library and Information Science Research* 26, no. 2 (2004): 140–61.

8. Jeffrey Rubin, *Handbook of Usability Testing: How to Plan, Design, and Conduct Effective Tests* (New York: Wiley, 1994).

9. Alison J. Head, "Web Redemption and the Promise of Usability," *Online* 23, no 6 (1999): 20–32.

10. Mike Scaife and Yvonne Rogers, "Kids as Informants: Telling Us What We Didn't Know or Confirming What We Knew Already," in *The Design of Children's Technology*, ed. Alison Druin, 27–50 (San Francisco: Morgan Kaufmann Publishers, 1999).

11. Alison Druin, "The Role of Children in the Design of New Technology," *Behaviour and Information Technology* 21, no. 1 (2002): 1–25.

12. Druin, "The Role of Children in the Design of New Technology."

13. Druin, "The Role of Children in the Design of New Technology."

14. Hugh Beyer and Karen Holtzblatt, "Contextual Design," *ACM Interactions* 6 (January–February 1999): 32.

15. Beyer and Holtzblatt, "Contextual Design," 40–41.

16. Elliot Soloway, Mark Guzdial, and Kenneth Hay, "Learner-Centered Design: The Challenge for HCI in the 21st Century," *Interaction* 1, no. 2 (1994): 36–48.

17. Soloway et al., "Learner-Centered Design," 39.

18. Soloway et al., "Learner-Centered Design," 41.

19. Yasmin B. Kafai, "Children as Designers, Testers, and Evaluators of Educational Software," in *The Design of Children's Technology*, ed. Alison Druin, 123–45 (San Francisco: Morgan Kaufmann Publishers, 1999).

20. Erran Carmel, Randall Whitaker, and Joey George, "PD and Joint Application Design: A Transatlantic Comparison," *Communications of the ACM* 36, no. 4 (1993): 40–48.

21. Carmel et al., "PD and Joint Application Design."

22. Carmel et al., "PD and Joint Application Design."

23. Michael Muller and Sarah Kuhn, "Participatory Design," *Communications of the ACM* 36, no. 6 (1993): 26.

24. Michael Scaife, Yvonne Rogers, Frances Aldrich, and Matt Davies, "Designing for or Designing With? Informant Design for Interactive Learning Environments," in *Proceedings of the SIGCHI Conference on Human Factors in Computing System*, ed. S. Pemberton, 343–50 (New York: ACM Press, 1997).

25. Scaife et al., "Designing for or Designing With?" 344.

26. Scaife and Rogers, "Kids as Informants."

27. Scaife et al., "Designing for or Designing With?" 350

28. Scaife et al., "Designing for or Designing With?" 346

29. Alison Druin, "Cooperative Inquiry: Developing New Technologies for Children with Children," in *Proceedings of the SIGCHI Conference on Human Factors in Computing Systems*, ed. S. Pemberton, 592–99 (New York: ACM Press, 1999). Quote is on page 593.

30. Alison Druin, Ben Bederson, Angela Boltman, Adrian Miura, Debby Knotts-Callahan, and Mark Platt, "Children as Our Technology Design Partners," in *The Design of Children's Technology*, ed. Alison Druin, 51–72 (San Francisco: Morgan Kaufmann Publishers, 1999).

31. Andrew Large, Valerie Nesset, Jamshid Beheshti, and Leanne Bowler, "'Bonded Design': A Novel Approach to Intergenerational Information Technology Design," *Library and Information Science Research* 28, no. 1 (2006): 64–82.

32. Scaife et al., "Designing for or Designing With?"

33. L. S. Vygotsky, *Mind in Society: The Development of Higher Psychological Processes* (Cambridge, MA: Harvard University Press, 1978).

34. Leanne Bowler, Andrew Large, Jamshid Beheshti, and Valerie Nesset, "Children and Adults Working Together in the Zone of Proximal Development: A Concept for User-Centered Design," in *Data, Information, and Knowledge in a Networked World*, Proceedings of the Canadian Association for Information Science, June 2–4, 2005, London, ON, Canada, www.cais-acsi.ca/2005proceedings.-htm (accessed June 27, 2005).

35. Ben Williamson, "The Participation of Children in the Design of New Technology: A Discussion Paper," *Nesta Futurelab* 2004: 6, www.nestafuturelab.org/research/discuss/01discuss01.htm (accessed June 27, 2005).

36. Large et al., "Design Criteria for Children's Web Portals"; Shazia Mumtaz, "Children's Enjoyment and Perception of Computer Use in the Home and the School," *Computers & Education* 36, no. 4 (2001): 347–62; Myron Orleans, and Margaret C. Laney, "Children's Computer Use in the Home: Isolation or Socialization?" *Social Science Computer Review* 18, no. 1 (2000): 56–72; Schacter et al., "Children's Internet Searching on Complex Problems"; G. Siann, and D. C. E. Ugwuegbu, *Educational Psychology in a Changing World*, 2nd ed. (London: Unwin Hyman, 1988); Chin-Chung Tsai, Sunny Lin, and Meng-Jung Tsai, "Developing an Internet Attitude Scale for High School Students," *Computers & Education* 37, no. 1 (2001): 41–51.

37. Large et al., "Design Criteria for Children's Web Portals."

38. Large et al., "Design Criteria for Children's Web Portals."

39. Large et al., "Design Criteria for Children's Web Portals."

40. R. A. Krueger, *Focus Groups: A Practical Guide for Applied Research*, 2nd ed. (Thousand Oaks, CA: Sage, 1994).

41. Andrew Large, Jamshid Beheshti, and Charles Cole, "Information Architecture for the Web: The IA Matrix Approach to Designing Children's Portals," *Journal of the American Society for Information Science and Technology* 53, no. 10 (2002): 831–38.

42. Bilal, "Children Design Their Interfaces for Web Search Engines"; Bilal, "Draw and Tell"; M. L. Guha, Alison Druin, G. Chipman, J. A. Fails, S. Simms, and A. Farber, "Mixing ideas: A New Technique for Working with Young Children as Design Partners," in *Proceedings of Interaction Design and Children 2004: Building a Community*, ed. Allison Druin, Juan Pablo Hourcade and Sharmon Kollet, 35–42 (New York: ACM Press, 2004).

43. Large et al., "'Bonded Design.'"

44. Andrew Large, Jamshid Beheshti, Valerie Nesset, and Leanne Bowler, "Designing Web Portals in Intergenerational Teams: Two Prototype Portals for Elementary School Students," *Journal of the American Society for Information Science and Technology* 55 no. 13 (2004): 1140–54.

45. Leanne Bowler, Valerie Nesset, Andrew Large, and Jamshid Beheshti,

"Using the Web for Canadian History Projects: What Will Children Find?" *The Canadian Journal for Information and Library Science* 28, no. 3 (2004): 3–24.

46. Andrew Large, Jamshid Beheshti, Valerie Nesset, and Leanne Bowler, "Children's Web Portals: Are Adult Designers on Target?" in *Access to Information: Technologies, Skills, and Socio-Political Context*, Canadian Association for Information Science, Winnipeg, June 2004, www.cais-acsi.ca/proceedings/2004/large_2004.pdf (accessed June 27, 2005).

47. Bowler et al., "Using the Web for Canadian History Projects."

48. Jacob Nielsen, "Kids' Corner: Website Usability for Children," *Alertbox* April 2002, www.useit.com/alertbox/20020414.html (accessed June 27, 2005).

10

Causes of Information-Seeking Failure: Some Insights from an English Research Project

Andrew K. Shenton

As the importance of helping young people to develop information skills grows and schools give increasing attention to this area, the frequency with which youngsters have been seen, by information professionals and researchers alike, to fail when looking for information is a matter of great concern. Yet empirical research specifically devoted to the phenomenon of information-seeking failure is meager. This chapter begins by tracing recent shifts in the teaching of information skills that have been designed to enhance their utility and, against this background, it explores the reality of information-seeking failure among young people that has been revealed by a wide ranging, recently conducted study undertaken in the northeast of England. Individual reasons are isolated as to why, for the young informants, many information needs went unmet, and these are illustrated via specific situations reported by the study participants. The chapter concludes by discussing the findings of this UK project in terms of previous work, and offers recommendations that may be made in the light of the investigation's results.

The last thirty years have seen major changes in the orientation of information skills teaching programs. As Rogers observes, in the 1970s the training in this area offered to young people tended to be restricted to "user education," with the instruction often tacitly underpinned by an assumption that information-seeking action would take place in a library environment.[1] This emphasis is evident in much of the contemporary published advice offered to educators with regard to the skills that they should inculcate and those that their charges should learn and implement. The algorithm presented by Stagg and Brew for "finding the book you want," for example, is aimed entirely at developing the skills of young users in relation to the library catalog.[2] A further strand within information skills instruction at this time operated at a more micro level—the teaching of techniques for exploiting individual types of publications found in the library environment. The program of "information training" proposed by Lindsay encompasses both dimensions—the use of library tools, including the subject guide, the classification scheme and the classified catalog, and information retrieval from materials such as dictionaries, encyclopedias, atlases, gazetteers, maps, and telephone directories.[3] Noting the low profile of the "library instruction" typically offered in UK secondary schools at this time, White and Coles are particularly critical of its frequent restriction to only first-year pupils and a tendency to associate it exclusively with the English department.[4] Weight to the former charge is given by Hamilton, who, in presenting ideas for how schools may wish to use their "library lessons," acknowledges that, at her time of writing, regular sessions of this kind in her British school did not continue beyond the first year.[5]

The 1980s saw a clear shift in favor of generic models in which skills involving the exploitation of the library catalog, the classification scheme and paper sources were increasingly addressed not in isolation but within integrated programs in which youngsters could understand how the decisions they made and actions they took at individual stages contributed in some way to an overall investigative process. Momentum in this direction was gained with the championing of the approach by influential figures in the discipline who recognized the importance of moving attention away from a predominant emphasis on specific sources and retrieval systems toward process schemes characterized by a more widely relevant, problem-solving orientation.[6] Mancall, Aaron, and Walker, for example, wrote persuasively of the need to shift the focus of information literacy teaching from a library-centered to an information-centered perspective. Broadly, the new models were aimed at equipping youngsters to develop skills and appropriate responses to generic prompts relating to such matters as

- the nature of the need;
- the information known to be required;
- the location of that information;
- the evaluation of the information;
- the use of the information in order to meet the need.

Marland's seminal "Information Skills Curriculum" and the model by Coles, Shepherd, and White provide early evidence of the increasing interest in these areas.[7] Today, comparable concerns underpin many information literacy schemes that remain prevalent in our schools.[8] Although models for teaching information skills frequently imply that the production of a curriculum assignment forms the principal context for the youngster's efforts, Chelton and Cool recognize that such programs have become "cast within the larger framework for developing skills for lifelong learning."[9] Some twenty years ago, commentators like Liesener and Cleaver were integral to the growth of this trend, with their appeals for the promotion of lifelong learning via the teaching of information skills in schools.[10]

One of the most important conceptualizations of information skills in recent years has been the "Seven Faces of Information Literacy" pioneered by Bruce. This model is *particularly* focused on generic issues, and differs from much preceding work in its inherently phenomenological emphasis—its concern lies in information literacy as it is experienced by information users themselves. Essentially, the "seven faces" refer to individual principles of shared understanding. These state that information literacy

- involves the use of IT for information retrieval and communication;
- relates to finding information within sources;
- is process-oriented;
- is associated with the control of information;
- emphasizes the construction of personal knowledge bases;
- sees knowledge and personal perspectives combined to allow the development of novel insights;
- allows information to be used wisely for the benefit of others.

Increasing levels of subjectivity form a key characteristic of these conceptions. In the first of Bruce's "categories" information is perceived to be objective—"something outside the individual." Yet, in the seventh, information is understood within the context of "one's own life experience" and is material that "can be used in qualitatively different ways."[11] Such a flexible orientation contrasts sharply with the rigid prescription of user education instruction that predominated in the 1970s.

The gradual shift in the direction of information literacy programs was accompanied to a degree by comparable changes in the focus of much research into the actual information-seeking behavior of young people. Writing in 1987 and using language that echoes that of Mancall, Aaron, and Walker, Varlejs detected that, some years earlier, there had been a movement in information-seeking research generally away from a materials emphasis to one that was, again, more information-centered.[12] By the mid-1980s, this change had become evident in the nature of studies of young people's information seeking. Interest in the different environments visited by youngsters and the different sources they use increased, while attention to the levels of demand for specific materials in a given library dwindled. Chelton and Cool believe that it was the beginning of the next decade, however, that saw the "rise of researchers who endeavored to develop a more general understanding of the information-seeking process among youth, across different contexts, and with a variety of information resources."[13] Certainly, over the last twenty years, even where young people's information seeking has been investigated within the confines of a particular curriculum project, coverage has not always been restricted to resources in library or school settings. Several studies, for example, have explored the variety of information-seeking methods used by youngsters undertaking academic assignments.[14] Further scrutiny of the whole information universes of their respective subjects is apparent in studies where researchers have not focused purely on information seeking to satisfy school obligations.[15] Cool argues that more work of this kind is needed. She writes,

> Researchers have for too long worked within a model that assumes that the school entirely defines the parameters of children's and young adults' information needs. Overcoming this neglect to consider the desire of youth to find out about their world, apart from specific classroom assignments, is necessary in order to develop more general models of youth information-seeking behavior.[16]

Despite greater interest in the different forms of information behavior undertaken by youngsters, much work over the last twenty years has concentrated not on issues or themes that have emerged across a broad base of diverse information-seeking activity but on patterns in relation to one of the following more specific areas:

- the location of information within particular books;
- the use made of libraries, especially school and public, and/or paper materials of various types;
- the exploitation of tools such as library catalogs or bibliographic databases;
- the methods adopted by inquirers working with the Web, CD-ROM software, and/or other forms of electronic encyclopedias;
- comparisons of youngsters' experiences with paper and electronic information sources;
- the behavior of young people seeking information on particular subjects.

Shenton and Dixon attempt to provide a more generic perspective in their examination of the issues that typically arise in information seeking; they do not restrict their investigation of such issues in terms of either curriculum work or the use of a particular type of information resource.[17] Given Walter's observation that, aside from the considerable research into young people's interactions with electronic resources, the body of knowledge devoted to youngsters' information seeking is "asymmetrical and fragmented,"[18] it is unsurprising that papers with such a specifically generic thrust are rare.

Problem situations, rather than user behavior per se, have seldom formed in their own right the focus of research, although notable work in this area has been done by Cooper, with regard to the difficulties faced by young children in library environments,[19] and by Akin in relation to the phenomenon of information overload.[20] Many studies have revealed more incidentally problems encountered by young people while undertaking information-seeking action, yet very little research has been devoted specifically to information-seeking failure and the circumstances in which it emerges. Especially when it is realized that work exploring these matters may have clear implications for information skills teaching and the design of information materials, user failure remains significantly underresearched. Essentially, knowledge in the area is limited to particular media and environments, and has been gained from research more generally concerned with young people's information behavior in these contexts. The integration that has been such a feature of the development of information literacy teaching programs in the last twenty-five years remains conspicuously lacking. Notwithstanding the moves toward the information-oriented research that Varlejs identifies, little has been done, either in new empirical studies or within syntheses drawing on the findings of existing work, to investigate user failure across the use of different sources and different locations in relation to action taken to address information needs of different kinds. This chapter aims to uncover, from this open perspective, factors that lead to failure when youngsters attempt to find information and assess the extent to which they are particular to youngsters of certain ages. More specifically, it examines what was learned in these respects from a research project undertaken in recent years in the UK.

THE RESEARCH PROJECT

Study Aims

The findings reported in this chapter emerged from a study that encompassed an area much broader than information-seeking failure. The research in question was a British Academy-funded PhD project that attempted to explore the information universes of young people as revealed by their words and ideas. The importance of this phenomenological approach is recognized by Amey, who observes, "To properly understand and serve adolescents we need to look at their behavior in their terms, not ours."[21] In full, the underpinning research question asked, "With regard to information, how do youngsters' attitudes and behavior as conveyed through their own perspectives change during the years of childhood?" Childhood, in this case, was represented as the period from four to eighteen years of age. Two particular information-related dimensions were isolated for coverage—young people's information needs and the actions they take in response to them. During the course of the investigation, many instances of user failure were revealed and, in order to gain further insight into the causes, the circumstances associated with these failures were explored in detail. Although information-seeking failure did not form one of the study foci per se, such situations came to light as the line of questioning taken with the informants traced situations from the emergence of an information need through to the effectiveness of any remedial action taken in response to the need and, within this context, problems accompanying information-seeking action became apparent.

The justification for uniting the strands of information needs and information seeking derives from the principle that the latter must be understood with reference to the needs that have inspired it. Eskola is one of the most vocal advocates of such an approach,[22] and Vakkari notes, "Methodically 'information needs' and 'seeking' are only analytical differentiations for the purpose of analysis. Methodologically they will be treated as functions of a broader task or problem situation to be coped with."[23] It was believed that this attitude would be shared by the young people from whom data would be collected. The viewpoints of Eskola and Vakkari reflect the rationale behind current trends toward the examination of information seeking in context. In the late 1990s, Dervin observed the increasing popularity of this movement.[24] Many researchers stress the close association between a person's information need and his or her subsequent information-seeking behavior, and believe that recognition of an information need actually marks the start of the information-seeking process for that individual.[25]

The investigator concentrated his attention on information seeking wherever it took place, in relation to the range of sources and materials that the informants exploited and in response to the full diversity of information needs experienced by the informants. Shenton distinguishes between research that addresses the "where"/"what" of information seeking and that devoted to the "how."[26] In the former, the preferences of individuals are examined in terms of the providers and sources they exploit, while in the latter the users' actual interactions with sources are scrutinized. The research study forming the subject of this chapter dealt with both dimensions.

Clarification of Terms

For the purposes of the project, an *information need* was considered to be the desire or necessity to acquire the material required by a youngster to—in his or her eyes—ease, resolve, or otherwise address a situation arising in his or her life. Such material might include facts, interpretations, advice, opinions, or other types of messages carrying meaning. Although these areas are largely analogous to the forms believed by Chen and Hernon, and Poston-Anderson and Edwards to constitute information,[27] it was decided specifically to exclude imaginative works on the basis that their inclusion would extend the scope of the study too far and possibly direct undue attention to, for example, the location of particular fiction books in libraries. The concept of "information need" was assumed to embrace needs and wants alike, partly because to concentrate exclusively on what the investigator might consider "necessary information" would involve the introduction of a judgmental approach on his part that seemed incompatible with the aim of examining information needs from the perspective of the youngsters. It may also be argued that since a researcher cannot experience the emotions and thoughts of an informant, the making of such distinctions is, as Line suggests, nigh impossible.[28]

A stance similar to that taken by several previous researchers was adopted with regard to the concept of *information seeking*, that is, it was understood to include any action taken by an individual to address a perceived information need.[29] Such actions are underpinned by decisions taken at a cognitive level relating, for example, to the selection of a particular source, resource, or organization to be approached and the manner in which it is to be exploited. The fact that, in the context of the project, attention was directed only to situations in which either a need was ignored or a conscious effort was made to satisfy it means that the accidental discovery of information and incidental information acquisition as described by Erdelez were beyond its scope.[30] *Information-seeking failure* was assumed to relate to situations in which a user, having decided to take information-seeking action, was unable to access material that contributed, in that person's eyes, to the adequate satisfaction of the need. Frequently, after experiencing initial failure, the youngster was subsequently more successful when he or she employed a fresh approach either with the same resources or with different information materials, although there were many instances, too, where the youngster took no further action and the need remained entirely unmet. This chapter addresses both the individual instances of failure and situations where, after several attempts were made, there remained a conspicuous lack of information-seeking success.

The term, *information universe*, is found in existing work much less frequently than "information need" and "information seeking." It was employed within the study to refer to the circumstances within which an individual requires and pursues information. The phrase is used by Latrobe and Havener for a similar purpose.[31] With regard to the information-seeking dimension, an information universe may relate to the sources available to and utilized by the person and the methods he or she employs for their exploitation. An individual's information universe thus includes, but goes beyond, his or her "information horizon," which Sonnenwald believes to consist of the variety of information resources accessible to that person.[32] Essentially, the concept is similar to that of an "information world,"[33] to Amey's construct of an "information environment,"[34] and to the notion of the "user's life world" postulated by Wilson, who defines such a world as "the totality of experiences centred upon the individual as an information user."[35]

Methodology

The techniques employed in the study did not derive from the wholesale adoption of one particular research paradigm. Rather, they were selected in response to the aims of the project and their implications. The philosophical justification for this approach is summed up by Patton, who believes the researcher to have an "intellectual mandate" for selecting whatever techniques he or she considers most suitable, regardless of their paradigm.[36] A similar argument is presented elsewhere.[37] Vakkari quotes a range of investigators concerned with information seeking who have employed in a single study techniques characteristic of the two different research frameworks—the naturalistic and the positivist—in order to meet their purposes.[38] Kuhlthau, Friel, and Burdick, whose projects have incorporated the two approaches, are particularly enthusiastic in their support for using qualitative and quantitative methods in concert.[39]

While there are commentators who point out that such mixing has become common,[40] this eclecticism is not shared by all. Merriam writes of the "ongoing debate" surrounding its validity,[41] and Silverman goes as far as to suggest that two "armed camps" have arisen as a result of commitments made by researchers to one or other of the paradigms.[42] Lincoln and Guba reside firmly in the qualitative domain. They assert unequivocally in relation to naturalistic inquiry, "Mix-and-match strategies are not allowed," arguing that an investigator must accept the whole paradigm and *all* the methods it entails.[43] Rossman and Wilson label proponents of such a stance "purists," and believe their steadfastness to stem from the perception that qualitative and quantitative approaches derive from "different, mutually exclusive epistemological and ontological assumptions about the nature of research and society."[44] In terms of the empirical study, it was feared that the adoption of the paradigm of naturalistic inquiry in its entirety could lead to the intended study foci becoming compromised simply to accommodate the naturalistic principles involved. This implies shifting the ends in light of the means rather than the more appropriate adjustment of the means to fit the ends.

The nature of the topic (i.e., information universes), the perspective taken (i.e., that of youngsters themselves), and the orientation of the work (i.e., explorative) combined to render the project nearer the naturalistic end of the research spectrum than the positivist as regards the methods that were adopted. In particular, qualitative data collection and analysis techniques were selected to allow detailed exploration of the contexts of the young people's needs and behavior and of the manner in which they had constructed meaning from their experiences. Nevertheless, in the account of results that follows, frequencies are given of the numbers of participants exhibiting particular forms of information-seeking failure in order to imbue the work with greater precision and transparency.

The Sample

Informants were drawn from six schools in the town of Whitley Bay. This area was chosen as the fieldwork location partly because, through his previous teaching experience, the investigator had developed a network of contacts in the town and could be confident that at least some Whitley Bay schools would agree to participate. Approximately ten miles from the city of Newcastle upon Tyne, Whitley Bay is located on England's northeast coast. It is situated in the metropolitan borough of North Tyneside, which itself lies within the county of Tyne and Wear. If it is considered to embrace the wards of Monkseaton, St. Mary's, Seatonville, and Whitley Bay itself, the town's population is around thirty-eight thousand. Ethnic minorities formed less than 2.5 percent of the population at the time of the most recent Census.[45] One of North Tyneside's more affluent areas, Whitley Bay enjoys low unemployment and an overwhelming majority of the town's seventeen-year-olds is involved in full-time education.

All fourteen nondenominational schools within Whitley Bay were given the opportunity to take part in the study. Of the six that agreed to do so, three were first schools (catering for children from three to nine years of age), two middle schools (for nine- to thirteen-year-olds) and one a high school (for youngsters between thirteen and eighteen). All the participating schools are open to boys and girls and are comprehensive, admitting youngsters regardless of ability, race, or religion. They are all funded by the local education authority and subject to its guidance. In the latter half of the 1990s, shortly before the study commenced, each was inspected by the British Office for Standards in Education (OFSTED), a national regulatory body responsible for monitoring standards in schools, and emerged with credit. Recurring themes in the OFSTED reports included substantial parental support, high levels of pupil attendance, consistently good behavior, few exclusions, and praiseworthy academic standards. Test and examination results in each school usually exceed the national average.

Informants in all six schools were drawn from one class in each year group. The class sampled and the individual pupils approached for data within that class were chosen at random. Each class consisted of mixed ability youngsters from the same year group. Random selection was believed the most effective strategy in helping to ensure that the youngsters taking part were broadly representative of those in the classes from which they had been drawn. Each Class Teacher verified that the sample taken from his or her class embraced a wide range of ability. In total, 188 pupils from fourteen year groups were involved; 95 were boys and 93 girls.

Data Gathering and Analysis Methods

Data were collected via twelve focus groups and 121 individual interviews conducted during the year 2000. No pupil took part in more than one data gathering session. A life-centered line of questioning was taken in all the dialogues, with informants initially asked,

> Think of a time recently when you needed help, when you needed to decide what to do, when you were worried about something or when you needed to find something out or learn something, either for school or your own interest. It might've been at home, at school or anywhere else. Could you tell me about what you remember of that time?

This approach was based on a strategy devised by Dervin et al. for their study of the information needs of Seattle residents.[46] After providing stories relating to the needs they had experienced, informants were asked to recall the action they had taken in response. The researcher ensured that the youngsters' accounts addressed the channel or resource they had utilized, the tactics employed in using it, any problems that they had encountered and their ultimate level of satisfaction with the outcome. Highly prescriptive information-seeking activities, in which the pupils had been asked by their teachers to employ a certain resource or approach, were not considered in the discussions. Each data collection session was tape recorded and a verbatim transcript prepared soon after the completion of the dialogue.

Although individual interviews and focus groups formed the principal methods of data gathering, where possible the data contributed by the youngsters were verified against documentary sources. In particular, data pertaining to information needs were triangulated against National Curriculum requirements[47] and internal school documents, such as curriculum programs of study and schemes of work. All data that had not been shown to be erroneous were manually coded inductively in accordance with the constant comparative method of Glaser and Strauss.[48] A key task during data analysis lay in using the coded and categorized data to define types. Broadly, these addressed information needs, information-seeking action and information-seeking problems/failures. This production of typologies moved the project firmly into the "interpretive" form of research described by Merriam.[49] The data pertaining to the two information-seeking dimensions were explored at three levels— unitary, contiguous, and multidimensional.

- *Unitary level.* Patterns of action and problems/failures were investigated in relation to each type of need that the informants sought to address. The data associated with these two information-seeking foci were also scrutinized in terms of the individual kinds of mate-

rial and resources, as well as with regard to each school phase of
the informants.

- *Contiguous level.* Patterns apparent in relation to various types of
need were examined. A similar approach was taken in terms of the
use of different varieties of information sources and environments,
and finally with regard to the youngsters as a whole, irrespective
of their school phases.
- *Multidimensional level.* In the highest form of analysis, the
researcher explored overarching patterns that were apparent across
different types of need, the use of different information sources
and informants of different ages.

The findings described in this chapter resulted from the application
of the three levels of analysis.

Criticisms and Limitations

No claim is made that the results of the project can be applied to populations outside those of the schools in which the fieldwork took place.
Although youngsters within the individual classes were selected randomly as this was considered the most effective strategy for increasing
the likelihood of their being representative of pupils in the classes from
which they were drawn, no attempt was made to ensure representative-
ness beyond this level.

It must also be acknowledged that the study relied heavily on self-
reported data. In addition to employing triangulation in the manner
already described, strategies were adopted to minimize the possibility
of informants deliberately misleading the researcher. In all the data collection sessions, the investigator attempted to establish an early rapport
with the participants, stressing the importance of honesty, indicating
that there were "no right answers" to his questions, and promising that
data would not be reported back to the pupils' teachers. To uncover any
deliberate lies, a system of iterative questioning developed by Shenton
was also adopted.[50] During a data collection session, the researcher
returned to points previously made by an informant in order to assess
the consistency of the data that the person supplied at different times in
the discussion. So as to reduce the danger of inaccuracies in the data
resulting from hazy memories of events, interest was directed only at

youngsters' recent experiences. Criticism may be made of the fact that each informant was approached for data only once during the fieldwork stage. Although this approach has frequently been used in research into young people's information seeking, it is not without opposition. Cool, who advocates a more longitudinal perspective, argues that it provides a "somewhat artificial snapshot" of the phenomenon under investigation.[51] Furthermore, the use of individual interviews with young children, in particular, is somewhat controversial. Mauthner considers them awkward for youngsters of this age,[52] and Cooper notes that where a child is not used to such a situation, he or she may view it as a test and this can affect the responses that are given.[53] Cooper further suggests that stress may be caused to the informant by removing him or her from the normal educational routine.

As the perspective taken in this chapter is that of exploring user failure on the basis of accounts of information-seeking action supplied by the participants, it lacks the particularly low-level insights that may be gained only through observation and, in IT contexts, the recording of computer keystrokes. The degree of detail of the work is in this respect very different from that offered by Chen, for example. In her investigation of the use of a computer catalog, she provides a highly specific breakdown of the types of error made by high schoolers.[54] In the same way, no data elicited in the Whitley Bay study indicated that failure resulted from users' spelling errors when entering search terms into computer systems, as informants may well either have been unaware that they had made such mistakes or have forgotten these details on recalling the incident at a later date. Yet, in work elsewhere it has been widely noted that poor spelling of search terms has been a significant problem when youngsters have employed computer catalogs.[55] A similar issue has arisen with regard to the entry of URLs when youngsters have used the Internet.[56] This chapter takes a more broad-brush approach, focusing less on the minutiae of specific tactics employed by inquirers in certain situations and more on uncovering generic patterns.

Results

Lack of Action as a Cause of Unmet Needs

A feature of the study was the alarming frequency with which informants reported that, in specific situations, their information needs were not met. By no means always, however, was this the result of unsuccessful action. Although most cases of unmet need emerged after ineffective attempts were made to find information, in some twenty-six instances a need was felt but no information-seeking effort was made. Generally such inaction resulted from users simply being unwilling to expend the effort necessary to make a search. Nevertheless, five of the youngest inquirers who wanted but did not actively seek subject-related information did not know where to start looking. Edgar (aged six), for example, was deterred because the type of materials he believed would be most likely to help him were not available at home. Wanting information on jungles, he was prevented from looking by his knowledge that "we haven't really got a jungle book." The lack of action taken to satisfy needs for affective support and empathetic understanding was even more frequent. In the former scenarios, informants required reassurance and/or sympathy in relation to a past, ongoing, or future situation that caused them concern, while in the latter youngsters were keen to learn more either about the motivations of a particular person generally or an individual's specific behavior at the time of a certain event. Eight youngsters who described experiencing needs for affective support did not seek information, perhaps believing that to acknowledge their desire for emotional backup was to admit to others a weakness in themselves. Curiously, however, they were quite willing to talk of such needs to the researcher.

One informant was loath to consult teachers, who might have been able to provide the required information, because she considered them unpleasant or potentially hostile. In the words of Pauline (aged eleven), "I wouldn't ask my teacher 'cos she's not very nice." Here, the personal dynamics associated with a face-to-face exchange proved an insurmountable deterrent. Thus, where an adult from whom information might be sought was known to the youngster, the quality of the relationship between the two parties was critical in the inquirer's decision as to whether or not to make an approach. Another informant who had considered asking teachers feared that his questions would be regarded as inappropriate for discussion within the school environment and did not know where else to seek advice. Adrian (aged fifteen), who wanted guidance on strategies that he should adopt to stop smoking, was critical of the way, he felt, his school did not address this matter, beyond dispensing didactic, anti-smoking messages designed to discourage pupils taking up smoking from the outset. Adrian detected a resistance among staff to advise pupils on how to stop smoking once the youngsters had made the decision to break their habit. He attributed this to the school's tendency "to pretend there isn't a problem."

Unsuccessful Information-Seeking Action

The factors associated with information-seeking failure can be grouped into five categories: need/source mismatch, knowledge deficiency, skills shortcomings, psychological barriers, and social unease and inhibitions. Figure 10.1 shows diagrammatically the individual issues within these broad groups, which are here recast as five "dimensions."

1. Need/Source Mismatch *The source was inappropriate to the nature of the topic on which information was sought.* This incongruity was particularly prevalent in the experiences of very young children

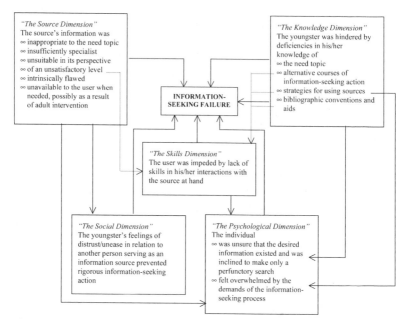

Figure 10.1. Diagrammatic Representation of Factors Leading to Information-Seeking Failure

who were seeking, from adults, information on personal interests. Nine informants aged five, six, or seven posed to members of the family questions that they were ill equipped to answer. Penelope (aged seven) was unsuccessful when seeking from her parents information on the Millennium Dome, a major tourist attraction that was generating much interest in Britain at the time of the fieldwork. When wanting to learn about the rules of soccer, Alan (aged six) asked successively his father, mother, and eventually his sister but on each occasion his need was not met. These incidents illustrate the fact that some youngsters in the early years of school were unclear as to the extent of the knowledge possessed by members of their family and had naïve expectations of the information they might be able to provide. Older informants tended to recognize that, when they needed in-depth information, either for their interest or for school purposes, it was unrealistic to believe that other people could supply such material, unless they were genuine subject experts.

The task of finding a particular person with sufficient knowledge of value in a more personal situation affecting an informant proved an insurmountable problem for Suzanne (aged eleven), who wanted to know "what it would be like" when she appeared as a contestant on a television quiz show. Those she normally approached for information, such as her parents and teachers, had very limited knowledge of the area. When personalized information of this kind was required, some of the most successful information seekers were those who used sources that had already been selected specifically for them by another party. Joy (aged seventeen), for example, developed a greater understanding of the post-viral fatigue syndrome from which she was suffering by reading leaflets supplied by her doctor.

Four informants made inappropriate use, leading to information-seeking failure, of tourist information centers. Alexandra (aged eleven), Pamela (aged thirteen), Dennis (aged thirteen), and Eric (aged thirteen) all went to these organizations in support of local studies projects for school and, on each occasion, the youngster's need remained unmet, largely because he or she had misunderstood the nature of the material that the agencies provided. When the centers were visited for their intended purposes, informants gained the desired results. Electronic resources, too, were twice used in unsuitable situations. Hilary (aged eleven) realized that her CD-ROM encyclopedia at home did not cover careers information. After trying unsuccessfully to learn about the work of a vet from this resource, she came to the conclusion, "You can't really get any programs that tell you about that." Another middle schooler, Neville (aged thirteen), made inappropriate use of a GOSIP point (i.e., the General On Street Information Point), which dealt in local information pertaining to Newcastle, the city in which it was located. Oblivious to its intended purposes, Neville interrogated the terminal to find out about television schedules and, unsurprisingly, was unable to retrieve the information he sought. An ignorance of the characteristics of two different types of paper sources led Tim (aged ten) to make poor initial decisions in terms of the materials that he should use. The boy confessed to being unsure of the differences between dictionaries and encyclopedias and acknowledged that, in several situations, it was only after failure in using a dictionary that he realized an encyclopedia was a more appropriate form of text. Information-seeking failure emerged, too, when unsuitable monographs from the home library were consulted. All the cases in which no information on the relevant topic could be found in domestic books of this kind involved informants in the older half of the sample. Fourteen-year-old Ed, for example, looking for information on the beliefs of the major political parties for a school assignment on Personal and Social Education, began his search with an entirely inappropriate book from the home library about "man and society." Ed admitted spending considerable time examining this volume simply because it was readily available to him, not because he had identified it as a promising source.

Although there was clearly a mismatch between the source and the nature of the need in all the situations described above, there would otherwise appear to be little in the way of a single, common pattern. The age of the youngest informants who approached unsuitable adults was so junior and their information-seeking experience and skills so meager that the use of other people formed virtually their only information-seeking option. Suzanne, too, considered that her one "real" course of action available lay in asking familiar adults, and ultimately this response proved to be inadequate. Unsuccessful users of tourist information centers, CD-ROM software, the GOSIP point, and some reference books were under genuine misapprehensions as to the nature of the information they could expect to find. Unsuitable monographs at home were frequently consulted because of convenience reasons.

In most instances where other people, tourist information centers and domestic books were used unsuccessfully, the inquirer was confident that the desired information at least existed. The youngster's challenge was simply to connect with it. Situations also arose in the study, however, where, unbeknown to the individual, the information might not exist, either in any recorded form or as knowledge within another person. Here, what the youngster wanted to know had to be discovered from practical experience. This was true in a range of instances in which the youngsters encountered problems in their everyday lives. Nathan (aged four) and Melissa (aged five), for example, both lost toys that they valued and sought information on where they might be found. Even some subject queries lacked clear-cut answers that could be discovered from information sources. The answer to Ian's (aged nine) question of how many stars there are in the galaxy, for example, has confounded even world renowned astronomers such as Carl Sagan, who once famously admitted he could provide no better an answer than "millions and millions."

The information offered by the source covered the general area of need but was insufficiently specialist. This was a problem in twelve situations when older middle schoolers and high schoolers consulted paper or electronic encyclopedias. Two twelve-year-olds, Dirk and Shane, became acutely aware of this issue when using children's encyclopedias in paper form. Shane recognized that his general encyclopedia of this type was a poor substitute for more specialist geographical texts, and, in almost every case of older informants using CD-ROM encyclopedias for school assignments, they were found to lack the in-depth information required. Lionel (aged thirteen), for example, reported how he had retrieved "hardly anything" when attempting to use *Microsoft Encarta* to find out about the Kalapalo Indians, and Louis (aged thirteen) made a similar criticism when consulting *Encarta* and *Encyclopedia Britannica* CD-ROMs for the same purpose. "The information wasn't good enough," he explained. "It didn't go into enough depth about the thing. It didn't actually specialize in the questions we had." Julia (aged sixteen), soon to complete her GCSE studies, indicated using *Encarta* mainly "to browse around." In terms of information for specific school assignments, she found its value limited. "It's not very detailed . . . it's really not got enough," she considered.

Efforts to find, from materials such as books, applied subject knowl-

edge dealing with particular objects of interest to youngsters and pertaining directly to their own social worlds were also usually
unsuccessful as what was found was insufficiently particular to the
inquirer's situation. June (aged six), who had wanted to learn more
about a fossil sent to her by her grandfather, recalled that the books she
looked at "didn't really tell me anything about *my* fossil. They just
showed me like pictures of fossils . . . and told me things more about
dinosaur fossils."

*The information offered by the source had not been prepared from
the perspective required by the user.* Despite the wealth of material
offered on the Web, twenty-two instances were reported where inquirers
found material in this environment that met their needs only partially.
Toby (aged sixteen) contrasted the ease with which he had, for his own
purposes, located on the Web a list of works by a particular poet with
his lack of success in finding, for school, information on the much more
nebulous topic of the causes of pollution and "urban sprawl" in Japan.
After using the Web for work on the Japan assignment, Toby was disconcerted by the fact that the onus now lay with him to construct information from disparate insights, which he had gained from the material
he had collected.

Similar problems to those of Toby, albeit with regard to different
information media, were recognized by Joan (aged nine) when undertaking a project on "endangered animals" and Francis (aged thirteen),
on two separate occasions, when he was investigating "how films have
treated aliens" and "war crimes and their punishment" respectively. In
each case, however, the inquirers countered the fact that they met with
initial failure when using search terms that closely reflected their real
area of interest by subsequently presenting new keywords to the index
of a book or an Internet search engine. Here their isolation of particular
elements led to reductionism. Their focus shifted to the coverage of
individual instances—a certain animal, a particular film or a specific
war. The overall picture for which they were searching proved impossible for the inquirers to obtain as packaged information within the
sources available to them.

*The material offered by the source was cognitively inaccessible to
the user.* Youngsters' needs in terms of the cognitive level at which they
required material were brought into sharp focus when information
retrieved by some informants was seen to be pitched unsuitably high

and was effectively useless to them. For Tony (aged seven), the content was too challenging linguistically. After examining his father's books on Newcastle United Football Club, he admitted struggling to read the information they offered because they were written "more or less for grown-ups." Elsewhere, information was too advanced conceptually. Norman (aged thirteen), who was interested in alternative medicine, explained how, when consulting his mother's college notes on the subject, he struggled to grasp the content. He admitted, "It's really submolecular stuff. I can only understand the basics." In both instances, had the information been couched in simpler language or expressed in less demanding terms, the information needs may well have been met since the material itself was relevant to the focus of the youngsters' interests. These issues recurred on five occasions when books from the adult collection of the public library were used or other volumes owned by parents or older siblings were consulted in the home.

The source suffered from serious intrinsic shortcomings. Four informants recalled how their information seeking had been thwarted when they identified serious weaknesses within a source that they had hoped to use. All were older informants who, in attempting to write an essay or revise for an examination, made searches of their class notes. For Petra (aged sixteen), these proved "illegible." Julia (aged sixteen) found hers to be "incomprehensible." Gareth (aged seventeen) recognized that they provided only a partial and superficial record of what his teacher had told the class. They were lacking in the required detail and both he and Bradley (aged eighteen) admitted that they were "probably inaccurate." All four pupils shunned their notes completely and resumed their information seeking elsewhere.

The fallibility of other people as information sources was reported on three occasions. In each scenario information given by parents in response to a skill-related query from their offspring was found to be inadequate. Mandy (aged sixteen) recalled how her father had unintentionally misled her when she had asked for help with her mathematics homework. Two adults provided information of the wrong kind. Isaac's (aged ten) father, whom he, too, had approached for assistance with mathematics homework, simply supplied what he believed to be the answers, which ultimately proved to be erroneous, rather than explaining how to tackle the questions. Jim (aged ten) reported a similar problem. In these instances, the temptation to pursue a convenient method appeared to outweigh the desire to make the effort demanded to consult a more authoritative source. Ultimately, however, the youngster realized in each situation that the quality or nature of the information elicited was such that the need had not been properly met.

Whether the source took the form of handwritten notes or another person, the informants chose to reject the material offered to them in each of the circumstances described above. In one further instance, however, shortcomings in the source meant that no appropriate information whatsoever was available. This was the case for Victor (aged seven), who discovered that information provided by BBC Television's "Ceefax" service did not relate to the installment of a television program in which he was interested. Rather, what was shown pertained to an earlier edition.

The youngster's ability to exploit a particular source was undermined by intervention from others. All but one of these instances involved the blocking at school of websites that may well have proved effective in helping to meet the inquirer's information need. Undertaking work for a Personal and Social Education assignment on "safe sex," Ben (aged fourteen) had initially searched the Web via the school computers but soon realized that they did not permit the retrieval of information on this subject and turned to his system at home. A similar discovery was made by Joy (aged seventeen) who, when seeking "stories about France," was supplied with no details about the activities of the far Right political movement. Joy knew that the content provided for her was "obviously censored" and "there's certain things that they don't let you on to." The lack of discrimination of the filter at school clearly presented unintended barriers to Benny and Joy, both of whom were intent on finding information for proper school purposes.

The youngest child to recall being affected by adult intervention was Penelope (aged seven) in a completely different situation. While looking for information at her local public library, Penelope was interrupted by her mother, who decided that they had spent long enough in the building and they should now return home.

The preferred source was unavailable at the time when information-seeking action was required, although no deliberate attempt had been made to inhibit the youngster's action or to curtail it prematurely. Nine of the ten instances of this kind again involved Information Technology. In eight of these scenarios a website that a youngster wanted to visit had either disappeared or had otherwise become unavailable. Christine (aged ten), however, found herself unable to use her family's home computer at all. Equipped with access to the Web and a range of CD-ROMs, the machine had been constructed by her father and, when he was not at home, Christine and her mother were unable to operate it as he was the only person in the household who had mastered the system's idiosyncratic switching on procedure.

A situation was also reported in which a youngster was unable to make contact with other people who had already been identified as the most promising information source. Wendy (aged nine) intended to learn about Australia, the topic for a Geography project she was undertaking at school, by talking to friends who had lived in the country. They would, Wendy hoped, be able to provide access to materials as well as to help her "with their knowledge." When her friends unexpectedly returned to Australia, however, Wendy found herself having to change her approach.

2. Knowledge Deficiency *The youngster's knowledge of the topic was insufficient to represent it in suitable keywords that could be used in approaches to a source.* Sixteen youngsters recalled situations in which the search words that they employed when interacting with IT resources failed to retrieve the information they desired yet only twice did young users admit that their knowledge of the subject was such that they "didn't know what to look it up under." For a homework assignment, Joe (aged eight) was required to learn about static electricity but this phrase was not used by the teacher who introduced the task. She merely demonstrated how a sheet of transparent plastic could be made to stick to another surface and asked her pupils to investigate why this was happening. Joe usually relished the opportunity to find out information from his children's encyclopedia but knew that this strategy was inappropriate in these circumstances. In discussing the matter with his parents, he was, however, able to draw out their knowledge in response to his account of the demonstration. Seven-year-old Tony had to use a similar approach when he wanted to know more about what he could see on examining a range of everyday materials and substances under a microscope. Again, the accepted names and terms for what he was observing were unknown to him. Still, on this occasion, he was able to show his parents exactly what he had seen.

The information seeker suffered from a lack of knowledge of alterna-

tive courses of action. Time and time again first-schoolers whose initial attempts to find information in particular situations did not deliver the anticipated results were unaware of the alternative courses of action open to them. Four of the youngest informants—Chantal (aged four), Brian (aged five), Gerald (aged five) and Austin (aged seven)—did not know, in specific situations, of any alternatives to asking others, and Anna (aged five) was unable to suggest how she could find out about dinosaurs beyond watching video recordings and looking at books—the two methods that she had employed. Although all five youngsters were discussing action taken in response to needs relating to their own interests, a similar paucity of ideas for information-seeking action emerged when first-schoolers were reporting their attempts to find material for academic purposes. Wes (aged nine), one of the oldest of the informants in this school phase, was unaware of anything else he could have done when looking for information on the United States for a school project apart from using the public library and the Internet. Faced with other needs, three middle-schoolers reported approaching specialist organizations, which here took the form of a drug awareness agency and an Islamic embassy, and, on each occasion, relevant information was obtained but in all three instances the approach was inspired by advice from a teacher. The three children admitted that they would not have taken this action without prompting.

Among older informants, where youngsters encountered difficulties in determining additional courses of action after initial information-seeking failure, the problem generally arose when they were faced with a need that was out of the ordinary or at least differed from those with which they were used to dealing. In the situation quoted earlier, where Suzanne (aged eleven) wanted to know what it would be like to appear on a television show, after her habitual courses of information-seeking action were found to be unsuitable and failed, she was unsure how to respond.

The youngster had an inadequate understanding of techniques for the effective exploitation of electronic tools and sources. Several of the techniques long recommended by teachers of information skills—systematic preliminary planning of a search, the application of Boolean logic and the use of tactics for varying the precision of a search in the light of preliminary results—were very seldom reported. Indeed, only two youngsters spoke of planning their searches in advance and of varying systematically the specificity of their search terms, while no one referred to using any Boolean operators. This is, of course, in addition to the problem of Joe and Tony, who were unable to conceive of any terms from the outset. The volume of information made available electronically was such that insufficient attention to Boolean logic and changes in keywords for searching induced feelings of resentment and frustration, leading to eventual information-seeking failure. After initially gaining unsatisfactory results with one particular tool or resource, the young users usually abandoned their efforts with it and went elsewhere, sometimes to less appropriate materials.

The information seeker was hindered by a lack of understanding of bibliographic conventions and traditional aids. These shortcomings were most apparent in the public library environment. In eight situations problems emerged from the most fundamental of bibliographic practices, especially the way in which nonfiction collections were organized. Middle-schoolers Nigel (aged ten), Larry (aged ten), and Harvey (aged eleven) were of the opinion that material of this kind was arranged in alphabetical order in accordance with the "name" of the subject. Christine (aged ten) was unaware of any order at all. This ignorance resulted in user failure on occasion. Elsewhere, failure was avoided because an adult, usually the child's mother, took the lead in finding information in the building, although clearly this may also have helped perpetuate the child's ignorance.

Gillian (aged ten) and Jonty (aged twelve) admitted to being overwhelmed by the scale of the adult collection in their local public library and recalled situations in which they were unable to find the information they required without adult aid. They appreciated that their failure was largely due to their inability to make effective use of the finding aids offered for their benefit. Their experience in their school libraries, which were more familiar to them, was of little value here as information could be found reasonably easily in these environments without consulting the bibliographic tools available and those provided were significantly different from those in the public library. In short, the specialization and detail of the material required by some inquirers was of a higher level than the youngster's understanding of the way in which information materials were arranged in their local public libraries. The actions of Norman (aged thirteen) and Kirsty (aged thirteen) in conducting a subject search using an inappropriate facility offered by their library's catalog are indicative of the uncertainties that dogged many youngsters in public libraries. In addition, two further inquirers—Curtis (aged eight) and Shane (aged twelve)—consulted neither staff nor any form of finding aid and practiced what might be described as "unguided wandering" within the library.

3. Skills Shortcomings   *Lack of skills hindered the user's ability to extract information from the source at hand.* Fourteen instances were reported where youngsters failed at the point when they were they were interacting with a particular information source. Six of the youngest children had to abandon their attempts to find information when confronted with a lengthy index at the back of a book and the alphabetical ordering skills that were demanded of them proved beyond their capabilities.

Poorly developed skills in key areas also contributed to user failure more indirectly. Even if a young child seeking information had been aware of other options that were available, he or she would have been unable to exploit the sources effectively. The unfamiliarity of a computer keyboard would have prevented the very youngest children using CD-ROM or the Internet, for example, and the very basic level of their reading would have rendered these resources inappropriate without significant adult assistance. Such deficiencies led to youngsters' reliance on other people as information sources, even though in certain situations this was highly unsuitable. In contrast to their more inexperienced counterparts, teenage participants had, over a period of time, established a good knowledge of specific materials, especially where the need involved a topic of ongoing interest, and possessed greater skills in exploiting them.

Nevertheless, the task of finding, within a certain book, information appropriate to a particular need led to significant problems for two teenagers as well as younger users. In situations that contrast with those reported earlier in relation to Joan (aged nine), Francis (aged thirteen) and Toby (aged sixteen), all of whom struggled to find information on diffuse topics, Duncan (aged seventeen) and Melvyn (aged eighteen) were unsuccessful when highly specific material was needed, the latter indicating that a major difficulty for him lay in determining the likely relevance of books whose titles suggested that they covered only general themes.

4. Psychological Barriers   *The individual was unsure that the desired information actually existed.* This form of uncertainty may be viewed as a variation on the theme of knowledge deficiency, although in these circumstances it was an awareness that the informant could not be sure that what was wanted actually existed—a phenomenon that may be dubbed a "knowledge of ignorance"—which caused the doubt and prompted the seeker to finish the search prematurely. When discussing instances of information-seeking action, most informants knew that the material would be available somewhere. This was especially the case with information for school assignments. The challenge lay in connecting with the information required. Pamela (aged thirteen), however, knew that the premise on which her need was based might be erroneous. Pursuing information about local hockey clubs playing in the highest national league, she at first believed that there must be at least some such teams competing at this level but, when her initial information-seeking action failed to produce the desired results, she became increasingly skeptical. Ultimately, fearing that "I might be looking for something that isn't, and can't be, there," she chose to abandon her efforts.

The individual felt overwhelmed by the demands of information-seeking. In situations where finding information proved more difficult than the youngsters had hoped, eighteen reported ending their searches without going beyond one or a few sources and the need remained unsatisfied. In thirteen of these cases the needs inspiring the information-seeking action related to leisure interests. Some users had formed in their minds a hierarchy of the importance of needs of different kinds. Gillian (aged ten), for example, felt that needs pertaining to her own interests were "less important" than those for school, and indicated that she would readily call off information searches when material that she did not consider a priority proved troublesome to locate. Four were deterred even at the outset by the time and effort required to make a search of the public library and chose not to visit the organization, although they acknowledged that suitable information might be available there.

Youngsters from first to high school age were discouraged from finding information when faced with materials—either on the Web or in paper form—that provided densely presented text. Glynis (aged fifteen), drew attention to her preference for books "aimed at younger children, 'cos they've got nice big print and pictures so they're easy to understand," even though they did not always provide information sufficiently specialist to meet her needs. She continued,

> I hate it when you've got paragraphs and paragraphs of tiny print. I just can't be bothered with it. Sometimes this small print goes on for pages and pages and I have problems reading through just one paragraph. Usually I've forgotten what was on line one when I'm on line four or whatever. I've just completely forgotten it.

This attitude led to Glynis abandoning much information-seeking activity when using paper materials.

While he was aware that the Internet could provide valuable material, Ed (aged fourteen) was highly disillusioned with Web searching, which might involve individual scrutiny of many different sites, most of which would prove unhelpful, and ultimately he usually aborted his efforts, opting for *Encarta* instead. Ed was particularly resentful at the prospect of reading large amounts of text on-screen. Rather than examine a range of different sites, he preferred to find an appropriate article on *Encarta* and print it off for later reading at his convenience. In truth, there were two problems here that conspired to defeat Ed. He was insufficiently knowledgeable in strategies for reducing the number of sites that resulted from his use of a search engine and his limited higher order reading skills rendered it difficult for him to form quick and accurate impressions of the relevance of the individual sites to which he was directed.

A sensation of being overpowered by the amount of material, whether in the adult collection area of a public library, in relation to the content within an individual book or when using a search engine to retrieve information from the Web, was widely reported, yet this did not always result in information-seeking failure per se. In these instances, the problems could have often been avoided had the user had a greater knowledge of effective strategies for exploitation and better developed skills in implementing them. A range of expedient solutions was developed by some informants to enable them to retrieve sufficient information to meet their need but other seekers simply terminated their efforts altogether. Sometimes the expedient method failed to yield any appropriate information. Usually, where a URL was inputted to take the user to a website, the address was either already known by the youngster or copied from reference material. Damien (aged nine), however, recounted how, when looking to restrict the scope of his search to sites that were wholly relevant to snakes, the subject of his science project for school, he had entered phrases such as "www.reptiles" and "www.-snakes" in the hope of finding suitable sites with those URLs. In each case his efforts met with no success. Damien was one of the youngest children to report using the Internet unaided and it is possible that inexperience played a part in his adoption of such an ineffective strategy.

With regard to paper materials, expedient strategies that resulted in failure more often than success in the incidents reported included flicking through pages of a book without prior consultation of the index or contents list, and selecting the first few volumes within a collection that were apparently relevant, rather than making a choice from the totality of materials available. Five informants taking such action appreciated that their behavior conflicted with other strategies advocated by their teachers and admitted that the advised procedures might be much more likely to produce effective results but considered them more onerous and inconvenient to employ. One such youngster was Wendy (aged nine). Well aware of the importance of contents lists and indexes, she nonetheless shunned them and chose to navigate via "the little captions" within individual books, thereby denying herself the opportunity to make a more thorough search. Likewise, Eric (aged thirteen) reported how his preferred strategy lay in turning the pages of a book for appropriate pictures that would provide cues to relevant text.

5. Social Unease and Inhibitions   *The youngster spurned the opportunity to pursue information at length from an adult as a result of unease or distrust.* Such behavior indirectly led to unsuccessful information seeking as the inquirers' negative attitudes toward certain people prevented their wholehearted exploitation when they might have been the most appropriate sources to meet particular needs. In choosing to consult elsewhere, youngsters effectively ruled out their best opportunity for information-seeking success, and either thereafter used materials that were less suitable or abandoned their efforts altogether. Michelle (aged eighteen) revealed how she had received highly dogmatic responses when asking school staff for guidance on how to strike a balance in allocating time for academic work and her part-time employment. She explained, "Most teachers just say, 'What's more important, work or school?' and then they'll say you should be doing more for school," without addressing the problem in a more helpful fashion. Michelle believed that such a response was due to the school's vested interest in pupils achieving academic success. Now doubting the willingness of her teachers to dispense impartial advice, Michelle felt discouraged from pursuing the matter further in school.

Summary

Study informants did not gain information to meet their needs when they

- took no action
  - because they did not want to expend the effort required to make a search;
  - in the belief that materials that would meet the need were inaccessible to them;
  - possibly through a reluctance to admit their need;
  - as they feared a hostile reaction from others.
- made an unsuccessful effort to find material. In these circumstances, one or more of the following scenarios applied:
  - the source was inappropriate to the nature of the topic on which information was needed;
  - the source provided insufficiently specialist information, although some content was pertinent to the general area of need;
  - the information available from the source had not been prepared from the perspective required by the user;
  - the level of the material offered by the source was unsuitable to the youngster in terms of its reading level and/or conceptual complexity;
  - the source may have been able to provide appropriate information but was known to be seriously flawed and of dubious value;
  - adult intervention in the information-seeking process curtailed or inhibited a thorough search by the user;
  - after making inquiries, the youngster discovered that his or her preferred source was unavailable;
  - the inquirer's knowledge of the topic on which he or she was seeking information was inadequate to allow the generation of effective search terms;

- the youngster was unaware of alternative information-seeking options in the event of initial problems;
- the inquirer had a poor grasp of effective information-finding strategies, particularly in relation to electronic materials, or very limited awareness of bibliographic conventions and aids;
- a lack of skills on the youngster's part, especially with regard to keyboarding and reading, undermined his or her ability to find information when interacting with a certain source;
- the user canceled the search at an early stage either because he or she was unsure that the desired information actually existed or because the anxieties or frustrations that resulted from the information-seeking process were insurmountable. Youngsters were particularly disconcerted by the time and effort necessary to make a rigorous search and when they found themselves having to find appropriate material within the masses with which they were presented;
- unease and distrust prevented the inquirer from pursuing information from other people intensively when their initial reactions proved unfavorable.

DISCUSSION

Despite the scarcity of work specifically examining the phenomenon of information-seeking failure, many of the themes prevalent in the Whitley Bay study echo past observations by information professionals and the results of previous research, as well as providing practical evidence of long-established theoretical constructs. For example, Nicholas draws attention to "unexpressed" information needs[57] and, in the Whitley Bay research, these were especially apparent, with many needs going unmet because they were simply not acted upon by the participants. In terms of such needs emerging among young people, other studies have also found youngsters to be reluctant to seek information on certain matters, Latrobe and Havener indicating "relationship issues" in particular.[58] The Whitley Bay study revealed that, in certain instances, a distrust or dislike of other people prevented the participants from pursuing information wholeheartedly from them. The former mindset is reminiscent of the wariness of some of the teenage girls interviewed by Poston-

Anderson and Edwards, who believed that the school library offered only "socially sanctioned information."[59] Although one may argue that, in the Whitley Bay study, the teenager, Michelle, had been provided with wise advice by her school, for the girl herself her information need was far from met because she doubted the integrity of the information given. The work of Walter offers further evidence of the tensions that may exist between youngsters and adult information providers.[60] Specifically, the author explains how the tone taken by grown-ups can alienate young people, who may prove more likely to take note of information given by peers. In addition, instances were reported in the Whitley Bay study in which simply inaccurate information was given to the participants by their fathers. Although Walter also notes the danger of misinformation to young people, in her research it was peers and the media, rather than parents, who were the providers.[61]

Very young children, in particular, were seen to approach one person then another successively in pursuit of eventual success when asking family members for information, and Watson has identified a comparable "trial and error" in relation to eighth-grade users of the Internet.[62] In view of the youngest children's ineffectiveness when seeking information from other people and the immature assumptions that they held in terms of the kind of knowledge that they could expect from family members, it is perhaps pertinent to note that several of the previous studies that have found the use of other people for information to be an especially successful strategy for youngsters have drawn their samples from teenagers, rather than young children.[63]

The difficulty that one participant, in particular, experienced when using the Internet to search on a general topic and the relative ease with which he found the material that he desired on a more precise matter corroborates the findings of Wallace and Kupperman[64] but contrasts with the conclusions of a substantial body of work that would appear to indicate that finding highly specific information is often harder than when what is required is more diffuse.[65] Schacter et al. suggest that searching on ill-defined topics is easier as there is a greater number of potential answers. Large reiterates this argument and adds that information pertaining to the vaguer area may be found in many different ways and on many different pages. He also believes that it may be easier to locate information on the matter in question by browsing—a method typically favored by youngsters. Williams, however, pursues a contrasting line of reasoning, writing, "the vast majority of pages [on the Web] are not indexed by humans and, in many cases, documents may be lost through the practice of using generic terms or concepts [when searching] rather than the natural language of the text."[66] If one associates the employment of generic search terms with more open-ended topics, Williams's explanation may go some way to accounting for the difficulty the participant experienced.

Past research suggests that, after locating material whose subject falls within their area of interest, young information seekers may find it difficult to construct for themselves the type of wider, generic insight that three of the Whitley Bay youngsters sought. In relation to information seeking on the Web, Bilal concludes that her research participants tended to pursue "specific answers to the task, [rather] than developing understanding of the information found,"[67] and Taylor comes to the same conclusion with regard to children using print media.[68] Comparable findings have emerged in several earlier studies. In their review of existing work, Armbruster and Armstrong detect that youngsters have been seen to be most effective when extracting information from passages that provide factual detail and are significantly less successful when required to distill an overall message within the text.[69] Noting the tendency of young children to struggle in forming broad generalizations from what they have read, Kintsch attributes this shortcoming to youngsters processing "text in a linear, element-by-element fashion," with readers concentrating their efforts on individual sentences or sentence pairs.[70] A similar habit is noted by Bereiter and Scardamalia.[71] These observations would appear to indicate a lack of skills associated with skim reading.

Shenton and Dixon recognize a tendency in research for the information needs of youngsters to be understood in terms of criteria such as the subject of the information required and the purpose to which the material is to be put.[72] The authors urge deeper investigation into information needs to address a range of other situational variables. Among the Whitley Bay youngsters, the cognitive level of material and its readability proved especially important criteria. Gross suggests that it is the fact that youngsters encounter difficulties in finding resources appropriate to their abilities that, at school, leads teachers to prepackage materials specifically for them.[73] What is perhaps surprising is that, in contrast with the evidence presented in other studies,[74] the Whitley Bay youngsters reported few problems in the readability of material they had found on the Web. A possible explanation for this is that almost all the youngest users of the Internet, whose reading and cognitive abilities were of an especially limited level, were working with an adult or older sibling who either directed the child's attention to suitable sites or simplified the content appropriately for the youngster. Williams has also found evidence of involvement of this kind by grown-ups.[75]

Previous work has indicated the problems that can emerge when interventions by adults unwittingly thwart honest information-seeking action. During the year in which fieldwork was conducted, the lack of discrimination of Web filters and their tendency to deny access to sites that would help to satisfy genuine information needs on the part of young people were highlighted in a report in the consumer magazine, *Which?* This revealed that a study by American librarians had found such filters to deny access to sites needed to answer users' inquiries in 35 percent of instances. Several of the filters tested by the magazine itself were seen to block "straightforward safe-sex advice."[76] Some four years later, little appeared to have changed, as Chelton was still commenting on the frequency with which school librarians anecdotally reported that Internet filters impeded "legitimate school-based information seeking."[77] One of the youngest Whitley Bay participants was prevented from taking more than cursory information-seeking action by the fact that she was entirely at the mercy of the decisions made by her mother with regard to how long they should spend in their local public library. This incident illustrates Gross's observation that factors associated with a dependence on adults can inhibit successful information-seeking among the young.[78]

Two situations in which a seven- and eight-year-old respectively reported being unable to form appropriate search terms to represent subjects on which they required information are indicative of wider challenges for youngsters noted by researchers in the context of library environments. Sandlian writes of the problems in "choosing the right words to initiate a search,"[79] and Cooper comments that young children, especially, "may know specifically what they want, however, they do not yet know the word for it."[80] If Hirsh's discovery in relation to the use of computer catalogs that subject knowledge is a key factor in search success[81] has general applicability in other information-seeking situations, clearly any youngster who does not have the appropriate vocabulary to represent even their broad topic of interest is especially disadvantaged. More specifically, the experiences of the two Whitley Bay youngsters emphasize the wider truth of a key criticism of the Web made by one of Watson's informants, namely, "If you don't have . . . [the subject], you can't find it."[82]

The ignorance that many informants exhibited in terms of the characteristics of individual types of information sources and the situations when their use is appropriate reflects the concerns of Fieguth and Bußmann, who emphasize the problems encountered by youngsters in "deciding upon the relevant medium to search."[83] Furthermore, one of the most significant information-seeking puzzles to emerge for Whitley Bay informants—that of not knowing what to do when a particular course of action did not deliver the desired result—has been recognized to be a particularly common problem in a library context.[84]

The lack of use of effective tactics for exploiting electronic resources has, again, been clearly evident in past investigations. Little advance planning of searches, for example, has been highlighted elsewhere,[85] although youngsters scrutinized by Bowler, Large, and Rejskind tended to give greater preliminary thought to the strategies they employed in their later search sessions.[86] A range of researchers has detected either a marked absence of Boolean operators or inappropriate use of them.[87] In terms of efforts to vary search results, the difficulties for youngsters of developing an alternative term if the initial attempt fails to produce the desired result have again been noted.[88]

The alienation of users that results from conventions employed within libraries, and which in the Whitley Bay research frequently led to user failure, has been a recurrent theme in LIS literature for many years. Sandlian, for example, isolates a wide variety of demands that are made on young users in this setting as a result of particular bibliographical practices.[89] The misuse of the library catalog by two middle-schoolers offers testimony to the continuing mystery of the library catalog. Little appears to have changed in the twenty-five years since Flint wrote of the "mystique" that surrounded this tool.[90] Neuman, who has also found evidence of youngsters' employment of inappropriate approaches when undertaking particular searches, attributes the problem to a conceptual naïveté in relation to the resources with which they are interacting.[91] It is unsurprising that the two reported instances of "unguided wandering" both failed to yield the desired results, given the assertion of White and Coles that a "casual approach to libraries will usually fail."[92] When assembled as a totality, these insights support the argument of Chelton and Cool that learning "to become a library user is a socialization process, and those who do not become socialized into the proper ways of using the library are blocked from access to it."[93]

Wilson considers information searching behavior to be a particular kind of information-seeking behavior, one especially associated with interactions with actual sources.[94] Efforts at this level are also recognized by Armbruster and Armstrong, who describe the essential process as one of "locating information,"[95] and by Ellis, who terms it "extracting."[96] At this stage, failure for the Whitley Bay youngsters often resulted from inadequate reading or alphabetical ordering abilities. The lack of basic skills among young children is also identified in several studies, with limited reading ability highlighted as a particular barrier.[97] It may be a reflection of the scale of the problems faced by such youngsters that LaBounty found that the highest number of information queries to an e-mail reference desk came from children of elementary school age.[98] Among older Whitley Bay informants, shortcomings included an inability to determine the relevance of books that seemed from their titles to offer only general perspectives. Gross has also found evidence of this problem.[99] Shortcomings in this area imply poor use of finding aids such as contents lists and indexes within individual books, and deficiencies in the youngsters' higher order reading skills, especially scanning. These observations are indicative of a more general pattern that is prevalent across a range of information media and has been discussed in previous studies. For example, the fact that some of the participants in Chen's project examining the searching behavior of high-schoolers using an online catalog "apparently did not recognize . . . answers when they appeared in the middle of a long list" would again seem to imply an absence of the requisite scanning skills.[100]

One youngster was unsure whether the material she wanted to satisfy a leisure-oriented information need actually existed. This uncertainty never emerged in relation to needs pertaining to school assignments, and in these situations participants never seemed to have any doubts. Previous studies suggest that the youngsters were correct in this belief. Gross, for example, recognizes that the questions teachers ask in such assignments "tend to be based on 'known' knowledge."[101]

Young children and older informants alike in the Whitley Bay study experienced situations when they felt overwhelmed by the amount of material in front of them and struggled to discriminate between what they needed and what was irrelevant. Rudduck and Hopkins, too, note the problems teenagers experience when using books other than the set texts recommended by their teachers.[102] They describe, in particular, how pupils struggle to recognize the information that they require when the materials they are using are less intellectually and linguistically accessible than those they usually consult. Some become anxious when required to look beyond one textbook, which had hitherto appeared to provide all the necessary information. Furthermore, the fact that one Whitley Bay youngster, in particular, was reluctant to read large amounts of text on-screen has been mirrored in previous projects.[103]

Informants of various ages employed expedient methods to find information when working with books and electronic resources and, again, comparable patterns have been widely reported in existing research. Liesener, in the mid-1980s, detected a tendency for young-sters to accept "what can be found in more efficient but less effective ways."[104] Much more recently, Large has reached a similar conclusion in relation to young people's use of electronic resources. He states unequivocally that his experience leads him to believe that "students (not surprisingly) will take the road of least cognitive effort."[105] The ineffectiveness of the naïve, expedient methods employed by one of the youngest users of the Web, who entered "speculative" URLs, perhaps offers one reason for the wider pattern detected by Lazonder, Biemans, and Wopereis that more expert young Internet users were seen to be more proficient than novices in locating sites on the Web.[106] Even some of the individual approaches employed by the Whitley Bay youngsters have been reported elsewhere. The popularity, especially among boys, of the tendency of one informant to turn the pages of books in order to locate appropriate pictures that may provide entry points into suitable information is observed, for example, by the Children's Literature Research Centre in England.[107] Broadly, the expedient methods employed by the Whitley Bay informants are analogous to the "satis-ficing" strategies discussed by Agosto.[108] With regard to Web-based information seeking, the author suggests that these are employed to bring about outcomes that are sufficient to meet the individual's pur-poses without ensuring optimum results. For the participants in the Whitley Bay study, however, their approaches often resulted in the location of no relevant material, rather than the minimum required level.

Much of the novelty of this chapter and with it the contribution that it has made to existing theory has derived from the way in which broad reasons for information-seeking failure have been isolated and explored in a range of situations. The evidence presented in terms of a particular reason has often related to situations involving different information materials and responses to various types of need. Nevertheless, although in some instances significant differences have emerged and new issues revealed, the findings can also broadly be seen to support and add weight to many of the individual discoveries that have been reported in existing disparate papers with respect to information-seeking failure.

CONCLUSION

The prevalence of unmet information needs was highly apparent in the study, yet this did not come as a complete surprise to the researcher, as much past work has given a similar impression. Walter's study, for example, found that many information needs among California's ten-year-olds were not fulfilled.[109] With regard to information-seeking failure in more specific situations, Pitts discovered a general lack of success among many of her teenagers using libraries,[110] and Edmonds, Moore, and Balcom realized that their youngsters appeared to lack the skills necessary to use either a card or electronic catalog effectively.[111] Particularly low levels of success in Internet use have been reported by Bilal.[112]

Ostensibly, it may be tempting to assume that information-seeking failure must be due in large measure to shortcomings on the part of the youngsters themselves, but the results of the project indicate that this factor is by no means always the cause. Clearly, some youngsters made inappropriate choices of source. The efforts of others were undermined by an ignorance of the subject they were pursuing, of the information-seeking options open to them, of the approaches most likely to be effective when finding information, and of basic conventions applied in "bibliographic situations." The skills of users were frequently inadequate for the task and many youngsters seemed inclined to give up their searches at a relatively early stage. Certainly, the implications of these shortcomings should not be underestimated. As Pickard identifies, "successful use of [information resources] is directly linked to the individual's capacity to acquire and apply the skills demanded."[113] Still, there were also instances of what may be termed "source/user dislocation," where either adult intervention disrupted the youngster's efforts or the inquirer was simply unfortunate that the source that had been selected was unavailable at the point of need.

One of the most significant broad findings of the study lies in the importance of the psychological dimension of information seeking. While educators may well bemoan the lack of planning in advance of information-seeking action reported by virtually all the informants and the marked absence of the use of Boolean logic during interactions with electronic tools and resources, these seldom caused user failure in themselves. Rather, they were frequently indirect factors as they contributed to inefficient action, which led to users becoming impatient and frustrated in the face of initial results that did not meet their expectations. For inquirers with this negative mind-set, what may have been temporary setbacks became causes of ultimate failure as searches seemed to be aborted all too quickly. A frequent tendency among youngsters to stop their searches for information before the achievement of a satisfactory outcome has also been reported in other studies. Exploring the behavior of youngsters using the Web, Agosto, for example, lists a wide range of reasons for such termination—boredom, repetition in the material, "information snowballing," the setting of specific time limits for the activity, and physical discomfort resulting from prolonged computer use.[114] Rarely did the Whitley Bay inquirers appear to consider in detail the reasons for an information-seeking problem that they encountered, and hardly ever did they use knowledge that they had gained from such a situation to inform their future action. This is consistent with conclusions reached by Pickard in relation to boys' use of electronic materials.[115] The researcher notes how the male teenagers in her study tended simply to blame the resource with which they were interacting, rather than look for deficiencies in their own actions. It seemed difficult for Whitley Bay youngsters to learn from the experience and modify their behavior accordingly to meet the need of the moment. In general, individuals simply chose to adopt the next option which, through habit, they were used to pursuing in a comparable situation.

Beyond these broad overall patterns, considerable variations were evident in the success of older and younger informants when information was being sought on matters of personal interest. The former were markedly more effective. In particular, where their interests were of long standing, some informants had, over a period of years, developed habitual courses of action that continued to serve them well, and their skills in exploiting the appropriate sources with the expenditure of the minimum effort required had been carefully developed. In contrast, whether the informants were teenagers or younger children, where subject information was required for school, it was generally found eventually, although not always in the first source exploited. Older pupils, especially, were often required to draw on various materials to meet the need in its entirety. Such information scatter has been found by Durrance to be a significant challenge for adult information seekers too.[116]

The fact that some similar problems appear to emerge across adults, teenagers, and young children perhaps implies that certain issues associated with information seeking may be viewed as "universals" at least as far as the age of the individual is concerned. In an old but still oft-quoted paper, one of the "generalizations" made by Faibisoff and Ely, for example, with regard to the behavior of adult information users—namely that they "are often unaware of sources and how to use them"[117]—could equally suitably be applied to the youngsters in the Whitley Bay study and, in relation to Web-based behavior, Large asserts quite unequivocally, "Their elders . . . replicate many of the difficulties encountered by youthful information seekers."[118] It may, therefore, appear churlish to focus specifically on young people and to identify the causes of their information-seeking failure without due acknowledgment of these wider patterns. Nevertheless, given the fact that the teaching of information skills appears to have developed considerably over the last thirty years, the nature and prevalence of the reported information-seeking failures remain alarming. Perhaps the most obvious feature would seem to be the grave disparity between the problem solving approach so widely advocated and the action articulated by many informants when discussing their actual behavior in natural information-seeking situations.

Implications

In Terms of Information Resources and Materials

Sources were often criticized by study informants on the basis of their inability to satisfy a particular information need or on the grounds of being difficult to use, but rarely were materials simply dismissed as "bad sources." Notable exceptions, however, were the subject notes that the older pupils made, especially during lessons. Even the eldest participants, of seventeen and eighteen years of age, found the skill of note taking difficult to develop, and the work produced was frequently illegible, inaccurate, and superficial, and made little sense on later reading. The informants had very little confidence in these materials and some considered them totally untrustworthy. Either more attention must be given to the teaching of effective note-taking skills or alternative pedagogical methods should be investigated.

Although many of the criticisms made of the Web as an information resource resulted from limited knowledge of appropriate information-seeking approaches or poorly developed skills on the part of users in accessing its material effectively, some problems arose from shortcomings for which the youngsters could in no way be blamed. Insufficiently discriminating Web filters, in particular, were seen on several occasions to block access to "innocent" material on a range of subjects needed for academic work. Clearly, much still has to be done to increase the sophistication and effectiveness of these tools.

In Terms of the Teaching of Information Skills

The findings of the project highlight the importance that should be attached to the following areas within programs for teaching information skills, using language and concepts appropriate to the developmental stages of the individuals involved:

- Draw attention to the options available to inquirers with regard to where, broadly, they may look for information.
- Promote within youngsters an understanding of the characteristics of these individual sources, resources, and materials in relation to the content that each can be expected to offer and what sorts of needs they may be expected to help meet.

- Raise awareness of the kinds of information that may be impossible—or at least are very difficult—to find.
- Inculcate a variety of skills that are required to exploit the information materials discussed. The overall teaching program may embrace, for example, generic areas like keyboarding and higher-order reading skills, especially skimming and scanning, as well as approaches for effective information-seeking action. The latter, such as the use of Boolean logic, may be more specific to informatics. It must be acknowledged, however, that higher-order reading skills are notoriously difficult to teach to some youngsters. Watson draws particular attention to how novices attempting to skim read "lack the confidence to free themselves from word-by-word and line-by-line decoding."[119] Large sounds a further note of caution, suggesting that, when reading material on the Web, skimming "can degenerate into such rapid movement that key information can easily be missed."[120] Where skills are particular to a certain source or an environment like a library collection, a background awareness of "bibliographic conventions" needs to be developed in learners prior to the teaching of the skills themselves. In these circumstances, connections should be made between the potentially intimidating public library and its more familiar school counterpart in order to convey how the underlying principles relating to the arrangement of information materials are similar.
- Encourage information seekers to construct flexible, holistic plans that outline, at the outset of an information search, the avenues of action that might be taken and how the precision of a search may be varied in accordance with the initial results obtained.

The ultimate aim must be to ensure that, time and time again, after making informed decisions on the sources, resources, or materials that should be used in their particular circumstances, youngsters are able to connect swiftly and effectively with what they require in order to meet their information need.

The areas listed above should be understood by the educator not as a series of disparate elements but principles that work in concert within an integrated whole, and the manner in which each affects other aspects of the information-seeking process should be recognized from the outset. The effective teaching of information skills, for example, not only renders the exploitation of a particular source more successful but also helps to widen the range of information-seeking options that inquirers believe to be available to them.

A key priority for information skills teaching lies in developing a more collaborative atmosphere with learners and shifting emphasis away from purely didactic instruction. All too often the focus of programs lies in imposing a recommended course of information-seeking action on learners. Opportunity must be given to engage interactively with pupils and for them to share ownership of the exchanges. Educators should be prepared to discuss with youngsters their ill-advised, expedient information-seeking actions and acknowledge, rather than at once dismiss, the arguments of their advocates. If, however, pupils can be shown how the methods that their teachers propose are more likely to deliver the desired results, the techniques are more likely to be adopted. Youngsters must also be encouraged to accept that problems form a natural part of the information-seeking process and are merely temporary setbacks. In contrast, Pickard, who has also found that young people quickly become discouraged when information resources do not perform as expected, draws attention to how, in the "real world," the hype surrounding electronic materials actually *emphasizes* feelings of failure within young people when they come to use them, as they have developed unrealistic expectations of what such resources can deliver.[121] The challenge for inquirers lies in using any unfavorable initial outcomes to inform corrective, future action.

NOTES

1. Rick Rogers, ed., *Teaching Information Skills: A Review of the Research and Its Impact on Education* (London: Bowker-Saur, 1994), 1.

2. Sylvia Stagg and Sarah Brew, "Finding the Book You Want: An Algorithm," *School Librarian* 25, no. 3 (1977): 221–22.

3. John Lindsay, "Information Training in Secondary Schools," *Education Libraries Journal* 19, no. 3 (1976): 16–21.

4. Chas White and Michael Coles, "Libraries and Laboratories," *School Librarian* 28, no. 3 (1980): 237–42.

5. Linda Hamilton, "Suggestions for Secondary School Library Lessons," *School Librarian* 25, no. 3 (1977): 217–20.

6. Michael B. Eisenberg and Michael K. Brown, "Current Themes Regarding

Library and Information Skills Instruction: Research Supporting and Research Lacking," *School Library Media Quarterly* 20, no. 2 (1992): 103–9; Carol C. Kuhlthau, "An Emerging Theory of Library Instruction," *School Library Media Quarterly* 16, no. 1 (1987): 23–28; Jacqueline C. Mancall, Shirley L. Aaron, and Sue A. Walker, "Educating Students to Think: The Role of the School Library Media Program," *School Library Media Quarterly* 15, no. 1 (1986): 18–27.

7. Michael Marland, ed., *Information Skills in the Secondary Curriculum* (London: Methuen Educational, 1981); M. H. Coles, C. A. Shepherd, and C. White, "The Science of Library and Book Skills," *School Librarian* 30, no. 3 (1982): 200–207.

8. Michael B. Eisenberg and Robert E. Berkowitz, *Information Problem-Solving: The Big Six Skills Approach to Library and Information Skills Instruction* (Norwood, NJ: Ablex, 1990); James E. Herring, *Teaching Information Skills in Schools* (London: Library Association, 1996); Carol C. Kuhlthau, *Teaching the Library Research Process*, 2nd ed. (Lanham, MD: Scarecrow Press, 1994); Barbara K. Stripling and Judy M. Pitts, *Brainstorms and Blueprints: Teaching Library Research as a Thinking Process* (Englewood, CO: Libraries Unlimited, 1988); David Wray and Maureen Lewis, "Extending Interactions with Non-Fiction Texts: An EXIT into Understanding," *Reading* 29, no. 1 (1995): 2–9.

9. Mary K. Chelton and Colleen Cool, "Introduction," in *Youth Information-Seeking Behavior: Theories, Models, and Issues*, ed. Mary K. Chelton and Colleen Cool, viii (Lanham, MD: Scarecrow Press, 2004).

10. James W. Liesener, "Learning at Risk: School Library Media Programs in an Information World," *School Library Media Quarterly* 14, no. 1 (1985): 11–20; Betty P. Cleaver, "Thinking About Information: Skills for Lifelong Learning," *School Library Media Quarterly* 16, no. 1 (1987): 29–31.

11. Christine Bruce, *Seven Faces of Information Literacy in Higher Education* (1997), http://sky.fit.qut.edu.au/~bruce/inflit/faces/faces1.php (accessed September 12, 2005).

12. Jana Varlejs, "Information Seeking: Changing Perspectives," in *Information Seeking: Basing Services on Users' Behaviors*, ed. Jana Varlejs, 67–82 (Jefferson, NC: McFarland, 1987).

13. Chelton and Cool, "Introduction," in *Youth Information-Seeking Behavior*, ix.

14. Louise Limberg, "Experiencing Information Seeking and Learning: A Study of the Interaction Between Two Phenomena," *Information Research* 5, no. 1 (1999), http://informationr.net/ir/5-1/paper68.html (accessed September 12, 2005); Joy H. McGregor, "Cognitive Processes and the Use of Information: A Qualitative Study of Higher Order Thinking Skills Used in the Research Process by Students in a Gifted Program" (PhD dissertation, Florida State University, 1993); Judy M. Pitts, "Personal Understandings and Mental Models of Information: A Qualitative Study of Factors Associated with the Information-Seeking and Use of Adolescents" (PhD dissertation, Florida State University, 1994).

15. L. J. Amey, "Neglected Enthusiasts: Adolescent Information Seekers," in *Meeting the Challenge: Library Service to Young Adults*, ed. Andre Gagnon and Ann Gagnon, 43–54 (Ottawa: Canadian Library Association, 1985); Kathy Latrobe and W. Michael Havener, "The Information-Seeking Behavior of High School Honors Students: An Exploratory Study," *Journal of Youth Services in Libraries* 10, no. 2 (1997): 188–200; Barbara Poston-Anderson and Susan Edwards, "The Role of Information in Helping Adolescent Girls with Their Life Concerns," *School Library Media Quarterly* 22, no. 1 (1993): 25–30.

16. Colleen Cool, "Information-Seeking Behaviors of Children Using Electronic Information Services During the Early Years: 1980–1990," in *Youth Information-Seeking Behavior: Theories, Models, and Issues*, ed. Mary K. Chelton and Colleen Cool, 31 (Lanham, MD: Scarecrow Press, 2004).

17. Andrew K. Shenton and Pat Dixon, "Issues Arising from Youngsters' Information-Seeking Behavior," *Library and Information Science Research* 26, no. 2 (2004): 177–200.

18. Virginia A. Walter, "Public Library Service to Children and Teens: A Research Agenda," *Library Trends* 51, no. 4 (2003): 576.

19. Linda Cooper, "Problems Associated with the Ability of Elementary School Children to Successfully Retrieve Material in the School Library Media Center and Some Alternative Methods of Classification Which May Help to Alleviate These Problems: A Case Study of the Common School Library, Amherst, Massachusetts," *Public & Access Services Quarterly* 2, no. 1 (1996): 47–63.

20. Lynn Akin, "Information Overload and Children: A Survey of Texas Elementary School Students," *School Library Media Research*, 1 (1998), http://www.ala.org/ala/aasl/aaslpubsandjournals/slmrb/slmrcontents/volume11998slmqo/akin.htm (accessed September 12, 2005).

21. L. Amey, "Thespians, Troubadours, Hams and Bad Actors," *Emergency Librarian* 13, no. 5 (1986): 9.

22. Eeva-Liisa Eskola, "University Students' Information Seeking Behaviour in a Changing Learning Environment—How Are Students' Information Needs, Seeking and Use Affected by New Teaching Methods?" *Information Research* 4, no. 2 (1998), http://informationr.net/ir/4-2/isic/eeskola.html (accessed September 12, 2005).

23. Pertti Vakkari, "Information Seeking in Context: A Challenging Metatheory," in *Information Seeking in Context*, ed. Pertti Vakkari, Reijo Savolainen, and Brenda Dervin, 457 (London: Taylor Graham, 1997).

24. Brenda Dervin, "Given a Context by Any Other Name: Methodological Tools for Taming the Unruly Beast," in *Information Seeking in Context*, ed. Pertti Vakkari, Reijo Savolainen, and Brenda Dervin, 13–38 (London: Taylor Graham, 1997).

25. Chun Wei Choo, "Closing the Cognitive Gaps: How People Process Information," in *Financial Times: Mastering Information Management*, ed. Donald A. Marchand, Thomas H. Davenport, and Tim Dickson, 245–53 (London: Financial

Times/Prentice Hall, 2000); Jacqueline A. Fourie, "Pupils as Curricular Information Seekers and the Role of the Public Library," *South African Journal of Library and Information Science* 63, no. 3 (1995): 129–38; Carol C. Kuhlthau, "Developing a Model of the Library Search Process: Cognitive and Affective Aspects," *RQ* 28, no. 2 (1988): 232-42; Gary Marchionini, "Information-Seeking Strategies of Novices Using a Full-Text Electronic Encyclopedia," *Journal of the American Society for Information Science* 40, no. 1 (1989): 54–66; Pitts, "Personal Understandings and Mental Models of Information"; Walter, "Public Library Service to Children and Teens"; Lynn Westbrook, "User Needs: A Synthesis and Analysis of Current Theories for the Practitioner," *RQ* 32, no. 4 (1993): 541–49; T. D. Wilson, "Models in Information Behaviour Research," *Journal of Documentation* 55, no. 3 (1999): 249–70.

26. Andrew K. Shenton, "Research into Young People's Information-Seeking: Perspectives and Methods," *Aslib Proceedings* 56, no. 4 (2004): 244.

27. Ching-chih Chen and Peter Hernon, *Information Seeking: Assessing and Anticipating User Needs* (New York: Neal-Schuman, 1982); Poston-Anderson and Edwards, "The Role of Information in Helping Adolescent Girls with Their Life Concerns."

28. Maurice B. Line, "Draft Definitions: Information and Library Needs, Wants, Demands and Uses," *Aslib Proceedings* 26, no. 2 (1974): 87.

29. Jarkko Kari, "Making Sense of Sense-Making: From Metatheory to Substantive Theory in the Context of Paranormal Information Seeking" (paper presented at the Nordis-Net workshop—(Meta)theoretical Stands in Studying Library and Information Institutions: Individual, Organizational and Societal Aspects, Oslo, 1998), http://www.paranet.fi/paradocs/tutkimuksia/kari1998a.pdf (September 12, 2005); James Krikelas, "Information-Seeking Behavior: Patterns and Concepts," *Drexel Library Quarterly* 19, no. 2 (1983): 5–20; Pitts, "Personal Understandings and Mental Models of Information."

30. Sanda Erdelez, "Information Encountering: It's More Than Just Bumping into Information," *Bulletin of the American Society for Information Science* 25, no. 3 (1999): 25–29.

31. Latrobe and Havener, "The Information-Seeking Behavior of High School Honors Students."

32. Diane H. Sonnenwald, "Evolving Perspectives of Human Information Behaviour: Contexts, Situations, Social Networks and Information Horizons," in *Information Seeking in Context*, ed. Pertti Vakkari, Reijo Savolainen, and Brenda Dervin, 176–89 (London: Taylor Graham, 1997).

33. Elfreda A. Chatman, "The Impoverished Life-World of Outsiders," *Journal of the American Society for Information Science* 47, no. 3 (1996): 195; E. Murell Dawson and Elfreda A. Chatman, "Reference Group Theory with Implications for Information Studies: A Theoretical Essay," *Information Research* 6, no. 3 (2001), http://informationr.net/ir/6-3/paper105.html (accessed September 12, 2005); Paul Solomon, "Discovering Information Behavior in Sense Making—1: Time and Tim-

ing," *Journal of the American Society for Information Science* 48, no. 12 (1997): 1099.

34. Amey, "Neglected Enthusiasts," 52.

35. T. D. Wilson, "On User Studies and Information Needs," *Journal of Documentation* 37, no. 1 (1981): 6.

36. Michael Q. Patton, *Qualitative Evaluation and Research Methods*, 2nd ed. (Newbury Park, CA: Sage, 1990), 193.

37. Robert Grover and Susan G. Fowler, "Recent Trends in School Library Media Research," *School Library Media Quarterly* 21, no. 4 (1993): 241–47; Dervin, "Given a Context by Any Other Name."

38. Vakkari, "Information Seeking in Context."

39. Carol C. Kuhlthau, "Information Search Process: A Summary of Research and Implications for School Library Media Programs," *School Library Media Quarterly* 18, no. 1 (1989): 19–25; and "Inside the Search Process: Information Seeking from the User's Perspective," *Journal of the American Society for Information Science* 42, no. 5 (1991): 361–71; Linda de Lyon Friel, "The Information Research Process with Low-Achieving Freshmen Using Kuhlthau's Six-Stage Model and the Interventions that Facilitate the Process" (PhD dissertation, University of Massachusetts Lowell, 1995); Tracey A. Burdick, "Success and Diversity in Information Seeking: Gender and the Information Search Styles Model," *School Library Media Quarterly* 25, no. 1 (1996): 19–26.

40. David A. Erlandson, Edward L. Harris, Barbara L. Skipper, and Steve D. Allen, *Doing Naturalistic Inquiry: A Guide to Methods* (Newbury Park, CA: Sage, 1993); Richard A. Krueger, *Focus Groups: A Practical Guide for Applied Research*, 2nd ed. (Thousand Oaks, CA: Sage, 1994); Matthew B. Miles and A. Michael Huberman, *Qualitative Data Analysis: An Expanded Sourcebook*, 2nd ed. (Thousand Oaks, CA: Sage, 1994).

41. Sharan B. Merriam, *Qualitative Research and Case Study Applications in Education* (San Francisco: Jossey-Bass, 1998), 8.

42. David Silverman, *Doing Qualitative Research: A Practical Handbook* (London: Sage, 2000), xiii.

43. Yvonna S. Lincoln and Egon G. Guba, *Naturalistic Inquiry* (Newbury Park, CA: Sage, 1985), 251.

44. Gretchen B. Rossman and Bruce L. Wilson, "Numbers and Words: Combining Quantitative and Qualitative Methods in a Single Large-Scale Evaluation Study," *Evaluation Review* 9, no. 5 (1985), 629.

45. National Statistics Online, *Census 2001: Neighbourhood Statistics*, http://neighbourhood.statistics.gov.uk/dissemination/ (accessed September 12, 2005).

46. Brenda Dervin, Douglas Zweizig, Michael Banister, Michael Gabriel, Edward P. Hall, and Colleen Kwan, *The Development of Strategies for Dealing with the Information Needs of Urban Residents, Phase One: The Citizen Study* (Seattle: School of Communications, University of Washington, 1976).

47. Department for Education, *The National Curriculum* (London: HMSO, 1995).

48. Barney G. Glaser, and Anselm L. Strauss, *The Discovery of Grounded Theory: Strategies for Qualitative Research* (Chicago: Aldine de Gruyter, 1967).

49. Merriam, *Qualitative Research and Case Study Applications in Education*, 38.

50. Andrew K. Shenton, "'What If Your Informants Lie?' Countering the Possibility of Dishonesty in Self-Reported Data," *Information Research Watch International* (February 2004): 2–3.

51. Cool, "Information-Seeking Behaviors of Children Using Electronic Information Services During the Early Years," 30.

52. Melanie Mauthner, "Methodological Aspects of Collecting Data from Children," *Children and Society* 11, no. 1 (1997): 16–28.

53. Linda Z. Cooper, "Children's Information Choices for Inclusion in a Hypothetical, Child-Constructed Library," in *Youth Information-Seeking Behavior: Theories, Models, and Issues*, ed. Mary K. Chelton and Colleen Cool, 181–210 (Lanham, MD: Scarecrow Press, 2004).

54. Shu-Hsien Chen, "A Study of High School Students' Online Catalog Searching Behavior," *School Library Media Quarterly* 22, no. 1 (1993): 33–39.

55. Cool, "Information-Seeking Behaviors of Children Using Electronic Information Services During the Early Years"; Sandra G. Hirsh, "Domain Knowledge and Children's Search Behavior," in *Youth Information-Seeking Behavior: Theories, Models, and Issues*, ed. Mary K. Chelton and Colleen Cool, 241–70 (Lanham, MD: Scarecrow Press, 2004); Paul Solomon, "Children's Information Retrieval Behavior: A Case Analysis of an OPAC," *Journal of the American Society for Information Science* 44, no. 5 (1993): 245–64; Virgina A. Walter, Christine L. Borgman, and Sandra G. Hirsh, "The Science Library Catalog: A Springboard to Information Literacy," *School Library Media Quarterly* 24, no. 2 (1996): 105–10.

56. Raya Fidel, Rachel K. Davies, Mary H. Douglass, Jenny K. Holder, Carla J. Hopkins, Elisabeth J. Kushner, Bryan K. Miyagishima, and Christina D. Toney, "A Visit to the Information Mall: Web Searching Behavior of High School Students," *Journal of the American Society for Information Science* 50, no. 1 (1999): 24–37; Yasmin Kafai and Marcia J. Bates, "Internet Web-Searching Instruction in the Elementary Classroom: Building a Foundation for Information Literacy," *School Library Media Quarterly* 25, no. 2 (1997): 103–11.

57. David Nicholas, *Assessing Information Needs: Tools, Techniques and Concepts for the Internet Age*, 2nd ed. (London: Aslib, 2000), 23.

58. Latrobe and Havener, "The Information-Seeking Behavior of High School Honors Students," 194; Virginia A. Walter, "The Information Needs of Children," *Advances in Librarianship* 18 (1994): 111–29.

59. Poston-Anderson and Edwards, "The Role of Information in Helping Adolescent Girls with Their Life Concerns," 28.

60. Walter, "The Information Needs of Children."

61. Walter, "The Information Needs of Children."

62. Jinx S. Watson, "'If You Don't Have It, You Can't Find It': A Close Look at Students' Perceptions of Using Technology," *Journal of the American Society for Information Science* 49, no. 11 (1998): 1024–36.

63. Larry Amey, "The Special Case for YA Programming," *Emergency Librarian* 12, no. 3 (1985): 25–26; Latrobe and Havener, "The Information-Seeking Behavior of High School Honors Students"; Pitts, "Personal Understandings and Mental Models of Information"; Poston-Anderson and Edwards, "The Role of Information in Helping Adolescent Girls with Their Life Concerns."

64. Raven Wallace and Jeff Kupperman, "On-line Search in the Science Classroom: Benefits and Possibilities" (paper presented at the annual meeting of the American Educational Research Association, Chicago, 1997).

65. Linda Dobson, "Navigating the Sea of Information: A Qualitative Study of Public Library Information Provision for Children in County Durham" (master's dissertation, University of Northumbria at Newcastle, 2000); Fidel et al., "A Visit to the Information Mall"; Andrew Large, "Information Seeking on the Web by Elementary School Students," in *Youth Information-Seeking Behavior: Theories, Models, and Issues*, ed. Mary K. Chelton and Colleen Cool, 293–319 (Lanham, MD: Scarecrow Press, 2004); John Schacter, Gregory K. W. K. Chung, and Aimée Dorr, "Children's Internet Searching on Complex Problems: Performance and Process Analyses," *Journal of the American Society for Information Science* 49, no. 9 (1998): 840–49.

66. Peter Williams, "The Net Generation: The Experiences, Attitudes and Behaviour of Children Using the Internet for Their Own Purposes," *Aslib Proceedings* 51, no. 9 (1999), 319.

67. Dania Bilal, "Research on Children's Information Seeking on the Web," in *Youth Information-Seeking Behavior: Theories, Models, and Issues*, ed. Mary K. Chelton and Colleen Cool, 277 (Lanham, MD: Scarecrow Press, 2004).

68. Nansi Taylor, "Find the Lady . . . Once and Future Skills," *School Librarian* 43, no. 1 (1995): 11–13.

69. Bonnie B. Armbruster and James O. Armstrong, "Locating Information in Text: A Focus on Children in the Elementary Grades." *Contemporary Educational Psychology* 18, no. 2 (1993): 139–61.

70. Eileen Kintsch, "Macroprocesses and Microprocesses in the Development of Summarization Skill," *Cognition and Instruction* 7, no. 3 (1990), 162.

71. Carl Bereiter and Marlene Scardamalia, "Intentional Learning as a Goal of Instruction," in *Knowing, Learning, and Instruction: Essays in Honor of Robert Glaser*, ed. Lauren B. Resnick, 361–92 (Hillsdale, NJ: Lawrence Erlbaum Associates, 1989).

72. Andrew K. Shenton and Pat Dixon, "Information Needs: Learning More About What Kids Want, Need, and Expect from Research," *Children and Libraries* 3, no. 2 (2005): 20–28.

73. Melissa Gross, "Children's Information Seeking at School: Findings from a

Qualitative Study," in *Youth Information-Seeking Behavior: Theories, Models, and Issues*, ed. Mary K. Chelton and Colleen Cool, 211–40 (Lanham, MD: Scarecrow Press, 2004).

74. Dobson, "Navigating the Sea of Information"; Kafai and Bates, "Internet Web-Searching Instruction in the Elementary Classroom"; National Council for Educational Technology, *Libraries of the Future: A Pilot Study of the Impact of Multimedia and Communications Technologies on Libraries in Education—Final Report* (Coventry, England: National Council for Educational Technology, 1996).

75. Williams, "The Net Generation."

76. Anon, "Through the Net," *Which?* (May 2000), 38.

77. Mary K. Chelton, "Future Direction and Bibliography," in *Youth Information-Seeking Behavior: Theories, Models, and Issues*, ed. Mary K. Chelton and Colleen Cool, 389 (Lanham, MD: Scarecrow Press, 2004).

78. Gross, "Children's Information Seeking at School."

79. Pam Sandlian, "Rethinking the Rules," *School Library Journal* 41, no. 7 (1995): 22.

80. Cooper, "Problems Associated with the Ability of Elementary School Children to Successfully Retrieve Material in the School Library Media Center and Some Alternative Methods of Classification Which May Help to Alleviate These Problems," 49.

81. Sandra G. Hirsh, "How Do Children Find Information on Different Types of Tasks? Children's Use of the Science Library Catalog," *Library Trends* 45, no. 4 (1997): 725–45.

82. Watson, "'If You Don't Have It, You Can't Find It,'" 1026.

83. Gert Fieguth and Ingrid Bußmann, *Children in Libraries: Improving Multimedia Virtual Access and Information Skills—Annual Report No. 1* (1997), http://chilias.isegi.unl.pt/chilias_int/anrep/anrep.htm (accessed October 5, 2000).

84. Penny Moore, "Children's Information Seeking: Judging Books by their Covers," *School Library Review* 8 (June 1988): 5; Penelope A. Moore and Alison St. George, "Children as Information Seekers: The Cognitive Demands of Books and Library Systems," *School Library Media Quarterly* 19, no. 3 (1991): 161–68.

85. Schacter, Chung, and Dorr, "Children's Internet Searching on Complex Problems"; Raven M. Wallace, Jeff Kupperman, and Joseph Krajcik, "Science on the Web: Students On-line in a Sixth-Grade Classroom," *Journal of the Learning Sciences* 9, no. 1 (2000): 75–104.

86. Leanne Bowler, Andrew Large, and Gill Rejskind, "Primary School Students, Information Literacy and the Web," *Education for Information* 19, no. 3 (2001): 201–23.

87. Bilal, "Research on Children's Information Seeking on the Web"; Bilal, Dania, "Children's Search Processes in using World Wide Web Search Engines: An Exploratory Study," *Proceedings of the 60th Annual Meeting of the American Society for Information Science* 35 (1998): 45–53; Sandra G. Hirsh, "Children's Relevance Criteria and Information Seeking on Electronic Resources," *Journal of*

the *American Society for Information Science* 50, no. 14 (1999): 1265–83; David J. Lyons, Joseph L. Hoffman, Joseph S. Krajcik, and Elliot Soloway, "An Investigation of the Use of the World Wide Web for On-Line Inquiry in a Science Classroom" (paper presented at the annual meeting of the National Association for Research in Science Teaching, Oak Brook, 1997); Diane Nahl and Violet H. Harada, "Composing Boolean Search Statements: Self-Confidence, Concept Analysis, Search Logic and Errors," *School Library Media Quarterly* 24, no. 4 (1996): 199–207; Schacter, Chung, and Dorr, "Children's Internet Searching on Complex Problems"; Wallace and Jeff Kupperman, *On-Line Search in the Science Classroom.*

88. Penny Moore, "Information Problem Solving: A Wider View of Library Skills," *Contemporary Educational Psychology* 20, no. 1 (1995): 1–31; Delia Neuman, "Learning and the Digital Library," *Library Trends* 45, no. 4 (1997): 687–707.

89. Sandlian, "Rethinking the Rules."

90. Cathy Flint, "Tomorrow's Children: Children in a Changing Society and their Changing Library Needs," in *Alternative Futures: Proceedings of the 20th Biennial Conference, Library Association of Australia, Canberra, 26–30 August, 1979,* ed. Judith Baskin, 72 (Sydney: Library Association of Australia, 1979).

91. Neuman, "Learning and the Digital Library."

92. White and Coles, "Libraries and Laboratories," 237.

93. Chelton and Cool, "Introduction," in *Youth Information Seeking Behavior,* xi.

94. Wilson, "Models in Information Behaviour Research."

95. Armbruster and Armstrong, *Locating Information in Text,* 2.

96. David Ellis, "A Behavioural Approach to Information Retrieval System Design," *Journal of Documentation* 45, no. 3 (1989): 176.

97. Children's Literature Research Centre, *Young People's Reading at the End of the Century* (London: Roehampton Institute, 1996); Cool, "Information-Seeking Behaviors of Children Using Electronic Information Services During the Early Years"; Gross, "Children's Information Seeking at School"; Melissa R. Gross, "Imposed Queries in the School Library Media Center: A Descriptive Study" (PhD dissertation, University of California, 1998).

98. Verna LaBounty, "Reference Desk on the Internet," *Book Report* 16, no. 2 (1997): 19.

99. Gross, "Children's Information Seeking at School."

100. Chen, "A Study of High School Students' Online Catalog Searching Behavior," 36.

101. Gross, "Children's Information Seeking at School," 217.

102. Jean Rudduck and David Hopkins, *The Sixth Form and Libraries: Problems of Access to Knowledge* (London: British Library, 1984).

103. Bilal, "Research on Children's Information Seeking on the Web"; Lesa Perzylo and Ron Oliver, "An Investigation of Children's Use of CD-ROM Multimedia Technology for Information Retrieval: Comparing Two Case Studies," *Australian*

Library Review 11, no. 2 (1994): 145–56; Wallace and Kupperman, *On-line Search in the Science Classroom.*

104. Liesener, "Learning at Risk," 20.

105. Large, "Information Seeking on the Web by Elementary School Students," 304.

106. Ard W. Lazonder, Harm J. A. Biemans, and Iwan G. J. H. Wopereis, "Differences Between Novice and Experienced Users in Searching for Information on the World Wide Web," *Journal of the American Society for Information Science* 51, no. 6 (2000): 576–81.

107. Children's Literature Research Centre, *Young People's Reading at the End of the Century.*

108. Denise E. Agosto, "Bounded Rationality and Satisficing in Young People's Web-Based Decision Making," *Journal of the American Society for Information Science and Technology* 53, no. 1 (2002): 16–27.

109. Walter, "The Information Needs of Children."

110. Pitts, "Personal Understandings and Mental Models of Information."

111. Leslie Edmonds, Paula Moore, and Kathleen M. Balcom, "The Effectiveness of an Online Catalog," *School Library Journal* 36, no. 10 (1990): 28–32.

112. Bilal, "Children's Search Processes in Using World Wide Web Search Engines."

113. Alison Pickard, "Young People and the Internet," *Library and Information Update* 3, no. 1 (2004): 32.

114. Agosto, "Bounded Rationality and Satisficing in Young People's Web-Based Decision Making," 24.

115. Pickard, "Young People and the Internet."

116. Joan C. Durrance, *Armed for Action: Library Response to Citizen Information Needs* (New York: Neal-Schuman, 1984).

117. Sylvia G. Faibisoff and Donald P. Ely, "Information and Information Needs," *Information Reports and Bibliographies* 5, no. 5 (1976): 9.

118. Large, "Information Seeking on the Web by Elementary School Students," 313.

119. Watson, "'If You Don't Have It, You Can't Find It,'" 1032.

120. Large, "Information Seeking on the Web by Elementary School Students," 303.

121. Pickard, "Young People and the Internet."

Bibliography

This list updates the one in the 2004 book.

Agosto, Denise. 2004. Design vs. content: A study of adolescent girls' website design preferences. *International Journal of Technology & Design Education* 14(3): 245–60.

Agosto, Denise E., and Sandra Hughes-Hassell. 2005. People, places, and questions: An investigation of the everyday life information-seeking behaviors of urban young adults. *Library and Information Science Research* 27(2): 141–63.

Alexander, Jonathan. 2006. *Digital youth: Emerging literacies on the World Wide Web.* Cresskill, NJ: Hampton Press.

Boekhorst, A. K., and J. J. Britz. 2004. Information literacy at school level: A comparative study between the Netherlands and South Africa. *South African Journal of Library & Information Science* 70(2): 63–71.

Branch, Jennifer L. 2001. Junior high students and think alouds: Generating information-seeking process data using concurrent verbal protocols. *Library and Information Science Research* 23(2): 107–22.

———. 2003. Instructional intervention is the key: Supporting adolescent information seeking. *School Libraries Worldwide* 9(2): 47–61.

Cooper, Linda Z. 2004. The socialization of information behavior: A case study of cognitive categories for library information. *Library Quarterly* 74(3): 299–336.

DiPerna, Paul. 2006. K–12 encounters the Internet. *First Monday* 11(5). http://firstmonday.org/issues/issue11_5/diperna/index.html (accessed May 6, 2006).

Drum, Allison. 2005. What children can teach us: Developing digital libraries for children with children. *Library Quarterly* 75(1): 20–41.

Eamon, Mary Keegan. 2004. Digital divide in computer access and use between poor and non-poor youth. *Journal of Sociology & Social Welfare* 31(2): 91–112.

Ebersole, Samuel E. 2005. On their own: Students' academic use of the commercialized Web. *Library Trends* 53(4): 530–38.

Fitzgerald, Hiram E. 2005. How low-income children use the Internet at home. *Journal of Interactive Learning Research* 16(3). http://www.editlib.org/index .cfm?fuseaction = Reader.ViewAbstract&paper_id = 5876 (accessed May 14, 2006).

Griffiths, Jillian R. 2005. Student searching behavior and the Web: Use of academic resources and Google. *Library Trends* 53(4): 539–54.

Gross, Melissa. 2005. The impact of low-level skills on information-seeking behavior: Implications of competency theory for research and practice. *Reference and User Services Quarterly* 45(2): 155–63.

———. 2006. *Studying children's questions: Information seeking behavior in school.* Lanham, MD: Scarecrow Press.

Gross, Melissa, Eliza T. Dresang, and Leslie E. Holt. 2004. Children's in-library use of computers in an urban public library. *Library & Information Science Research* 26(3): 311–37.

Halttunen, Kai. 2003. Students' conceptions of information retrieval: Implications for the design of learning environments. *Library & Information Science Research* 25(3): 307–32.

Hamer, Judah S. Coming out: Gay males' information seeking. *School Libraries Worldwide* 9(2): 73–89.

Hansen, Derek L., Holly A Derry, Paul J.Resnick, and Caroline R. Richardson. 2003. Adolescents searching for health information on the Internet: An observational study. *Journal of Medical Internet Research* 5(4). http://www.jmir.org/ 2003/4/ (accessed April 23, 2006).

Harris, Frances Jacobsen. 2005. *I found it on the Internet: Coming of age online.* Chicago: American Library Association.

Heinstrom, Jannica. 2005. Fast surfing, broad scanning, and deep diving: The influence of personalilty and study approach on students' information-seeking behavior. *Journal of Documentation* 61(2): 228–47.

Huffaker, David. 2004. Spinning yarns around the digital fire: Storytelling and dialogue among youth on the Internet. *Information Technology in Childhood Education Annual* 2004(1). http://www.aace.org/dl/index.cfm/fuseaction/currentjournal/ journal/ITCE (accessed May 14, 2006).

Hultgren, Frances, and Louise Limberg. 2003. A study of research on children's information behaviour in a school context. *New Review of Information Behaviour Research* 4(1): 1–15.

Hung, Tsai-Youn. 2004. Undergraduate students' evaluation criteria when using Web resources for class papers. *Journal of Educational Media & Library Sciences* 42(1): 1–12.

Hyldegård, Jette. 2006. Collaborative information behaviour—Exploring Kuhlthau's information search process model in a group-based educational setting. *Information Processing & Management* 42(1): 276–98.

Large, Andrew, Valerie Nesset, Jamshid Beheshti, and Leanne Bowler. 2006. "Bonded design": A novel approach to intergenerational information technology design. *Library & Information Science Research* 28(1): 64–82.

Leino, Kaisa, Pirjo Linnakyla, and Antero Malin. 2004. Finnish students' multiliteracy profiles. *Scandinavian Journal of Educational Research* 48(3): 251–70.

Lenhart, Amanda. 2005. Protecting teens online. *Reports: Family, Friends & Community.* PEW Internet & American Life Project. http://www.pewinternet.org (accessed April 23, 2006).

Lenhart, Amanda, and Mary Madden. 2005. Teen content creators and consumers. *Reports: Family, Friends & Community.* PEW Internet & American Life Project. http://www.pewinternet.org (accessed April 23, 2006).

———. 2005. Teens and technology. *Reports: Family, Friends & Community.* PEW Internet & American Life Project. http://www.pewinternet.org (accessed April 23, 2006).

Lenhart, Amanda, and Lee Rainie. 2001. Teenage life online. *Reports: Family, Friends & Community.* PEW Internet & American Life Project. http://www.pewinternet.org (accessed April 23, 2006).

Levin, Doug, Sousan Arafeh, Amanda Lenhart, and Lee Rainie. 2002. The digital disconnect: The widening gap between Internet-savvy students and their schools. *Reports: Family, Friends & Community.* PEW Internet & American Life Project. http://www.pewinternet.org (accessed April 23, 2006).

Lin, Chia-Ching. 2004. Taiwanese adolescents' perceptions and attitudes regarding the Internet: Exploring gender differences. *Adolescence* 39(156): 725–34.

Loertscher, David V., ed. 2005. *Understanding in the library: Papers of the Treasure Mountain Research Retreat #12, Oct. 5–6, 2005—Gilmary Retreat Center, Pittsburgh, PA.* Pittsburg, PA: Hi Willow Research & Publishing and F & W Associates.

Oblinger, D. 2003. Boomers, Gen-Xers & Millenials: Understanding the new students. *EDUCAUSE Review* 38(4): 37–47.

Rainie, Lee, and Paul Hitlin. 2005. The Interent at school. *Reports: Family, Friends & Community.* PEW Internet & American Life Project. http://www.pewinternet.org (accessed April 23, 2006).

Rothbauer, Paulette. 2004. People aren't afraid anymore, but it's hard to find books: Reading practices that inform the personal and social identities of self-identified lesbian and queer young women. *Canadian Journal of Information & Library Sciences* 28(3): 53–74.

Sangee, Kim. 2005. HIV/AIDS knowledge, attitudes, related behaviors, and sources of information among Korean adolescents. *Journal of School Health* 75(10): 393–99.

Scott, Thomas. 2005. Analyzing student search strategies: Making a case for integrating information literacy skills into the curriculum. *Teacher Librarian* 33(1): 21–25.

Shenton, Andrew Kenneth, and Pat Dixon. 2005. Information needs: Learning more about what kids want, need, and expect from research. *Children & Libraries: The Journal of the Association for Library Service to Children* 3(2): 20–28.

Slone, Debra. 2003. Internet search approaches: The influence of age, search goals, and experience. *Library & Information Science Research* 25(4): 403–18.

Tarleton, Beth, and Linda Ward. 2005. Changes and choices: Finding out what information young people with learning disabilities, their parents and supporters need at transition. *British Journal of Learning Disabilities* 33(2): 70–76.

Todd, Ross J. 2003. Adolescents of the information age: Patterns of information seeking and use, and implications for information professionals. *School Libraries Worldwide* 9(2): 27–46.

Trevor, P. D. Taylor. 2002. The Internet and youth engagement: An exploration of how youth spend their time online and its relation to civic involvement. PhD dissertation. Wilfrid Laurier University.

Valenza, Joyce. 2006. They might be gurus: Teen information-seeking behavior. *Voice of Youth Advocates*. http://www.voya.com (accessed April 8, 2006).

Weiler, Angela. 2005. Information-seeking behavior in Generation Y students: Motivation, critical thinking, and learning theory. *Journal of Academic Librarianship* 31(1): 46–53.

YALSA Research Committee, ed. 2006. Current research related to young adult services, 2000–2005. *Young Adult Library Services* 4(3): 35–46.

Youn, Seounmi. 2005. Teenagers' perceptions of online privacy and coping behaviors: A risk–benefit appraisal approach. *Journal of Broadcasting & Electronic Media* 49. http://www.highbeam.com (accessed March 3, 2006).

Index

About the Editors and Contributors

Denise E. Agosto is an assistant professor in the College of Information Science and Technology at the I School at Drexel University. Her major research interests include young people's information seeking in digital environments, and Hispanic and multicultural issues in children's and young adult literature and library services.

Jamshid Beheshti is associate dean of education at McGill University. His research interests include information retrieval, interface design, and virtual reality. He is currently involved in several projects on development of virtual environments for children.

Anthony Bernier is an assistant professor at San Jose State University where he specializes in the administration of youth services in public libraries. His current research interests include developmentally appropriate library design aesthetics and explorations of public space equity for young people.

Leanne Bowler is a doctoral student at McGill University. Her research interests lie in the area of young people's information behavior. Her dissertation will investigate the metacognitive knowledge of adolescents during the information search process.

Donna Braquet is an assistant professor and life sciences librarian at the University of Tennessee (UT) Libraries. Though trained as a science librarian, much of Braquet's research and service deals with broadening libraries' and librarians' roles in regard to issues of diversity and social justice. She currently serves on the UT Libraries' Diversity Committee; her focus is creating outreach opportunities that allow the UT Libraries to provide diversity-related resources and services to the campus and the community at large. For more information on the University of Tennessee Libraries' Diversity Committee, see the home page at http://www.lib.utk.edu/diversity/.

Mary K. Chelton is a professor in the Graduate School of Library and Information Studies, Queens College, City University of New York. She received her doctorate from Rutgers University after completing a dissertation on adult-adolescent service encounters. An award-winning librarian prior to her doctorate, Chelton's primary research interests focus on marginalized users and services in library contexts. She is a cofounder, with Dorothy Broderick, of *Voice of Youth Advocates*.

Colleen Cool is an associate professor in the Graduate School of Library and Information Science, Queens College, City University of New York. She received her PhD from the School of Communication, Information and Library Studies at Rutgers University. Dr. Cool's primary theoretical interests are in applying social interaction theory to the study of HCI. Her research has centered around the study of human information seeking behavior and the design of information systems that effectively support people in their interactions with information. She is currently a co-PI on an IMLS-funded project to design more effective Help mechanisms for novice users of digital libraries.

Manjeet K. Dhillon is an academic librarian and lecturer at Birmingham College of Food, Tourism and Creative Studies in the UK. Her research interests include online information seeking, particularly by students in higher education; usage of online resources; teaching and learning methods in information literacy; and librarians as teachers.

Karen E. Fisher is an associate professor in the Information School of the University of Washington, and chair of the MLIS program. Her research specialty is information behavior in everyday life. Her latest books include *Theories of Information Behavior* (2005) and *How Libraries and Librarians Help* (2005). Her current research is funded by the National Science Foundation, Microsoft, and the Institute of Museum and Library Services. She won the 2005 Shera Award for Distinguished Published Research, the 1999 ALISE Research Award, and the 1995 ALISE Hannigan Award. She is a member of several editorial boards as well as the Permanent Program Committee of the Information Seeking in Context (ISIC) Conference series, and was the 2004–2005 chair of ASIST SIG USE.

Vivian Howard teaches in the School of Information Management, Faculty of Management, Dalhousie University in Halifax, Nova Scotia. She is also the editor of *Hot, Hotter, Hottest: The Best of the YA Hotline* (Scarecrow Press, 2002) and is on the National Executive of IBBY Canada. She is currently completing her doctoral dissertation on the role of pleasure reading in the lives of young teens through the University of Wales, Aberystwyth.

Sandra Hughes-Hassell is an associate professor in the College of Information Science and Technology at the I School at Drexel University. She teaches in four areas: resources for young adults, social and professional aspects of information service, instructional role of the information specialist, and online searching. Her research interests include the delivery of information services to children and young adults, the social impact of information technology, and the information needs of disadvantaged youth.

Shan Jin graduated from Dalhousie University's MLIS program in 2004. She mainly works in the archives and records management field. Now she is a records analyst in the Nova Scotia Department of Transportation and Public Works.

Carol F. Landry is a PhD student at the University of Washington Information School. She has collaborated in several key studies for the Information Behavior in Everyday Contexts (IBEC) research program. Her research interests are information seeking in everyday life, information poverty, the digital divide, and the affective dimension of information behavior.

Andrew Large is CN-Pratt-Grinstad Professor of Information Studies at McGill University. His major research areas are human-computer interaction, information retrieval, and information-seeking behavior. His current projects focus upon the design and development of Web-based information retrieval tools for elementary school students.

Lynne (E. F.) McKechnie is an associate professor on the Faculty of Information and Media Studies at the University of Western Ontario, and Beverley Cleary Professor in Youth Services (visiting) in the Information School at the University of Washington. Dr. McKechnie's research and teaching interests center around the role of public libraries in the development of children as readers, information materials for children, and children's everyday life information behavior.

Elizabeth Marcoux is an assistant professor in the Information School at the at the University of Washington. Her focus is on the information needs of children and youth. Her current research interests involve understanding the information habits of youth as they migrate out of childhood into young adulthood, and in understanding the actions of information professionals who work or will work with children and youth. She also works to provide access to information to marginalized children such as the Native American children's communities. She participates actively in various initiatives nationally as well as in Washington State that contribute to improved information services to children and youth.

Bharat Mehra is an assistant professor in the School of Information Sciences at the University of Tennessee. Broadly, Mehra's teaching and research philosophy brings a deeper understanding of users and their social and cultural contexts (including socioeconomic and sociopolitical factors) into library and information science education. Specifically his work explores diversity and intercultural issues and has focused on community informatics or the use of information and communication technologies to enable and empower local and global communities to meet their needs and aspirations. It has involved addressing issues of social justice and social equity in the information professions for representing minority and disenfranchised populations. For more information about Mehra, see his home page at http://www.sis.utk.edu/people/faculty/mehra.

Eric Meyers is a research assistant and doctoral student at the University of Washington. His research interests include school library media programs, youth information behavior, and information fluency in formal and informal contexts. Formerly a teacher, school librarian, and technologist, he consults with school professionals on information services, library spaces, and technology curriculum.

Valerie Nesset is a doctoral student at McGill University. Her research interests relate to elementary school children and their information-seeking behavior. Her dissertation research examines the information behavior of grade-three students in the context of a class project.

Jennifer Burek Pierce is an assistant professor in the School of Library and Information Science at the University of Iowa, where she teaches courses including young adult literature. Her research examines aspects of sexual and reproductive health information, particularly in relation to adolescent reading guidance in the late Victorian and early Progressive Eras. She is writing her first book, *Sex, Brains, and Video Games: A Librarian's Guide to Understanding Teens in the Twenty-First Century*, which is forthcoming from ALA Editions.

Andrew K. Shenton divides his time between his responsibilities as a research supervisor at Northumbria University in northeast England and working with youngsters in the Study Center of Monkseaton Community High School. He gained a doctorate in 2002 after a detailed investigation of the information-seeking behavior of children and young people. By this time, he had already received the Dawson Prize and Instant Library Award in recognition of outstanding academic achievement at Northumbria University. Dr. Shenton has now had some thirty-five research papers published in the United States and his native Britain.

Joanne Silverstein is the director of research and development at the Information Institute of Syracuse and an assistant research professor at

Syracuse University's School of Information Studies. Her research addresses user-based system design, and the evolving role of human intermediation in Web-based, scalable information for the education and library communities.

Joyce Kasman Valenza has been the librarian at Springfield Township High School (Pennsylvania) since 1998. She is currently working on her doctorate at the University of North Texas. Her major research interests include youth services, information literacy, technology and young people, virtual libraries, online learning, databases and searching, the evolving role of the teacher-librarian, Internet2 in libraries, and Web 2.0/Library 2.0.